Sport in the Global Society

General Editor: J A Mangan

FOOTBINDING,
FEMINISM AND FREEDOM

CASS SERIES: SPORT IN THE GLOBAL SOCIETY
General Editor: J A Mangan

The interest in sports studies around the world is growing and will continue to do so. This unique series combines aspects of the expanding study of *sport in the global society*, providing comprehensiveness and comparison under one editorial umbrella. It is particularly timely, with studies in the political, cultural, social, economic, geographical and aesthetic elements in sport proliferating in institutions of higher education.

Eric Hobsbawm once called sport one of the most significant practices of the late nineteenth century. Its significance is even more marked in the late twentieth century and will continue to grow in importance into the next millennium as the world develops into a 'global village' sharing the English language, technology and sport.

Footbinding, Feminism and Freedom

The Liberation of Women's Bodies
in Modern China

FAN HONG

De Montfort University

FRANK CASS

LONDON • PORTLAND, OR

145932

First Published in 1997 in Great Britain by
FRANK CASS & CO. LTD.
Newbury House, 900 Eastern Avenue
London, IG2 7HH

and in the United States of America by
FRANK CASS
c/o ISBS, 5804 N.E. Hassalo Street
Portland, Oregon, 97213-3644

British Library Cataloguing in Publication Data

Hong, Fan
    Footbinding, feminism and freedom : the liberation of
    women's bodies in modern China. – (Sport in global society)
    1. Women's rights – China – History   2. Exercise for women –
    China – History   3. Footbinding – China
    I. Title
    305.4'2'0951

    ISBN 0 7146 4633 4

    Library of Congress Cataloging-in-Publication Data:

    A catalog record for this book is available
    from the Library of Congress

Typeset by Regent Typesetting, London

Printed in Great Britain by
Bookcraft (Bath) Ltd, Midsomer Norton, Avon

Contents

⋊⋋⋌⋄⋋⋌⋉

Illustrations

❈❈❈❈❈

Acknowledgements

THIS BOOK was originally a doctoral dissertation undertaken at the International Research Centre for Sport, Socialisation and Society, University of Strathclyde.

When I began my research some four years ago I was only too well aware that it would not be easy. There was a long and difficult linguistic, conceptual and empirical route to travel. In particular, I had to climb a steep linguistic 'track'. In this journey through the landscape of the English language my guide, Professor Mangan, supported my faltering steps with the attention to my efforts that every student hopes for. He saved me from stumbles beyond reckoning, and when I slipped he quietly and firmly picked me up. It was his quality of supervision: speedy in response, meticulous in textual scrutiny, always readily available for discussion and continually encouraging and enthusiastic in approach, which ensured that I completed my journey.

I have reason to be most grateful to those scholars in the field of women's studies who gave me their time freely and who commented constructively on my work: Professors Roberta Park, Patricia Vertinsky, Synthia Slowikowski, Marlene Adrian, Joanna Davenport.

Within the Faculty of Education of Strathclyde University I should like to thank Dr Gerry Finn for his professional help, especially with the thesis footnotes. I owe special thanks to Mr Iain Smith and Professor Douglas Weir for their very practical assistance.

Thanks are due to the staff of the Jordanhill Campus Library, especially Irene Stirling, Iain Allan and David Alcock for their efficient help with Western sources. Thanks are also extended to George Payne, who brought me a huge box of source material from China after his holiday there. I would like to thank, in addition, the staff of the Department of Educational Studies, Strathclyde University, especially Dr Peter Martin and Margaret Davies for giving me the administrative support that allowed me to complete most of my thesis in the Department. I would also like to express my thanks to the School of Physical Education, Sport and Leisure, De Montfort University, Bedford for the time provided to complete my thesis. Deryck Uprichard, an expert with computers, also kindly helped me resolve the problems of transforming my manuscript into a readable typescript. I am most grateful.

I do not wish to overlook, and will not forget the Faculty of Education of Strathclyde University and the International Research Centre for Sport, Socialisation and Society, which jointly funded the research for this study. Without the persistence, determination and vision of J. A. Mangan, Alistair Nicholson and Iain Smith this study might never have been started, let alone completed.

Robert Easton and Jacqueline Lewis of Frank Cass provided invaluable professional advice and assistance.

I should like to make the usual acknowledgements with gratitude to the editors of *The International Journal of the History of Sport* and *Women in Sport and Physical Activity Journal* for permission to use material in the Prologue and Chapters Two and Three respectively.

The most profound thanks go to my Chinese colleague Yan Xuening, editor of *The Journal of Chinese Culture and Sports History*. Her continual help in locating valuable sources was of crucial importance. I am also indebted to my Chinese colleagues Tan Hua, Professor at the Research Centre of Sports History, Chengdu Physical Education Institute, Wang Zhengming, Professor at Xi'an Physical Education Institute, Fan Wei, lecturer at the Chengdu Physical Education Institute, and Xiong Xiaozhen, Editor of *The Journal of Chinese Culture and Sports History*, who provided me with numerous sources that I would never have found alone. Acknowledgement is made also to the Sports History Working Committee of the Ministry of Sport in Beijing, which gave me full and free access to significant archival sources, and to the staff of the Committee for giving me their invaluable support in various ways. Thanks are also extended to my uncle, Fan Fan, and cousin, Fan Ruchuan, in Taiwan, who provided with me sources unavailable in mainland China.

Thanks also go to Craig Gill for his patience, encouragement and help. Finally, let me express my deep gratitude to my family, without whose support, I would never have come this far.

Notes on Translation

❧✦❧

THIS THESIS employs the Pinyin system for the translation of Chinese names. This system first used in China in the 1950s. It is now the official romanisation system in the People's Republic of China, and has been adopted by the United Nations. It is currently becoming standard around the world. Thus familiar names such as Mao Tse-tung, Peking and Yenan appear in the text in the slightly more novel forms of Mao Zedong, Beijing, and Yan'an.

This thesis uses Pinyin romanisation throughout except for some personal names that are long familiar in the West or difficult to recognise in Pinyin. Thus personal names such as Sun Yat-sen and Chiang Kai-shek remain in the old form. In citing Western language sources that use the older Wade-Giles romanisation system, however, references to persons and places are left unchanged.

In China, 'tiyu' refers to exercise, physical education, competitive sport and physical culture. I have translated it according to its contexts.

Finally, unless otherwise indicated, all translations are my own renditions.

Series Editor's Foreword

❧❧❦❧❧

SHORTLY AFTER THE Second World War, when Joseph Needham, the Cambridge Marxist and superlative scientific synthesist, decided to dedicate himself to his *magnum opus Science and Civilisation in China*, the Cambridge scientific community was not impressed with this intellectual exercise in Eastern 'esotericism'. His Asiatic obsession, in their eyes, was seen as self-indulgent, ludicrous, even irresponsible. In modern science the West was where it had all happened. Today Napoleon's 'sleeping giant' has recently awoken from 'hibernation', eager for a role on the world's stage, hungry to obtain redress for earlier Western humiliations, ambitious to confront Japan for the leadership of South East Asia – and Europe and the West have much to learn, quickly, about this vast and potentially powerful nation – so hopefully scientists of *all* persuasions will now need little urging to set about the task. For them this book should be required reading.

Modern China is no socialist Utopia. It is still, if less acutely than in the past, an oppressed society, and official corruption is still endemic, totalitarianism is still extant. Much of the harsh past characterises the present – while the people continue to demonstrate impressively the qualities of stoicism, fortitude and humour. Some things, however, have changed somewhat for the better and in this remarkable book, in the role of a cultural fugleman, Fan Hong describes and explains the process in recent Chinese history of the gradual release of women from physical tyranny. In her carefully chosen words, '. . . female emancipation cannot be separated from physical emancipation'. It was a process, as she rightly stresses, that was a prerequisite of fuller emancipation – of minds and emotions. In placing her emphasis uniquely on the body she underlines a fundamental feature of Chinese culture which others, as she reasonably remarks, seem to have insufficiently appreciated and inadequately understood – the crushing, spiritual, emotional and physical impact of the excruciating, appalling and cruel custom of female footbinding. As she writes: 'Without normal limbs, unmutilated extremities and unrestricted movement there was little possibility of physical and psychological health, educational access, occupational opportunity and political assertion. More than this, without access to modern exercise there were distinctly reduced possibilities of personal pleasure, self-realisation, self-fulfilment, social status and gender enhancement'.

There is much that is original in this volume. Making good use of Chinese archival sources – virtually unknown and consequently mostly unconsidered in the West – the author explores, for example, the role of women in the Communist 'soviets' of the nineteen thirties, and draws attention to the pragmatic realisation of the Communist Party of the value of women's muscle in the struggle against the Japanese and the Nationalists, and the consequent calculated and cautious Party endorsement of *selective* women's rights, illustrating nicely a sensible recognition of the fact, to distort Alfred Adler's famous aphorism only slightly, that it is easier to get others to fight for your principles than for you to live up to them! This study of Eastern female emancipation is not only a prototypical contribution to the cultural history of China, it is a prototypical contribution to the cultural history of modern sexuality, gender and society. It offers academia evidence, argument and analysis at several levels.

In his mould-breaking study of men in the rise of Imperial German, *Gold and Iron: Bismarck, Bleichroder and the Building of the German Empire*, Fritz Stern wrote 'I hope the book does more than offer facts . . . It is not only the functioning of a society that is meant to be depicted here . . . something of its spirit should emerge as well. There are attitudes, clusters of ideas and prejudices, gestures that bespeak manners, silences that express values . . .'. This study of women during and after the decline of Imperial China is similarly mould-breaking in approach. And it has similar hopes. For my part, I hope that its originality will be recognised, appreciated and applauded. It is no more than it deserves.

J. A. Mangan

Modern China: Women, Emancipation and Exercise

❊❊❊❊❊

Conceptual Concerns

EXERCISE IN THE modern world is a global phenomenon with significant political, cultural, social, educational, economic, spiritual and aesthetic dimensions.[1] For this reason it is a phenomenon which has been increasingly investigated in recent years by anthropologists, educationalists, historians and sociologists.[2]

In the case of the Occident the relationship between modern female exercise and emancipation has been scrutinised by academics in Britain and America.[3] They have argued that exercise for women has served as a means of self-realisation, self-fulfilment and liberation.[4] These studies have brought new evidence, arguments and perspectives to studies of contemporary Western cultures and societies.[5]

In Western academia various feminist theories exist within feminist studies of exercise.[6] There has been an uneasy co-existence between these theories. Generally speaking, however, liberal feminist theory has contributed a great deal to an understanding of the cultural liberation of women through exercise.[7] Marxist, radical and socialist feminist theories have developed theoretical and empirical critiques of the deeply gendered structure and values of the world of exercise. These feminists argue that because exercise is an important institution in the construction of male supremacy and capitalist patriarchy, women's participation in exercise strongly challenges conservative culture and a male-dominated society.[8] More importantly, they assert that women's participation in exercise also helps them to expand their possibilities for emancipation – it can be a form of self-assertion and a means of liberation from conventional values and restrictions. This book attempts to provide historical evidence of relevance and value to these various theoretical schools and, in an

Oriental context, to offer empirical evidence to underpin further theorising.

In the case of the Orient the academic situation is very different. There has yet to be, for example, an *evolutionary* study of women's exercise and its relationship to their emancipation within modern Chinese society from the momentous arrival of the Western powers in 1840 which changed China for ever. To date no academic work has discussed women, exercise and emancipation within the social, cultural and political setting of China from the mid-nineteenth to the mid-twentieth centuries. Inquiry into the evolving relationship between women's exercise and emancipation over this period is necessary, and overdue, if there is to be a full understanding of modern China in an era of gender reconstruction. More than this, the dramatic and brutal patriarchal traditions of physical repression of the female body in Chinese history, particularly the inhuman institution of footbinding, make the physical emancipation of Chinese women in this period an issue of special significance and a valuable case-study in the history of the emancipation of the modern female body.

This book will explore the relationship between women's exercise and emancipation in modern China, and try to assess the impact of women's emancipatory exercise on the status of women in modern Chinese society. Although a number of studies are restoring Chinese women to history,[9] none has used the evolution of women's exercise, from the period of the first 'opening' of China in the middle of the nineteenth century, as a window into social custom and, more particularly, social change. This book, therefore, will analyse women's exercise in China between 1840 and 1949 in its social, cultural and political contexts in order to define its critical importance for female physical liberation.

Chinese women's physical liberation has developed under unique circumstances. In modern China, modern women's participation in physical activity has not only challenged traditional patriarchy and its definitions of women, but has also helped women construct a vision of freedom. For Chinese women, to a marked extent, exercise has served as an avenue to wider liberation. It has been a progressive force which has helped, and helps, shape new, ameliorative, benevolent and humane values. It is interesting that such a significant aspect of modern history has been so neglected. Academic myopia has lasted too long.

Paradoxically this short-sightedness is probably due to both the perceived insignificance *and* the actual significance of the subject: academic rhetoric asserts women's value, while academic action denies it,[10] yet women in those famous and ringing words hold up 'half the [Chinese] sky'. It is this contradiction that makes the subject especially fascinating and deserving of attention.

The concepts of hegemony, exercise and empowerment are fundamental to this study. At one level of analysis, exercise is a cultural sphere in which a dominant group may attempt to legitimate its power. But the hegemony established in this way by superordinates is always incomplete and open to challenge from subordinates. In other words, the ruling group places ideological, moral and structural constraints on others' thoughts and activities, but these constraints do not fully determine outcomes; individuals and groups retain the ability to act as historical agents, thinking critically and acting transformatively.[11] Exercise, as any other major cultural sphere, is often dominated by the values of the superordinate group, but it does not prevent subordinate groups from restructuring and redefining exercise in their own ways in order to meet their needs.[12] Exercise, therefore, may be conceptualised as a contested cultural terrain. Its interpretation and implementation are invariably subject to struggle[13] and nowhere more clearly than in modern China.[14]

Studies of women's exercise and emancipation in China, it is suggested, should concentrate on two issues: the first is the way in which exercise constitutes an important cultural sphere where ideological meanings of gender are produced, presented and enacted. This requires an examination of the role of exercise in the definition and redefinition of gender characteristics, the social construction and reconstruction of gender in formal and informal education programmes, the production and presentation of images of women and women's exercise, and the relationship of exercise to women's cultural identity.[15]

The second issue should concentrate on the empowering[16] of women through the empowerment of their bodies through exercise. As Ann Hall argues, exercise should call upon the body's capacities and skills to determine what it can achieve.[17] Yet patriarchal culture has often defined women as 'other object', more specifically as 'sex-object', often specifically by virtue of the presence or absence of freedom to exercise.[18] According to Hall, exercise can be empowering for women, but its purpose and its outcome, in fact, have been more often to enhance women's sexual 'objectification'. Research by Hall, Park,

Hargreaves and others offers us an understanding of the processes whereby the female body becomes sexualised, controlled and oppressed.[19] More importantly, it shows how exercise paradoxically plays a vital role in both reinforcing the male-dominated status quo in Western countries, while emancipating women from traditional repression.[20] Both these processes have occurred, and occur, in China and to advance our understanding of female emancipation, not only in the West but also in the East, these processes require scrutiny.

While the concepts of exercise, hegemony and empowerment are fundamental to this inquiry, three areas of social existence are equally fundamental: religion, culture and politics.[21]

Religion, Emancipation and Exercise

For many anthropologists, religion contributes to the uniting of communities through shared experiences and common explanations of the purpose of life. For many sociologists and social psychologists religion also serves social ends. For them, too, it exists to ensure the cohesion of the community. Historians, for their part, describe religion in terms of events resulting from beliefs.[22]

Chinese society and character have been tempered and shaped in history by several religions. In addition to Taoism and Confucianism, foreign-born religions, particularly Buddhism and Christianity, have exerted an impact upon Chinese culture and society. Prior to 1840 it was Confucianism, however, which played a crucial role in the construction of social order and the images of masculinity and femininity in China.

Confucianism based its doctrine on the ancient yin–yang doctrine of polarity.[23] Yin represents the negative, passive, weak and destructive, whereas yang stands for the positive, active, strong and constructive. As they act and interact a harmony is achieved and recreated time and time again. Yin and yang constitute all the elements, and reproduce the cycle of life and the seasons, so that a harmony of nature is created. Both individuals and society are also composed of these two opposites. While femininity is yin – negative, soft, dark and weak, masculinity is yang – positive, hard, bright and strong. According to this doctrine, in order to achieve a complementary social harmony, women should operate in the domain of yin, which is fundamentally passive. Confucianism incorporated the yin–yang doctrine into its rationalisation of human interaction. It advocated a strict and inflexible social hierarchy by emphasising the static social roles of different categories of people and especially of women in their relationship to men.

Confucianism, essentially, is a system of social ethics. The concept of Li (namely rites, rituals, rules of propriety, or codes of behaviour) lies at the heart of the system.[24] The origin of Li can be traced back to the need to control the self-seeking nature of man in early feudal Chinese society.[25] Using the rules of propriety as a means of social control to contain and yet provide satisfaction for human desires, the Confucian institution of Li has left very distinctive marks on Chinese culture and mentality. It succeeded in enclosing the personality of the individual within the parameters of his or her prescribed roles, to the extent that individuality was hardly differentiated from those roles. For this reason, in a traditional Confucian society, all interpersonal relationships were held together by a hierarchy of social roles. Each role functioned in the manner prescribed in the Confucian texts.[26]

In Confucianism, one harsh reality was that the yin–yang doctrine was adopted to confine women to a subordinate position. Women were relegated to an inferior role because they were designated weak by nature. Female education consequently taught women total submission to men. Physical constraints, in particular footbinding, served as a practical means to confine women to the home. Female bodies, therefore, were restrained to actualise and symbolise their subordinate role.

Exercise had a place in the Confucian texts. It was an educative tool. Its purpose was to achieve a well-developed morality through non-competitive physical activity. It also served as a cohesive ritual helping to maintain the social *status quo*. As a result, Chinese physical activities under Confucianism lost their earlier degree of competitiveness. It was replaced by an emphasis on harmony of movement representing coherence and cohesion.[27]

Christianity came to China in a series of invasions by Western countries in the nineteenth century. It did not make many Christians out of the Chinese, but it exerted considerable influence on Chinese culture and custom, above all, on the transformation of women's bodies. Christianity spread throughout China, due to an influx of thousands of Christian missionaries from abroad representing both Catholic and Protestant theologies.[28] After 1860 missionaries were to be found in every province, in almost every important city and in many villages. Churches were erected, missionary schools established, hospitals and dispensaries set up. A multitude of philanthropic enterprises were undertaken and the number of Chinese Christians grew to three million in a very short period of time.[29]

Although to many Chinese observers the purpose of the Christian missionaries remains a subject of dispute[30] – was it spiritual conversion or was it cultural conquest through conversion? – it nevertheless had a strong impact on Chinese life. Christianity contained concepts of individuality, equality and humanitarianism, which boldly challenged the established prevailing values of Chinese culture, and was, therefore, favoured by progressive forces. However, Confucian conflict with the alien religion went beyond the boundaries of religion. It spilt over into the social, cultural and political domains. Christianity confronted traditional mechanisms of social order – not least in the area of women's lives, their bodies and their physical constraint. Opposition to Confucianism lay at the heart of this conflict.

In times of change, it has often been argued, religion plays an important role in transmitting new ideas, mobilising communities, offering them new and wider vistas and stimulating them to re-evaluate social existence. The liberal ideals of Christianity went comfortably hand in hand with the progressive forces in the changing China of the nineteenth century. As far as women were concerned, it provided comparatively more opportunities for freedom along with a happier vision of their future than Confucianism. Christianity brought to Chinese women the normality of *unmutilated* limbs – the basic requirement of physical emancipation. Religion is thus a critical dimension of this inquiry.

Culture, Emancipation and Exercise

The West's beneficial influence on Chinese women's bodies inspired nothing less than a physical revolution. The availability of modern exercise for women in China, as argued above, owed much to the introduction and influence of Western religious and associated educational principles and practices. An exploration of the interaction between Western and Chinese culture in the nineteenth and twentieth centuries and its relevance for Chinese society, will bring us to a long overdue understanding of the evolution of Chinese women's physical emancipation – the necessary precursor of a more extensive emancipation.

Unlike Western culture, which from the time of the Renaissance onwards viewed exercise as part of education, Chinese culture mostly ignored the educational cultivation of the human body. Furthermore, as already discussed, while Western exercise in part stressed competition Chinese exercise emphasised non-competition. In addition, Western medicine in the mid-nineteenth and early twentieth centuries greatly influenced exercise, especially women's exercise. As Vertinsky and McCrone point out, from the mid-nineteenth century onwards, based on a bold rejection of conservative scientific principles and medical theories, female doctors, feminists and educationalists encouraged women to take part in physical exercise.[31] Innovatory medical ideas eventually had a beneficial influence on Western women's freedom to participate in physical exercise and public opinion gradually began to accept the value of women's exercise.[32] In contrast, Chinese medicine had a negative influence on women's exercise. It rode in harness with Confucian culture. Chinese medicine was based on the doctrine of yin–yang and transcendental experience.[33] It stressed the unchangeable and fragile nature of the female body. Female physical fragility was considered natural, desirable and static.[34] In short, Western exercise when it arrived in China provoked confrontation with Chinese concepts of the physical encapsulated in traditional cultural beliefs.

Some Chinese patriots[35] insisted on the retention of traditional physical activities. They held that China should maintain traditional activities with their non-competitive nature as a way of maintaining good health, as a symbol of national identity and as a source of national solidarity. They strongly advocated non-participation in Western competitive exercise, which they saw as a danger to the Chinese culture of thousands of years standing.[36] They wholly failed to see that the non-competitive nature of Chinese exercise had helped to make China incapable of facing up to, and successfully adapting to new trends and new forces in the world. More than this, they refused to endorse women's involvement in modern exercise. This philosophy helped to form a nation that tended to be backward looking, satisfied with past circumstances and resistant to any radical social progress. However, certain progressives – for example, Lu Xun (1881–1936), one of the greatest period thinkers and writers in China – were hostile towards ancient Chinese exercise and to its exclusivity.[37] They regarded it as an unscientific remnant of an anachronistic culture. They hoped that modern physical culture would speed the demise of feudal tradition.[38]

Proselytisers of progress argued that the ancient culture and its associated physical forms of activity failed to meet the new needs of society. New social challenges required a new robustness for men *and* women. Western exercise met this requirement.[39] Confrontation between conservative and radicals led to a complete transmogrification of the feudal Chinese exercise system into a modern exercise system. Its evolution, with its emancipatory consequences for women, is crucial to this inquiry. It represented a *cultural revolution* of some significance.

Politics, Exercise and Emancipation

Exercise is frequently a crucial means of transmitting political ideological values.[40] In this role it operates at several levels. At one level it is, to use a well-worn but nevertheless insightful cliché, 'war without weapons', a means of asserting the bloodless supremacy of one political ideology over another.[41] At another level it can be a calculated internal political distraction, promoting escapism and wooing the hearts of both political 'outsiders' and 'insiders'. At yet another level, especially relevant to this study, it can focus acceptable attention on movements and their ideologies. Women's emancipatory zeal in all its manifestations has been closely and continually monitored and controlled by the political authorities in twentieth century China. The history of both Chinese women and Chinese women's studies clearly illustrates this.[42] In this study an attempt will be made to assess the impact of official ideology on the relationship between empowerment, emancipation and exercise.[43]

The evolution of modern Chinese women's exercise and emancipation is characterised by three periods: birth (1840–1911); growth (1911–49) and maturation (1949–present). Each period, in turn, is characterised by different political systems and their associated ideologies.

In the past, traditional forms of women's exercise certainly existed. This was especially true of the Tang Dynasty (960–1100), a period often regarded as the Golden Age of Feudal China.[44] Subsequently, when Confucianism became the dominant ideology, women were marginalised in society and traditional Chinese women's exercise went into a drastic and terminal decline. Then the period 1840–1911 saw both the birth of modern women's exercise and their emancipation movement.

In the mid-nineteenth century there were profound ideological challenges to the established normative order in China. Confucian orthodoxy was questioned, particularly with regard to its tenets on women. Exogenous and indigenous reformers then took up the issue of women's rights.[45] Exercise became one platform from which to launch the liberalisation of the Chinese woman.[46]

In the ideological clash between Chinese Confucianism and Western liberalism radicals came to realise that without women's physical liberation, women's intellectual, moral and emotional emancipation could not be fully realised. They believed that Western exercise, its theories and practices, could bring a new vigour to feudal Chinese culture and to the Chinese people, and that central to this process was the need for women to achieve the emancipation of their bodies.[47] In these relatively supportive circumstances, but not without setbacks, modern Chinese women's freedom to exercise became possible. It was an early and critical manifestation of a more comprehensive humanitarian ideal of freedom.

After the 1911 Revolution,[48] China became a Republic. This change of political system brought a new, incomplete and short-lived democratic direction to national political ideology. The May Fourth Movement (1919), which strongly opposed traditional Chinese values and customs, for its part offered a brave set of political ideals to a still considerably conservative civilisation, and *inter alia* created an amenable environment in which physical activities for women were more encouraged. Occidental ideals of liberty, equality, and individualism now had a revolutionary influence on Chinese feudal philosophy, structure and traditions, stimulated change in Chinese society and, in turn, in attitudes to women and their bodies. In consequence, there appeared in China in this period a new physical culture characterised by democratic philosophical ideals. Women had greater opportunities to take part in physical activities and women's physical education departments in schools and colleges were set up.[49] In the cities, the seed-beds of radical thought, there was an increasing possibility for women to demonstrate their new physical independence.

Significantly, it was in this period that Chinese sportswomen participated in the Far East Asian Games and even attended the Olympic Games.[50] Their participation confronted traditional Chinese cultural beliefs, values and ethics. Olympism stressed the freedom of the individual, the spirit of competition, and the ideal of equality. It met Chinese women's need to do away with Confucianism and its traditional, repressive and exploitative directives. Their outstanding performances internationally gave them enhanced social status and, to a degree, assisted the general struggle for emancipation. Thus, a new athletic ideology and culture appeared in China which steadily if gradually endorsed, supported and illustrated a wider set of emancipatory ideological imperatives. In this way a closed circle was created.

It is important to recognise that the requirements of political survival in a war-torn China in the 1930s were crucial stimulants to the advance of emancipatory exercise. Both Communists and Nationalists endorsed and organised women's involvement in modern exercise – not least in the symbolically significant area of competitive sport[51] – to ensure their political, military and economic contribution to the survival of the respective systems.

The emphasis in this book, as stated above, will be on the period 1840 to 1949. However, it will end with a brief consideration of 1949 to the present. The 1949 revolution brought a rupture with the past in many ways, but at the same time the communist state which resulted was a product of the past. It was a consequence of history. That history was in its memory and it made the New China and was responsible for the new attitudes to women – their bodies and their minds – that characterised the New China. In a real sense the impact of the struggle for the freedom of the female body in the years before 1949 can only be fully assessed from a consideration of the years after 1949.

The new state, the People's Republic of China, was built on Marxist ideology and constituted a highly centralised socialist society. This change brought an unprecedented growth in Chinese women's opportunities for exercise. The adoption of Marxist ideology pushed a still extant male chauvinism to the margins of society – at least in theory.[52] Chinese government leaders, as Marxists, were ideologically committed to the principle of female equality in society as part of the superiority of their socialist system.[53]

In addition, this 'young' Marxist-Leninist state tried to establish itself in the world as a socialist society worthy of international respect. It quickly appreciated that exercise in the form of international competitive sport offered it a superb opportunity to bask in the full glare of the limelight of world publicity. This was particularly important for the Chinese who had been humiliated by powerful Western states economically, militarily and politically for over one hundred years. Furthermore, the patriotic pride generated by athletic success, especially against the world's strongest nations, helped to unite an ethnically diverse society and to forge a nation politically and culturally. Then again, for Chinese Communist leaders, sport was one of the most visible and effective means of explaining to people all over the world the advantages that socialism had over capitalism. For the Party leaders, attaining sporting supremacy, particularly through the Olympic Games, was principally for the purposes of gaining recognition and prestige for Communist China and for Communism generally.[54] They fully appreciated the importance of sport in state political life – as a vehicle of political propaganda.

For all these reasons, after 1949 Chinese women's sport at a representative level accrued to itself a major political role and won encouragement from the government. The rise of Chinese women's sport, ideologically, financially and administratively, in the post-war decades was not accidental but was purposefully established and sustained. It was, and is, promoted to emphasise to, and to inculcate in the young the chosen primary political values of the society. It comprised, and comprises, an important means of ensuring political cohesion, conformity and continuity.[55] Arguably, the best example is the victory of the women's volleyball team in the 1980s which clearly showed that women's sport was a way of creating a political identity, national confidence and international status for China and its communist ideology, structure and system.[56]

Undoubtedly, as the product of political change, women's widespread participation in exercise has, to a certain extent, changed the traditional image of women. It has helped to reduce their oppression, to establish a new way of life for them, and to improve their social status. Emancipation is not complete. Change can be painfully slow. Nevertheless, women's active and general participation in exercise[57] is precipitating, reinforcing and reflecting changes in the role of women. Ever more positive prospects are clearly discernible for women both in exercise and in society as China slowly (at present) accommodates itself to new ideological pressures, and the third phase of Western ideological hegemony (contemporary capitalism) comes to pass in the decades spanning the twentieth and twenty-first centuries.[58] But, of course, such change will bring its problems for women.[59]

11

Conclusion

This book then is concerned with understanding the nature of the evolving role of women in modern Chinese culture and society and, more specifically, with the role of women's exercise in relation to women's status in their modern physiological, psychological, educational, cultural and political progress towards emancipation. It is a study of a cultural revolution, at one level complete in itself as a study in exercise in culture, and at another level contained within and part of a wider cultural revolution – the physical transformation of women's bodies and the ideologies and actions associated with them. Both revolutions are the products of political, religious and cultural upheaval in the nineteenth and twentieth centuries.

The study brings Chinese women – half the population of by far the largest national population in the world – to the centre of the Chinese cultural stage. The story is an astounding history of the struggle to reclaim their bodies, to reject mutilation on a gargantuan scale, to achieve physical normality, and finally, to seek through the exercise of their released bodies, health, pleasure, confidence, independence and achievement. More than this, and crucial to the thrust of this analysis, physical emancipation was the prerequisite of further emancipation, and it was thus crucial to the whole emancipatory movement. To recognise this fact is to fill in a large and hitherto missing piece in the cultural jigsaw that comprises a picture of women and their struggle for freedom in modern China.

Notes

1. J. A. Mangan in his article 'The Social Construction of Victorian Femininity: Emancipation, Education and Exercise', in The *International Journal of the History of Sport*, Vol. 6, No. 1, May 1989, p.1, argues as follows: 'To avoid confusion, and to ensure comprehension, sport here is used as a generic term covering physical activities intended to improve physical, mental and moral health'. I adapt this definition and treat *exercise* as the generic concept that subsumes within it the elements of physical education and sport. In short, I define exercise as a generic term covering physical activities which are intended to improve physical, mental and moral health.
2. Hobsbawm, E. J., 'Mass-producing Traditions: Europe, 1870–1914', in Hobsbawm, E.J. and Ranger, T. (eds), *The Invention of Tradition*, Cambridge, 1983; Mason, T. (ed.), *Sport in Britain*, London, Faber & Faber, 1988.
3. Fletcher, S., *Women First: the Female Tradition in English Physical Education 1800–1980*, London: Athlone, 1984; see also Vertinsky, P., *The Eternal Wounded*

Woman, Manchester: Manchester University Press, 1990.

4. McCrone, K.E., 'Play up! Play up! And Play the Game! Sport at the Late Victorian Girls' Public Schools', in Mangan, J.A. and Park, R., (eds), *From 'Fair Sex' to Feminism*, London: Zed: 1987, pp.97–129; Park, R., 'Sport, Gender and Society in a Translantic Victorian Perspective', in Mangan and Park, op. cit., pp.58–96.

5. Multifaceted analysis of women, emancipation, inequality and exercise, for example, have been offered by Birrell, Boutiller, Blue, Fletcher, Guttmann, Hall, Hargreaves, Mangan, McCrone, Park and Vertinsky among others.

6. See Hall, M. A., 'Knowledge and Gender: Epistemological Questions in the Social Analysis of Sport', *Sociology of Sport Journal*, Vol. 2, 1985, pp.25–42; Vertinsky, P., 'Gender Relations, Women's History and Sport History: A Decade of Changing Enquiry 1983–1993', *Journal of Sport History*, Vol. 21, No. 1, spring 1994, pp.319–42.

7. Messner, M.A. and Sabo, D.F., 'Toward a Critical Feminist Reappraisal of Sport, Men, and the Gender Order', in Messner M.A. and Sabo, D.F. (eds), *Sport, Men and Gender Order*, Champaign: Human Kinetics, 1989, p.4.

8. Beck, B., 'The Future of Women's Sport: Issues, Insight, and Struggle', in Sabo, D.F. and Runfola, R. (eds), *Sports and Male Identity*, Englewood Cliffs, NJ: Prentice-Hall, 1980, pp.299–314.

9. Croll, E., *Feminism and Socialism in China*, London: Routledge & Kegan Paul, 1978; see also Andors, P., *The Unfinished Liberation of Chinese Women 1949–1980*, Bloomington: Indiana University Press, 1983; Curtin, K., *Women in China*, New York: Pathfinder Press, 1979; Kristeva, J., *About Chinese Women*, London: Marion Boyars, 1977; Ono Kasuko, *Chinese Women in a Century Revolution*, Stanford: Stanford University Press, 1989.

10. In China studies of women, emancipation and exercise were carefully controlled by the Party.

11. Gruneau, R., (ed.), *Popular Culture and Political Practices*, Ontario: Garamond Press, 1988, pp.11–27; see also M. Bennett *et al.*, *Popular Culture and Social Relations*, Milton Keynes, 1986, pp.68–82.

12. See Mangan J.A., *Athleticism in the Victorian and Edwardian Public School: the Emergence and Consolidation of an Educational Ideology*, Cambridge: Cambridge University Press, 1981; Holt, R., *Sport and the British*, Oxford: Clarendon Press, 1989.

13. See Mangan, J.A., 'The Social Construction of Victorian Femininity', op. cit.; Mason T., op. cit., p.345.

14. See below, especially Chapters Five, Six and Seven.

15. Scraton, S., 'Boys Muscle in Where Angels Fear to Tread – Girls Sub-cultures and Physical Activities', in Horne, J., Jary, D., and Tomlinson, A., (eds), *Sport, Leisure and Social Relations*, London: Routledge & Kegan Paul, 1987, pp.160–83.

16. Hall, M.A., 'How Should We Theorize Sport in a Capitalist Patriarchy?' *International Review for Sociology of Sport*, Vol. 1, 1985, pp.109–13.

17. Young, I., 'The Exclusion of Women From Sport: Conceptual and Existential Dimensions', *Philosophy in Context*, 1979, Vol. 9, p.46.

18. Lenskyi, H., *Out of Bounds: Women, Sport and Sexuality*, Toronto: Women's Press, 1986.

19. Hargreaves, J., 'Where's the Virtue, Where's the Grace', *Theory, Culture and Society*, Vol. 3, No. 1, pp.19–39.

20. Hall, M.A., 'The Discourse of Gender and Sport: From Femininity to Feminism', *Sociology of Sport*, 1988, Vol. 5, pp.330–40.

21. Hoberman, J.M., *Sport and Political Ideology*, London: Heinemann, 1984, pp.1–19.

22. Davies, D., 'The Study of Religion', in *The World's Religions*, a Lion handbook, Lion Publishing, 1982, pp.10–19.
23. Berthrong, J., 'Sages and Immortals: Chinese Religions', in *The World's Religions*, op. cit., 1982, pp.245–53.
24. Ching, Jujia, *Confucianism and Christianity*, Tokyo: Kodansha, 1977, p.41.
25. Tin, F., 'Utopias East and West: The Relationship between Ancient and Modern Chinese Ideals', *Alternative Future*, 1980, Vol. 3, No. 3, pp.18–20.
26. Wu, J.C.H., 'Confucians and Chinese Culture', *Journal of the China Society*, 1978, Vol. 15, pp.14–23.
27. Liu, Binguo, 'Kongzi yu tiyu' [Confucianism and Sport], *Chengdu tiyu xueyuan xuebao [Chendu Institute of Physical Education Journal]*, 1983, Vol. 4, pp.7–11.
28. Chen, Jinpan, *Zhongguo jindai jiaoyushi* [Modern Chinese Education History], Beijing: *Renmin jiaoyu chubanshe* [People's Education Press], 1979, p.61.
29. Wu, Chih-kang, 'The Influence of the YMCA on the Development of Physical Education in China' (unpublished Ph.D thesis), University of Michigan, p.41.
30. Zhongguo tiyushi xuehui [Chinese Society for History of Physical Education and Sport], hereafter CSHPES, *Zhongguo jindai tiyu shi* [Modern Chinese Sports History], pp.5–7.
31. See McCrone, K., *Sport and the Physical Education of English Women 1870–1914*, London: Routledge, 1988, *passim*; Vertinsky, P., *The Eternal Wounded Woman*, op. cit.
32. See Reekie, Shirley H.M., 'The History of Sport and Recreation for Women in Britain, 1700–1850', (unpublished Ph.D thesis), Ohio State University, 1982; Vertinsky, P., *The Eternal Wounded Woman*, op. cit.; Hargreaves, J. *The Sporting Female*, op. cit.; Fletcher, S., *Women First . . .*, op. cit.; McCrone, K.E., *Sport and Physical Education of English Women 1870–1914*, op. cit.
33. Needham, Joseph, *Science and Civilization in China*, Cambridge: Cambridge University Press, 1983, Vol. 5, pt. V, pp.125, 209.
34. Van Gulik, R.H., *Sexual Life in Ancient China: A Preliminary Survey of Chinese Sex and Society from ca. 1200 BC. until 1644 AD*, Leiden, The Netherlands: E.J. Brill, 1961.
35. Such as Jiang Weiqiao, Wang Geng and Chen Duizen. See Jang, Weiqiao, 'Wode tiyu guan' [My View of Exercise], *Changsha tiyu zhoubao* [Changsha Sports Weekly], No. 1, Jan. 1920, pp.19–20; Wang, Geng, 'Guocui tiyu' [On Traditional Exercise], *Xuedeng* [Study Guide], Oct. 1921, pp.30–1; Chen, Duizen, 'Fuxing minzhu Yu tichang guoshu zi yiyi' [On the Restoration of the Nation and the Promotion of Traditional Exercise], *Guoshu zhoukan* [Traditional Chinese Exercise Weekly], Oct. Nov. and Dec., 1934, No. 127, p.1, No. 128, p.2, No. 129, pp.2–3.
36. Ibid.; see also the Editor's article, 'Lun guoming tiyu' [On Sports and the Nation], *Dagong Bao* [Dagong Daily], 7 Aug. 1932.
37. Lu, Xun, 'Shuigan lu' [My View], *Xin qingnian* [New Youth], Vol. 5, No. 5, May 1918, pp.5–6; and 'quansu yu quanfei' [On Traditonal Exercise], *Xin qingnian* [New Youth], Vol. 6, No. 2, Feb. 1919, pp.9–10; see also Long, Liuquan, 'Pi jing-zou' [Denouncement of Traditional Exercise], *Changsha tiyu zhoubao* [Changsha Sports Weekly], No. 1 Jan. 1920, pp.105–16; Yuan, Denli, 'Shijie aohui de jianzhi ji duiyu woguo tiyu de yingxiang' [The Influence of the Olympics on Our Exercise], *Tianjin tiyu zhoubao* [Tianjin Sports Weekly], Vol. 1, No. 5, May 1932, pp.15–19; Wu, Yunrui, 'Jinhuo zi guomin tiyu wenti zi wojian' [My View on the Development of National Exercise], *Tianjin tiyu zhoubao* [Tianjin Sports Weekly], Vol. 1, No. 33, Sept. 1932, pp.2–3.
38. Ibid., and see also Xie Siyang, 'Da Dagong Bao shelun' [In Answer to the *Dagong*

Daily Leading Article of August], *Sports Weekly*, 27 Aug. 1932.

39. Jiang, Xiangqin, 'Tiyu jiujin shi shenmen?' [What is Sport?], *Jiaoyu rensheng* [Education and Human's Lives], No. 1, Oct. 1923, pp.2–4; Fang, Wanbang, 'Woguo tiyu xianxin shida wenti ji jiejue tujin' [Ten Problems of our Exercise and Sport and their Resolutions], *Tiyu jikan* [Sports Quarterly], Vol. 1, No. 3, July 1935, pp.353–61.
40. Mangan, J.A., 'Sport, Academic Myopia and A New Vision', *Zhongguo tiyu bao* [China's Sports Daily], 24 April 1992.
41. Hoberman, E.J., op. cit., pp.16–19.
42. See , for example, Chapters Five to Epilogue.
43. See, for example, Chapters Five to Eight.
44. See Fu Liannong, 'Lun Tanren Jianmei guan de bianhua' [The Changing Image of Beauty and Fitness in the Tang Dynasty], MA thesis, Chengdu tiyu xueyuan [Chengdu Physical Education Institute], 1989; Zhang Weiyi, 'Lun Tangdai funu de tiyu huodong' [On Women's Physical Activity in the Tang Dynasty], MA thesis, Chengdu tiyu xueyuan [Chengdu Physical Education Institute], 1986.
45. See below, especially Chapters Two and Three.
46. Zhang, Zhidong, 'Quan xu pian' [Exhortation to Study], 1898, trans. by Teng, Ssu-yu and Fairbank, J.K. *China's Response to the West, A Documentary Survey, 1839–1923*, New York: the Viking Press, 1967; Burton, M.E., *The Education of Women in China*, New York: Fleming H. Revell, 1911.
47. Burton, M.E., op. cit.
48. In October 1911 the Revolutionary Alliance launched its uprising in the city of Hankou. New Army troops led by Yuan Shikai joined the uprising against Qing. The Revolution led the fall of the Qing Dynasty and China became a Republic in February 1912.
49. CSHEPS, *Zhongguo jindai tiyu shi* [Modern Chinese Sports History], Beijing: Beijing tiyu xieyuan chubanshe [Beijing Physical Education Press], 1989, p.22.
50. Fan, Hong and Wang, Daping, *Tiyu shi manhua* [Sport History], Beijing: Kupu chubanshe [Chinese Science Press], 1989, pp.20–23, and 35–8.
51. See Chapters Five to Eight.
52. See the 1995 report of the State Council, 'The Situation of Chinese Women', *Beijing Review*, June 1994; see also the speech of Jiang Zemin (The General-Secretary of the Party) at the Opening Ceremony of the International Women's Conference in Beijing, Sept. 1995, (Conference document). They are a frank recognition of continuing discrimination in communist China.
53. Croll, E., *The Women's Movement in China*, Nottingham: Russell Press, 1973, p.11.
54. Riordan, J., *Sport, Politics and Communism*, Manchester: Manchester University Press, 1991, pp.131–2.
55. Hoberman, J.M., op. cit., p.222.
56. Riordan, J., op. cit., p.144.
57. Of course, it is fully recognised that sport is only one agency in this process. The point to be emphasised is that its role has not been sufficiently recognised by scholars.
58. It may be argued that there have been three stages in Western ideological hegemony (with different degrees of success): Christianity, Democracy and Capitalism.
59. Not least the emergence of 'Confucian Capitalism' with the attendant physical exploitation of women in various forms.

ONE

Culture, Challenge and Change in Late Feudal China: A Clash of Ideals and the Consequences

Traditional Chinese Culture before 1840

TERMS SUCH as restlessness, reaction, reform, revolution appropriately describe the political, cultural, social and economic conditions of China between 1840 and 1911.[1] To provide an introductory set of images for the exploration of female emancipation it will be helpful here to paint in broad strokes, before providing the finer brushwork to the Chinese canvas of the period, and then – in later chapters – enlarging the canvas with imagery beyond 1911 and up to 1949.

The conflict with the British opium traders and subsequent British expeditionary forces in 1840 was a turning point in modern Chinese history.[2] The Chinese mandarins as well as the general public were petrified and confused by defeat in the Opium War. These narcissistic and conceited Chinese officials, who had never before doubted the superiority of their power, culture and civilisation, had to swallow an unpalatable fact: they had been defeated by a people they had always called 'barbarians'.[3] This event had a devastating impact upon Chinese political, cultural, social and economic life. Eventually, Confucian conservatism – the 'cement' of one of the world's oldest civilisations began to crumble.[4] An alien culture, in the wake of military, economic and political invasions, began to challenge the Chinese way of life at the root of which lay Confucianism.[5]

For nearly two thousand years, as a philosophy of life, at every level[6] Confucianism had provided the political, social and moral foundation to Chinese culture.[7] It had sustained an inflexible social hierarchy and had ensured a static social structure.[8] The lengthy grip of Confucianism was a product of the geographical structure and the social and economic conditions of ancient China. Geographically, China was cut off from rest of the world by mountains and desert to the west and south-west, the formidable Pacific Ocean to the east and south, and the vast impenetrable grasslands and forests to the north. Family-based agricultural farming was the dominant form of productivity. The Chinese family hence constituted the nucleus of a social network, at the head of which sat the major bread-earner, the father of the family, who owned and controlled the family enterprise.[9] Century after century, a rural culture existed centring itself on the concepts of patri-archal power and filial piety, relying on trust, fidelity, fear of losing face and time-honoured rules of civilised conduct, all of which were later highlighted, standardised and exalted by Confucius and his neophytes through a set of precepts known as the Confucian Ethics.[10]

Confucianism is too large a doctrine to discuss in detail here. However, what is relevant is that under Confucianism there were 'Three Bonds': absolute loyalty and obedience were due from ministers to prince, from son to father and from wife to husband.[11] These bonds may be seen as the essence of Confucianism. These imperatives formed the foundation of monarchical despotism and social inequality, dividing people into rigid status groups with different rights and duties, not only according to social custom but also in law. It was this stable core of Confucian doctrine which, for almost two thousand years, ensured that it served as an official creed. The chief precept of Confucian ethics was filial piety. This was the basis of the monarchical as well as the family system. Filial piety and loyalty to the prince were twin concepts in Confucianism, for the prince was regarded as the father of the people, and a man's 'filial' obligations were fulfilled only when he extended his loyalty unreservedly to the prince. The rationale for 'piety' was social order at all levels. The core of Confucianism was Li (the rules of propriety) which were supposed to be based on the principle of benevolent control. It is important, however, that Confucian concepts are con-sidered within their actual historical context. In reality, in Chinese history, they were often nothing more than a manipulative means by which an absolute ruler enforced conformity. The rules of propriety were inflexible. They defined privileges and obligations in accordance with the individual's status, and they were sanctioned by law. In addi-tion, they were principles which ran directly contrary to modern ideals of liberty and equality. Eventually, this fact proved to be their Achilles heel.

18

The Confucian code resulted in a major abuse of the principle of equality – the unequal treatment of women. Among other things it imposed a ruthless double standard in sexual mores. According to Confucian concepts of chastity, for example, a woman whose husband died was supposed to remain a widow throughout her life and a girl was expected to commit suicide if she should have the misfortune to be raped. Furthermore, the wider requirement of chastity applied only to women. It was insistence on this unilateral 'inhuman' virtue that called forth the strongest protest from early modern progressive thinkers, such as Chen Duxiu (1880–1942), Hu Shi (1891–1962), and Lu Xun (1881–1936).[12] Lu Xun, China's foremost writer and thinker of the twentieth century saw clean through Confucianism and savagely attacked it as human 'cannibalism' in his *Diary of a Madman* (1918), the first book to be written in vernacular Chinese.

The story succinctly conveys the author's attitude towards the Confucian tradition. Suffering from a persecution complex, the mad-man thinks that all those around him, including his immediate family (very significant in the light of Confucian tradition) are going to kill and eat him. To confirm his suspicions, he delves into a book of Chinese history: 'The history recorded no dates, but over every page was scrawled the words "benevolence, righteousness, truth, virtue". Since I couldn't sleep, I made a close scrutiny of this book, until by midnight I discovered all over it a succession of two words between the lines: "Eat men".'[13] In spite of the Confucian protestation of stability and decency as its central tenets, for Lu Xun and many pro-gressive Chinese, traditional life consisted of nothing but moral cannibalism. In such hypocritical circumstances Confucian culture eventually brought about the moral stagnation of Chinese society, and led the Chinese to develop such cultural characteristics as obsequiousness, submissiveness and compliance.[14]

Confucianism, as discussed above, based on the economy of an autarchic family-based agriculture, honoured and safeguarded patri-archal power. It must be admitted that it was not wholly negative in impact. In the early stages of its existence, it was compatible with the economic development of China and contributed to the creation of positive social values which maintained both the stability and living standards of the autarchical family.[15] Nevertheless, in time, it became a reactionary force ritualised and bureaucratised by rulers to serve as a means of maintaining the status quo. As a result, the progress of the nation was thwarted for centuries. Gradually the people became less energetic, less enterprising, and less innovative and, eventually, the vigour of the whole nation was affected.[16] Interestingly, the change of form and emphasis in traditional Chinese physical activities nicely illustrates this cultural deterioration. From the moment that Confucianism came into being, it permeated the whole of Chinese society, reinforced existing social values, emphasised the concept of hierarchy, and, with deleterious results, infiltrated, and remoulded traditional Chinese physical culture. This had immediate and sub-sequent consequences for the moral mandates underpinning the cultural concepts of masculinity and femininity.

For instance, sports of an originally competitive nature, such as archery and the martial arts (wushu), lost their competitive nature through the influence of centuries of Confucianism. Archery, by way of an example, once a highly competitive contest with well-established rules and regulations, declined into a highly ritualised 'archery cere-mony',[17] with complicated ceremonial procedures. The social status rather than the performance of the participants was stressed. Distinctive bows, arrows and accompanying music were strictly allo-cated according the social status of the participants.[18] Another example of the impact of Confucian ethics on traditional Chinese sport involves Chuju, Chinese classic football. It was originally an aggres-sively competitive game, played by two opposing sides with two goals.[19] Due to its competitiveness, the game was often used by mili-tary mandarins to train soldiers in order to cultivate their fighting spirit and improve their physiques during the Han (206 BC–220 AD) and Tang (618–907 AD) Dynasties. However, as time passed, two goals merged into one in the Song (960–1279 AD) and Yuan (1260–1368 AD) Dynasties.[20] Vigorous competition was replaced by a much gentler phenomenon: less competitive and primarily exhibitive. Grace-fulness and harmony of movement were given priority.[21] Arguably the legacy of this evolution could still be found in recent modern Chinese sports. Perhaps this is one reason why, until recently, the Chinese have done better in gymnastics than in sports of a more directly confronta-tional nature. Other forms of traditional Chinese sport, swimming, for example, which could have easily developed into a competitive sport as did its Western counterpart, ceased to evolve and remained essentially a form of recreation, though it had been widely practised as early as the Qin Dynasty (221–207 BC).[22] And Chinese polo, competitive and popular both in and out of court in the Tang Dynasty (618–907 AD), simply disappeared.[23]

When Confucianism, therefore became the dominant official doctrine, physical culture, as an instrument of the wider culture, was adapted to serve as a means of reinforcing the new moral values, and the social status quo. Chinese traditional sports also lost some of their original aesthetic features. In Confucianism appreciation of the beauty of the human body was simply non-existent. It was forbidden for men to show large parts of the body or even to talk about the human physique. Even stricter rules applied to women.[24] Eventually, Chinese traditional sports accurately reflected widespread social values and conditions and could no longer draw any competitive energy from society. Their stagnation was inevitable. The source of this stagnation can be traced directly to Confucian culture, which was not only accountable for the reorientation of traditional Chinese exercise, but also prevented women from participating in it.

Women's role and status were clearly and unequivocally defined in Confucianism, which borrowed its essential wisdom from an even more ancient concept of the first millennium BC. This was the concept of 'yin' and 'yang', according to which, the universe was composed of two interacting elements: 'yin' and 'yang'. 'Yin' symbolised femininity: dark, weak, passive; 'Yang' symbolised masculinity: bright, strong, active. The whole universe and its elements fell into two categories; the sun and the moon, day and night, summer and winter. This dualism might be an insightful concept when applied cautiously and selectively to the natural world in which some things can be divided into two interacting and complementary parts, but when in classic Chinese philosophy it was used to explain all of human society, simplistically and fallaciously, it heaped all kinds of positive and superior traits upon men and left women with negative and inferior characteristics.[25]

This cosmological belief was incorporated into the teaching of Confucius and his followers in the second century BC and became part of the official value system since it helped to maintain feudal rule – the son of Heaven was 'yang' and the ruled were 'yin'. According to this concept, men and women were as different as heaven and earth: men were noble and women were ignoble. And their roles were distinct: 'While a man does not talk about internal affairs (affairs inside the house), a woman does not talk about external affairs (affairs outside the house).'[26] Accordingly, women were regarded as ignorant, limited and inferior. A series of cruel restrictions were imposed upon them. They had to 'obey the father when at home, submit to the husband when married, and listen to the son after the husband dies'.[27] Their life became one of subjugation. They were oppressed by imperial, feudal and patriarchal power.

In order to have women completely in its control and at its disposal, the Confucian-dominated society also invented and forced upon women an odd and appalling concept of feminine physical beauty – the small, bound foot. It became the symbol of women's subservience.

The bound foot was euphemistically known as the 'golden lily' or the 'perfumed lily'. Girls usually began to bind their feet from four to five years of age. The toes were broken and bent under the sole of the foot, and the foot was then bound with several metres of bandages that stopped the blood circulation. This physically restrictive process lasted ten to fifteen years. During that time, girls could not at first get up for several months even with the aid of the cane. After one year they could only get about by being carried in sedan chairs. J. W. Maxwell has described the nature of footbinding:

> The practice consists in the application of a short, heavy bandage, neatly and tightly bound to the feet of growing girls. The great toe is merely compressed. . . . The other four toes, however, are bent under the foot, where they are eventually walked on and their compression and atrophy enhanced . . . a foot is thus shortened and in addition, owing to constant pressure and insufficient circulation, the plantar length thereof may be as short as three inches, or a little less.'[28]

The practice of footbinding seems to date back to the Han Dynasty (206BC–24AD), and it became fashionable at the beginning of the tenth century between the Five Dynasty (907–960) and the beginning of the Song Dynasty (960–1279). This development was attributed to Li Yu (937–978), the second emperor of the Southern Tang Dynasty. He was supposed to have compelled his favourite concubine, Yaoniang, to dance with small bound feet on the image of a large lotus flower.[29] It became the fashion. Men praised its aesthetic and erotic qualities. The small feet, measured steps and gentle swaying gait were thought to be reminiscent of the willow or poplar in the wind. The slight body looked ready to fall at the slightest touch. In men's eyes, 'looking at a woman with bound feet walking is like looking at a rope-dancer, tantalising to the highest degree. The bound foot is indeed the highest sophistication of the Chinese sensual imagination'.[30] The small, elegant feet occupied an important place in

Li Yu (937–978), the second emperor of the Southern Tang Dynasty, compelled his favourite concubine, Yaoniang, to bind her feet and dance on the image of a large lotus flower. (From Yao Lingxi, (ed.), *Cai fei lu* [The Record of Tiny Feet], Tianjin: Shidai gongshi and Tianjin shuju, 1936–38).

'Golden Lotus touches the Ground'. (From Yao Lingxi, (ed.), *Cai fei lu* [The Record of Tiny Feet], Tianjin: Shidai gongshi and Tianjin shuju, 1936–38).

sensual poetry and song.[31] There was even a book which classified the bound feet into five main divisions and eighteen types.[32]

Bound feet were associated with security, mobility and status. As Lin Yutang, a famous early twentieth century Chinese writer stated, 'Mothers who wanted their girls to grow up into ladies and marry into good homes had to bind their feet young as a measure of parental foresight, and a bride who was praised for her small feet had a feeling analogous to filial gratitude.'[33] A small-shaped foot was a girl's pride. Bound feet became an essential prerequisite for an advantageous marriage and indeed, for any form of successful social mobility.[34] For women the bound foot was the passport to all that was good in life. It was, for both men and women, the dominant form of sexual attractiveness. Therefore footbinding became customary.

Under such conditions, Chinese women's health and fitness went into decline. With their small feet and weak bodies, self-evidently, they could do little. The only traditional physical exercise available to them comprised of nothing more than court entertainments, such as court polo and dancing to amuse men, and very undemanding sports, such as weiqi (Chinese chess),[35] rope skipping, touhu, (throwing arrows into a bottle),[36] and some seasonal activities like crossing a bridge or taking a stroll on Chinese New Year's Eve to drive away the evil spirits, gentle hill walking on the ninth day of the Ninth Lunar Month and playing on a swing on the fifth day of the Fourth Lunar Month. As regards competitive sports, for reasons already discussed above, there were almost none for men, and certainly none for women.[37]

Before 1840, therefore, orthodox Confucianism held a dominant position in traditional Chinese culture. Its essence was the 'principle of hierarchy', which governed political structure, social life and traditional ethics. Ancient Chinese exercise, as a product of China's culture and history, closely reflected the social relationships of a male-dominated, hierarchical society. Women's bodies also neatly demonstrated this state of affairs. Physical freedom was repressed.

Cultural Challenges (1840–60)

In the eighteenth century, the British East India Company's export trade of Indian fabrics to Britain was curtailed by various Acts of Parliament in order to protect Britain's own growing textile industry, and the Company turned its attention to the importation of tea from China. In theory, the tea was to be paid for in silver specie. However, there was a problem. Prior to this moment, China had been a despotic country which relied on self-sufficiency, despised the concept of foreign trade, and provided no opportunities for foreign companies. Thus, in practice, tea was obtained by the illegal export of Indian opium to China by private merchants working in conjunction with the Company and encouraged by the British government. The eventual restriction imposed on this arrangement by the Chinese authorities irritated these aggressive entrepreneurs, who demanded free trade and diplomatic immunity – to no avail. The Chinese government considered opium highly undesirable and in 1839 sent Commissioner Lin Zexu to Guangzhou (Canton) to suppress the opium trade. Lin expelled the British and destroyed the opium stock. In consequence, in June 1840, a British expeditionary force blockaded Guangzhou (Canton) and on 20 June the Chinese were forced to sign the Chuanpi Convention, whereby they undertook to cede Hong Kong Island to the British. Later, in August 1841, the British set off north occupying, in quick succession, Xiamen(Amoy), Tinghai, Ningpo, Shanghai, and Zhenjiang and the Manchu government was forced to sign the 1842 Treaty of Nanking (Nanjing). This officially ended the Opium War on 29 August 1842. In accordance with its terms, Xiamen, Fuzhou, Ningpo, Shanghai and Guangzhou were all to be opened to British trade. It was the beginning of a series of humiliating treaties imposed by force on the declining Chinese empire. China's door, having been closed for centuries, had been forced open by the British. This event marked the beginning of China's modern history.[38]

The military confrontation with the British opium traders and troops brought China's face to face with a strange people and culture. This fact now gradually influenced the development of the country and created both an immediate crisis and acute instability for the Chinese establishment. However, this foreign invasion also brought opportunities for the progressive forces in the country to take action against the ruling class and the dated Confucian ethics. The first incident of this kind[39] was the Taiping Tianguo (Kingdom of Heavenly Peace) Uprising, which took place between the years 1850 and 1864.

The beginning of the nineteenth century found the Manchu (Qing Dynasty, 1644–1911) regime in trouble and in slow, irreversible decline. The Qing Dynasty had reached its prime in its early years after replacing the Ming Dynasty (1368–1644) and had indeed, for a time, pumped some vigour into the nation. However, soon after it had secured absolute power and control over the country, like all totalitarian regimes in history, it developed all kinds of sick symptoms, such as administrative inefficiency, widespread corruption, peculation, a drained treasury and an incipient economic crisis. These symptoms foretold the fall of the Dynasty in a not too distant future. Foreign invasion accelerated the decline. By the middle of the nineteenth century, all the symptoms coalesced into a serious political cancer. Government corruption, foreign encroachment, a large floating population and local revolutions began to beset the aged empire. In 1850 a period of great turbulence started with the most radical and violent rebellion in Qing history, the above mentioned Taiping Tianguo Uprising.[40]

Led by Hong Xiuquan, the Taiping Rebels, united under doctrines of quasi-Christianity, started out from Guangxi Province and soon spread all over the Qing Empire. It was the first time in China's history that the Chinese people had risen openly against the feudal empire, imperial government, and the emperor, the son of the Chinese Heaven, who had been worshipped as a sacred icon. [41] Influenced by a new religious ideology based on Protestant ethics gleaned selectively from Western missionaries, and fashioned after their own understanding of the Bible, the rebels directed their attacks against 'the Son of the Chinese Heaven'. Hong proclaimed that he was the younger son of God and the brother of Jesus Christ. He took as his responsibility the introduction of the worship of the Christian God into China and inaugurated a campaign which took on many of the outward features of Western Protestant Christianity. [42]

The sect, 'the Worshippers of Shangdi' (a Chinese term for God), led personally by Hong himself, became very popular. Its cult contained many elements of Chinese provenance: the cult was a bizarre syncretism of misunderstood Christian and Chinese beliefs, which justified the sect's political actions.[43] They strove to overthrow the Manchu regime and to reform China by reshaping its existing social values in line with what they understood of Christian religious theology and Western political ideas.[44] Serious efforts were directed at land reform, the creation of a common treasury, the restructuring of hierarchic and discriminatory social patterns,[45] and, most importantly from the perspective of this study, the establishment of equality between men and women and the improvement of women's social status.[46] This included the abolition of foot-binding [47] – a practice that was both an abstract affirmation of women's restricted status in feudal China, and a concrete means of confining women within the home. Of course, these reformatory ideas and actions clashed with established social values and met the powerful resistance of Confucian tradition. The reform movement alienated the landed class, petty officialdom and the educated, whose learning was largely composed of Confucian doctrine. It was asking a lot of the rebels to fight against so many enemies at the same time, especially the power of Confucian precepts. Nevertheless, since they were all linked it was necessary to fight them all.

For their part, the women of the Taiping Rebellion were acutely conscious of the inequality that society imposed upon them and demanded equality with men in such issues as rights of land owner- ship and the right to education including 'physical education'[48] – the prerequisite of women's military contribution to the success of the rebellion. And militarily women did contribute successfully.[49] Some women even held the position of senior commander,[50] and poems were written in praise of their courage, fighting spirit and intelligence. One such verse acclaimed a female fighter Su San-niang:

> Crowd thronged on the streets like cattle,
> To see Su San-niang returned from her battle,
> Blessed as daughter of God she fought,
> Praised were her military merits by all.[51]

Of another woman warrior, it was proclaimed:

> Under her command,
> Two hundred gallant soldiers stand,
> Tens of thousands enemies to be
> Stand no chance but to flee.[52]

While of another it was recorded:

> In the hundred battles that she fought,
> Never ever beaten was the report.[53]

Crude as these extracts from ballads of the time are, they offer clear evidence of the acceptance of women military leaders.[54] Triumphantly returning women victors and high-ranking commanders certainly improved women's image in society.

As we have seen above, in the Taiping Tianguo Uprising, Christianity indirectly played a positive part in improving women's social position. Inspired by imported Protestant ethics, the rebels came to hold the view that because both were children of God, all men and women should be equal and they should have the same rights. Accordingly, the ultimate aim was to set up an earthly 'Kingdom of Heavenly Peace', in which men and women would live happily in egalitarian harmony. To achieve this Utopia, the rebels believed that men and women must fight together against patriarchal power, which was regarded as the foundation of feudal rule. The 'historically unprecedented, glorious, and progressive liberation of women', as Fan Wenlan, the distinguished Chinese historian, once put it, would then 'become a reality in the unfolding course of this peasant revolution'.[55] Reformers thus began their campaign by attacking the traditional sexist patriarchy, the ancient family structure and institutionalised discrimination against women. This attack was of great significance, for by instilling in people a slavish morality the patriarchal order provided the psychological foundation for autocratic monarchical rule and patriarchal domination. Unsurprisingly, Zeng Guofan, an out-and-out advocate of Confucianism, and later the commander of the government army, stated that the rebellion was ' an unprecedented crisis in the history of ethical principles' and a threat to the Confucian moral order.[56]

The rebels' overt proclamation against the ruling class inevitably provoked the Manchu regime and incurred immediate repression. But it was their threat to Confucian morality that was utilised to crush the rebellion. Zeng Guofan, instead of calling for support to fight for the dynasty or for the son of Heaven, appealed to the country's gentry by saying, 'What they (the rebels) want is not a change only concerning our great Qing Dynasty. No, it is a vital change that concerns our nation's entire moral tradition. They make our Confucians . . . weep in the world. How can anyone who can read and write remain silent and just sit there with hands in sleeves, without thinking of doing something about it?'[57]

The rebellion was finally defeated in 1864.[58] A foreign religion, a challenge to fundamental Confucianism, and a threat to the established patriarchal power were all too much for the Confucian culture to permit. More time and a much stronger seed of the progressive ideal were needed to push aside the deeply rooted Confucian culture of centuries of growth in the cultural soil of China. Military action at this moment in time on the part of the liberals was not able to achieve this, no matter how zealous the reformers were nor how many

Western military advisers were hired by them.[59] However, although this first conflict ended with the defeat of the progressive forces, exogenous cultural influence was not to be eliminated with military defeat. Western theology, culture and ideas advocated by the Taiping Rebels, especially a progressive advocacy (for the time in both West and East) of equality between men and women and the abolition of footbinding essential for women's eventual physical liberation, had brought a glimmer of light, that would glow progressively brighter in the long dark tunnel of the feudal regime.

Unlike the urban origins of the emancipation of women in Europe,[60] the emancipation of Chinese women arose out of a rural revolution – and physical transformation. It was the rural 'female barbarians with unbound feet' of the Taiping Movement, who pulled back the curtains of modern history for Chinese women and allowed them on to the public stage. Thus started an era when women's issues and the role of women in Chinese society slowly began to come to the fore in Chinese history.

Cultural Confrontation (1860–94)

Due to the domestic disturbances and foreign incursions, some progressive Qing bureaucrats now began to appreciate the extent of the crisis which the nation was facing. They united and planned the reform of Chinese culture, economy and politics, and to this end they launched a movement known as 'Westernization' (1861–94).[6] The movement had two objectives: the purchase of Western weaponry to strengthen national defence in conjunction with the introduction of Western machinery and technology to industrialise the country; and the revival of traditional Chinese Confucian culture. These measures were aimed at saving the declining Qing Empire.

Inevitably, however, with Western modern equipment and technology came Western influences, which were at odds with Confucian ethics. Western missionaries, educationists, merchants and sailors flooded into the Chinese ports, Western-style buildings arose in large cities and harbour towns. Telegraph offices and foreign banks were introduced. Translations of Western books flourished. The government even felt the need to send students abroad to study and began to show a degree of tolerance for Western ideas.[62] Thus, this period saw not only the introduction of Western merchandise and technology,

30

but also witnessed an influx of Western cultural institutions, such as missionary education, military training and physical culture. The latter was greatly favoured by the government. Sensibly, it believed that military power was the bulwark of the Empire and, in addition, that mass military physical exercises which stressed unity and discipline helped maintain a unified regime. As a result, these exercises, borrowed from the successful Western forces, spread rapidly and widely all over China.

This military-orientated physical exercise was known as Tichao – gymnastics. It provided most of the physical training that was available in Chinese schools during this period. The fundamental purpose of the physical exercise programme was to make boys good soldiers. Marching, saluting, and military terminology were stressed in imitation of a military camp. This tradition of military drill held a strong position of influence for the greater part of the last twenty years of the nineteenth century.[63] It is not to be overlooked. Western military exercises as a contribution to military success won the approval and support of the Chinese authorities because they were significant instruments of political control. However, they also created a climate of acceptability for Western practice that eventually had implications for women and their physical freedom, but first their feet had to be unbound.

Other kinds of Western exercise, such as basketball, baseball, volleyball, tennis, and track and field events were ignored by the Qing government and received little official attention, though they existed in missionary schools and through the YMCA and YWCA in some large cities. Western military exercises were the dominant form of exercise in this period in China.[64] But the potential of more readily recognisable kinds of Western exercise should never be underestimated. The seeds of change had been planted and were germinating. The missionary had a large role to play in the physical liberation of Chinese women as the next chapter will reveal in some detail.

Germination occured mostly in Western-style schools and academies established during this period.[65] In these schools, Western military exercises were taught as a major subject and physical education was a compulsory course. The physical education curriculum in the North Western Navy Academy included fencing, boxing, football, high jump, long jump, swimming, skating and gymnastics.[66] In 1872, the Qing government selected 120 young boys to be sent to the United States to study as part of the national self-strengthening programme.[67] On return from abroad, after seven to nine years' study, they became the major advocates of Western ideas, technology and physical activity.[68] Team games also made their first appearance in this period in some girls' schools – on a voluntary basis and between classes.[69] The reasons for this, as mentioned above, will be considered in depth shortly. At this point it should simply be observed that missionary rather than military zeal provided the stimulus.

The Westernisation Movement, then, was an opportunity for the feudal government to absorb new ideas. As part of the process, Western exercises, together with Western science and technology, were introduced into China. As these exercises became part of the Chinese cultural domain, there were eventually to be important consequences for Chinese women.

Change and Continuity (1895–1911)

China's Westernisation Movement came to a halt when China was defeated in the first Sino-Japanese War (1894–95).[70] The dream of restoring China's power and strength through the Westernisation Movement was shattered. If the defeat by the Western powers came as a shock, the defeat by Japan, its small neighbour, brought nothing but utter humiliation to the Chinese. For Japan had been regarded until then by the Chinese as a cultural colony, whose modernisation had been recently completed through its Meiji Restoration launched only in 1868.[71] The defeat had immediate and extensive repercussions at home and caused Chinese progressives to review the progress of their own efforts at Westernisation.

They found that their attempt to modernise China was nothing more than building castles in the air. Foreign ideas and practices could not simply be raised on China's traditional cultural foundations. They realised that if China wanted to grow strong in order to catch up with the developments of the Western world, major changes to its political system and its culture, including reforms of moral, intellectual and physical institutions and the introduction of a new educational system, were all essential. These ideas were simply too much for a minor reform to accommodate. There would have to be a major revolution. Many Chinese intellectuals, therefore, now demanded radical reconstruction. Thus in 1898, another movement, known as the One Hundred Days Reform (or the Constitutional Reform

Movement),[72] led by Kang Youwei (1858–1927), Liang Qichao (1873–1929), Tan Sitong (1865–98), Yan Fu (1853–1921) and others, was launched with the aim of bringing the Western democratic ideal and political system to China.[73]

More and more academics came to realise China's serious political and cultural decline and attributed much of it to Confucianism. The 1898 reform movement were able to gain influence with the Guangxu Emperor and persuaded him to issue edicts calling for the creation of a political advisory council, the abolition of sinecures in the bureaucracy, the promotion of industry and commerce, and the creation of a national school system which would include Western learning in the curriculum. The reform movement endorsed many Western cultural institutions, among them Western exercise.[74] The leaders of the movement, as others of the Qing government before them, considered that Western military exercises and physical exercise programmes were conducive to boosting their revolutionary ideas, which they saw as embodied, to some extent, in the energy, developed fitness, stamina, strength and self-reliance produced by such exercise. Yan Fu, a student newly returned from England, who translated Thomas Huxley's book *Evolution and Ethics* into Chinese, in an essay entitled 'On Strength',[75] pointed out that Darwin's evolutionary theories and Spencer's sociological writing had implications for transforming and strengthening society. Above all, there was the need to strengthen people's bodies. Therefore, Chinese culture, which ignored the value of a strong body, needed to be changed. To reform China, stated Yan, it was crucial to develop strength through (Western) exercise.

His was far from being a lone voice. Kang Youwei, the leader of the Constitutional Reform Movement, wrote a memorandum to the Qing government recommending the abolition of traditional Chinese military training and examinations and the creation of Western style military schools throughout China to train Chinese soldiers and students.[76] Thus the idea of saving the country, in part, by promoting Western patterns of physical exercise, came into being.[77] The leaders cherished the hope that cultural reform, in turn, would bring about a change in political institutions. However, a hostile conservative reaction, headed by the Empress-dowager Cixi, led to the arrest of the leading reformers, the crushing of the movement, and the placing of Guangxu under house arrest.[78]

Although the Empress-dowager Cixi showed some sympathy for

elements of Western modern culture, she would not permit the whole-sale transformation of her Chinese traditional culture, and would never tolerate any significant change in the indigenous social and political systems. Hence, when she perceived that Western cultural influence had become a threat to the Chinese feudal legacy, she resorted to military action to suppress the Constitutional Reform Movement. She then supported the Boxer Rebellion,[79] an anti-Western revolt, which started in 1898 as a movement to drive out foreigners and to protect the Qing dynasty.[80] The Empress-dowager Cixi freely used xenophobic sentiments in an attempt to restrict, and better still to get rid of, Western influence in the country. It had grown too powerful and had become a threat to her power.

In 1899, however, the counter-reform movement began to get out of hand. Several foreign missionaries were killed and Chinese Christians were attacked by the Boxers. Railways and telegraph lines, which were associated with the hated foreigners, were destroyed. Finally, when the Boxers besieged the foreign legations in the capital, Cixi rode the anti-foreign wave by declaring war upon the foreign powers. This untimely decision failed to gain support from the provincial governors in the South who protected foreign lives and property in their own domains and thus prevented the spread of the conflict. Cixi's decision was not even fully supported in the court. Hence, when in 1900 the Western allies (comprising Britain, the USA, Japan, Russia, Germany, France, Austria and Italy) sent an expeditionary force [81] to Beijing to relieve the legations, the Qing government could not put up an effective resistance. A quick and harsh settlement was imposed, including the payment of an indemnity and the permanent stationing of foreign troops between Beijing and Tianjin.

The defeat by the Western allies smashed the Qing government's dream of restoring the empire by military force. From then on, the government continued to make concessions to the foreign powers, and also began to adopt reforms in the hope of reviving the dying empire. For the first time in its long feudal history, China's government was brought into the whirlpool of modern world politics and, among other things, made to re-evaluate its educational policy. The Empress-dowager Cixi herself, having vaguely realised *inter alia* the weaknesses of the Chinese educational system, and in a desperate attempt to secure the survival of the dynasty, launched a series of educational reforms. These included the abolition of the traditional

34

imperial civil service examination system (of some 1,300 years' standing) based on the Confucian classics, its replacement in 1905 by a national system of modern schools,[82] and the encouragement of study abroad, particularly in Japan, which was regarded as an inspirational example of Asiatic modernisation.

Western ideals and methods of education were now introduced into schools. These included physical exercise, gymnastics and modern games and were prescribed by the Qing government. In 1903, the government stipulated two or three hours per week of physical exercise for upper and lower elementary schools.[83] Subsequently, physical education was made a required course in middle schools, higher schools, lower normal schools and lower agricultural schools. In 1909, schools were required to offer physical education as a required course[84] and the time allotted for gymnastics and physical exercise in schools was raised to four hours per week.[85]

Through these major changes in educational practice attention was drawn gradually and increasingly to Western exercise, sport and games, although due to an admiration of things Japanese (German-influenced), gymnastics still held pride of place in the formal curriculum. As we have seen earlier, these Western innovations represented progressive elements in China, who saw in them the embodiment of a new spirit that could revitalise the dying Empire. Traditional Chinese exercises, inevitably associated with traditional Chinese culture, were now neglected and were excluded from the curriculum of modern schools. They began to move from the centre to the margin of the cultural stage, especially in large cities, which were the main locations of the developing westernised culture. From now on, the rapid expansion of Western exercises, sports and games and the decline of traditional Chinese activities went hand in hand.

Reports in national and regional newspapers and periodicals in the early years of the twentieth century provide clear evidence of the new fashion. The first report of a basketball game appeared in the *Tientsin Bulletin* of the municipal YMCA on 11 January 1896: 'A game of basketball will be played this afternoon. All young men interested in athletics are welcome to join the game at 4 p.m.'[86] Basketball soon spread to other schools and became the most popular ball game in China. In 1907 baseball was brought into China.[87] In addition, football matches between some Chinese college teams, such as Hsieh Ho and Huiwen, and Western legation guards' teams became a regular event.[88] Track and field events were organised both in missionary schools and government schools. By 1908, track and field meetings were held frequently in Tianjin, Beijing, Shanghai, Fuzhou, and at least ten other cities. The earliest events include Baoding (1904), Beijing (1905), Chengdu (1905) and Nanjing (1907).[89]

In 1910 newspapers reported the First National Athletic Meeting which contributed greatly to Chinese interest in modern sports. This Meeting was held from 18 to 22 October and was the first modern sports event at the national level. The activities included many of the recently introduced Western sports and games, such as track and field, tennis, football and basketball. Each day, on average, some 40,000 spectators attended. Interest was intense. *The North Herald* reported that, 'The First National Athletic Meet in China bids fair to leave as significant a mark on the country as the meeting of the National Assembly in Peking.'[90] The *Association Men* remarked about the same time that 'China is getting athletic. This event tells us that the Chinese youth is awakening . . . Many schools and other organisations are eager to get involved in physical training activities. All this will mean an improvement of the physique of young China.'[91]

An amusing sidelight to this national meeting, which nicely illustrated the conflict between modern Western culture and traditional Chinese culture in China in those years, was offered by the case of Sun Baoqing, a high jumper from Tianjin. Sun had performed poorly in the opening round, because his long pig-tail constantly knocked the bar off its stands. He was so angry that the same evening, without a second thought, he cut off his long queue – the source of his identity, according to Manchu law.[92] He came back the next day to become high-jump champion of China.[93] His action was more than a symbolic gesture! The point to be made again and again is the significance of the body in the metamorphosis of Chinese culture in its great period of challenge and change in the second half of the nineteenth century. For men, but more especially for women, the body became an icon of modernity, reconstruction and rehabilitation. The role of the physical in the redefinition of the moral capacity of Chinese culture, society and politics deserves more than a footnote in contemporary Chinese history. Yet to date it has been insufficiently considered in both text and footnote.

Involvement in Western physical activities, of course, was the mere tip of a revolutionary iceberg – large, powerful and inexorable. In the social and political spheres, disenchanted Chinese, especially the intelligentsia, disillusioned with the Qing regime and faced with a changing world, began to ponder upon the appropriateness of Confucian ideas and ethics. They wanted to see China revive and become strong and powerful again. They saw the weaknesses of traditional Chinese culture and wanted it reformed through Westernisation. By studying Western philosophical works and observing European and American societies, they came to the conclusion that the vigour which had accounted for the advance of the Western powers resided in the strong individual development of mind *and* body. In their attempt to create a social environment which would help to free individuals from traditional bondage and improve individual creativity, the reformers eventually turned their attention to the greatest 'undeveloped resource' – Chinese women. Thus women's emancipation – physical, mental and moral – was, for the first time in China's history, brought into sharp focus in society.

In summary, the second half of the nineteenth century was a time of drastic change in China, which not only provoked strong resistance from the ruling regime but also from fellow-travellers – die-hard Confucians. Disenchantment with the ethics of these fundamentalists and their contribution to political, economic and cultural decline stimulated criticism and confrontation. The consequences were internal cultural conflicts provoked by Western cultural diffusion (including a new conceptualisation of physicality – for men and women). Several attempts at reform were made and failed. However, change was seen as necessary and slowly came about. A direct consequence was a new role for women in a new society.

With the broad brushwork of the late nineteenth-century canvas completed it is now appropriate to paint in the finer detail – the reconstruction of women's physicality, a reconceptualisation of women's physical capabilities and a redefinition of women's physical rights. Leading the reformatory charge for this reconstruction, reconceptualisation and redefinition, were the Christian missionaries from the West, who will be considered in Chapter Two.

Notes

1. Spence, Jonathan D., *The Search for Modern China*, London: Hutchinson, 1990; McAleavy, Henry, *The Modern History of China*, London: Weidenfeld and Nicolson, 1967; Rodzinski, Witold, *The Walled Kingdom: A History of China from 2000 BC to the Present*, London: Fontana Paperbacks, 1984, pp.164–229; Heren, L., Fitzgerald, C.P., Freeberne, M., Hook, B. and Bonavia, D., *China's Three*

Thousand Years: The Story of A Great Civilization, London: Times Newspapers Ltd, 1973, p.170.

2. Latourette, K.S., *The Chinese: Their History and Culture*, New York: Macmillan, 1964, p.302.

3. Hu, Sheng, *Cong yapian zhanzheng dao wusi yundong* [From the Opium War to the May Fourth Movement], Shanghai: Shanghai renmin chubanshe [Shanghai People's Press], 1982, pp.11–13; Jian, Bozhan (ed.), *Zhongguoshi gangyao* [The History of China], Beijing: Renmin chubanshe [People's Press], Vol. 4, 1982, p.4; Teng, Ssu-yu and Fairbank, John K., *China's Response to the West: A Documentary Survey, 1839–1923*, op. cit., pp.53–4; Spence, Jonathan D., *The Search for Modern China*, op. cit., p.196.

4. Ho, Pingti, 'The Significance of the Qing Period in Chinese History', in Levenson, J.R. (ed.), *Modern China: An Interpretive Anthology*, New York: Macmillan, 1971, p.25.

5. Smith, D.H., *Confucians*, London: Temple Smith, 1973, p.18.

6. Berthrong, J., 'Sages and Immortals: Chinese Religions', in *The World's Religions*, A Lion Handbook Series, London: Lion Publishing, 1982, p.245; Needham, J., *Within the Four Seas*, London: Allen & Unwin, 1969, p.63.

7. Smith, D.H., op. cit., p.158.

8. Jaywardena, K., *Feminism and Nationalism in the Third World*, London: Zed, 1987, p.170.

9. McAleavy, Henry, op. cit., pp.4–11.

10. Smith, D.H., op. cit., pp.72–3; Berthrong, J., op. cit., pp.246–51.

11. Chen, Jinpan, op. cit., p.13.

12. For details of Chen Duxiu, Hu Shi and Lu Xun, see Chapter Four, notes, 51, 60 and 66.

13. Lu, Xun, *Kuanren riji* [Diary of a Madman], English translation see *Lu Xun quanji*, Beijing: Foreign Language Press, 1957, Vol. 1, pp.6–21.

14. Liang, Qichao. 'Xin min shuo – lun shang wu' [New People – On Promotion of Military Exercise], *Xin min congbao* [The Journal of New People], No. 1, 1903, pp.7–14.

15. Croll, E., *Feminism and Socialism in China*, op. cit., p.22.

16. Feng, Gesheng, 'Jun guomin pian – yuanyin yu tipo zhe' [On Military Exercise – Weak Bodies Cause the Weakness of the Nation], op. cit.; Liang, Qichao, 'Xin min shuo – lun shang wu' [New People – On Promotion of Military Exercise], op. cit.

17. Zhou, Xikuan, *et al.*, *Zhongguo gudai tiyu shi* [The Physical Education and Sport History of Ancient China], Chengdu: Sichuan guji chubanshe, 1986, p.57.

18. Ibid.

19. Gong, Shixun, 'Shilun handai zhuqiu' [On Chinese Football in Han Dynasty], *Tiyu weishi* [The Journal of Sports Culture and History] hereafter *TWS*, No. 1, 1989, pp.44–55.

20. Tang, Hao (ed.), *Zhongguo tiyu chankao zhiliao ji* [Chinese Sports History Record], Beijing: Renmin tiyu chubanshe [People's Sports Press], 1958, Vol. 1, p.48.

21. Qiao, Keqin and Guan, Wenmin, *Zhongguo tiyu shixiang shi* [Chinese Physical Culture History], Lanzhou: Gansu minzu chubanshe [Gansu Minorities Press], 1993, pp.98, 140.

22. Gu, Shiquan, *Zhongguo tiyu shi* [Physical Education and Sport in China], Beijing: Beijing tiyu xueyuan chubanshe [Beijing Physical Education Institute Press], 1987, p.26.

23. Sui, Peiyie, 'Tangdai maqiu' [The History of Chinese Polo], *Chengdu tiyu xueyuan xuebao* [The Journal of Chengdu Institute of Physical Education], No. 3, Sept. 1985, pp.31–6; see also his MA thesis 'Lun maqiu de qiyuan he fazhan' [On the

Origin and Development of Chinese Polo], Chengdu tiyu xueyuan [Chengdu Physical Education Institute], 1985.

24. Croll, E., *Feminism and Socialism in China*, op. cit., p.13; Qiao and Guan, op. cit., p.117.

25. Berthrong, J., 'Sages and Immortals: Chinese Religions', op. cit., p.244.

26. Quoted in *Xin qingnian* [New Youth], Vol. 2, No. 4, Dec. 1916, p.3.

27. Quoted in Headland, I.T., *Home Life in China*, London, 1914, p.69 (np).

28. Snow, Helen, *Women in Modern China*, The Netherland: Mouton, 1967, p.18.

29. Bao, Chuzi, 'Quan jie chanzu' [On Release from Footbinding], *Wanguo gongbao* [International News], Vol. 710, 14 Oct. 1882.

30. Lin, Yutang, *My Country and My People*, London: Williams, 1936, p.159.

31. Levy, H.S., *Chinese Footbinding: The History of a Chinese Erotic Custom*, London: Neville Spearman, 1966, p.41.

32. Lin, Yutang, *My Country and My People*, op. cit., p.160.

33. Ibid.

34. Pruitt, I., *A Daughter of Han: An Autobiography of a Working Woman*, Stanford: Stanford University Press, 1967, p.22.

35. Yong, Gaotang *et al.*, (eds), *Tiyu baike quanshu* [The Encyclopedia of Chinese Sport], Beijing: Zhongguo baike quanshu chubanshe [Chinese Encyclopedia Press], 1980, p.341.

36. Ibid., p.278.

37. Qiao and Guan, op. cit., pp.115–18.

38. Jian, Bozhan, op. cit., pp.1–10; Hu, Sheng, op. cit., pp.33–82.

39. Hu, Sheng, op. cit., pp.116–25.

40. Ibid., pp.125–62; also see Jian, Bozan, op. cit., pp.19–27; Heren *et al.*, op. cit., p.149.

41. Michael, F., 'Regionalism in Nineteenth Century China', in Levenson, op. cit., p.48.

42. Rodzinski, W., op. cit., pp.186–7.

43. Boardman, Eugene Powers, *Christian Influence Upon the Ideology of the Taiping Rebellion*, Wisconsin: University of Wisconsin Press, 1952.

44. Michael, F., 'Regionalism in Nineteeth Century China', op. cit., p.48.

45. See *Taiping tianguo* [The Taiping Rebellion], Shanghai: Shengzhou chubanshe [China Press], 1954 (editor's name is not available).

46. Ibid., p.155; see also Guo, Tinyi, *Taiping tianguo shisi rizhi* [Taiping Rebellion History], Taibei: Commercial Press, 1963, pp.149–50; Chen, Zhongyu, 'Taiping tianguo de funu zhenche' [The Policy towards Women in the Taiping Rebellion], in Bao, Jialin (ed.), *Zhongguo funu shi lun ji* [the Selected Works on Chinese Women's History], Taibei: Daoxiang chubanshe, 1992, pp.240–45.

47. Ono, Kazuko. op. cit., p.11.

48. CSHSPE, *Zhongguo jindai tiyu shi* [Modern Chinese Sports History], op. cit., pp.20–21.

49. Zhong, Dejian. 'Zheqing huozhuan – wei nuguan zhan' [The Report of Taiping Rebelllion – Military Women], in *Taiping tianguo* [The Taiping Rebellion], op. cit., No. 3, pp.110–11.

50. Ibid., pp.94, 105; also see Ono Kazuko, op. cit., pp.8–10.

51. Quoted in Long, Qirui, *Wanyue shanfang shicao* [Poems Collection of Wanyue san-fang], Beijing: Zhonghua shuju, 1962, p.35.

52. Guangxi sheng Taiping tianguo wenshi diaoca tuan [The Research Team of Taiping Rebellion in Guangxi Province], *Taiping tianguo qiyi diaoca baogao* [Research Report of the Taiping Rebellion in Guangxi], 1956, p.70.

53. *Taiping tianguo* [The Taiping Rebellion], op. cit., No. 4, p.572.

54. For more examples see Chen Zhongyu, op. cit., pp.240–43.
55. Fan, Wenlan, *Zhongguo tongshi* [The History of China], Beijing: Renmin chuban-she [People's Press], 1952, Vol. 1, p.135.
56. Shih, Y.C., *The Taiping Ideology: Its Sources, Interpretations, and Influence*, Seattle: University of Washington Press, 1967, p.18.
57. Quoted from Michael, F., 'Regionalism in Nineteenth Century China', op. cit., p.48.
58. Hu, Sheng, op. cit., p.6; Fairbank, John K., *The Cambridge History of China: Late Ching, 1800–1911*, 1978, Cambridge: Cambridge University Press, *passim.*
59. Chen, Jinpan, op. cit., p.33.
60. Ono, Kazuko, op. cit., p.22.
61. The 'Westernisation Movement' was also known as the Self-strengthening Movement or the Restoration Movement. It was advocated by a group of highly placed, prominent officials of the Qing government. The essence of the Movement was to learn from foreigners, equal them and finally surpass them. The Movement did not, however, envisage a consistent programme of modernisation, since it intended to leave the semi-feudal political and economic structure intact. For further details about this Movement see Spence, Jonathan D., *The Search for Modern China*, op. cit., pp.197, 225; Rodzinski, W., op. cit., pp.210–11; Jan, Bozhan, op. cit., pp.44–9; Gray, J., op. cit., pp.103–4.
62. Latourette, K.S., op. cit., p.302.
63. Su, Jinchen, 'Junguomin tiyu zhi yingxiang' [The Influence of Military Drill on Chinese Physical Education], *TWS*, No. 3, 1987, pp.55–8.
64. CSHSPE, *Zhongguo jindai tiyu shi* [Modern Chinese Sports History], op. cit., pp.53–4.
65. These included North Western Navy Academy (1881), Tianjin Weaponry Engineering College (1885), Guangdong Navy Academy (1887), Fuzhou Ship-building Institute (1866), Tianjin Telegraph School (1880), Shanghai Telegraph School (1882), South Western Navy Academy (1890), Hubei Weaponry Engineering College (1895), and Nanjing Army Academy (1895). See CSHSPE, *Zhongguo jindai tiyu shi* [Modern Chinese Sports History], op. cit., pp.54–5.
66. Wang, Anpo, '63 lian qian de tiyu huodong' [Sporting Activities 63 Years Ago], in Tang, Hao, op. cit., Vol. 3, pp.121–3.
67. CSHSPE, *Zhongguo jindai tiyu shi* [Modern Chinese Sports History], op. cit., p.56.
68. Ibid.
69. Qin, Ji, 'Yantai tiyu zhi bianhua' [Change of Sport in Yantai], *Tiyu zhoubao* [Sports Weekly], Nos. 12, 13, 1932, pp.5, 9.
70. The war between China and Japan was declared on 1 August 1894. China was routed on both land and sea, and was forced to sign the humiliating Treaty of Shimonoseki on 7 April 1895. The Treaty stipulated a huge indemnity of 230 million taels, the opening of Chongqing, Suzhou, Hangzhou and Shanxi to trade, the right of Japanese nationals to engage in manufacturing in China, and the ceding of Taiwan and Liuqiu Islands.The treaty signalled a new stage in China's decline towards colonial status.
71. For a discussion of the Meiji Restoration see Lehmann, Jean Pierre, *The Image of Japan: from Feudal Isolation to World Power*, London: George Allen & Unwin, 1978; Irokawa, Daikichi, *The Culture of the Meijin Period*, trans. by Jansen, M.B., Princeton, New Jersey: Princeton University Press, 1970; Backmann, G.M., *The Modernization of China and Japan*, New York: Harper and Row, 1962.
72. Heren *et. al.*, op. cit., p.172.
73. Rodzinski, W., op. cit., p.242.
74. Qiao and Guan, op. cit., pp.168–76.

75. Yan, Fu, 'Yuan qiang' [On Strength], in *Huoguan Yansi congshu* [Collected Works of Yan Fu], Vol. 3, 1895, p.3.
76. Kang, Youwei, 'Qing tingzhi gong ma shi wu shi gaishe pinxiao zhe' [Memorandum: Requesting a Ban on Traditional Military Training and the Establishment of a Modern Military Academy], in Kang, Youwei, *Wuxu zougao* [Memorial in 1898], 13 Aug. 1898, pp.8–11.
77. CSHSPE, *Zhongguo jindai tiyu shi* [Modern Chinese Sports History], op. cit., p.62.
78. Jian, Bozhan, op. cit., pp.91–2.
79. The Boxer Rebellion (1898–1900) was an anti-Christian, anti-foreign uprising. It originated in northern Shandong and ended with the siege of the Foreign Legation in Beijing. Participants were mostly poor peasants who practised a type of martial art that gave the name 'boxer' to the movement. The uprising ended when a combined Western military expedition entered Beijing, forcing the Empress dowager Cixi and her court to flee to Xi'an.
80. Rodzinski, W., op. cit., p.242.
81. Hu, Sheng, op. cit., pp.762–801; Spence, Jonathan D., *The Search for Modern China*, op. cit., pp.234–5; Gray, J., op. cit., pp.126–46; Heren *et al.*, op. cit., p.174; Fairbank, J.K., *The Cambridge History of China: Late Qing, 1800–1911*, op. cit.
82. The following statistics illustrate a sharp increase in the provision of modern schools at this time:

Year	1907	1912
No. of schools	37,888	87,272
No. of students	1,024,988	2,933,387

See Chen, Jinpan, op. cit., pp.70, 167–8.
83. See 'Zhouding xiaoxuetang zhangcheng 1903' [the 1903 Authorised Imperial Primary School Act], 'Zhouding zhongxuetang zhangcheng 1903' [the 1903 Authorised Imperial Middle School Act], and 'Zhouding youji shifan xuetang zhangcheng 1903' [the 1903 Authorised Imperial Normal College Act], in Chengdu tiyu xueyuan tiyushi yanjiushuo [Chengdu Sports History Institute], hereafter CSHI (ed.), *Zhongguo jindai tiyushi zhiliao ji* [Modern Chinese Sports History Reference], Chengdu: Sichuan jaoyu chubanshe, 1988, pp.138–44, 157–61.
84. See 'Xuebu biantong xuetang xinzhang zhi yiwen' [On the Authorised Imperial Acts], *Shi bao* [Times], 18 May 1909.
85. See 'Xuebu zhouqing biantong cudeng xiaoxue gangcheng zhe' [The 1909 Authorised Imperial Act of Schools], *Jiaoyu zazhi* [Education Journal], No. 5, May 1909.
86. *Tientsin Bulletin*, Tianjin, Vol. 3, 1896.
87. Fan and Wang, *Tiyu shihua* [History of Sport], op. cit., p.46.
88. For further details see the 'Report of YMCA, Beijing, 1907–1908' (A copy of this report can be found in the Historical Library of the YMCA, New York City). See also CSHSPE, *Zhongguo jindai tiyu shi* [Modern Chinese Sports History], op. cit., p.64.
89. 'Jinshi daxuetang kai diyichi yundonghui gao laibin wei' [The Report of the First Sports Meeting of Beijing University], *Sichuan xuebao* [Journal of Sichuan Education], No. 3, 1905; 'Baoding shifan xuetang diyiqi yundonghui' [The Report of the First Baoding College Sports Meeting], *Chengdu ribao* [Chengdu Daily], 19 Sept. 1904; 'Sichuan sheng diyichi yundonghui zhangcheng' [Rules of the First Sichuang Provincial Sports Meeting], *Sichuan xuebao*, No. 19, 1905; 'Nanjing diyichi xuexiao lianhe yundonghui' [The First Nanjing Colleges' Sports Meeting],

in Tang, Hao, op. cit., No. 4, 1958, pp.72–3.

90. *The North Herald*, 23 Oct. 1910.
91. *Association Men*, Beijing, Vol. 4, 1910. 'Association Men' was a journal of the YMCA.
92. The hairstyle of Manchu men consisted of a high shaved forehead and a long braid down the back. Originally it was developed to keep long hair out of the face in battle. By Manchu decree, issued by Dorgon in 1645, all Chinese men had to adopt this hairstyle or risk execution. Cutting the queue braid was regarded as an act of defiance against the Qing government.
93. Wu, Chi-kang, op. cit., pp.123–7.

TWO

Missionaries and Reformers:
The Reconceptualisation of Femininity
in Modern China

THE ORIGIN AND development of the Chinese women's emancipation movement cannot be understood without first placing it in the context of the changing image of the female body, and this fundamental change in Chinese culture in the late nineteenth and early twentieth centuries cannot be understood itself without an examination of the influence of the Christian missionaries and their powerful impact on Chinese women's physical education and education. The task of this chapter, therefore, is to examine and assess first, the significance of the missionary influence as an 'agent of change',[1] and second, Chinese reformers resulting attitudes and actions. The focus is on the body, cultural confrontation and social change resulting from exogenous and indigenous ideas and actions.

The Body: Natural Fact or Cultural Performance

Over time, debate as to whether 'being female constitutes a natural fact or a cultural performance'[2] has resolved itself into two opposing viewpoints: essentialist and constructionist. For essentialists, 'the body is real and accessible, always there and directly interpretable through the senses'.[3] The body is a physical given. It stands outside social and cultural influence. In the nineteenth century physiological and medical experts, for example, asserted that women were inferior to men because of their essential biological functions. It was simply a matter of nature. In contrast, constructionists assert that 'the body is always . . . culturally mapped, it never exists in a pure or uncoded state'.[4] Patricia Vertinsky, for instance, has claimed: 'Objective science

43

would have the body stand outside society, history and language, but
. . . there is no natural way of presenting the body. Not just the
scientist, but science itself is subjective, . . . a cultural and social
product.'[5] As Bryan S. Turner has argued: ' What it is to be man or
woman is a social definition, since physiology is always mediated by
culture.'[6] Such arguments permit the view that women's unequal
position in society is socially rather than naturally constituted,
embedded in and shaped by the social and cultural order.[7]

The feminist historian Joan Kelly has insisted that 'the invisibility of
women as a distinctive social group in traditional history must not be
ascribed to female nature, to an 'essential' femaleness, but to the issue
of women's status in society in relation to men'.[8] In the eyes of contemporary feminists, sex and sexual difference become a way of signi-
fying cultural construction, the social phenomenon of power, and the
social relationship of power. Joan Scott succinctly reflects this in her
statement that sexuality is a social category imposed on a sexed body.[9]
In short, the relationship between the body and sexual inequality is
established and sustained by a social system, and at the same time is
fundamental to that social system.

Such constructionist interpretations have ensured that the female
body has become a special site of investigation and re-theorising in
terms of its ability to provide explanations for women's social subordination.[10] Michel Foucault is of the opinion that historically the
idea that women were inferior to men was naturalised and thus legitimated because 'deployments of power are directly connected to the
body – to bodies, functions [and] physiological processes'.[11]

It is certainly true, of course, from the viewpoint of natural science,
that the body is a natural object. Physical differences between man
and woman self-evidently exist. Nevertheless, when we put the body
into a cultural and social context, it is interpreted within the framework of the social system. In this context, the female body can become
a subject of social subordination. It is formed in response to society's
pressures, preconceptions and even prejudices. In short, at one level
the body is not a social but a physical entity; at another level, it is a
social phenomenon. Woman is born a woman, a natural fact, but is
made inferior by, among other things, patriarchal culture.

However, in asserting this outcome care must be taken to recognise
that theories of patriarchy often tend to assume 'a consistent or
inherent meaning for the human body – outside social or cultural
construction'.[12] Such a position is both simplistic and ahistorical.

Arguably, one answer to such theoretical inadequacy, as Vertinsky has pointed out, is available in Derrida's concept of deconstruction 'which demands a constant reappraisal and contextual analysis of the way in which any binary opposition between male and female operates'.[13] This assertion has an immediate relevance for the evolution of traditional Chinese culture. Chinese society has been historically organised on the principle of patriarchal power, in which the behaviour of female subordinates was regulated by the solid phalanx of King, father and husband.[14] But over time this regulation has changed in emphasis and extent. In Chinese society, therefore, the body – and the female body in particular – is a location for debate about the changing nature of ideology, power, social structures and cultural systems.

Footbinding: Sexuality, Security and Social Control

Women in nineteenth-century China, living within a symbolic feudal system and a declining traditional society, were marked with minus signs: they were considered a negative force, in constant dialogue with death and evil. They were handicapped by inferior property rights, disenfranchisement and poor education, all because of their alleged physical and mental weaknesses. This state of affairs permitted, among other things, the continuance of a long tradition in pursuit of a perceived feminine physical ideal – the crippling binding of women's feet discussed briefly earlier.[15]

At first, the bound foot was the privilege of monarchy and aristocracy. Soon it spread throughout the whole population and became 'the symbol of the castration of women which Chinese civilisation was unique in permitting'.[16] Why did this custom last in China for more than one thousand years? First, the body is a site of enormous symbolic imagination. Its culturally defined deformities are stigmatising, while at the same time its culturally defined perfection brings praise and admiration. Chinese men admired the bound foot and regarded the beauty of the tiny foot as a mark of gentle refinement and eroticism. The small foot along with its little staggering dancelike walk – thought to be erotic – entered courtly literature and stimulated waves of adoration among the poets. It became the most erotic part of the female body. Second, women suffered willingly in order to please men. Women have always shown a willingness to maim themselves

45

Footbinding: sexuality, security and control. (From Yao Lingxi (ed.), *Cai fei lu* [The Record of Tiny Feet], Tianjin: Shidai gongshi and Tianjin shuju, 1936–38).

to achieve male-defined standards of beauty and to win love and admiration. The tiny foot was appealing, valuable and respectable. It was a way into a man's arms, heart and hearth. It was a necessary condition for success in the marriage market. Parents eventually believed that their daughters' chances on the marriage front would be seriously impaired unless they had made the correct choice for their

An upper-class lady bares her Golden Lotuses. (From Yao Lingxi (ed.), *Cai fei lu* [The Record of Tiny Feet], Tianjin: Shidai gongshi and Tianjin shuju, 1936–38).

daughters' feet: 'When their daughter was between four and eight years old parents would speak harshly to her and frighten her with severe expressions. They would oppress her in every conceivable manner so that the bones of her feet might be broken and the flesh putrefy. They would tell her that she would then be happy in her parents' hearts, knowing that when she later got married they would be very proud of her.'[18] Great families favoured footbinding, lesser families followed in imitation. For women, the bound foot was the passport to all that was good in life.

Third, footbinding was a tool of social control in a male dominated society. It created firm social boundaries and expressed clear-cut social relations. Patriarchal culture 'tends to assume a fixed state of male oppression over women and rests on a single variable of physical difference'[19] and has defined women as an object of ownership. Bound feet physically prevented women from moving about freely and unchaperoned and rendered them immune to the social disease of conjugal infidelity. A Chinese manual for women reasoned that footbinding was a restraining device. 'Why are feet bound? It is not because they are good looking with their bowed arch, but rather because men feared that women might easily leave their quarters and therefore have their feet bound tightly in order to prevent this.'[20] Footbinding, in short, was a convenient and effective way to express and enforce the concept of female chastity. A chaste girl would rush to submit her tiny feet to her marriage. After so many years of suffering, this action presented a unique opportunity to gain the respect and recognition of the in-law and husband as undeniable proof of her capacity to suffer and obey. She would stay in the house and would not be seen in the streets. Throughout the nation, the tiny foot became a symbol of chastity and a vital part of the national moral ethic;'It is a trifling matter to die of starvation, but a grave matter to lose one's chastity'.[21] The bound foot transformed a woman into a fetish but it also enforced a social morality, established sexual boundaries and expressed social relations. As Francis Hsu pointed out: 'Footbinding seemed a reasonable addition to differences between the sexes.'[22] It helped to maintain a clear divide between men and women and emphasised conformity to the social dictum that women had to differ from men in every visible physical aspect.

Footbinding was also part of a set of morals which defined women as inferior. Over the years this definition produced protest. From the Ming Dynasty (1368–1644) to the Qing Dynasty (1644–1911), enlightened and liberal thinkers in Chinese history criticised footbinding. The list includes unconventional philosophers like Li Zhi (1527–1602), who expressed radical opinions on women's education; novelists like Cao Xueqin (1715– c.63), who created many symbols of female rebellion against feudal dogmatism in the *Dream of the Red Chamber*; poets like Yuan Mei (1716–98), who advocated women's education; thinkers like Wang Chong (1744–94), who advocated free social intercourse among men and women and opposed the customary proscription against the remarriage of widows; satirists like Li Ruzhen (1763–1830), who had women playing the roles of men in his novel, *Flowers in the Mirror*; and liberal scholars like Gong Zizhen (1792–1841). All pointed to the waste of talent caused by the underestimation and mistreatment of women. Li Ruzhen criticised the sometimes farcical extremism of the practise of admiring tiny feet: 'If a women has a three-inch bowed foot but a short neck and thick waist, how can she ever give a light appearance when walking, as if she were skimming over the waves.'[23] While their arguments, however, drew attention to the inappropriateness of exclusively admiring bound feet while disregarding other attributes of beauty, they didn't destroy the evil practice. They failed to change or even slightly to modify the traditional view.

Footwear for the 'Golden Lotus'. (Thanks are due to Linda Wrigglesworth, Chinese Costume and Textiles, London, for permission to reproduce this photograph.)

When the Manchus from the North conquered China in the seventeenth century they attempted to abolish footbinding because they regarded it as culturally backward. They did not prevail. Traditional Chinese views were not seriously challenged. Instead, the influence of footbinding and other aspects of Chinese culture were increasingly felt by the Manchu themselves as the years went by. Manchu men came to prefer tiny feet, and their wives either bound their feet in response or attempted simulation by wearing high-heel shoes in which the foot, though not bound, appeared to be deformed and diminutive.

Some have argued correctly that during this long feudal period Chinese women did, in fact, participate in exercise.[24] However, from paintings, poems and other written records,[25] it is clear that these were not strenuous physical activities, rather they were restricted amusements for special occasions. [26] It is hard to imagine that women with bound feet, who 'past the gate can't retreat' [27] could participate in any vigorous movement. As Li Yu, the famous poet of the Ming Dynasty described in his poem 'Beauties': 'I have seen two beautiful women playing in the sunshine of early spring. After only a few minutes their small feet were tired. They were too exhausted to talk to each other.'[28]

The Christian Missionary: Early Agent of Physical Liberation

It was Christian missionaries, rather than radical critics, who effectively challenged traditional Chinese culture and created the opportunity for women to free themselves, first physically and then mentally. Western powers invaded China in mid-nineteenth century, not only with military forces but also with strong ideological forces in the form of religious dogma. It was the contention of many Westerners who came to China in the nineteenth century that the Chinese were uncivilised, uneducated and irreligious.[29] Western missionaries, therefore, were sent to China to convert the Chinese to their superior *weltanschauung*.

The earliest treaties with the West, such as the treaties of 1842, 1844 and 1860,[30] made it legal for missionaries to live in the treaty ports and travel to the interior of China. After 1860 they were also permitted to buy or lease land and to build houses or churches. Due to the most-favoured-nation clauses of the treaties, by which privileges granted to any one nation were automatically extended to others, missionaries of all nationalities had these rights and could go everywhere in China.[31]

The latter part of the nineteenth century saw the expansion of missionary work in the form of missionary societies and organisations embracing, for example, the Church of the Holy Trinity; the Union Church; the Baptist Church of the Bund; the Deutsche Evanglische Kirche; a variety of Catholic Churches in the French and International Settlements; the traditional Protestant Churches, the Salvation Army; the YMCA and YWCA.[32] Addison P. Scotan has pointed out that 'For Christians, certainly one of the greatest achievements to be noted is the spread of Christianity and the growth of the Church.'[33]

Although there were differences in structure, style and proselytisation, the aim was always the same – to Christianise the Chinese. The missionaries were convinced that they had received God's call to conversion, that Christianity was a major component of Western progress, and that they must share their faith with the as yet backward and unbelieving heathen.[34] Their antipathy towards the Chinese world has been remarked upon by Jonathan Chao: 'They regarded many Chinese religious and social customs as cultural barriers to the Gospel, which needed to be removed. Accordingly, many missionaries saw themselves as wilful destroyers of the traditional culture and as builders of a new Christian civilisation for China.'[35]

The late part of the nineteenth century saw a significant change in the type of missionary sent to China. They now came as Bible translators, educationists, doctors, scholars and social reformers. These better-educated missionaries, influenced by recent developments in the West concerning women, brought new emancipatory perspectives to the task of ministering to the 'Women's Issue'. Their aim was to influence Chinese women's religious beliefs, but their historic function, as it turned out, was to help transmit new ideas and images to Chinese women and to free women from feudal bondage. In the interests of spiritual imperialism missionaries, therefore, ensured women's freedom from temporal imperialism. It was missionary education that constituted the first step up the women's emancipatory ladder.

For well over a thousand years in China the opinion of Confucius in regard to the education of women held general sway. Women's education was very different from that of men. *The Four Books* and *Five Classics* of men's education,[36] were not considered in any way an essential part of women's education. Women had their own five classic books: *Women's Disciplines; The Records of Illustrious Women of Ancient Times; Female Filial Piety Classics; Women's Instructions; The Classics for Women.* They portrayed the major components of women's successful education as:

1. An appreciation of the state of subjection and weakness in which women were born.
2. A knowledge of the duties of a woman when under the power of a husband.
3. The unlimited respect due to a husband, and the constant self-examination and restraint necessary to achieve this .
4. A recognition of the obedience due to a husband and to his parents.
5. An awareness of the qualities which render a female lovable, divided into those relating to her virtue, her conversation, her dress and her occupations.

In these texts women's education aimed at perfect submission not personal development.

There were no schools for girls in Confucian China and only a few women could read and write. China saw no value in women's education and was strongly of the view that its effect on women would be undesirable. So half of the nation was left uneducated. When William Dean, the first American Baptist missionary, arrived in China in 1859[37] he was surprised to find that

> the Chinese classics say that among the ancients, villages had their schools, districts their academies, departments their colleges, and principalities their universities. These are for the benefit of the boys, for while Chinese writers speak of the importance of female education, we never see their girls in schools, and have seldom seen a Chinese woman who could read her own language. The chief stimulus for boys to study – the prospect of office and wealth – is taken away from the girls. . . . The very few Chinese women we have met who could read have learned from a brother or father at home.[38]

Adele Fielde, one of the earliest women missionaries to China, reported that: 'Native girls' schools are almost unknown . . . In the whole empire probably not more than one woman in a thousand knows how to read.'[39] Another missionary offered an even smaller estimate: '. . . with very rare exceptions women are never educated. Of heathen women possibly one in two or three thousand can read.'[40] Arthur H. Smith announced at the Shanghai Missionary Conference of 1890, 'among the thousands of women whom we have met, not more than ten had learned to read'.[41] The testimony of the Chinese was even more bleak. In 1897 Song Hen lamented the fact that 'the education of Chinese women had been non-existent and only one in ten thousand women can read'.[42]

Generally speaking, then, before 1840 when China was opened up to the outside world, Chinese women were illiterate. The major reason for this situation was the low position of women in Chinese culture. Confucian belief held that it was 'a law of nature that women should be kept under the control of man and not allowed any will of their own'.[43] Furthermore, it held that women were incapable of being educated because of their natural slow wits. The unflattering estimate of, and prejudice towards women's intelligence was so strong that women themselves accepted it. Mrs Cilman, one of the educational missionaries in Hainan City, said, 'when the women are asked if they would like to learn to read, the idea is so new that they think they could not'.[44] Miss Howe, a missionary in Kin Kiang City, stated that when she visited some homes and asked the women to learn to read, they appeared amused and surprised at this idea and then refused: 'No, indeed, I am not so strong-minded as that.'[45]

In addition, other cultural mores had a bearing on the historic scholastic restrictions of Chinese women. There were practical constraints on female education in that girls were not permitted to be instructed or taught by men and there were practically no educated women in China to fill this teaching gap. Furthermore, it was not in accordance with the ideas of Chinese propriety that girls should be seen going to and fro on the streets to school. Even supposing the above attitude could be overcome, it was still impossible for girls to get to school by themselves because of their maimed feet.

Clearly for women opportunities for education were virtually non-existent in the period before the missionaries brought fresh ideas about women's education into China. However, through the advent of these missionaries the outlook for women in China changed. It is with the arrival of the missionary, therefore, that a new era in women's education in China began.[46]

The first school for girls was opened in Ningpo in 1844, shortly after the Opium War, by Mary Ann Aldersey, an Englishwoman.[47]

She was one of the first missionaries of the Society for Promoting Female Education to arrive in the East. She supported 'a flourishing girls' school in China, chiefly from her own private funds'.[48] Other missionaries followed in Mary Ann Aldersey's footsteps.[49] Fuzhou Girls' Boarding School, for example, opened in Fuzhou city in 1859 [50] and Eliza Bridgman of the American Board opened a school for girls in Beijing in 1864. These women and others like them built schools for girls with the express purpose of preaching the gospel and freeing them from feudal bondage. By 1876 there were more than 2,000 female students studying in at least 121 missionary schools for girls.[52] Jessie G. Lutz claimed in his book, *China and the Christian Colleges, 1850 – 1950*, that 'numerous primary and secondary schools for girls were founded during the nineteenth century'.[53] Recruitment of pupils, however, was not easy. So unwilling were parents to allow their children to attend the missionary schools in those days that it was customary to offer pupils food, clothing and shelter, to say nothing of free books and tuition. The missionaries undertook the seemingly impossible task of persuading the Chinese that they meant only good for their daughters, and of convincing them that their daughters were both capable of education and worthy of it. Their success was limited, but the consequences were extensive.

From these difficult beginnings there developed institutions of four types: elementary day schools; intermediate boarding schools with, in some cases, a high school attached; women's Bible-training schools; and nurses' training schools. In 1902 there were more than 4,000 female students studying in missionary establishments.

It would be naive to assume that missionaries were concerned only with education and religious matters. In fact, from the beginning, they concerned themselves with a total reconstruction of China through the transmission of Western ideas and values to the Chinese, including Chinese women.[54] Consequently, these girls schools were modelled on English or American schools[55] and physical education was part of the curriculum. Siu Bobby presents details of the curriculum of five representative schools for girls under American mission boards in Southern, Eastern, Northern and Central China. A close study of this curriculum suggests that the exclusive purpose of missionary schools was to mould Chinese women in the Western image.[56] Cheng Sumei, a student of the missionaries school in Tianjing run by the Northern Methodist Episcopal church, declared:

All the lessons were given in English. . . . It was not long before I could speak a little English. I was dressed and my hair was arranged now in European fashion. . . . With my English clothes, a hat which was the first I had ever had on my head, the skirts which I now wore instead of trousers, I felt very much 'in the role' . . . I learned how to drink tea as the English take it, with sugar and milk; how to eat bread and butter and toast; how to use a knife and fork instead of chop-sticks, and *how to take exercise*. [emphasis added][57]

The missionaries met the strongest resistance from exponents of that fundamental element of Chinese culture – the custom of footbinding. Few Chinese girls could go to school with their bound feet and few could take part in the schools' physical exercises and activities. Chinese women suffered not only mentally but physically. The missionaries, therefore, were obliged to concern themselves with both aspects of this suffering.

In the missionaries' eyes tiny-footed girls usually looked as if they were in pain, for instead of jumping about happily they needed help in walking, as if they were wounded. Footbinding was consequently denounced as an evil which crippled approximately half the population, added to the misery of the poverty stricken, increased child deaths, prevented women from supporting themselves and from caring adequately for their children, inhibited 'the cheer and cleanliness' of their homes, and confined women and their thoughts to the narrowest of spheres. This state of affairs caused the missionaries to concern themselves with social reform.[58] As Jerome Chen has pointed out: 'The missionaries were the first to draw Chinese attention to the irrational, traditional ways in which men treated women.'[59] They began strenuously to oppose the unchallenged custom of footbinding. They combined women's education and the abolition of women's footbinding, seeing them jointly as the only way to achieve Chinese women's emancipation – physical, moral and intellectual.

Missionaries therefore founded anti-footbinding societies and enlisted support in many areas of China in the early and formative years of the abolition movement: 'A major factor in bringing the evils of footbinding before a large audience was the missionary community, which worked devotedly for this cause and gradually influenced public opinion against it.'[60] The Natural-foot Society in Shanghai, led by Mrs Archibald Little, an Englishwoman and an influential leader in

Footbinding in China – a native Christian poster, advocating the abolition of footbinding. (From the early missionary literature advocating the abolition of footbinding.)

the Anti-footbinding Movement,[61] published upwards of 30 pieces of literature, edicts, proclamations, posters, poems and folders of photographs.[62] Its intention was to oppose inhumane customs and 'to petition the Emperor that children born after 1897 should not be recognised as of standing unless they had natural feet'.[63] Anti-footbinding societies used various techniques to advance their objectives. Memorials and letters were sent to provincial governors. Public meetings were held in provincial capitals and large cities. Over a million tracts, leaflets and posters were sent out from Shanghai alone, in addition to a large number from other cities.[64] They slowly made an impact. For instance, the account of the Anti-footbinding Society in Amoy in 1874 stated that those women who were willing to promise not to bind their daughters' feet were 'putting their marks' to a pledge to that effect.[65]

The actions of these societies steadily attracted public attention and increasingly won support from liberal intellectuals and influential officials. These included prominent viceroys like Zhang Zhidong, the governor-general of Hunan and Hupei provinces, who contributed an article to *Zhixin bao* (New Knowledge News) advocating the Anti-footbinding Movement.[66] Even orthodox Confucianists gradually joined their ranks. A lineal descendant of Confucius named Ko Huichang said:

> I have always had my unquiet thoughts about footbinding and felt pity for the many sufferers. Yet I could not venture to say it publicly. Now there are happily certain benevolent gentlemen and virtuous daughters of ability, wise daughters from foreign lands who have initiated a truly noble enterprise. They have addressed our women in animated exhortations and founded a society for the prohibition of footbinding.[67]

Christian missionaries exerted an unrelenting influence and were instrumental in bringing about change at the highest social level. In 1895 ten influential Christian women of different nationalities formed a natural-foot society and, in order to request support from the Empress Dowager Cixi,[68] drew up a memorial to which 'nearly all foreign ladies in the Far East added their names'.[69] The memorial is believed to have eventually reached the Palace,[70] and it is said that the Empress Dowager finally issued the Anti-footbinding Edict of 1902 'after sustained pressure from foreign women of various nationalities'.[71]

The missionaries were also instrumental in bringing about change at a lower social level. Footbinding among converts was discouraged. Sometimes this was made a condition for entering the Church.[72] Converts would vow not to bind the feet of their daughters, and every effort was made to influence the parents of daughters against this profitless and injurious custom.[73] Missionary girls' schools were not subject to Chinese custom or law, but were under their own jurisdiction. They drew up their regulations to the effect that girls with bound feet were not accepted into their schools unless they renounced the practice.[74]

In short, Christian missionaries made a significant contribution to the Anti-footbinding Movement. As Mrs Archibald Little stated, 'footbinding, although still widely practised, has received its deathblow among intelligent Chinese. Too much credit for this reform cannot be given to the noble band of women missionaries who fought the stubborn battle for years and are fighting today.'[75] Through their efforts these women released thousands of Chinese women from the physical restriction of footbinding and for the first time girls were able to take part in physical exercise in school.

Physical exercise, as mentioned earlier, was practised in most of the missionary schools for girls. For instance, in missionary girls' schools in Zhenjiang, Jiangsu province, gymnastics was a compulsory activity.[76] In the British Mary Vaughan School for girls in Shanghai, students had exercise for an hour every day.[77] In almost all the missionary girls schools it was the aim that 'from 1 p.m. to 4 p.m., students will be encouraged to do some physical exercise'.[78] When Miss Dodson, a friend of a missionary, visited one of the schools she found that 'the fashion of small feet had, of course, disappeared and the fair students wore top boots and I suppose had drill exercise. What a wonderful change for China.'[79] William Dean found that 'Now the girls enjoy fully all their playtimes.'[80]

Chinese girls in the missionary schools then developed both their minds and bodies. Their progress, without exaggeration, was remarkable. Dean noted that when a Chinese girl returned to her home town she attracted great interest: 'it was the wonder of all that region that here was a girl who could read . . . They were awestricken and looked upon her as something superhuman . . . When they heard the words which proceeded from her lips they were afraid of her and treated her with the greatest respect.'[81] Educated women, thus distinguished from the generality of their sex, attracted people's curiosity. People began

to be convinced that women could perhaps effectively learn something in school. The stubborn attitude to women's inability slowly
began to change.[82]

In 1906, when 50 boys' schools in Hankou took part in an athletics
meeting, six girls' schools attended. This was probably one of the first
occasions when Chinese girls appeared before the public performing
exercises.[83] The public didn't complain. Traditional prejudices were
weakening.

Physical release, unbound feet and vigorous exercise brought a
sudden and hitherto unknown freedom to girls. It led them to rather
dramatic and somewhat high-handed methods of expressing themselves and stimulated bold emancipatory ambitions. For example in
Chengdu, the capital of Sichuan province, girl students with unbound
feet wore the same semi-foreign uniform as boy students when they
walked on the streets. In so doing they flouted the long established
traditions of not going alone in the street and of not wearing
garments similar to those of the male. In Hangzhou, when an education official failed to give girls the high grades they desired, they
refused to receive their diplomas publicly from his hand.[84] In Ginling,
Luella Miner, the President of North China Union Women's College
was challenged by her students, who publicly opposed her conservatism, in an annual meeting.[85] Two of the large schools in
Paotingfu had student rebellions. In one of these cases,

> The Girls' High School was invited to attend the field day exer-
> cises of the graduating class of the large military school. The
> young ladies were willing to put aside their studies for the day
> and attend. The proctor was willing to chaperone them but the
> lady director withheld her consent. Nevertheless part of the
> school, led by the proctor, did attend. This insubordination
> rapidly led to the resignation of the proctor and to a school strike
> by the students who had attended. The strike . . . was in force for
> about half a month.[86]

Self-assertion was catching. Some boys, as well as some girls, began
to voice their opposition to traditional custom, for example, arranged
marriages, and expressed themselves in favour of a readjustment of
the traditional relationship between men and women – the foundation of Chinese society. They knew something of the relations which
existed between men and women of the West and were eager to
imitate them. Boys and girls pressed against the parameters of social

etiquette. They invited each other, for example, to attend parties without a chaperone. Even the missionaries, who had introduced their Western ideas with the best of intentions, now expressed concern. The principal of one girls' school argued at a conference of missionaries in 1908 that 'one of the most important features of educational work for girls during the present crisis is the privilege it gives us of helping them to adjust to their new condition. Their present condition is very uncertain and we should do all we can to help them find themselves.'[87]

The missionaries quickly realised that the struggle for winning the souls of Chinese women partly through caring for their bodies and alleviating their physical sufferings, was getting out of hand. Many Chinese women rushed to embrace the Western ideal of personal liberty. They believed that China's old social system should pass away, and that women, in this transition period, should take the opportunity to free themselves from feudal bondage. They energetically challenged long-established tradition and their behaviour obviously went beyond that expected, and indeed welcomed by the missionaries. The missionaries came to China to convert the Chinese to Christianity: 'From the time they arrived in China until the time they left, the missionaries lived and worked in the highly organised structure of the mission compound, which resulted in their effective segregation – psychological as well as physical – from the surrounding Chinese society . . . For the missionaries really did not want to enter the Chinese world any more than they had to. Their whole purpose was to get the Chinese to enter theirs.'[88] However, this entry was clearly defined and circumscribed. When the Chinese women began to fight for their freedom in their own way, the missionaries could not understand them. The American Board Deputation commented, 'the emancipation of women is one of the watchwords of the advance movement in China, but . . . the sudden access to freedom and vagueness of the ideal which the leaders sometimes set before themselves constitute an element of real danger'.[89] They suggested that more Christian women be sent from the West to China to guide the Chinese women's emancipation movement in a controlled manner.

It is not easy to assess just how much the missionaries, who came from a totally different culture and locked themselves into self-imposed isolation, understood of Chinese women's educational and emancipatory needs within the framework of their own society. However, irrespective of their understanding or lack of it, the missionaries may be seen from a sociological perspective as major 'agents of change'. They saw education correctly as the key by which the door to the social transformation of Chinese society could be opened. Through the practice and promotion of Western education, the missionaries attempted to abolish footbinding and to change cultural attitudes towards Chinese women's bodies, health, education and status. Above all, by caring for bodies (especially broken feet) and alleviating physical sufferings, they hoped to win souls and to liberate Chinese women from feudal culture – spiritually, mentally and physically. In their ambitions they were not without success.

The further significance of the work of missionaries in relation to Chinese women's physical emancipation was that they brought physical education from the West to China. As Song Ruhai, a well-known educationist and social reformer in China of the period, stated: 'It is the missionaries who introduce and practice the physical education and sports activities for women.'[90] New physical exercises provided a pathway to women's physical well-being. Chinese women demanded both freedom from culturally founded physical sufferings, and the destruction of cultural prejudices against women's participation in physical activities. These demands laid the foundation for a change in women's image and position in Chinese society. Even more importantly, however, missionary action stimulated Chinese reformers concern with women's issues in China. This eventually produced marked social change. As Jane Hunter has pointed out: 'For years, missionaries had advanced a consistent program for Chinese women with little to show for it. Only when Chinese nationalist reformers made the course of female education their own did Chinese attitudes begin to change. The reformers sought the advice of Western female educators, and welcomed their aid, in their own efforts to bring China to self-sufficiency.'[91]

Patriotism and Progressivism: Chinese Reformers

Leading reformers, such as Kang Youwei, Liang Qichao, Tan Sitong, and Yan Fu, heavily influenced by missionary ideas and practices regarding women's education, made the liberation of women an integral part of the patriotic and progressive reform movement of 1898. Kang Youwei (1858–1927) pointed out that for thousands of years Chinese women had suffered in feudal culture and society.

They were not permitted to be independent, or to manage a business, or to hold office. Being unable to be citizens, or members of the assemblies, they are even kept from pursuing scholarship, from publishing their views, from gaining a name for themselves, from social intercourse, from throwing parties, from going sightseeing or from leaving the house. Furthermore their waists are corseted, their faces veiled and their feet bound.[92]

He argued that former sexual boundaries should be abolished so that women may 'attain the joy of equality, independence, and oneness with all'.[93]

Tan Sitong (1865–1898), another noted reformer, went even further than Kang Youwei. He did not attack the inequality of men and women as an isolated phenomenon, but rather saw it as merely one part of the same immorality. Tan Sitong claimed:' Men and women are both the flowers of the universe, both having infinitely rich and great tasks.'[94] He asked for the master–slave relationship between man and woman to change into one in which 'the right of self-sovereignty' existed.

Liang Qichao (1873–1929), a well-known journalist and social reformer, for his part, rebuked his fellow-country men and women for their lack of initiative: 'Women's education is popular at present', he exclaimed, 'It is a contribution of the Westerners. It is the missionaries who established girls' schools to educate Chinese women. Not the Chinese themselves. What a shame.' [95] Kang Tongwei,[96] daughter of Kang Youwei, a female radical, went a step further and advocated the establishment of girls' schools by the Chinese themselves to educate Chinese women: 'The missionaries opened schools for our Chinese women in the port cities. We Chinese have scholars, why don't we set up schools to teach our women?'[97] Gradually, the public began to accept the argument that the Chinese should have their own girls' schools: 'We should establish *our* schools for *our* girls.' (emphasis added)[98]

Missionaries, then, had set an example for Chinese society. Due to their efforts some Chinese women had been given opportunities for self-development. Precedent had been established and modern European ideas about women's education were embraced for the first time by Chinese reformers. But how to liberate the women of China? The reformers had different ideas to the missionaries. The missionaries had put the emphasis first on establishing schools and then abolishing footbinding. Education was their first concern. The Chinese, for their part, concentrated initially on abolishing footbinding – first physical release and afterwards mental provision.

Naïve patriotism was at the root of the difference in approach. Chinese reformers were convinced that one of the major reasons for the weakness of China was the physical weakness of the progeny of the 'bound-feet women'. Since the primary function of women was considered to be the bearing and raising of children, women's health became a form of insurance to guard against the further decline of China, or more particularly, of China's sons. No scheme of reform was now thought to be effective unless it included measures for the improvement of women as 'mothers'. The assertion was that:

> The bound feet of women will transmit weakness to the children, weakening the bodies of healthy generations . . . When the weakness becomes inherited, where shall we recruit soldiers? Today look at Europeans and Americans, so strong and vigorous because their mothers do not bind their feet and, therefore, have strong offspring. Now that we must compete with other nations, to produce weak offspring is perilous.[99]

Yan Fu, a well-known political reformer, put it more succinctly: 'When the mother is healthy the infant will be plump. When the inherent nature is nourished, the species will advance.'[100]

The Chinese now were acutely anxious about their national fate and spoke of 'preserving the nation', and 'preserving the race'.[101] The state had to be strengthened and the race had to be pressured to evolve. But how to achieve these goals? Women's bodies and their health became a major issue linked to the nation's survival or demise and its strength or weakness. Outmoded vestiges of the past had caused both loss of China's 'international face' and the continued feebleness of its women: 'There is nothing so much as footbinding to make the foreigners laugh at us and criticise us for being barbarians.'[102] On this patriotic basis, in conjunction with the pioneering work of Western missionaries, the Chinese Women's Movement[103] was launched for the abolition of footbinding, female education and, ultimately, female emancipation.

Sustained theoretical attacks, as we have seen already, had been launched on footbinding in the last decade of the nineteenth century. Two of the chief protagonists, as mentioned earlier, were Kang

Youwei and Liang Qichao. Kang Youwei wrote a eloquent Memorandum which he submitted to the throne in 1898. In it he traced the unilinear progress over time toward a more enlightened culture, showing, for example, how China's ancient criminal penalty of severing two feet was later nullified by benevolent sovereigns. He then described in painful detail the abnormal and inhuman treatment of the young and innocent girl, whose limbs were so impaired that she had to 'get up by holding on to the bed and cling to the wall for support when walking'.[104] He proposed that prohibition orders against footbinding should be circulated and enforced by a system of penalties. Remiss officials should be deprived of their privileges and householders should be fined for every pair of bound feet in their family.[105]

Liang Qichao approached the problem from a broader perspective and thought in terms of raising the social status of women. He wrote forceful essays in favour of the abolition of footbinding. These essays persuaded even those people who felt antipathy to ideas they believed were imported from abroad. In one of his essays he asserted:

> Men and women share things equally. Heaven gives them life and parents give them love . . . But women are trained either to fulfil a series of duties or to serve as playthings. In Africa and India they pressed a stone against women's head to make it level; in Europe they wanted the women to have a slender waist by pressing wood against her waist; in China the women had to have their feet bound, a punishment like cutting off the lower legs. These three punishments produced imperfect women throughout the world. I don't know when bound feet started, but the originator must have been a corrupt prince, an immoral ruler, a robber of the people, or a despicable husband. Alas! Good things in the world are done only with the greatest caution and hesitation, but evil things are transmitted very easily from one to another. These cruel, despicable and frightening things spread their wings everywhere and for countless ages! Parents force their daughters into footbinding, while others make this the basis for selecting their son's brides. And a man esteems his wife for this reason. The child is punished this way when it has still not lost its first set of teeth. Its bones are broken and its flesh deteriorates, with blood scattered about and injury widespread.

Parents ignore its signs, do not pity its weeping, are cold to its entreaties, and deaf to its screams.[106]

Liang's essays throbbed with emotion. It was said that some parents were so moved on reading them they that at once decided against having their daughters' feet bound.[107]

After Kang Youwei and Liang Quichao many progressives wrote articles, poems and songs to popularise the anti-footbinding cause, denouncing especially the suffering caused by footbinding.[108] These cries of protest were passed by word of mouth to those many women who were unable to read. In imitation of the missionaries, Kang Youwei started an 'Anti-footbinding Society' in Guangdong (Canton) in 1883. Soon, the reformers had set up anti-footbinding societies and natural-foot societies throughout the whole country. Societies were set up, for example, in Shanghai (1894); Aomen (Macao) (1897); Hunan (1897); Shunde (1897); Longshan (1897); Fujian (1897); Sichuan (1897) and Zhejiang (1898). Members were advised not to bind the feet of their daughters. Those who had already had their feet bound were encouraged to free them. Marriage to girls with natural feet was encouraged.[109] This move struck directly at the basic social tenet that bound feet were a necessary prerequisite to a good marriage. According to the *North China Herald*, the custom only received its deathblow when a growing number of Chinese men joined the societies and took the oath that neither they nor their sons would marry a 'small-footed' woman.[110]

Chinese anti-footbinding societies flourished and spread quickly all over the country. The most militant group was in Hunan province. The headquarters of the anti-footbinding association was in the office of the newspaper, *Xiang bao* (Hunan Daily). The *Xiang bao* ceaselessly preached in favour of unbinding women's feet. The editor, Tang Caichang, claimed: 'If I do not shout loudly about the coming world disaster, then may my body be forever condemned to hell in all successive reincarnations, never returning to the ranks of the living.'[111] The *Xiang bao* continued to print the names of those who joined, gave contributions to, and sponsored the anti-footbinding society. The total was more than 1,300.[112] The Hunanese reformers attempted to protect women with natural feet from discrimination in marriage. They distributed the 'Song to Stop Footbinding' free of charge and encouraged discount sales of the new 'cloud-toe square shoes' for unbound feet. Eventually, the Hunan Government Censor,

Huang Zunxian, issued an order prohibiting footbinding. He declared that it was a crime of the same magnitude as infanticide and should be severely punished.[113] The campaign was widely supported. It was recognised that in view of new political, social and economic ambitions society could not afford to have women in the house doing 'nothing'. Branches of the anti-footbinding society continued to spring up one after the other. Even as far away as the mountains of Yuling Xian, Shanhua county, a branch of the anti-footbinding society appeared.[114] Footbinding among Hunanese women now decreased[115] and statistics reveal the rapid breakdown of this centuries-old tradition in other provinces. In Dingxian County, for example, 125 miles south of Beijing, there was a sharp increase in women with unbound feet, the proportion rising from 18.5 per cent in 1905 to 40.3 per cent between 1905 and 1909.[116] The anti-footbinding movement successfully challenged Confucian ideas about, and attitudes towards women, changed women's social image in society and paved the way for their further economic, cultural and political liberation.

It will be recalled that Kang Youwei wrote his 'Memorandum Requesting a Ban on the Binding of Women's Feet' in 1898. In it he was clearly trying to mobilise Chinese women's protests in order to strengthen the state through the abolition of footbinding and the improvement of women's capacities as mothers.[117] Unfortunately, his and others ideas for reform fell momentarily on deaf ears and with the defeat of the One Hundred Days Reform[118] in 1898, some anti-footbinding societies were closed down. But those societies organised by missionaries grew in number and continued to advance the anti-footbinding cause. Consequently and amazingly, as mentioned earlier, in 1902 the Empress Cixi issued the decree exhorting 'the gentry and notables to influence their families to abstain from the evil practice and by this means abolish the custom forever'. [119] For the first time the movement had received official support at the highest level. In consequence, officialdom now took action. The governor of Nanjing, for example, issued an ordinance banning footbinding: 'From 1902, girls under ten years of age are not allowed to have their feet bound, and fines for violation, or rewards of observance of the rule, will be given out accordingly. Anti-footbinding societies should be extensively established.'[120]

To reiterate, then, the abolition of footbinding was a necessary foundation for women's participation in physical exercise. In turn, this participation was the prerequisite of sound health, personal vigour and physical fitness. It was in the context of the abolition of footbinding that women's general education became a crucial issue. It was commonly acknowledged that only the abolition of footbinding could free them from physical bondage and that only modern education could free them from intellectual bondage, there being no modern Chinese education for women. Liang Qichao advocated just such an education, claiming that women's education was 'internally to broaden the mind, and externally to help one make a living'.[121]

Mission schools had provided an exemplary model for the Chinese: 'The mission schools, with their high teaching standards and foreign equipment seemed to provide the most advanced courses for Chinese women.'[122] Chinese radicals, however, emulated the mission schools not only because of their standards, but also because as patriots these reformers were reluctant to leave the education of Chinese women entirely in the missionaries' hands. They began to sponsor the establishment of new indigenous schools.

The first girls' school opened by the Chinese was founded in Shanghai in June 1898.[123] The main sponsor was the reformer Jing Yuanshan. He had consulted missionary women on its effective management before opening the school[124] and it was set up largely in the image of missionary girls' schools: 'Its purpose was to develop women's minds, to strengthen women's bodies and to teach women the new morality.'[125] Footbinding was banned and physical exercise was compulsory.[126] Many respectable and important people now devoted entire family resources and even their lives to founding girls' schools. Sponsoring girls' education became widespread.[127]

Virtually all of these new private schools were modelled on the missionary schools' curriculum, teaching methodologies and administrative regulations. The schools were ostensibly to teach arithmetic to girls from 'good' families, but other subjects were taught such as English, reading, spelling, geography, drawing, handicrafts and physical education. The Zhong-meng Girls School in Shanghai offers a typical example. The Headmistress Tong Tongxue had been to Western Europe [128] and under her instruction the school became a rallying point for those who wanted a more Western-style education for Chinese girls. The curriculum included Chinese literature, ethics, psychology, foreign languages, mathematics, history, geography, education, music, religion and gymnastics.[129] Her girls were members of the first generation of Chinese females to enjoy the right to physical

67

education and to take part in modern exercise. They were living symbols of the early stages of emancipation.

The importance of this moment, therefore, for the future of exercise for women should not be underestimated. Here was the beginning of a long road to the eventual (unexceptional) freedom to take part in, to enjoy and to compete in the life-enriching physical activities of the modern world.

Women's education was further popularised after 1907. A statute for girls' schools had originally been excluded from the Authorised Imperial Act of Education when it was first drafted in 1902. However, when the Imperial Commission returned from abroad in 1906 after visiting educational institutions in the West, it urged the Board of Education to set up a national system of women's education in China. This led to the issue of a new code stating: 'the good education of the citizens of the empire depends upon the good education of its women'.[130] Provision was now made for establishing government-sponsored schools for girls. Soon girls' schools were established wherever possible in prefectural cities and even in county towns.[131] By 1909, there were 114 girls' schools in 17 big cities and provinces.[132] Daughters and wives persuaded their fathers and husbands to subscribe to the new institutions, which provided them with access to new ideas and a route to free themselves from traditional physical, mental and cultural bondage.

Gymnastics was part of the curriculum in every school according to the Authorised Imperial Act of Girls Schools in 1907 and the Authorised Imperial Act of Women's Normal Colleges in 1907.[133] All schools now laid great emphasis on the students' intellectual, moral *and* physical development and there can be little doubt that these schools laid the foundation for the future development of modern Chinese women's exercise, physical education and sport.

The development and rapid expansion of physical exercise in girls schools called for a scientific system of physical education and qualified teachers of gymnastics and games. Educationists and reformers founded women's colleges devoted to Western physical education theory and practice. The courses ensured the provision of urgently needed teachers.[134] As a result, qualified teachers quickly emerged. This marked the beginning of physical education as a discipline and stimulated the development of Western exercise. These developments, of course, had considerable relevance eventually for female emancipation as later chapters will reveal.

Conclusion

By the early twentieth century missionaries and reformers had jointly brought about a reconceptualisation of femininity and a redefinition and reshaping of the female body in accordance with Western perceptions of female normality, desirability and propriety. In time, this had a profound significance for the relationship between the sexes, the cultural roles of men and women, and the nature, manifestation and demonstration of social power. Initially, it touched the lives of only the more wealthy, privileged and fortunate – but it was a beginning.

Notes

1. Chenng, Yuet-Wah, *Missionary Medicine in China: a Study of Two Canadian Protestant Missions in China before 1937*, Lanham: University Press of America, 1988, p.3. See also Spence, Jonathan D., *The Search for Modern China*, op. cit., pp.204–10; Barnett, Suzanne W. and Fairbank, John K. (eds), *Christianity in China*, Cambridge, MA: Harvard University Press, 1985; Stauffer, Milton T. (ed.), *The Christian Occupation of China*, Shanghai: China Continuation Committee, 1922; Lutz, Jessie G. (ed.), *Christian Missions in China, Evangelists of What?*, Boston: D.C. Heath and Company, 1965.
2. Vertinsky, Patricia, 'The Social Construction of the Gendered Body: Exercise and the Exercise of Power', paper delivered to the North American Society for Sports History Conference, Halifax, May 1992, p.5.
3. Ibid., p.1.
4. Ibid.
5. Ibid., p.21.
6. Turner, Bryan S., *The Body and Society*, Oxford: Basil Blackwell, 1984, p.59.
7. Vertinsky, P., 'The Social Construction . . .', op. cit., p.1.
8. Ibid.
9. Scott, Joan Wallach, *Gender and the Politics of History*, New York: Columbia University Press, 1988, pp.32, 42.
10. Vertinsky, P., 'The Social Construction . . .', op. cit., p.4.
11. Foucault, Michel, *History of Sexuality*, New York: Partheon, 1978, p.152.
12. Scott, Joan Wallach, op. cit., p.34.
13. Quoted in Vertinsky, P., 'The Social Construction . . .', op. cit., p.3.
14. Blunder, Caroline and Elvin, Mark, *Cultural Atlas of China*, Oxford: Phaidon, 1983, pp.214–15.
15. See Chapter One.
16. Quoted in Kristeva, Julia, op. cit., p.83.
17. Lin, Yutang, *My Country and My People*, op. cit., p.159.
18. Huang, Haoshen, 'Zhongguo chanzu yibing shizu ziqiang zhiji bingshao jianglai buchehuo shuo' [On the Relationship between Footbinding and Strength of the Country], *Shiwu bao* [Current Affairs], No. 35, 8 Aug. 1907.
19. Vertinsky, P., 'The Social Construction . . .', op. cit., p.2.
20. Zhao, Lanxin, *Nu-er Jing zhu* [The Explanation of the Rules for Women], published in the Ming Dynasty, 1368–1644.

21. Quoted in Chen, Dongyuan, *Zhong guo funu shenghuo shi* [The History of Chinese Women's Life], Shanghai: Sangwu chubanshe [Commercial Press], 1937, p.137.

22. Hsu, Francis L. K., *Under the Ancestors' Shadow: Chinese Culture and Personality*, London, Routledge, 1949, p.109.

23. Quoted in Jia, Shen. 'Zhonghua funu chanzu kao' [Footbinding in China], in Bao Jialin, op. cit., p.190.

24. Zhang, Weiyi. 'Tangdai funu tiyu' [Women's Sports Activities in Tang Dynasty], *TWS*, 1983, No. 3, p.24; see also her MA thesis, 'Silun tangdai funu de tiyu huodong' [On Women's Physical Activity in the Tang Dynasty], op. cit.; Xu, Hong, 'Lun zhongguo gudai funu cuju' [On Women's Ball Games in Ancient China], *TWS*, 1984, No. 2, pp.41–2; Liu, Binguo, 'Mingdai gudian xiaoshuo zhongde tiyu' [Sport in the Literature of the Ming Dynasty], *TWS*, 1989, No. 1, pp.60–2.

25. Zhen, Surong, 'Gongshun daniang meiyou wujian' [On Gongsuen daniang's Sword Dance in the Tang Dynasty], *TWS*, 1985, No. 1, pp.13–15; Chen, Changyi, 'Lun Tangdai funu de cuju' [On Women's Ball Games in the Tang Dynasty], *TWS*, 1985, No. 3, pp.18–20; Fu, Liannong, 'Tangren Jianmeiguang de gaibian' [The Changing Image of Beauty and Fitness in the Tang Dynasty], MA thesis, op. cit.

26. Wang, Kunlun, 'Qingdai funu-de taqing huodong' [Women's Entertainment in the Qing Dynasty], *TWS*, 1986, No. 3, p.48.

27. Quoted in Croll, E., *Feminism and Socialism in China*, op. cit., p.78.

28. Quoted in Lin, Sitong, *Zhongguo tiyu wuqian nian* [Chinese Sports History], Xi'an: Xi'an tiyu xueyuan xuebao bianjibu [Xi'an Physical Education Institute Press], 1984, p.16.

29. Fairbank, John K., 'Introduction: the Place of Protestant Writings in China's Cultural History', in Barnett, Suzanne W. and Fairbank, John K., op. cit., p.4.

30. Spence, Jonathan D., *The Search for Modern China*, op. cit., pp.158–63.

31. Feuerwerker, Albet, *The Foreign Establishment in China in the early Twentieth Century*, Ann Arbor: Centre for Chinese Studies, the University of Michigan, 1976, p.39; Chang, Mark, 'A Brief History of Christianity in China', in Dacid, M.D. (ed.), *Western Colonialism in Asian and Christianity*, Bombay: Himalaya Publishing House, 1988, p.108; Cohen, Paul A., *China and Christianity: the Missionary Movement and the Growth of Chinese Anti-Foreignism 1860–1870*, Cambridge, MA: Harvard University Press, 1963, pp.68–70; Stauffer, Milton T. (ed.), *The Christian Occupation of China*, op. cit., *passim*.

32. Stauffer, M.T., op. cit., pp.11–13.

33. Scotan, Addison P., 'Missionary Attitudes and Preparation Seen in the Light of History of the Mission to China', *Presbyterian*, Vol. 4, 1988, p.16.

34. Varg, Paul A., 'A Survey of Changing Mission Goals and Methods', in Lutz, Jessie G. (ed.), *Christian Missions in China, Evangelists of What?*, op. cit., pp.1–10.

35. Chao, Jonathon, 'Western Impact and Social Mobility in China', *Missionary Monthly*, Aug./Sept. 1987, p.12.

36. The Four Books include *The Analects, The Great Learning, Mencius, The Doctrine of the Mean*. The Five Classics include *The Book of Change, The Book of History, The Book of Songs, The Book of Rites* and *The Spring and Autumn Annals*.

37. Dean, William, *The China Mission: Embracing a History of the Various Missions of All Denominations among the Chinese*, New York: Sheldon, 1859, p.95.

38. Ibid., p.23.

39. Fielde, Adele M., *Pagoda Shadows: Studies from Life in China*, Boston: W.G. Corthell, 1884, p.3.

40. Quoted in Dennis, James S., *Christian Missions and Social Progress*, Edinburgh: Anderson & Ferrier, Vol. 2, 1906, p.190.
41. Quoted in Burton, Margaret E., *The Education of Women in China*, New York: Fleming H. Revell Company, 1911, p.24.
42. Song, Hen, *Song Pingzi wencao* [Collected Works of Song Hen], Beijing: Renmin wenxue chubanshe, 1951, p.49.
43. Quoted in Li, Sitong, *Zhonghua tiyu wuqian nian* [Chinese Sports History], op. cit., p.53.
44. Burton, M. E., op. cit., p.31.
45. Ibid., p.24.
46. Lutz, Jessie G., *China and the Christian Colleges 1850–1950*. Ithaca: Cornell University Press, 1971, p.131; Fairbank, John K., 'Introduction: the Many Faces of Protestant Missions in China and the United States', in Fairbank, John K. (ed.), *The Missionary Enterprise in China and America*, Cambridge, MA: Harvard University Press, 1974, p.13.
47. For further details see Latourette, Kenneth S., *A History of Christian Missions in China*, New York: Paragon Book Gallery, 1975, pp.225, 252 and 267.
48. Dean, W., op. cit., p.141.
49. McGilivary, D. (ed.), *A Century of Protestant Missions in China 1807–1907*, Shanghai: The American Presbyterian Mission Press, 1907, pp.10–13; Paterno, Roberto, 'Devello Z. Sheffield and the Founding of the North China College', in Kwang, Ching Lin (ed.), *American Missionaries in China*, Cambridge, MA: Harvard University Press, 1970, p.44; Lutz, Jessie G., *Christian Missions in China*, op. cit., pp.130–34; Latourette, K.S., op. cit., pp.267–8.
50. Lutz, Jessie G., *China and the Christian Colleges*, op. cit., pp.132–3.
51. Dean, William, op. cit., pp.143–4.
52. Chen, Jingpan, op. cit., p.73.
53. Lutz, Jessie G., *China and the Christian Colleges*, op. cit., p.132.
54. Lutz, Jessie G., *Christian Mission in China*, op. cit., pp.vii, xix.
55. Lutz, Jessie G., *China and the Christian Colleges*, op. cit., p.131.
56. Siu, Bobby, *Women of China, Imperialism and Women's Resistance 1900–1949*, London: Zed , 1981, p.18.
57. Quoted in Hunter, Jane, *The Gospel of Gentility, American Women Missionaries in Turn-of-the-Century China*, London: Yale University Press, 1984, p.231.
58. Ibid., p.22.
59. Chen, Jerome, *China and the West: Society and Culture 1815–1937*, London: Hutchinson, 1979, p.380.
60. Levy, Howard S., op. cit., p.85.
61. Mrs Archibald Little was the wife of an English merchant. For her thoughts and actions see her two books: *In the Land of the Blue Gown*, New York: D. Appleton & Co., 1909, and *Intimate China: The Chinese as I Have Seen Them*, London: Hutchinson & Co. (n.d.).
62. The spokesperson for the Natural-foot Society announced in April 1895: 'The Society has been organised to print and distribute pamphlets, leaflets, and pictures among the Chinese on the subject of the prevailing practice of foot-binding, to encourage the formation of leagues and in other ways influence native opinion . . . Our aim is obviously a Christian one, at the same time we invite the help and sympathy of those who are moved by considerations ethical, economic or simply by pity for millions of little girls.' See *North China Herald*, 19 April 1895, p.598; see also Soothill, William B., *Timothy Richard of China*, London: Seeley, Service & Co., 1924, p.179; Croll, E., *Feminism and Socialism in China*, op.cit., p.48.

63. Quoted in Levy, op. cit., p.78.
64. Ibid., p.81. For further details see Chau, Virginia Chui-tin. 'The Anti-footbinding Movement in China (1850–1912)', MA thesis, Columbia University, 1966, *passim*.
65. Dennis, J.S., *Christian Missions and Social Progress*, op. cit., Vol. 2, p.356.
66. Zhang, Zhidong. 'Bu-chanzu-hui xu' [Foreword on Anti-footbinding Association], *Zhixi bao* [New Knowledge News], No. 29, 28 Aug. 1897.
67. Quoted in Levy, op. cit., p.81.
68. Cixi (1835–1908) was a concubine to Emperor Xianfeng and mother of Emperor Tongzhi. She was known to Westerners as 'the Empress Dowager'. From the time she became regent to the boy-emperor Tongzhi in 1861 until her death 48 years later. She held *de facto* power over the Qing government, naming two successive emperors to the throne.
69. According to the *North China Herald* (17 Dec. 1897) over one thousand Western women in the Far East signed their names. See also Couling, S., 'Anti-footbinding', *Encyclopaedia Sinica*, London, 1917, pp.29–30 and 186–7.
70. Charles Denby, the United States Minister to China, agreed in October of 1896 to forward the memorial to the Zongli yamen (the State Council), with the request that that body transmit it to the Empress. The Zongli yamen replied on 30 October 1896: 'In reply, we beg to state the memorial of the said society evidences the fact that the object in view is to do good. But the usage and customs prevailing in China are different from those of western countries. The binding of feet is a practice that has been in vogue for a very long time. Those who oppose the binding of their children's feet are not compelled to do so, while on the other hand those who wish to carry out the practice cannot be prevented from doing so. Custom has made the practice. Those in high authority cannot but allow the people to do as they are inclined in the matter of binding the feet of their children; they cannot be restrained by law.' See *North China Herald*, 20 Nov. 1896. The Zongli yamen refused to present the memorial to their Majesties. However, Mrs Little and Minister Denby made their request again. See *North China Herald*, 12 Feb. 1897. Eventually, the memorandum was submitted to the Court, where it was reported to have been seen in the Palace. See *North China Herald*, 17 Dec. 1897.
71. Hunter, B.S., op. cit., p.24.
72. McNabb, R.L., *The Women of the Middle Kingdom*, Cincinnati and New York, 1903, pp.100, 116.
73. Ross, Edward A., *The Chinese: The Conflict of Oriental and Western Cultures in China*, New York: (n.p.), 1912, p.179.
74. Ibid., p.179.
75. Bashford, James W., *China, an Interpretation*, New York: (n. p.), 1919, p.139; see also Mrs Archibald Little's books: *In the Land of the Blue Gown* and *Intimate China: The Chinese as I Have Seen Them*, op. cit.; and Bird, Isabella. *The Yangtze Valley and Beyond*, London: Virago, 1985. (It was first published in 1899 by John Murray Ltd).
76. CSHSPE, *Zhongguo jindai tiyu shi* [*Modern Chinese Sports History*], op. cit., p.63.
77. Hunter, B.S., op. cit., p.240.
78. CSHSPE, *Zhongguo jidai tiyu shi* [Modern Chinese Sports History], op. cit., p.63.
79. Quoted in Burton, op. cit., p.187.
80. Ibid., p.81.
81. Dean, William, op. cit., p.118.
82. Chen, Jinpan, op. cit., p.380.
83. Burton, op. cit., p.188.

84. Ibid., p.189.
85. Hunter, B.S., op. cit., p.252.
86. *North China Herald*, 12 June 1909.
87. Burton, op. cit., p.192.
88. Feuerwerker, Albet. *The Foreign Establishment in China in the Early Twentieth Century*. op. cit., p.48.
89. Burton, op. cit., p.193.
90. Song, Ruhai. 'Jidujiao qingnianhui de zhongguo tiyu zhi gongxian' [The Contribution of the YMCA to Chinese Sport], in *Zhonghua jidujiao qingnianhui 50 zhounian jinianche* [50 Years of the YMCA in China], published by the YMCA China Committee, Beijing, 1935, p.59.
91. Hunter, B S., op. cit., p.21.
92. Kang, Youwei, *Datong shu* [Book of a Universal Commonwealth], Beijing: Guji chubanshe, 1956, p.130.
93. Ibid., p.131.
94. Tan, Sitong. 'Ren xue' [Study of Humaneness], in *Tan Sitong quanji* [Collected Works of Tan Sitong], Beijing: Sanlian chubanshe [Joint Publishing], 1954, p.19.
95. Liang, Qichao, 'Changshe nuxuetang qi' [Promotion of the Establishment of Girls Schools], *Shiwu bao* [Current Affairs], 15 Nov. 1897, No. 45, and *Nuxue bao* [Journal of Women's Education], 24 July 1898, No. 1.
96. Kang Tongwei, daughter of Kang Youwei. However, because she is a woman, there seems to be no extant record of this female radical.
97. Kang, Tongwei, 'Nuxue libi shuo' [The Advantage and Disadvantage of Women's Education], *Zhixin bao* [New Knowledge News], 11 May 1898, No. 52.
98. Liu, Renglan, 'Lun cuangli zhongguo nuyixue' [On the Establishment of a Chinese Women's School], *Nuxue bao* [Journal of Women's Education], 20 Aug. 1898, No. 4.
99. Kang, Youwei, 'Qingjin funu guozu zhe' [Memorandum Requesting a Ban on the Binding of Women's Feet], in Kang, Youwei, *Wuxu zougao* [Memorial in 1898], 13 Aug. 1898, p.44.
100. Yan, Fu. 'Yuan qiang' [On Strength], in Yan Fu, *Yan jidao shiwei cao* [Collected Works of Yan Fu], Shanghai, 1922, Vol. 1, pp.55–9; also see Wang, Shi (ed.), *Yan Fu ji* [Selected Works of Yan Fu], Beijing: Zhonghua shuju, 1986, pp.468–9.
101. Zhen, Jinhui, 'Lun chanzu de li yu bi' [Argument on Footbinding], *Xiang bao* [Hunan Daily], 10 Sept. 1898, No. 151; Zhang, Zhidong, op. cit.
102. Kang, Youwei, 'Qingjie funu guozu zhe' [Memorandum Requesting a Ban on the Binding of Women's Feet], op.cit., p.45.
103. The term 'Women's Movement' is used to embrace all those groups, formal and informal, involved in women's issues.
104. Kang, Youwei, 'Qingjie funu guozu zhe' [Memorandum Requesting a Ban on the Binding of Women's Feet], op. cit., p.44.
105. Ibid., p.45.
106. Liang, Qichao, 'Jei chanzu hui xu' [Preface of Anti-footbinding Society], *Shiwu bao* [Current Affairs], 3 Jan. 1897, No. 16.
107. Lin, Yutang, *Shunxi jinghua* [The Swift Change of Beijing], Taibei, Dongya Press, 1984.
108. Works of the populists included Bao Chuzi's 'On the Abolition of Footbinding' (Oct. 1882), in *Wanguo gongbao* [International News], 14 Oct. 1882, Vol. 710; Chen Zhe's 'Release the Footbound', in *Jindai shiliao – wuxu pianfa* [Archives of

Modern Chinese History – the Reform Movement of 1898], Beijing: Kexue chubanshe, 1957, p.228; Jia Fu's 'On Footbinding' (Aug. 1896), in *Wanguo gongbao* [International News], 14 Oct. 1882, Vol. 710; Zhao Zengze's 'On Releasing the Bound Foot' (April 1897), ibid., April 1897, No. 99; Hang Haosheng's 'The Weakness of Footbinding in China' (Aug. 1897), in *Shiwu bao* [Current Affairs], 8 Aug. 1897, No. 35; Lin Shu's 'The Song of Suffering from Footbinding' (Jan. 1898), ibid., 24 Dec. 1897, No. 49 and 3 Jan. 1898, No. 50; Hong Wenzi's 'On the Abolition of Footbinding' (March), in *Xiang bao* [Hunan Daily], 23 March 1898, No. 15.

109. Liang, Qichao, 'Shiban buchanzuhui jianming zhangcheng' [Concise Rules of the Experimental Anti-footbinding Society]; *Shiwu bao* [Current Affairs], 2 May 1897, No. 25; Zhang, Shaobo *et al.*, 'Aomen buchanzu-hui bieji zhangcheng' [The Rules of Aomen (Macao) Anti-footbinding Society], *Zhixin bao* [New Knowledge News], 17 May 1897, No. 18; Tang, Sitong. 'Hunan buchanzu hui jianqu zhangcheng' [The Rules of Marrage in the Anti-footbinding Association in Hunan], in Cai, Shang-shi (ed.), *Tan Sitong qiuanji* [Collected Works of Tan Sitong], Beijing: Zhonghua shuju, 1981, pp.396–7.

110. *North China Herald*, 10 Aug. 1906.

111. Tang, Caichang, 'Jiu jin chanzu gei Hong Wenzhi de yifong xin' [Letter to Hong Wenzi on the Banning of Footbinding], *Xiang bao* [Hunan Daily], July 1897, No. 17.

112. Rong, Tiesheng, 'The Women's Movement before and after the 1911 Movement', *Chinese Studies in History*, Nos. 3–4, 1983, p.164.

113. Lewis, Charlton M., *Prologue to the Chinese Revolution: The Transformation of Ideas and Institutions in Hunan Province, 1891–1907*, Cambridge, MA: Harvard University Press, 1976, p.56.

114. Rong, Tiesheng, op. cit., p.165.

115. Lewis, C.M., *Prologue to The Chinese Revolution*, op. cit., p.56.

116. Gamble, S.D., 'The Disappearance of Footbinding in Tinghsien', *American Journal of Sociology*, Sept. 1943, pp.181–3.

117. Quoted in Croll, E., *Feminism and Socialism in China*, op. cit., p.50.

118. The One Hundred Days Reform (summer 1898) was a three-month period during which Kang Youwei and his supporters influenced Emperor Guangxu to issue edicts on political and economic reform. It was ended when Cixi staged a coup, imprisoning the emperor and executing six reformers. For details see Chapter 1 of this work and Spence, Jonathan D., *The Search for Modern China*, op. cit., pp.216–24.

119. Quoted in Levy, op.cit. p.86.

120. Quoted in Croll,E., *Feminism and Socialism in China*, op.cit., p.50.

121. Liang, Qichao, *Wuxu zengbian ji* [Record of the 1898 Reform], Shanghai: Zhonghua shuju, 1936, *passim*.

122. Croll, E., *Feminism and Socialism in China*, op. cit., p.51.

123. 'Nuxue xiansheng' [The Report of the Opening Ceremony of the First Chinese Girls School], *Xiang bao* [Hunan Daily], July 1898, No. 124.

124. 'Quncai dahui – 1897 nian 10 yue 6 hao' [The Report of the Women's Meeting on 6 Dec. 1897], *Nuxue bao* [Journal of Women's Education], 3 Aug. 1898, No. 2.

125. 'Nuxuehui shusu kaiguan zhangcheng' [The Rules of The Chinese Girls School], *Zhixin bao* [New Knowledge News], Oct. 1898, No. 9.

126. Ibid.

127. In Beijing, seven girls' schools were founded before 1909. In Shanghai, between 1902 and 1908, 18 girls' schools were set up. In Jiangsu 28 girls'

schools appeared between 1902 and 1906. In Zhejiang, there were 12 girls' schools by 1906. In Guangdong (Canton), the first girls' school was set up in 1902, and was soon followed by 14 more. Others appeared in Fujian, Hunan, Hubei, Jianxi, Anhui, Guizhou, Sichuan, Shandong and Shanghai provinces. The source is from 'Nuxue yi lan biao' [The Statistics of Girls' Schools], in CWF, op. cit., Vol. 1, pp.341–9.

128. See the report, 'Zhong-meng nuxuetang' [Zhong-meng Girls School], *Jingzhong bao* [Alarm Bell], 2 March 1903.

129. See the report, 'Zhong-meng nuxuetang zhangcheng' [The Rules of Zhong-meng Girls School], *Jingzhong bao* [Alarm Bell], 9 Sept. 1904.

130. Anon., 'The Feminist Movement in China', *Review of Reviews*, Jan. 1909, p.101.

131. In the capital, where there had been only five schools in 1907, the number rose to 26 in 1908 (see *North China Herald*, 18 July 1908); in Tianjin, between 1905 and 1908, 20 new girls' schools were founded; 12 girls' schools with a total of 800 pupils came into being in Shanghai; another 49 government-sponsored or private-funded modern schools with a total of 1,897 students flourished in Sichuan province (see Burton, op. cit., pp.126–9).

132. The actual number of girl students is disputed. However, the widespread growth of female education is quite clear from all the statistics. See 'Nuxue yi lian biao' [The Statistics of Girls' Schools], in Zhonghua quanguo funu lian-hehui funu yundong lishi yanjiushi [Chinese Women's Federation – Women's Movement Research Centre], hereafter CWF (ed.), Zhongguo jindai funu yundong lishi zhiliao [The Historical Archives of the Chinese Women's Movement], Beijing: Zhongguo funu chubanshe [Chinese Women's Press], Vol. 1, 1991, pp.341–9; Croll, E., *Feminism and Socialism in China*, op. cit., pp.53–4.

133. Zhongguo lishi xuehui [Chinese History Association] (ed.), *Daqing Guangxu xin-faling* [New Authorised Imperial Acts], Beijing: Shangwu yinshuguan, 1953, pp.35–47.

134. Colleges founded included the Shanghai Chinese Gymnastics School for Women (1908), The China Physical Education Teachers' College for Women (1908) and the Shanghai Liangjiang Women's Physical Education Institute (1909). The source is from CSHI, *Zhongguo jindai tiyushi zhiliaoji* [Modern Chinese Sports History Reference], op. cit., pp.292–300; and CSHSPE, *Zhongguo jindai tiyu shi* [Modern Chinese Sports History], op. cit., pp.78–9.

THREE

Strong Bodies for Strong Action: The Chinese Women's Enlightenment Movement (1895–1913)

❧❧❦❧❧

W HAT IS ENLIGHTENMENT? Immanuel Kant argued that 'Enlightenment is man's emergence from his self-inflicted immaturity. Immaturity is the incapacity to use one's own understanding without the guidance of another. This immaturity is self-inflicted if its cause is not a lack of understanding but a lack of courage to use understanding without the guidance of another. *Sapere aude!* Dare to know! Be guided by your own understanding! This is the watchword of enlightenment!'[1] Modern Chinese women's search for 'enlightenment' reflects the exigencies of their own history. Theirs is a history marked by the quest for emancipation from an imposed feudal worldview, cultural oppression and social inferiority.

Studies of Chinese history restrict the so-called Chinese Enlightenment period to the years 1915 to 1921.[2] However, in the case of women, this period should adjusted to cover also the years 1895 to 1913. This allows for a more complete consideration of those special factors involved in the Female Enlightenment Movement in modern China. Military defeat in the first Sino-Japanese War in 1895[3] destroyed the dream of restoring China's power and strength by means of the 'Westernisation Movement' initiated by the Qing government.[4] Chinese radicals – men and women – began the search for a political elixir of life to revive China in what seemed to be almost its political death-throes. Now was the time for Chinese women to use their intelligence to find their way without paternal authority, to develop their new-found sense of individuality and independence. At this moment in Chinese history, Chinese women inherited the energy, idealism and optimism characteristic of the European Enlightenment of the eighteenth century.

It is argued throughout this book that if the Chinese women's emancipation movement is to be studied meaningfully, it has to include the evolution of women's struggle for physical freedom, expression and enjoyment as part of a cultural redefinition of femininity within China. The study of the definition of women's bodies in Chinese culture is, in large measure, a study of social control, social order and social fashion. One of the significant ambitions of the Chinese women's emancipation movement, therefore, was to free women's bodies from Confucian cultural control, order and fashion. In its efforts to achieve this freedom, it firmly linked exercise to liberation. The relationship between women's emancipation, the changing images of women's bodies and the development of physical exercise ideologies and activities during the period 1895 to 1913, referred to here as the period of 'female enlightenment in modern China', forms the subject of this chapter.

The Ideal Woman – Good Wife and Healthy Mother

By the end of the nineteenth century Chinese radicals had begun to seek a new image for Chinese women. A conservative image, which went back literally thousands of years, was strongly challenged. Pressure from Christian missionaries and Chinese reformers had led to the imperial reforms discussed in the last chapter. Chinese radicals were ready to accept unreservedly the foreign claim that 'the position of women was one of the dark blemishes in the social life of the Chinese'.[5] These radicals now devoted considerable energy to reform. However, Chinese receptivity to Western images of women and the impulse to redefine femininity accordingly, depended less on the intrinsic merits of those images than on China's humiliating and precarious international position. Women's physical health had therefore become a foremost concern and almost every reformer now stressed the need to 'unbind' the feet of Chinese women and advocated physical exercise for women to ensure fit mothers for a fit nation.[6] Indirectly, in consequence, the bodies of women became the battleground for redefining a fundamental human relationship, that of woman and man. For conservatives, traditional sexual inequality was a requisite barrier to full, and in their minds, improper egalitarianism, [7] while for liberals sexual equality was a necessary requirement to full egalitarianism. [8] What aided the reforming liberals in their struggle was China's political feebleness and military humiliation by the European powers in the second half of the nineteenth century. China, claimed these liberals, needed healthy mothers to bear healthy sons to preserve and promote the state. Women's traditional bodies were described by liberals as 'political anomalies'. They required reconstruction. In essence, therefore, this reconstruction was not the consequence of idealistic progress but the outcome of practical purpose.[9] It was born of ineluctable political necessity.

Women, now, were to be supported by, but subordinate to the state. The general principle laid down for women's education was 'to nurture women's moral restraint, to provide necessary knowledge and skills, while *paying attention to physical development*'[10] (emphasis added). Footbinding was banned. Physical education was advocated to promote 'the regular growth of the body and smoothness of movement' of the four limbs. Health measures such as sound diet, hygiene and physical exercise became increasingly centred upon the functions of reproduction and child-rearing.[11]

Many male reformers, however, opposed women's demands for full equality on the grounds that a female's physical nature, represented by her body but understood most clearly in her reproductive function, disqualified her from public life and thus from full participation in society. *Min Bao* [People's News], the official organ of the revolutionary party, Tongmenghui [The Revolutionary Alliance] led by Sun Yat-sen, for example, published a total of 26 issues between 1905 and 1910 but not one contained a single article devoted to the women's emancipation movement.[12] The other leading party, the conservative Constitutional-Monarchical Party, made not the slightest attempt to represent women's views in its party organ – *Xinmin zhoubao* [New People's Weekly].[13] The widely read *Dongfang zazhi* [The East] adopted a traditional tone and carried article after article persuading women to be virtuous wives and good mothers. One of the articles quite explicitly urged female students not to use 'unseemly foreign vocabulary', such as 'national spirit, representation, sacrifice, society, conflict . . .', because these words dealt with subjects beyond women's proper concerns.[14] In this allegedly modern magazine women remained characterised collectively and idealistically by physiological and psychological properties such as passivity, sensitivity and gentleness. Untrammelled by any doubt or uncertainty one of the articles, entitled 'A Woman's Knowledge and the Demands of the Times', curtly warned young women that they must attend to 'essentials' and avoid stressing 'non-essentials', because essentials were 'nationally necessary'. Women should not 'waste their efforts' on non-essentials, thereby 'exhausting themselves both physically and mentally'. What were the 'essentials'? In the author's view: 'To honour your parents, to respect your friends, to have diligence and patience'.[15] This was simply a rehash of Confucian doctrine: 'the three obediences and the four virtues'.[16]

It gradually became clearer and clearer that some male reformers had neither the commitment nor the courage to further the Women's Movement. Far from refusing to have any truck with reactionary opinion, their understanding of women's liberation was limited to the idea of healthy mothers in the interest of healthy sons. As the well-known reformer Liang Qichao (1873–1923) claimed, 'The equality of men and women meant *not* [emphasis added] that women could do whatever men could, but that the different endowments of the sexes – modesty, gentleness, tenacity and patience on the part of women; boldness, strength, and grasp of general principle on the part of men – were to be equally respected, and made an equally important contribution to society.'[17] In short, for many progressive men, through their bodies women still represented and confirmed earlier social realities. The 'new woman' was to be a helpmate to her husband, a source of instruction for her sons; in her immediate surroundings, she would give ease to the family, and in a wider sphere she would improve the race.[18] Traditional prejudices were not set aside but rather incorporated into the language of reform.

Strong Bodies for Strong Action: Women's Active Role in the Revolution

Although advocacy of the virtuous wife and healthy mother held the field among most radical men in the first decade of the twentieth century, there was a growing number of educated women who were not satisfied with this narrow perception of their gender role. They were destined to play a crucial part in determining their country's future. In China the Women's Movement never enjoyed the status of an independent movement. From the beginning it was enmeshed in, and shaped by, nationalism.

During 1902–1903 several significant articles and translations of significant works touching on the question of women became available. In 1902 an hagiographic biography of Mme Roland of the

French Revolution was published in which her 'many-sided talents . . . , her natural gifts for leadership, the political intrigues, the pathos of her death, were all vividly set forth'.[19] 'Lolan furen' [Mme Roland] passed into the vocabulary of feminist and revolutionary writers as an exemplar of the forceful and determined woman patriot. In 1904, the 'Ballad of a French Heroine', a verse biography of Roland, which urged Chinese women to take emancipatory action for the sake of their country, appeared.[20] Joan of Arc was similarly lionized. Her biography was first written in journal form in 1900 and appeared in book form in 1904.[21] These Western heroines became role models. With their lives now available in Mandarin to a Chinese female audience the scope of their influence increased considerably.[22] However, the most important stimulus for change was the influence of those radical female students, inspired by revolutionary idealism, who travelled with their male colleagues to Japan – at that time in the throes of urgent Westernisation.[23] It was through these idealists that certain cultural breakwaters were breached.

Chinese students sought an education abroad from the middle of the nineteenth century onwards, most of them attending European and American universities.[24] This situation changed after defeat in the Sino-Japanese War of 1895.[25] There were three reasons: first, Japan's victory provoked Chinese envy and interest. There was a new consciousness of similarities with Japan in the areas of culture, language, custom and geography. Then there was the mutual problems of foreign aggression and modernisation.[26] In contrast to Chinese leaders of the time, the leaders of Japan's Meiji Restoration seemed to have the ability to handle these two significant problems to Japan's advantage.

Second, the Japanese education system attracted the attention of the Chinese. They considered that the secret of Japan's success was the promotion of modern education. The essence of the Japanese education system was militarism modelled, for the most part, on that of Germany. In Qing eyes, Bismarck had achieved victory over France in 1870 through compulsory education. Other nations, including Japan, had followed the Prussian example and China felt the need to do the same. Ancient China's martial spirit resembled that of modern Japan. The problem now was to revive it. Furthermore, the aims of Japanese education were patriotism and fidelity to the emperor. Consequently, to learn from Japan was smiled upon by the Qing government and it now sent educationists to Japan to observe the education system.[27] Perhaps curiously but certainly logically, radicals, as well as the Qing government, had come to the conclusion that China should learn from Japan if China was to resist foreign aggression and revive national fortunes.[28] As a consequence of this combined commitment, in 1903, China's first modern educational system was modelled on that of Japan.[29]

Third, the sudden abolition in 1905 of the Chinese civil examination system[30] as part of the modernisation of the country left many thousands of scholars, who had been preparing for many years to take the examinations, in the lurch. They formed a large intelligent group easily able to assimilate the radical ideas pouring in from the West, and Japan was the nearest and cheapest place to go for 'Western learning'.[31] So for the sake of the future of China, with the encouragement of the government in particular and society in general, a large-scale migration of students to Japan now began. The number of Chinese students in Japan thus snowballed from 13 in 1896 to 13,000 in 1906.[32] There were some female students among them.[33] A contemporary newspaper estimated that in 1906–1907 there were about one hundred Chinese girls attending various Tokyo schools, and still more studying outside the school system.[34]

It is a safe assumption that the Chinese girls and women who studied in Japan, as in the case of those studying in China, were from well-to-do families – a status which not only provided them with the wherewithal for travel and study, but also with the confidence to believe that they might take advantage of the opportunity.

Wives accompanying husbands were a common phenomenon. Wives were sent in part to keep the young student husband from 'going Japanese', but once there took the chance to study on their own in the less restrictive atmosphere of Japan. Some wives accompanied their husbands for other reasons. Li Ziping, wife of Feng Ziyu, followed her husband to Japan in 1903. While there they worked for revolution. He Xiangning, believed to be one of the first women to join the Revolutionary Alliance, also joined her husband in Tokyo for the same purpose in 1904, after selling her dowry jewellery for the needed funds.[35] Some girls travelled to Japan under the auspices of provincial governments, several of which became involved in sponsoring girls' study abroad. Fengtian province was among the first, having in 1905 negotiated an agreement whereby the Japanese Aoyama Girls' Vocational School would accept 15 girls from Fengtian each year. By 1907, 21 girls from Fengtian were actually studying under provincial sponsorship.[36] In 1905, Hunan province also sent 20 girls for short training courses in education.[37] However, most of the female students in Japan seem to have made their own financial arrangements.[38]

It was in Japan, therefore, that many Chinese men and women became acquainted with Western learning, joined in debate on the future of China, set up revolutionary organisations – and took their first steps in mastering the modern philosophy and practice of physical education. It was a far from insignificant element of their studies. They greatly valued the subject since they saw physical education as a significant means of developing a national spirit of *muscular unity* which would enable China to emerge as a modern state capable of defending herself. For this reason, almost all of the Chinese students took enthusiastic part in the physical training courses available in Japan.[39] As Din Hongchen, the governor of Sichuan province in the late Qing dynasty, wrote in his diary when he visited Japan in 1898, all Chinese students took gymnastics – the military-oriented physical exercise of the time – as a compulsory course.[40] The Qing government was more than content. As we have seen it held to the unexceptional view that military power was the bulwark of the Empire – a lesson China had to relearn painfully. In addition, in the view of the Qing authorities, military physical exercises, which stressed disciplined unity, would help maintain an ordered and unified regime. Thus Japan's physical training system set within the framework of a tightly controlled, corporate culture seemed a perfect model for China. The result was that the Chinese government sent more and more students to Japan to enrol in programmes of physical education and physical training (known generically as 'gymnastics').[41] From 19 June to 17 September 1906, for example, the Chinese government sent 104 students to Japan to learn 'gymnastics'.[42] Of the total Chinese student population in Japan, women made up only a small percentage, but they were highly motivated and often radical.[43] These women, for the first time freed from the constraints of family and, to an extent, culture, were both psychologically and physically able to demonstrate abilities that in their eyes justified an equal status with men.

As they had done for male students, some Japanese schools opened branches designed to offer short courses for Chinese women – taught in both Chinese and Japanese. Among the first to accept Chinese female students was the school of the Imperial Women's Association, whose headmistress was the Japanese educationist Shimoda Utako.[44] The Tokyo Women's School of the Fine Arts and the Women's College also opened their door to the Chinese.[45] The Chinese Girls' School of Tokyo was established in 1903; Shimoda Utako was superintendent of studies.[46] Eventually the best known of the Japanese schools for Chinese students was the Chinese Overseas Student Division of the Girls' Practical School established in 1901 by Shimoda Utako. Zhang Shichao, former editor of a radical Chinese newspaper *Subao* [Jiangsu News],[47] taught Chinese literature, but the rest of the teaching staff consisted of Japanese men and women who lectured through interpreters. The programme included courses in history, physics, chemistry, geography, mathematics, domestic science, music, needle-work, handicrafts *and* physical education.[48]

The specific aim of these schools was to train Chinese women to be educators. On returning to China, most of these women became educationists and many became physical educationists. For the most part, they were confirmed feminists and revolutionaries, and played an active role in both the national salvation movement and in the Women's Movement of the early twentieth century.[49]

Prior to the overthrow of the Qing government in 1911, male and female students returning from abroad, particularly from Japan, initiated a radical movement: 'Saving China with Tichao [Gymnastics]'. [50] This was in tune with the times. Social Darwinism, when it came to China, allowed intellectuals to hope that a means could be found to save the country from losing out in the global struggle involving the survival of the fittest. In Chinese vocabulary, Tichao (gymnastics), from the moment of its emergence, was closely connected with political purpose.[51] As Henry B. Graybill, Acting President of Canton Christian College in 1911, noted: 'We find a nation, once opposed to physical education and distinguishing the student from the soldier as the official from the coolie, now making a new class of soldier-students for the defence and glory of the nation.'[52] A modern tradition was born that has lasted right up to the present. Today the popular slogan 'Develop sport to vitalise China' characterises Communist China.[53] The turn of the century saw the invention of a tradition of some longevity.[54]

In the first decade of the twentieth century Tichao represented most of the physical training and physical education programmes available in Chinese schools.[55] In the 1920s it was replaced by another term, 'tiyu' (physical education and sport).[56] However, between 1910 and

1930 a large percentage of the leading personalities in the Chinese physical education movement were students trained in Japan.[57] This was certainly one of the reasons why modern Western games and sports were relatively ignored by Chinese society in this period.[58] These students from Japan, in effect, were responsible for the development of a modern education movement. They set up new schools[59] where gymnastics was a compulsory course and former Japanese students were employed as academic teachers and physical training instructors.[60] In general, these teachers were familiar with gymnastics but unfamiliar with Western ball games. As one student remembered, 'When I was in Hunan Teachers' College, Mr Liu Jiepei had just returned from Japan and became our physical educator. He taught us gymnastics, military exercise and dance. We had a high respect for him. But he couldn't play ball games.'[61] Women students who returned from Japan either founded, administered or taught in girls' schools. The Wusi Kenghua Girls' School, with 70 pupils, was established by three women who had studied in Japan.[62] Yang Changta was later a member of Shanghai women's revolutionary auxiliary committee in 1911 and principal of the Jiangsu Provincial First Girls' Normal School.[63] In 1906 the wife and daughter of a Mr Yen, who had both been educated in Japan, established what was said to be the first girls' school in Baoding, Hebei province.[64] Qiu Jin, a former student in Japan, who later led an abortive feminist and revolutionary uprising,[65] taught gymnastics in Minde and Xunxi Girls School, Zhejiang province in 1906.[66] It was the same story in virtually every province.[67]

Most of the early modern physical education and gymnastic books and articles used in China were translated, or written and introduced by these former students who saw the need to propagate the ideal of 'Saving China with Gymnastics' among their less-enlightened brothers and sisters. According to Gu Luanguang's *The Records of Translation*, six physical education and gymnastics books were published in China between 1901 and 1904, and five of them were translated by students who had returned from Japan.[68] In addition, between 1883 and 1911, more than 200 journals and newspapers were published in China. Translated papers and articles on gymnastics and physical exercise appeared in every one of them.[69] Furthermore, during the first decade of the twentieth century, many physical education colleges and societies and gymnastic training institutes opened, most of them founded or run by students who had studied in Japan.[70]

Those students had both an influential and inspirational effect on China's physical education. Before them, of course, the Christian missionary schools and YMCA had introduced modern physical activities,[71] putting China on the road towards modern physical education and games,[72] but their work was limited to large cities and missionary schools. Furthermore, their physical education ideals were not widely accepted, chiefly because of the growing anti-Western feeling in China in the late nineteenth century.[73] There was, in addition, the language gap. In contrast, the students trained in Japan were Chinese speaking and mostly patriots. It must not be overlooked that their 'gymnastics' was not simply, or indeed essentially, exercise for individual fitness, but exercise for national regeneration. Physical education was to be a means of political liberation. Little by little, the subject was incorporated into the curriculum of both government and private schools throughout China.[74] An examination of the curriculum implemented at the time reveals the importance of physical education in the years immediately prior to the overthrow of the Qing dynasty. Primary-school (ages 7–12) courses covered a period of five years. Eight courses were taught uniformly throughout the five years in a 30-hour week. Two hours a week were to be devoted to ethics, 12 to Chinese classics, four to Chinese literature, six to mathematics, one to history, one to geography, one to science, and three to gymnastics and physical exercise. In 1909 a change was made in this curriculum, reducing the time spent on a number of subjects such as history, geography and natural science, but the time spent on gymnastics and physical exercise remained unchanged. In the higher primary school (ages 15–19) gymnastics and physical exercise were compulsory and their aim was to give the students the strength to defend the nation. Physical education became very popular,[75] with gymnastics (military physical exercise) being stressed in school time and (Western) sports given space after school.[76] The Chinese soon felt comfortable with physical exercise, modern style. This played its part in establishing a more positive attitude toward Chinese women's right to exercise which, in turn, led more and more Chinese women steadily, if slowly, towards greater physical emancipation.

Access to 'gymnastics' for girls was an extension of female entry into the academic school world. As mentioned above, it was initially largely taught by the students who had studied in Japan. They had come to appreciate the patriotic value of exercise and they were eager to share this appreciation with students who had remained in China.

Xu Yibin (1881–1922), for example, one of the first and most famous reformers of Chinese female physical education, who studied in Dasheng Gymnastic College in Tokyo between 1905 and 1907, believed that 'gymnastics' would improve girls' health, stimulate study and impart such valuable qualities as determination, resourcefulness, independence and courage which were necessary for the country's regeneration.[77] When he came back from Japan in the autumn of 1907 he taught physical education in Shanghai Patriotic Girls School and then in 1908, in Shanghai, with his friend Tang Jianer, a female physical educator returned from Japan, he founded the first women's gymnastic school in China. It was called simply the Chinese Women's Gymnastic School.[78] Its aim was to furnish Chinese women with a balanced intellectual and physical training.[79] Most of the teachers in this school were graduates of Japanese colleges. In their professional hands gymnastics was intended to make students fit to serve both their anticipated professions and China. The motto of the Chinese Women's Gymnastic School was 'Build up the Chinese People's Health and Throw away the Humiliation of the Title of "Sick Man of East Asia"'.[80] Most graduates from this school became 'gymnastic' teachers in state and private schools and colleges and some of them established new women's physical education schools modelled on the Women's Gymnastic School in Shanghai.[81] They radiated an emancipatory vigour which thrust them into traditional male territory, asserting that women were the equal of men and should have the right to lead similar lives and share the same national responsibilities. They, and others like them, were not without influence. In the first 30 years of the twentieth century, an unprecedented number of independent and innovative young women existed in Chinese society.[82]

Meanwhile, one of the most widely admired male educators, Cai Yuanpei (1876–1940),[83] also recognised the important conjunction between mental and physical development and sought to produce girl students who were healthy as well as intelligent.[84] He and his friends founded the Patriotic Girls School in Shanghai in 1902,[85] with physical exercise as part of the curriculum.[86] Cai insisted that women had the right to develop their bodies as well as their minds. He sought to make his students physically fit in order to prove that women could share with men the role of active saviours of their country.[87] Cai was a revolutionary. He included in the curriculum a philosophy course on Nihilism, a history course on the French Revolution and added for good measure chemistry courses in bomb-making![88] His actions helped to create a cadre of radical women. These women firmly believed that their feminism was an integral part of nationalism. They lived in, and shared in, the atmosphere of ardent nationalism that grew in the student and intellectual circles of China and Japan. They were at least as committed to saving China as their male counterparts; but as women, they defined China's special weakness in terms of the familial and unacceptable existence allotted to the female half of the population.

A number of girls' schools, like the Patriotic Girls' School, Xunxin Girls' School, Minggao Girls' School and Mingjiang Girls' School had organisational connections with revolutionary groups like Guangfuhui [the Restoration Society] and Tongmenhui [the Revolutionary Alliance].[89] These schools provided a useful cover for their more extreme radical activities. The new demand for such schools presented an excellent chance to establish a respectable image within the community, generating the support of that segment of the population which supported reform while creating a base for its more covert and extreme activities. Those ties demonstrated that the movement for the education of women was not just a part of the general nationalistic fervour of the time for education. The schools themselves, through their staffs and students, took an active political role in the nationalist movement.

Other Chinese soon followed the lead of these radical intellectuals and established similar girls' schools. The very founding of such a school was a radical act in itself, in that it was contrary to long established social practice. The *North China Herald* reported that by 1907 some 1,000 girls were attending school in the Shanghai concession area, in some 12 missionary and 12 indigenous institutions.[90] Between 1902 and 1906, seven schools for girls were established in Hunan.[91] By 1908, there were 25 girls' schools in Canton,[92] and 20 girls' schools in Beijing. Nanjing had 12 girls' schools in 1909 with 753 pupils.[93] In Jiangsu and Zhejiang provinces 77 girls' schools were established between 1898 and 1911.[94]

These schools were established with clear and declared aims: the advancement of women's knowledge and the universalisation of women's education – mental and physical.[95] As stressed earlier, the development of women's physical abilities was most important to this general advancement. For the majority of middle-class girls and women who attended girls' schools and women's colleges, in conjunction with preparation for patriotic struggle, self-realisation through physical endeavour was a most profound ambition. For the first time in Chinese history, not without reason, this educational élite of Chinese women believed that freedom would come largely through exercise. This is no exaggerated assertion. Chen Jiefen,[96] by way of illustration, who in 1902 founded and edited the first women's magazine, *Nubao* [Women's Journal],[97] pointed out in an article on physical education the following year[98] that Chinese women's education had three elements: moral, intellectual and physical. Of the three, she asserted, physical development was the fundamental element. Physical education was not simply as important for women as moral and intellectual education, it formed their very basis. For women in a physically weak condition could do nothing, not even perform their traditional duties of companion and mother. In her view, women's moral growth and intellectual development could not be achieved without putting physical education *first*.

Chinese women had no tradition of exercise and they did violence to their bodies through footbinding, inactivity, and ignorance. They had accepted too readily the male ideal of feminine beauty as physical fragility because in their hearts they wished to please men. But real beauty depended on good health; the popular image of beauty was simply that favoured by 'dead-hearted, foolish males for the sake of making it easy to treat women disrespectfully and oppress them . . . if these men who created this ideal really consider it desirable, why didn't they apply it to themselves instead of making only women follow it?' Chen hoped, therefore, that her women comrades – poor worms – would henceforth realise their predicament and turn, and encourage each other to turn. Chen claimed,

> For several thousand years we have been sunk in a dark hell. Only since the importation of women's rights has there been a ray of light . . . but if we wish to escape the status of slaves and dogs and horses, we must reform ourselves, and the way forward lies with physical education. Women's emancipation should start from physical release through physical education. Let Chinese women have healthy bodies to shoulder the responsibilities of society and themselves.

Chen was wedded to the reformers' view of women's education and physical education.[99] As an educated woman with a knowledge and sense of history, she was in a position to be acutely aware of the extent of the historic handicap of Chinese women in their pursuit of an education – *crippled limbs.* She was adamant that a strong body was a prerequisite of strong action – an approach she favoured. In her view, women's emancipation could only be achieved through violent national revolution. With Medea-like vituperation, she pointed out, 'Chinese women live in an age of revolution; if they join together and seize the opportunity, develop their strength and fill their hearts with venomous hatred, destroying and then creating, then those who shed blood, who complete the enterprise, will be equal to men. In an age of change, if they fulfill their duties equally with men, then their rights will be equal as well.'[100]

Chen was a revolutionary who spoke for herself and others – but others also spoke for themselves. Similar militant aspirations associated with women's physical education were articulated by female and male radicals in various national journals.[101] Invariably these radical writers were hostile to the old Confucian beliefs and had unbounded trust in a new liberal morality. They declared that women should fight to obtain the right to develop themselves mentally and physically. This new image of women as militaristic, intelligent, strong and determined was gradually accepted by a minority in middle class, urban society. The best example of this militant ethos was Qiu Jin (1875–1907) who was an educationist, physical educationist and revolutionary heroine. She was a leading pioneer of Chinese women's emancipation and can be seen as an ideal period representative of feminism, radicalism and revolution.[102]

Qiu Jin was born into a wealthy conservative family. She had a traditional education, bound feet and an arranged marriage. The turning-point of her life came in 1900 when she went to Beijing with her husband. She was distressed by the presence of Western troops and this experience led her to develop strong anxieties about China's future. She was convinced that China was on the brink of disaster and that all Chinese needed to work for their country's salvation. It was nationalism that inspired many of her future actions. Distressed by her powerlessness and inspired by her aspiration to save her country, in July 1903 she decided to leave her husband and to sell her dowry in order to study in Japan.[103] On arriving in Japan she was determined to make the most of her new freedom. She unbound her feet and threw herself into a plethora of activities. From now on her life revolved around the three interlocking themes: education, feminism and revolution. She argued forcefully that exercise would develop women's determination, and kindle women's desire to contribute to the nation's well-being.[104] Furthermore, she asserted that it would ensure a positive contribution towards a new China. Eventually patriotism, she stated, would demand revolution, for only if China's rottenness, epitomised by the Qing dynasty, was dug out and only if China's ignorant populace was educated, would the country gain the qualities required to survive and then to flourish.

Qiu Jin blamed women themselves for their traditionally subservient position. Women had been forced to mutilate their bodies and hide themselves indoors. They had surrendered their rights and abilities by acquiescing in an indoctrination that destroyed independent thought and action. She believed that women should develop new mental and physical qualities in preparation for a new era.[105] She practised what she preached. In 1904 Qiu Jin enrolled in a Japanese language school in Surugadai in the Kanda area of Tokyo and later transferred to Shimoda's Vocational School.[106] This school emphasised physical exercise and provided a one-year training course for teachers. The physical education component was compulsory.[107] In 1905 Qiu Jin wrote to her brother: 'I am in the College. I am tough and healthy. I take part in gymnastics everyday to keep me fit.'[108] Beside attending the physical education course in the school, Qiu Jin learnt sword fencing and archery at the Martial Arts Society in Tokyo.[109] She dressed in men's clothing, carried a short sword, practised bomb-making and marksmanship, and drank considerable quantities of wine.[110] This behaviour was closely tied to the image of a 'masculine heroine' protesting energetically against traditional restrictions, in love with physical power and attracted to playing a traditionally male role in the cause of feminine liberation. As Qiu Jin exclaimed: 'My aim is to dress like a man! . . . In China men are strong, and women are oppressed because they are supposed to be weak. I want somehow to have the mind of a man. If I first take on the appearance of a man, then I believe my mind too eventually will become like that of a man.'[111] She also gave herself a second name, Jin Xiong, which meant 'able to compete with men'.[112]

Feminism was not simply a gender issue for Qiu Jin. It was an integral part of any answer to the political problems to which she sought solutions. In 1904 she reorganised Gongaihui [the Humanitarian Society] with Chen Jiefen who, as mentioned earlier, had written an influential article on women's physical education. The aim of this organisation was to promote Chinese women's education and rights.[113] In the spring of 1905, she joined Guangfuhui [the Restora-

Qiu Jin holding a short sword as a clear symbol of her imitative masculinity. (From the Archives of Chinese Sports Culture and History, Beijing.)

tion Society], a well-known revolutionary party.[114] In August, she became one of the first female members of the new revolutionary party – Tongmenghui [Revolutionary Alliance] led by Sun Yat-sen.[115] In 1906 Qiu Jin returned to China to be a teacher of physical education, language and history in the Minde and Xunyang girls' schools.[116] In January 1907, she and her close friend Xu Zhihua,[117] founded *Zhongguo nubao* [the Chinese Women's Journal] in Shanghai. Its aim was to urge women to leave home to gain their rightful place in society.[118] In this journal she gave full and clear expression to her views on female emancipation.[119] She attacked the traditional evil treatment of women such as foot binding, arranged marriage, enforced chastity, confinement and denial of education. To break away from this legacy of oppression Qiu Jin stressed that girls should seek a modern education so that they might earn a living, thereby winning the respect of their families, ensuring their independence, underlining their social importance and developing relationships beyond the home. In February 1907 Qiu Jin had an opportunity to put her ideals into practice when she became Principal of the Datong Normal College in Shao Xing, Zhejiang province.[120]

This college had been founded by revolutionaries in 1905.[121] There was a physical education institute attached to it for the express purpose of training revolutionary soldiers. When Qiu Jin inherited the fruits of a two-year effort by her friends from the Restoration Society, she extended its revolutionary endeavours beyond the college and used sports clubs as locations for the preparation of violent revolutionary action. First, she reorganised the old Sports Society in Shao Xing and changed its name to the Datong Sports Society.[122] Then she established a new sports society called the Sports Society of North District.[123] She also tried to found a Women's Sports Society but she failed due to the opposition of local conservatives and decided, therefore, to train women soldiers in the Datong Normal College.[124]

In her role as Principal of the College, Qiu Jin introduced her revolutionary ideas into her teaching, placing a great emphasis on military exercises such as fencing and riding.[125] She herself rode, fenced and boxed well.[126] As one student recalled, Qiu Jin always wore men's clothes, rode horseback astride and insisted on girls doing physical training.[127] A poem of the time expressed general admiration of her: 'A Heroine [Qiu Jin] is part of the male society, her military spirit and physical ability are well-known in Zhejiang. She advocates physical exercise and nobody can compare with her. All admire her'[128] Qiu Jin ensured that women in her care were physically capable of taking a strong and active part in her revolutionary schemes. Her aim was nothing less than the development of Chinese women with active minds *and* bodies, an appreciation of China's crisis and an acceptance of their responsibility for solving it – if necessary, by force. Her poem, 'Women's Rights,' best expressed her emphatic opinions: 'men and women are born equal, Why should we let men hold sway? We will rise and save ourselves, ridding the nation of all her shame.'[129] She had the resolve of a Joan of Arc and her concept of the relationship between women's freedom and revolution reflected an intensely personal commitment that earned her an early death. She established a local reputation as a scholar and teacher, but also as a deviant and dangerous non-conformist. A woman in her position and with her views was certain to become an object of curiosity and ultimately fear and hatred among the traditionally minded.[130]

In May 1907 she and her comrade Xu Zilin[131] decided to mount simultaneous uprisings in Zhejiang and Anhui on the 19 July. However, plans for the armed revolt in Zhejiang were leaked and, in early July, Xu was forced to act prematurely. His uprising failed. He was executed on the 6 July. The relationship between Xu Zilin and Qiu Jin was discovered by the Qing government and on 13 July Qiu Jin learnt that government troops were coming to arrest her. The situation was hopeless but she was too emotionally committed to flee in order to try again at a later date. With her students she resisted the soldiers in a brief battle and was captured.[132] In her minor role of physical educator, Qiu Jin was accused of anti-government activity.[133] The government were careful to avoid any mention of the fact that she was a college Principal – a figure of authority. The Governor of Zhejiang pronounced the death sentence and Qiu Jin, in the role of subversive physical educator of Datong Physical Education Society, was executed at the age of 32 on 15 July 1907. After her death, the government closed all the sports societies in Zhejiang province. The term 'physical education' was banned. It now implied 'revolution'.[134] Throughout society anxiety spread. Conservatism was re-established with a vengeance. Young girls, who had given up footbinding, feared that they might be considered revolutionary and reverted to the practice. Girls were taken from schools and there was a general reaction against modern ways.[135] However, all was not lost. Qiu Jin remained in the memories of her admirers. In the summer of 1912, after the 1911 Revolution to overthrow the Qing government, at the fifth anniversary memorial service of Qiu Jin's execution, the members of the Restoration Society, decided to 'reinstate the sports society which was founded by Qiu Jin and establish Zhejiang Sports School in her memory'.[136]

More than this, Qiu Jin came to symbolise the new woman of strong mind and strong body pledged to the strengthening of the nation through women's liberation. She proved an inspiration to her sex. There had been little assertion and confrontation before 1900. Now girls and women became, in some ways, one of the more important groups to gain prominence in China in the first phase of social revolution (1900–1911).[137] They proved to be principled, committed and energetic in their espousal of change. For their part, of course, women believed that in the long term they would benefit from reform, sexual restrictions would be swept away along with other old evils and in a new China, driven by liberal values, men and women would strive harmoniously together to reach shared goals to the benefit of all.[138] In the short term, the revolutionary movement offered women the opportunity to join in the great work of saving the nation, to prove themselves through heroic action, and thus earn the right to future equality.[139] For many radical women in this period, therefore, Qiu Jin was a model of female accomplishment and her spirit was frequently invoked during the 1911 Revolution. Despite her political martyrdom and the subsquent cultural retrenchment women steadily became a more vital force in the nation. This vitality was purposefully promoted by organised programmes of physical exercise in schools and colleges to the extent that it now came into the category of 'political ritual'. Allied to, and to some extent the foundation of, growing intellectual and emotional assertion, this new physical assertion lent its weight to the dramatic events of 1911.

The 1911 Revolution was a revolution to overthrow the Qing government and, finally and irrevocably, to end the feudal social system which had dominated China for thousands of years. It was the product of decades of dissension and discontent, breaking out on 10 October 1911 in the city of Wuchang, Hubei province. It rapidly and successfully spread to almost every province of China. On 1 January 1912, the Republic of China was formed in Nanjing with Sun Yat-sen as interim president.[140] In February of the same year the Qing emperor abdicated and the dynastic system of two thousand years came to an end. The 1911 Revolution had triumphed.

When the uprising broke out in Wuchang, the people rushed to join the forces of the revolution. In some noted instances, women were in the vanguard. Li Yuanhong, the Military Governor and Commander-in-Chief of the Revolutionary Army, for example, received a report, on 23 October 1911, that a student, Chao Daoxin, from the Wen Hua Girls School, had applied to join the army. Li rejected her application and explained that because the troops were composed entirely of men, the recruitment of women would be difficult.[141] A few days later, on 31 October 1911, Li received another letter from Wu Shuqing, who was a female student in Fengtian Normal College, requesting to join the revolutionary army.[142] She argued in her letter that there was no difference between men and women in the fighting of a revolutionary war, and that women had trained for such a moment in the gymnasiums of their schools. Li finally acceded to her request and agreed to organise a women's regiment in Wuchang.

Elsewhere in China, for instance in Shanghai, a number of women's forces were established in rapid succession. There was a Women's Military Guard led by Xue Shuzen, who was a student of Shang Xia Girls School;[143] a women's Northern Expeditionary Regiment led by Chen Wanyan;[144] a Women's Military Training Regiment led by Zhang Zhaohan (a physical educator of Shanghai, she used the Women's Gymnastic School as the training centre);[145] and a Women's Military Training Alliance led by Wu Mulan,[146] who was a student of Qiu Jin, and who after Qiu's death went to Japan to study for three years.[147] These radical women had prepared *inter alia* through their physical training in their school and college days for this moment. They were ready – 'healthy, brave and intelligent'[148] – and now set their minds on participating fully in the revolution.

Zhejiang, where Qiu Jin had given her life, was an area in which women were most active in the revolution. According to a report in the *Min bao* [News of People], women, led by Lin Zhongxue, now established Zhejiang Women's Military Regiment.[149] These women had been stirred by Qiu Jin's death and were determined to fulfil her revolutionary aims and honour her sacrifice.[150] Yun Weijun, a female physical education instructor,[151] was the Commander of the Women's Zhejiang Northern Expeditionary 'Dare-to-Die' Regiment. In the fighting for Nanjing, her troops fought in the front line. People lauded her as a second 'Maria'[152] and she has been revered as a shining star in the history of the republican revolution ever since.[153]

What led these Chinese women to such overt political aggression so far removed from the 'Three Bonds–Three submissions' which characterised their sex in the old society? First, external political pressures were certainly a factor. The Manchu government appeared incapable of resisting the imperialist powers, and female revolutionaries felt that the fate of the nation rested – at least in part – in their hands. Political crisis created an atmosphere in which modern anti-imperialism mixed with traditional anti-Manchuism – revulsion at government corruption and incompetence, anger at the Confucian family system, and a commitment to republicanism and individual liberty surged through these women. They were drawn to the idea of revolution as a decisive, dramatic event that would dispel at a stroke the impotence, decadence and injustice of existing society. They therefore placed political revolution ahead of feminist goals, and devoted their greatest energy to it. And, of course, after the feudal structural had been destroyed, sexual equality would be achieved – or so they believed.

Second, the awareness of these radical women of their 'new' abilities, especially their physical abilities, was another motive force. 'No longer were women viewed as victims of the temperamental nature of their own bodies, or of an intensely patriarchal society'.[154] They ignored physiological differences between men and women, the gender discrimination inflicted by society, and the self-restriction that women imposed on themselves as the 'weaker' sex. They believed that if society trained men and women equally – in body and mind – men and women could demonstrate the same capacities in military or any other matters. Female radicals, especially those who were physical educators, therefore, advocated and developed the strong female body for strong political action.

These women, of course, came from the élite layer of society, in which women were most likely to absorb Western ideas and have the education to take advantage of new opportunities. It must be made quite clear that they did not try to make this freedom available to the poor and uneducated women in rural villages or urban working class districts. They did not develop programmes either for reforming the national family system, in which men dominated women, or for destroying it entirely by concerted social action in city and countryside. They were locked into the narrow concerns of their class and all they advocated was that women of their position strive to become independent as an act of personal rebellion. After the 1911 Revolution, therefore, these women were quick to attempt to take advantage of the new situation at a personal level, asking for a share in the fruits of the Revolution and equal rights with men in the Republic on a one to one basis.

Confucian Revivalism

Women élitist radicals greeted the birth of the Republic of 1911 with high hopes. With euphoric optimism they believed that the overthrow of the dynasty would purge the country of corruption, remedy weakness and inaugurate a new era of social justice, national strength and individual freedom. Collectively, they had the sweet dream of men and women as equals. They followed the precedent established by Western women and asked for the right to vote. In their view this was the political foundation of gender equality. Women's groups, originally formed for military and relief activities, now reorganised to demand political suffrage.

The first such reorganised group was the Society of Comrades for Women's Suffrage, which was formed in Shanghai on 30 November 1911.[155] The founder was Lin Zongsu, a former student in Japan and the author of *Nu jie zhong xu* [Preface to the Bell of Women] written in 1903, who had called for an uprising of women before 1911.[156] The aim of the Society of Comrades for Women's Suffrage was 'To spread political studies and knowledge among women, to cultivate the political capabilities of women and prepare them for full political rights as citizens.'[157] The Nanjing Provisional Government was established on 1 December 1911. Lin Zongsu represented the Society of Comrades for Women's Suffrage and won support from the Provisional President Sun Yat-sen in Nanjing on 8 January 1912. Sun Yat-sen expressed the progressive and optimistic view that, 'In the future, women's right to vote will surely be affirmed. Women too should gain knowledge of law and politics and strive to understand the truth about freedom and equality.'[158]

Sun's optimism was premature. His speech evoked strong opposition from conservatives, especially the United Party of the Republic of China which was formed after the 1911 Revolution by former members of the Revolutionary Alliance. At the instigation of the United Party, the Federation which comprised the Revolutionary Alliance, the United Party and a group of supporters of a constitutional monarchy questioned Sun's judgement: 'Would the results of women participating in government be in accord with good social custom? . . . It is rumoured that whenever a certain woman makes a request, the president immediately grants it.'[159] Chang Taiyan, the head of the United Party, extolled the marriage system, the family system, 'the beautiful customs and good laws of traditional China' and stated that all should be carefully preserved.[160] The Federation suggested menacingly that 'The President should be careful about what he said'.[161]

Under this pressure from the conservatives, Sun Yat-sen went back on his earlier words, and declared that his speech was merely a personal view outlined in 'a personal chat'.[162] As the progressive Sun Yat-sen retreated, the radical women attacked. They were intransigent. They had expected their social position to improve after the establishment of the Republic of China and they were determined to fight for the right to vote to be included in the coming Constitution.[163] From January to March of 1912 women suffrage organisations 'popped up' like mushrooms in Shanghai, Guangzhou, Nanjing, Zhejiang province and Hunan province.[164] On 27 February 1912, some 'heroines' of the 1911 Revolution,[165] sent a petition to the Provisional Parliament in which they asserted that in the realm of obligations and rights men and women were identical. Now the political revolution had succeeded and the social revolution was about to follow, the equality of the sexes and the recognition of women's right to vote must be enacted. The text of the Constitution, the petition maintained, should contain a sentence that stated 'equality is uniform, regardless of sex; this appertains in the right to vote and the right to be elected to office'.[166]

The National Provisional Parliament was composed of delegates appointed by the provincial governors, including 120 members from the revolutionary parties and from among the old bureaucratic politicians. They were all men. Male determination to maintain the status quo, drew together male conservatives *and* radicals.[167] They would all share the rewards of domination. In the face of this entrenched power the prospects for the women's demands were hopeless. On 11 March 1912 the Provisional Constitution of the Republic of China was announced. It contained no clear ruling concerning women's rights. In section II, Article 5, on the people, the Constitution stated that 'all the people of China are equal, without distinction as to race, class, or religion,' but it didn't mention sex or women.[168] Twenty-six representatives of women's suffrage societies now petitioned the Provisional President Sun Yat-sen, demanding immediate constitutional revision.[169] They also demanded legislation supporting the rights of women. Their contumacy received no sympathy and they were ignored.

In March 1912, led by Tang Qunying, the founder of the Chinese

Suffrage Society in Beijing and a former student in Japan, more than 20 women demanded to be allowed to have the right to sit in on the deliberations of the National Parliament. Their request was rejected. The next day, Tang and other women again requested to enter the National Provisional Parliament as observers, but were turned away by armed guards. It was the last straw. The women were so angry that they broke the windows and injured the guards in the parliament building.[170] This action was criticised as unfeminine behaviour by the male-dominated parliament and press.[171] Tang and her followers were unrepentant. On 21 March 1912, she and five representatives of women's suffrage societies went to see the Provisional President Sun Yat-sen. He attempted a compromise, putting forward a proposal for enlarging the National Provisional Parliament to include women, thus temporarily mollifying women radicals.[172] This action was temporary through no fault of his own since Sun soon lost the political struggle[173] and on 1 April 1912 he resigned as provisional president. He was replaced by Yuan Shikai, a conservative.[174]

Under Yuan Shikai, the eclat with which the women's suffrage movement burst on the Republican era faded. Yuan Shikai founded the so-called Confucian Religion Society in 1912 to promote the values of filial piety that he deemed necessary for loyal citizenship.[175] In September 1913, an order was issued through the Education Ministry that the birthday of Confucius should be observed in all schools by a holiday and the holding of a celebratory meeting. This would purify the minds and steady the ambitions of the nation.[176] In October 1913, the national worship of Confucius was reinstated by law because Yuan believed that 'the masses of people were unenlightened and the revival of old ceremonies was a practical measure to check the moral decline since the revolution.[177] In 1914, the Education Act contained an edict that all schools should encourage students to worship Confucius and to learn Confucian doctrine.[178] Thus the official worship of Confucius was restored and Yuan Shikai gave liberally for the rehabilitation of the Hall of Classics and the Confucian Temple.

Under such conditions, the traditional position of women within the family and social structure was increasingly reinforced by legislation. Women were legally 'batoned' by authority, their role remaining that of 'a model housewife and an ideal mother'.[179] Even the concept of equality within different spheres sought by reformers of the late Qing government was rejected. Radical women watched hopelessly as the vast majority of the Chinese people submitted themselves to Confucian rituals. It was as if a revolution had never taken place. History seemed to be travelling in a circle. By way of example, in March 1912 the headquarters of Tongmenghui [the Revolutionary Alliance] had issued a nine-article policy outline, which included a clear statement 'advocating male–female equality'. Only five months later, in August 1912, when Tongmenghui was reorganised into the Guomintang [The Nationalist Party], equality for men and women was simply eliminated from its political platform.[180] As a new party, the Nationalist Party, angling for the support of conservative forces, carefully avoided support for the Women's Movement.

In the same year, the election law confirmed that only 'male citizens of the Republic of China' would have the right to vote.[181] In 1913, a series of laws were passed which repressed all suffragette political and social associations and their publications, and forbade women to publish magazines and join in any political groups or to attend meetings which included political discussion. In November 1913, an order for the dissolution of the Women's Suffrage Alliance was issued by the government and its 11 provincial branches were disbanded.[182] The Chinese women's suffrage movement, as many studies of Chinese society have observed,[183] came to an abrupt end. It was a case of feminism traduced. Exercise had proved a poor handmaiden of enlightenment. Self-reliance had proved a poor prop for self-advancement.

Why were the hopes of the women's movement so easily dashed in so short a time? The answer lies not only in political actions, already widely noted by historians,[184] but also in cultural reasons deeply rooted in Confucian prejudice. The basic function of the female body – child-bearing – was always a useful weapon for Confucian society to use in resisting women's liberation. In an era of Confucian revivalism both conservatives and radicals insisted that women should not be seen 'fallaciously' as simply objects of male control. Women themselves contributed to their condition. They adopted a subordinate posture in response to the strain of their role, were inactive because of the sheer burden of their own physiology and were weak because of the physical realities of their lives. Once again old sexual platitudes were strenuously aired with increasing success. Women's bodies and minds were best suited, went the argument, to family responsibility, not social duty, which was too heavy for them to bear. Having children was the natural responsibility of women and it took up all their energy. Their bodies lacked the vigour for wider roles.[185] The traditional concept of femininity was an accurate reflection of the propensities of the female body, and had been long recognised and accepted as such by Chinese culture and society – so sang the patriarchal chorus. The strong and active image of women in unstable revolution was neither remembered nor welcomed in the new stable society. A procrustean process trimmed and adjusted the image. Chinese culture reverted to reactionary ideals and images. The past became the present.

The result was that women who had founded schools (such as Hu Zhonghan in Guangzhou, Bai Tianzhen in Quizhou, Liu Qinhua in Henan), who had given support to the revolution and had advocated women's physical and mental emancipation and the creation of the Republic were slandered and viciously attacked as 'immoral women' because they were widows, and as such custom demanded that on the death of their husbands they withdraw from all public affairs.[186] Their confident and active involvement in political and social affairs was regarded as disgraceful and undesirable. In some newly established girls' schools and women's educational institutes, symbolically and significantly, physical education and physical training courses were now ignored[187] In the established girls' schools, physical exercise was changed from full body gymnastics to restricted *hand gymnastics*. Military training, which had been advocated in the revolutionary era as a proof of the equality between the sexes, was banned from the female students' curriculum.[188] At the same time the conservative Yuan Shikai urged male students to adopt the spirit of militarism and to develop strong bodies.[189] Exercise still played an important part in male students' education. Physical education once again became largely a man's prerogative, reflecting men's power to dictate cultural and curricula priorities. The ideal woman once again was supposed to be fragile, gentle and passive.

Nothing better illustrates the regression to past attitudes and practices than the fact that from 1910 to 1919 China held three National Games[190] and seven Huabei (Regional) Competitions (in the cities of Beijing and Tianjing and in the provinces of Hebei, Henan, Shandong, Shanxi, Dongbei),[191] and took part in the Far East Olympic Games four times.[192] On all these occasions women were excluded. The reforming efforts of the Japanese-trained female pioneers of girls' exercise were set aside. Had they continued women may well have had a place in these competitions. Exercise once again became a predominantly masculine preserve in both theory and practice. The truth of the matter was that sexual difference, couched in the traditional language of superiority and inferiority, gave men the confidence to control male and female relationships to their advantage. Consequently, male reformers failed to create an equal world. More to the point, many, it appears, did not want fundamentally to change sexual roles. They wanted women to be their assistants but not their partners. When faced with women's demands to share the world equally, they resisted them. Physiological difference served as their best argument – it had the weight of tradition. Limited physical exercise, in their view, was to be used simply to train women to be healthy mothers, not independent citizens.

In the final analysis radical women, as already stated above, were a small, educated group coming from the middle and upper classes. In 1907, for example, the Shanghai foreign concessions contained a total of 67,000 young women, and only 1,000 were studying in the new schools, while 30,000 were workers in the various factories.[193] The Women's Movement only involved some of the former. How could such a small group with so little power and in such a short time hope to overcome several thousand years of entrenched masculine authority? It was always a tall order.

Conclusion

By the end of the nineteenth century reformers had made some effort to emancipate women in the interests of healthy motherhood – for healthy manhood. By 1911, the feminists had forged productive links between patriots, revolutionaries and emancipationists. They were conscious that no meaningful change for women could be achieved within a humiliated country whose very existence seemed to be precarious. They saw the question of women's rights as intimately connected with the life or death of the Chinese nation. Thus the Women's Movement in this period played an integral if subsidiary part to the nationalist movement. The identification of the interests of women with those of the nation-state would later become a source of weakness for the Women's Movement, when they found themselves allied to a Nationalist movement which was basically inimical to the goal of liberating women from their traditional submissive status. The Women's Movement then became a fully independent movement.

However, the identification with nationalism was at first beneficial, a source of support for feminists.

It must also be recognised that the Chinese Women's Movement was clearly a product of a Chinese female élite in this early period. The feminists spoke of 'two hundred million sisters' as if they represented the interests of all Chinese women, though they had little knowledge of the nature of the existence of peasant and factory women and gave scant thought to practical emancipatory solutions to their predicament. In this complete lack of contact with the masses, feminism was out of touch with the population at large. It was in fact nationalism which eventually rescued Chinese feminism from this narrow élitism and provided the impetus for its democratisation. And it was communism which served as the eventual vehicle for the legitimatised emancipation of women – as we shall discover later.

Nevertheless, limited as it was in numbers, social vision and immediate impact, the Women's Movement in this period kept in motion a process of change. It served, directly, as the foundation for all later progress. Virtually all the Chinese women active in politics in the Women's Movement in the first decade of the twentieth century had been among that small band of pioneer schoolgirls, whose ambition was to replace feudal tyranny with national freedom – and who strengthened their bodies to be powerful enough to achieve that purpose – by force if necessary. They passed on their ideals to later generations. They sowed a revolutionary seed that, fed and watered in a more favourable political environment, eventually if erratically, grew into a tree of liberty.

Notes

1. Kant, Immanuel, 'What is Enlightenment?', in Reiss, Hans, (ed.), *Kant's Political Writings*, London: Ward Lock, 1970, p.54. Reiss's 'notes to the Text' were particularly helpful in interpreting why, for Kant, the question 'what is enlightenment?' was as important as the question 'what is truth?'. See Reiss, op. cit., p.192; also see Schwarcz, Vera, *The Chinese Enlightenment: Intellectuals and the Legacy of the May Fourth Movement of 1919*, Berkeley: University of California Press, 1986, p.1; Lively, J.F., *The Enlightenment*, London: Longman, 1968, p.xiii.
2. Schwarcz, V., 'A Curse on the Great Wall – The Problem of Enlightenment in Modern China', *Theory and Society*, Vol. 3, No. 3, 1984, p.457.
3. See Chapter One, note 70.
4. See Chapter One, note 61.
5. Jia, Fu, 'Chan zhu lun' [On Footbinding], *Wanguo gongbao* [International News],

No. 91, Aug. 1896.

6. Huan, Zhexian, 'Hao xian gao shi' [The Bulletin on Footbinding], *Xiang bao* [Hunan News], 9 May 1898.

7. 'Na nu pindeng zhi yuanli' [The Theory of Sexual Equality], in *Qing yi bao quan bian* [The Complete Works of Newspapers of the Qing Dynasty], Beijing, Vol. 25, No. 1, 1936.

8. Jin, Yi, (1874–1947) His real name was Jin Tianyu. He was a progressive educationist and a member of the Chinese Education Society at that time. His paper entitled *Nu jei zhong* [Bell of Women] was one of the most influential papers of the period. It was published by *Aiguo nu xuexiao* [The Patriotic Girls School] in Shanghai in August 1903.

9. Zhang, Zhidong, 'Bu chanzhu hui xu' [The Preface of the Anti-footbinding Society], op. cit.

10. 'Xuebu zhouding nuzi xiaoxuetang zhangcheng' [Rules of the Ministry of Education for Girls' Elementary Schools], *Zhongguo xinnujie* [China's New Women], No. 3, April 1907, p.175.

11. Jia, Hong, 'Ai nu jie' [For Women], *Nuzi shijie* [Women's World], No. 8, 24 Aug. 1904; Gao, Yabin, 'Fei gang pian' [On Abolishing the Three Obediences], *Tian yi* [The Will of Heaven], Nos. 11–12, 1907.

12. Rong, Tiesheng, op. cit., p.190.

13. Ibid., p.191.

14. See *Dongfang zazhi* [The East], 1904, No. 3, p.64.

15. Ibid.

16. The three obediences: to the father before marriage, to the husband after marriage, and to the son after the death of the husband. The four virtues were morality, proper speech, modest manner and delight in work. These were the spiritual fetters imposed on women by feudal society.

17. See Allen, Young J., 'The Difference between Men and Women', translated into Chinese and published in Li, Youning and Zhang, Yufa (eds), *Jindai Zhongguo nu quan yundong shiliao* [Source Materials on the Feminist Movement in Modern China], Taibei, 1975, pp.382–8; 'Lun Zhongguo bianfa zhi benwu' [The Basic Tasks of Chinese Reform], ibid., pp.388–90.

18. This view was advocated by Liang Qichao and several reformers at that time. See Liang, Qichao, 'Chuang she nuxuetang qi' [Advocacy of Establishing Girls' Schools], op. cit.; see also Zheng, Guanyin, 'Zi jiyizi zhuren lun tan nuxiexiao shu' [On Jiyizi's Letter about Women's Education], in Zheng Guanyin's *Shen shi weiyan* [My Opinion on the Current Issues], Shanghai, Vol. 2, 1900, pp.70–71.

19. Reference to this book is made in Chu, T.C., 'Magazines for Chinese Women', in The China Continuation Committee (ed.), *China Mission Yearbook 1917*, Shanghai: The Christian Literature for China, 1927, p.454.

20. A Ying, *Wan Qing xiaoshuoshi* [A History of Late Qing Fiction], Taibei: Commercial Press, 1968, p.158.

21. For further details see Feng, Ziyou, *Keming yishi* [History of the Revolution], Taibei, Commercial Press, 1953, p.151.

22. Chen, Jinpan, op. cit., pp.168–77.

23. Rodzinski, Witold, op. cit., p.251.

24. Chen, Jinpan, op. cit., p.96.

25. The war began in August 1894 and ended in February, 1895. For further details see Chapter 1, note 70. The military defeat of 1895 had an added edge of shame for Confucian literati used to thinking of Japan as the 'land of the eastern dwarfs', a condescending allusion to Japan's extensive borrowing from China as far back as the Tang dynasty (618–907). Shame, however, became

translated into an intense curiosity about Japan, especially about the Meiji Restoration of 1868.

26. Chen, Yan'an, 'Quan nuzi liuxie shuo' [On Women's Studying Abroad], *Jianshu*, No. 3, 25 June 1903; see also 'Gongaihui tongren quan luxie qi' [the Humanitarian Society Advocacy of Chinese Women's Study Abroad], *Jiangshu*, No. 6, 21 Sept. 1903.

27. Chen, Jinpan, op. cit., p.190.

28. Kang, Youwei, *Riben bianzhen kao* [The Search for Japan's Restoration], in *Zhongguo jidaishi zhiliao congkan: Wuxu bianfa* [Reference to the One Hundred Day Reform], Shanghai: Shengzhou guoguang chubanshe, No. 4, 1953, p.254.

29. Peake, Cyrus H., *Nationalism and Education in China*, New York: Columbia University Press, 1932, p.80.

30. The Chinese civil examination system (also called the Imperial Examination System) started in 606 AD in the Tang dynasty. It selected officials through a series of examinations based on ethical ideals and flowery literary expressions from the Confucian: Four Books and Five Classics. After the failure of the Opium War in 1840, the reformers asked for the creation of a system of modern education which focused on Western subjects, especially technological science with application to contemporary problems. In August 1905, the Qing government abolished the old examination system and established a modern education system which included new schools and colleges and Western curricula. The traditional education system which had been practised in China for more than 1,300 years came to an end. For more details, see Chen, Jinpan, op. cit., pp.167–8; Chu, K., 'Education', in Chen, Zen Sophia, (ed.), *Symposium on Chinese Culture*, Shanghai: China Institute of Pacific Relations, 1931, pp.206–23; Grey, J., op. cit., pp.131–3.

31. Peake, Cyrus H., op. cit., p.71.

32. Lin, Sitong, 'Jianlun Zhongguo jindai xuexiao binchao de xinshui' [Brief History of Military Drill in Chinese Schools at the Turn of the Century], in CSHSPE, *Lunwei ji* [Selected Works], Vol. 2, 1986, p.33.

33. Ji, Yihui, 'Zhongguo nuzi liuxue riben' [On Chinese Women Studying in Japan], *Dalu* [Journal of the Continent], No. 1, 1902.

34. See the report of *Zhongguo xin nujie* [Chinese New Women], No. 1, Feb. 1907, p.73.

35. Feng, Ziyou, *Keming yi shi* [History of Revolution]. op. cit., pp.101, 229; 'Guomindang Archives', 330/2651, p.2.

36. Reported in *Dongfang zazhi* [The East], No. 4, 1907, p.178; also see Huang, Fu-ch'ing, *Qingmo liuxuesheng* [Chinese Students in Japan in Late Ch'ing Period], Taibei: Institute of Modern History, Academis Sinica, 1983, p.59.

37. The report was in *Dongfang zazhi* [The East], No. 8, 1905, p.202.

38. Japan had the greatest number of Chinese women students, but some managed to travel even further afield, to Europe and the United States. Liang Qichao recalled three women among the 50 Chinese students he met on his 1903 US trip. A contemporary account showed 19 Chinese women attending American institutions of higher learning in 1905. See Wang, Y.C., *Chinese Intellectuals and the West 1872–1949*, Chapel Hill: University of North Carolina Press, 1966, pp.72–3.

39. Xiao, Cong, 'Shilun Qing mo liu ri xuesheng dui uo hua de riben tiyu chuanru Zhongguo shuoqi de zhuoyong' [On the Importance of the Returned Students from Japan in introducing 'Europeanised' Japanese Sports in the Late Period of the Qing Dynasty], in CSHEPS, *Lunwei ji* [Selected Works], Vol. 3, 1987, p.149.

40. Din, Hongchen, *Dongyin yuecao riji* [Diary of Trip to Japan], 1900, p.28.

41. Zhang, Tianbai, 'Tichao yichi yiru kao' [When did the word 'Gymnastics' come to China?], *TSW*, No. 6, 1988, p.14.

42. The statistics come from *Sichuan xuebao* [Sichuan Journal], No. 1, 1907.

43. In 1902, female students studying in Japan numbered no more than ten. The figure rose to more than one hundred in 1907. See 'Liu ri nuxuesheng hui' [The Society of Overseas Chinese Female Students in Japan], *Zhongguo xin nujie zazhi* [The Journal of New Women in China], No. 1, 5 Feb. 1907; see also Huang, Fuch'ing, op. cit., p.60.

44. Shimoda Utako (1854–1936) was a famous female educationist and a well-known scholar of the time. She founded the Imperial Women's Association in 1898 and set up a girls' school attached to the Association in 1899. In her life-time she opened and supervised several girls' schools and colleges, for example, a Chinese institute founded in 1908 in Tokiwamatsu. By 1914 well over 200 overseas women students had graduated from it. For more details about her, see Ono Kazuko, op. cit., pp.55, 214, 215.

45. Fan, Zhaoying, *Qingmo Michu yangxue xuesheng timing lu chuchi* [Preliminary List of the Names of Overseas Students in the Late Qing and Early Republic], Taibei: Sinica, 1962, p.45.

46. See *Dongfang zazhi* [The East], No. 1, 1904; *Youxue yipian* [The Journal of Translations], No. 1, 1903, p.37.

47. *Subao* [Jiangsu News], one of the most radical journals of the time. It was founded in 1896 and closed in 1903 by the Qing government.

48. See the report in *Zhongguo xin nujie* [New Women in China], No. 1, 1907.

49. Huang, Fu-ching, op. cit., p.60. Female students, such as Qiu Jin, Chen Jiefen, Tang Qunyin and Wang Changguo, became leading figues in the Chinese women's emancipation movement.

50. Feng, Hesheng, 'Jun gumin pian – yuanyin yu tipo zhe' [On Military Exercise], op. cit.; Xu, Yibing, 'Zhendun tiyu shang jiaoyubu shu' [A Memo to The Ministry of Education on Reorganising Physical Education], *Tiyu zazhi* [Sports Journal], No. 2, June 1914, p.1.

51. Cai, Yuanpei, 'Dunyu jiaoyu fangzhen zhi yijian' [My Educational Principles], *Dongfang zazhi* [The East], No. 10, April 1912, pp.2–3; Fan, Yuanlian, 'Jinri shi-jie dazhan zhong zi woguo jiaoyu' [The Present State of our Education], *Zhonghua jiaoyujie* [China's Education], No. 23, Nov. 1914; Han, Xizhen, 'Xu Yibing tiyu shixiang zi wo jian' [My View on Xu Yibing's Physical Education Thoughts], in CSHPES, *Lunweiji* [Selected Works], Vol. 2, 1986, pp.63–5.

52. See Graybill, Henry B., *The Educational Reform in China*, p.63, quoted in Peake, Cyrus H., *Nationalism and Education in China*, op. cit., p.68.

53. Zhang, Zhengting, 'Tiyu yu zhengxi Zhonghua zhi guanxi' [On the Relation-ship between Sport and the Reinvigoration of China], *Xin tiyu* [New Sports], 1984, No. 2, p.10.

54. Ibid.

55. Peake, Cyrus H., op. cit, p.67.

56. Fan, Hong, 'Tiyu yichi suyuan' [The Historical Change of the Word 'Tiyu' – Sport and Physical Education in China], in Fan and Wang, op. cit., p.170.

57. Han, Xizhen, 'Xu Yibing tiyu shixiang zhi wo jian' [My View on Xuyibing's Physical Education Thoughts], op. cit., p.64.

58. Xiao, Cong, 'Shilun Qing mo liu ri xuesheng dui uo hua de riben tiyu chuanru Zhongguo shuoqi de zhuoyong' [On the Importance of the Returned Students from Japan . . .], op. cit., pp.148–9.

59. For example, in Changsha, the capital of Hunan province, 26 secondary schools were established between 1902 and 1911. The founders were all

students trained in Japan. See Lewis, Charlton M., *Prologue to the Chinese Revolution: the Transformation of Ideas and Institutions in Hunan Province, 1891–1907*, Cambridge, MA: Harvard University Press, 1976, pp. 149–52; Lin, Sitong, 'Zhaoqi Zhongguo liu ri xuesheng dui Zhongguo jindai tiyu de xinqi you na xie gongxian' [The Contribution of Returned Students from Japan to Chinese Modern Sport], in Lin, Sitong, op. cit., pp.178–9. Jinghua Girls' School in Jiangsu province was also set up by a returned student. This fact was reported in *Shenzhou nubao* [Chinese Women's Journal], No. 8, Jan. 1913, p.1, and mentioned in Hashikawa, Tokyo (ed.), *Chugoku bunkakai jimbutsu sokan* [Who's Who in Chinese Cultural Circles], Beijing, 1941, p.109. However, we don't know her or his name. Xu Xilin, who later attempted to assassinate the Governor General of Anhui, established the Mingdao Girls' School in Shaoxing, Zhejiang. See Liu, Wang Li-min, *Zhongguo funu yundong* [The Chinese Women's Movement], Shanghai, Commercial press, 1933, p.29; Hu, Sheng, op. cit., pp.927–8. Chen Mengxiong founded the Ming Jiang Girls' School, Zhejiang province. See *Hubei xuesheng jie* [Hubei Students' Journal], No. 2, 1903, p.113.

60. For example, Minde Secondary School employed Huang Xin (1874–1916), who later became a famous leader of the 1911 Revolution; the First Teachers' College employed Lu Jiepei, who was a well-known physical educator in Hunan province; and Jian Baoshan and Liu Wuting, who both graduated from Japanese physical education institutes, became teachers of Chang Jun Secondary School in Changsha city and Hunan Provincial Technology Institute respectively. See *Hunan tiyu shiliao* [The Reference to Hunan Physical Education History], published by Hunan tiyu wenshi weiyuanhui (Changsha), Vol. 2, 1985, p.23; Vol. 3, 1986, p.40.

61. Ibid., Vol. 4, 1987, p.1.

62. The report was in *Dongfang zazhi* [The East], No. 2, Jan. 1905, p.159.

63. Liang, Chanmei, *Zhongguo funu fendou shihua* [A Historical Discussion of Chinese Women's Struggle], Chongqing: Huaxia chubanshe, 1943, p.71; see also *Funu zazhi* [Women's Journal], Jan. 1915, p.1.

64. See *Beijing nubao* [Beijing Women], 9 Aug. 1906.

65. Qiu Jin is discussed in this chapter, see below.

66. There is some confusion about Qiu Jin's life. Some studies mentioned that Qiu Jin was a teacher at Xunxi Girls' School. Others mentioned that when she came back from Japan Qiu Jin was a teacher in Minde School. In fact, Qiu Jin was a teacher in both schools for a short time. For further details see Wu, Jiang and Chen, Qubin, 'Xu Zhihua', in *Funu zazhi* [Women's Journal], No. 1, Feb. 1915; Han, Xizhen, op. cit., p.69.

67. Xu, Yibing, '20 nianlai tichao tan' [Review of the Development of Gymnastics in the Past 20 Years], *Changsha tiyu zhoubao* [Changsha Sports Weekly], Jan. 1920, pp.61–6.

68. See CSHSPE, *Zhongguo jindai tiyu shi* [Modern Chinese Sports History], op. cit., p.77.

69. See Zhang, Jinlu, *Zhongguo jindai chuban shiliao chubian* [Books in Press in Modern China], Shanghai: Commercial Press, 1954; *Zhongguo jindai chuban shiliao bubian* [Revised Books in Press in Modern China]; Shanghai: Commercial Press, 1957.

70. For instance, Jiangsu Provincial Gymnastic Institute (1905); Chongqing Physical Education College in Sichuan province (1905); Yunnan Provincial Gymnastic College (1906); Chengdu Gymnastic Institute attached to Chengdu Normal College in Sichuan province (1906); Sichuan Provincial Physical Education College (1906); Sichuan Wang's Suren Gymnastic College in

Chengdu city (1907); Henan Provincial Gymnastic Institute (1907); Yiaozhi Physical Education Institute (1907); Zhejiang Provincial Gymnastic Institute attached to Zhejiang Normal College (1907); Fengtian Gymnastic Institute attached to the Fengtian Normal College in Hebei province (1907); Chinese Gymnastic School in Shanghai (1907); Chinese Women's Gymnastic School in Shanghai (1908); Wuxi Physical Education Society (1903); and Shongkou Physical Education Society (1907). See CSHSPE, *Zhongguo jindai tiyu shi* [Modern Chinese Sports History], op. cit., pp.78–9.

71. Nie, Xiaohu, 'Zhaoqi jidujiao qinnianhui yu Zhongguo jidai tiyu de shehuihua qushi' [The Early YMCA and the Socialising Tendency of China's Modern History of Physical Culture]; Luo, Shiming, 'Qiantan jidujiao qinnianhui zai Zhongguo jindai tiyushi shang de zhuoyong' [A General Discussion of the Role Played by the YMCA in China's Modern History of Physical Culture]; Wang, Qihui, 'Wuhan jiaohui xiexiao de tiyu huodong' [The Sports Activities of Wuhan Christian Schools]. These three articles were published in CSHPES, *Lunwenji* [Selected Works], Vol. 2, 1986, pp.70–91.

72. Kolatch, J., *Sports, Politics and Ideology in China*, New York: Jonathan David, 1971, p.30.

73. One scholar who has studied the era of revolution, Mary Wright, characterised the Boxer Year of 1900 and the ensuing decade as a period of intense nationalism shared by nearly every segment of Chinese society. She defines this 'massive nationalism' as 'an intense and widespread fear that China would be partitioned and the Chinese disappear as a people'. Chinese from all walks of life and all political persuasions were determined that this fear would not be realised, and acted in various ways to implement their ideas. See Wright, Mary C. (ed.), *China in Revolution: The First Phase, 1900–1913*, New Haven: Yale University Press, 1968, p.8. With regard to Western physical educational ideals as epitomised by the missionaries and YMCA, these represented playing for pleasure rather patriotism. Japanese gymnastics with their militaristic emphasis were directly related to national survival. Furthermore, the Japanese were Asians.

74. CSHSPE, *Zhongguo jindai tiyu shi* [Modern Chinese Sports History], op. cit., pp.70–2. Kolatch, J., op. cit., p.5.

75. Peake, Cyrus H., op. cit., p.69.

76. Ibid., p.32.

77. Liao, Hui, 'Shandai ai tiyu: fang zhumin zhuojia Xu chi' [Interview with Yu Yibin's Son, Xuchi], *Xin tiyu* [New Sports], 1983, No. 3, pp.13–14.

78. Chu, Jianhong, 'Shanghai Zhongguo nuzi tichao xuexiao jianshi' [The History of the Chinese Women's Gymnastic Institute in Shanghai], in Tao, Hao, op. cit., Vol. 6, 1965. pp.23–8.

79. Duan, Guangchen, 'Jidai zhuming tiyujia Xu Yibin xianshen' [Xu Yibin – A Modern Physical Educationalist in China], in Tao, Hao, op. cit., Vol. 7, 1965, pp.12–19.

80. Fei, Shishi, 'Zhongguo tichao xiexiao jianshi' [A Brief History of the Chinese Gymnastic Institute], *Guomin tiyu* [Citizens' Sport], No. 1, Sept. 1941, pp.7–8; see also *Zhejiang tiyu shiliao* [Reference of Zhejiang Physical Education History], Hangzhou: Zhejiang tiyu wenshi weiyuanhui, No. 1, 1982, p.23.

81. Graduates from the Chinese Women's Gymnastic School and Chinese Men's Gymnastic School founded several physical education institutions and schools. For example, Fu Qiu and Pang Xinyao founded Shanghai Gongya Physical Education Institute; Hua Haowu opened the Chinese Women's Physical Education Institute; Lu Lihua set up Shanghai Liangjiang Women's

Physical Education School; Cai Quwu founded Zhejiang Hangzhou Physical Education School; Yang Zhenfeng opened Guangdong Physical Education Institute; Zu Zhongmin founded Suzhou Physical Education Institute; Yang Chenglie set up Chenglie Physical Education College; Sang Shiyuan founded Fengtia Physical Education Institute. See Fei Shishi, op. cit.; CSHSPE, *Zhongguo jindai tiyu shi* [Modern Chinese Sports History], op. cit., p.80.

82. Rankin, Mary B., 'The Emergence of Women at the End of the Ching: The Case of Ch'iu Chin', in Wolf, M. and Witke, R. (eds), *Women in Chinese Society*, Stanford: Stanford University Press, 1975, p.54.

83. Cai Yuanpei (1896–1940) was born to a wealthy family in Zhejiang. He obtained his classical jinshi degree in 1890. In the last years of the Qing Dynasty he served as an education official in his native Zhejiang, and then as a teacher and sponsor of radical schools and anti-Qing societies. He joined the Revolutionary Alliance, but was studying philosophy in Germany when the 1911 Revolution began. Returning to China in 1912, he served briefly as the Minister of Education under both Sun Yat-sen and Yuan Shikai. He travelled again to Germany and France, where he helped establish a work-study programme for Chinese students. Appointed president of Beijing University in 1917, Cai defended the rights of his faculty and students to speak out, claiming that they were all seeking 'education for a world view' and that the function of a university president was to be 'broad-minded and encompass tolerance of diverse points of view'. Four days after the 4 May demonstration Cai resigned in protest at the arrest of his students. He was reappointed in late 1919 and continued in office through the subsequent stormy years, remaining a staunch defender of human rights and freedom of intellectual inquiry.

84. CSHSPE, *Zhongguo jindai tiyu shi* [Modern Chinese Sports History], op. cit., p.88.

85. The founders of the Patriotic Girls' School were Jin Yuanshan, Cai Yuanpei, Li Shaoquan, Wu Yanfu and his wife Xia Xiaozhen and daughter Wu Yala, Wu Rulan, Chen fan and his daughter Chen Jiefen, Wei Zhoupei and Zhen Yi. However, there is a problem in identifying when the school was founded. Cai Yuanpei recalled that it was in 1901 (see *Cai Yuanpei zishu* [Cai Yuangpei's Autobiography], Taibei: Zhuangji weixue chubanshe, 1967, pp.38–9); *Nuxue bao* reported that it was founded in 1902 (see *Nuxue bao* [The Journal Of Women's Education], No. 4, 1902, p.27; Feng Zhiyou said it was in 1903 (see Fen, Ziyou. 'Xinzhonghui geming tongzhi' [Revolutionaries of the Xinzhong-hui], in *Xinhai Geming* [the 1911 Revolution], Shanghai, Commercial Press, Vol. 1, 1956, p.192). The school became a centre for anti-Manchu activities in the Shanghai region and was directly involved in revolutionary activities. The school was closed in 1909 for financial reasons. It was revived after the Revolution and continued as a leading Shanghai school while maintaining connections with some of the original founders. See Jiang Weiqiao, 'Zhongguo jiaoyuhui zhi huiyi [Reminiscences of the Chinese Education Society], in *Xinhai Geming* [the 1911 Revolution], op. cit., Vol. 1, 1956, p.487.

86. Chen, Jinpan, op. cit., pp.216–17.

87. Cai, Yuanpei, 'Zai Aiguo nuxuexiao zhi yanshuo' [The Speech at the Patriotic Girls' School], *Dongfang zazhi* [The East], No. 1, Jan. 1917.

88. Feng, Ziyou, *Geming yishi* [Revolution History]. op. cit., Vol. 2, p.78. Rankin, Mary Backus, *Early Chinese Revolutionaries: Radical Intellectuals in Shanghai and Chekiang 1902–1911*, Harvard East Asian Series, No. 50. Cambridge: Harvard University Press, 1971, notes, p.1.

89. Guangfuhui [the Restoration Society] was an anti-Manchu group founded in 1904 in Shanghai by revolutionaries Cai Yuanpei, Tao Chengzhang and Zhang

Binlin. It merged with Tongmenhui [the Revolutionary Alliance] in 1905. Tongmenhui was an anti-Manchu group founded in 1905 in Tokyo by the exiled Sun Yat-sen and Chinese students studying in Japan. It sponsored propaganda, fund-raising, and insurrectionary activities that culminated in 1911 with the Wuhan uprising and the fall of the Qing dynasty.

90. *North China Herald*, 18 July 1907, p.117.
91. Lewis, Charlton M., *Prologue to the Chinese Revolution*, op. cit., p.152.
92. Burton, M., op. cit., p.128.
93. Ibid.
94. *Nuzi shijie* [Women's World], No. 2, July 1907, pp.115–17.
95. *Zhejiang chao*, [Zhejiang Journal], No. 10, Dec. 1903, p.125; *Jiangsu* [The Journal of Jiangsu], No. 3, 1903, p.162.
96. Chen Jiefen (born in 1883) was a famous journalist, a feminist and revolutionary. She founded the Patriotic Girls' School in Shanghai with Cai Yuanpei and others. She was the daughter of Chen Fan, the editor of *Subao*, a progressive newspaper, and she founded *Nubao* [Women's Journal] in 1902. After her father's journal *Subao* was suppressed by the Qing government she was exiled to Japan with her father. She went to Japan in the autumn of 1903 and soon became a close friend of Qiu Jin. After she graduated from a Japanese college, she went to the United States to study and there married the revolutionary Yang Jun.
97. The journal's name was changed to *Nuxue bao* [The Journal of Women's Education] in early 1903 by Chen Jiefen. See Ge, Gongzhen, *Zhongguo baoxue shi* [Chinese Press History], Taibei: Taiwan xuesheng shuju, 1964, p.172.
98. Chen, Jiefen, 'Lun nuzi yijiang tiyu' [On Women's Participation in Physical Education and Exercise], *Nuxue bao* [The Journal of Women's Education], No. 2, April 1903.
99. Six years earlier, Liang Qichao and Kang Youwei had made a declaration of support for women's education, but defined this support almost completely in terms of the benefit to men and the nation. See Chapter 2 of this book.
100. Chen, Jiefen, 'Gong xi yao pingdeng', [Daughters-in-law must be equal], *Nuxue bao* [The Journal of Women's Education], No. 2, April 1903, pp.11–16.
101. These included *Nuzi jiaoyu* [Women's Education] in 1903; *Funu shijie* [Women's World] in 1904–5; *Juemin* [Awakening People] in 1904; *Xinnuxin* [China's New Women] in 1907; *Yunnan* in 1909–10.
102. Wu, Yuzhang, *Xinhai geming* [On the 1911 Revolution], Beijing: Renmin chubanshe [People's Press], 1962, p.87; Ayscough, Florence, *Chinese Women's Yesterday and Today*, London: Jonathan Cape, 1938, p.151.
103. See Liang, Guanggui, 'Qiu Jin yu tiyu' [Qiu Jin and Physical Exercise], in CSHI (ed.), *Ti yushi weiji* [A Sport History Collection], Chengdu: Chengdu Physical Education Institute Press, 1984, p.82; Yi, Jiandong, 'Yidai fengshao, yidai yingmin' [Hero and Heroine in Chinese History], *Wenshi zhishi* [The Knowledge of Literature and History], No. 4, Aug. 1993, p.113.
104. Wu, Zhiren, 'Qiu Jin yu tiyu' [Qiu Jin and Physical Exercise], in Tang, Hao, op. cit., Vol. 3, pp.23–5; Liang, Guanggui, op. cit., p.83.
105. Qiu, Jin, 'Jinwei shi' [Jinwei Stone], in *Qiu Jin ji* [Collected Works of Qiu Jin], Shanghai: Zhonghua shuju, 1960, pp. 122–5, 148–9.
106. Ono Kazuko, op. cit., 1978, p.61.
107. Wang Shiche, 'Huiyi Qiu Jin' [Recollections of Qiu Jin], in The Committee on Written Historical Materials of the Chinese People's Political Consultative Conference, (ed.), *Xinhai geming huiyi lu* [Recollections of the 1911 Revolution], Beijing: Zhonghua shuju, 1962, Vol. 4, p.227; Ge, Yanli, *Qiu Jin nianpu* [A

Chronological Biography of Qiu Jin], Jinan: Qilu shushe, 1983, op. cit., p.63.

108. See Ge, Yanli, ibid., p.64.

109. Ibid., p.63.

110. Bao, Jiali, 'Qiu Ji yu Qingmo funu yundong' [Qiu Jin and the Women's Movement in the Late Qing Period], in Bao Jiali, op. cit., pp.353–7; Chen, Qubin, 'Jianhu nuxia Qiu Jin Zhuan' [Qiu Jin's Bibilography], in Qu, Canzi (ed.), *Qiu Jin nuxia yiji* [Selected Works of Qiu Jin], Taibei: Zhonghua shuju, 1958, pp.2–3; Xu Zihua, 'Jianhu nuxia mubiao' [Qiu Jin's Life], in Qu, Canzi, *Qiu Jin nuxia yiji* [Selected Works of Qiu Jin], ibid., p.9.

111. Quoted in Ono Kazuko, op. cit., p.60.

112. Ibid.

113. Gongaihui [The Humanitarian Society] was founded by a group of Chinese overseas women students in Japan on 8 April 1903 before Qiu Jin arrived in Japan. 'The Rules of the Humanitarian Society' were published in the journal *Jiangsu*, 27 May 1903, No. 2. For reasons that are not at all clear the society ceased its activities some time later. When Qiu Jin arrived in Japan in 1904 she and her friend Chen Jiefen reorganised the society. This was announced in *Jing shizhong* [The Alarm Bell], 3 Oct. 1904. For further details, see the report 'Gongaihui da shexin' [The Establishment of the Humanitarian Society], *Jingzhong ribao* [The Alarm Bell News], 3 Oct. 1904; and 'Gongaihui zhangcheng' [The Rules of the Humanitarian Society], *Jiangsu* [The Journal Of Jiansu], No. 2, 27 May, 1903.

114. See Qiu, Canzi, *Qiu Ji geming zhuan* [Qiu Jin's Revolutionary History], Taibei: Sanmin shuju, 1960, p.46.

115. See Ge, Yanli, op. cit., p.63; Wang Shiche, op. cit. p.227.

116. See Liang, Guanggui, op. cit.; Bao, Jiali, 'Qiu Jin yu Qingmo finu yundong' [Qiu Jin and the Women's Movement in the Late Qing Period], op. cit.

117. Xu Zhihua was born in Shimen, Zhejiang province. She was famous for her poems. She met Qiu Jin in February 1906 when she was a teacher at Nanxun Girls School in Zhejiang. Qiu Jin went to see her and found her responsive, intelligent, sympathetic, and wholly delightful. For the next six months the two women worked together in close intimacy. Qiu Jin had at last found a 'zhiji' (a comrade). In the summer of 1906 they left the school and went to Shanghai where they founded the monthly journal *Zhongguo nubao* [Chinese Women's Journal]. The journal stopped after two issues because of a shortage of funds. Xu Zhihua met Qiu Jin for the last time on 17 March 1907 before Qiu Jin's uprising. Qiu Jin asked Xu Zhihua to bury her beside the tomb of the Song hero Yue Fei, on the bank of West Lake in Zhejiang, if she failed in the uprising. Xu Zhihua promised to take care of her friend's funeral and after Qiu's death Xu fulfilled her promise. Xu wrote some poems to commemorate Qiu Jin and these poems were published in *Nuzi zazhi* [Women's Journal] in Jan. 1915. See Wu, Jiang, and Chen, Qubin, 'Xu Zhihua zhuan' [The Biography of Xu Zhihua], *Nuzi shijie* [Women's World], No. 1, Jan. 1915.

118. Qiu, Jin, 'Zhongguo nubao fakan chi' [The Manifesto of the Chinese Women's Journal], *Zhongguo nubao* [Chinese Women's Journal], No. 1. Jan. 1907.

119. Ibid.; also see Ayscough, Florence, op. cit., pp.161–2.

120. Tao, Chengzhang, 'Zhe an ji lue' [The Record of the Zhejiang Uprising], in *Xinhai Geming* [the 1911 Revolution], op. cit., No. 3, 1956, pp.58–60; Chen, Qubin, 'Jianhu nuxia Qiu Jin zhuan' [Biography of Qiu Jin], in Qiu, Canzi (ed.), *Qiu Jin nuxia yiji* [Selected Works of Qiu Jin], op. cit., pp.57–68.

121. CSHSPE, *Zhongguo jindai tiyu shi* [Modern Chinese Sports History], op. cit., pp.91–2; Yao, Tinhua, 'Tatong xuetang kao' [Datong Normal College Textual

Research], *Zhejiang tiyu shiliao* [The Historical Materials of Zhejiang Sports History], No. 1, 1984, p.23.

122. Ibid.

123. Xu, Yougeng, 'Shaoxin beiqu tiyuhui jianwen' [The History of Shaoxin Northern District Sports Societies], *Zhejiang tiyu shiliao* [The Historical Materials of Zhejiang Sports History], No. 1, 1984, p.34.

124. Qiu's friend Tao Chanzhan wrote that Qiu Jin always wore men's clothes, and on horseback led students to military and physical training on a playground outside the city. Her appearance and behaviour offended the conservatives of the city, especially those with daughters. She was regarded as a dangerous example for girls in the city. Such was the hostility she inspired that on one occasion when Qiu Jin and her students came back from their exercise she was attacked by reactionaries. See Tao, Chenzhang, 'Zhe an ji lue' [The Record of the Zhejiang Uprising], op. cit.; see also *Zhejiang tiyu shiliao* [The Historical Materials of Zhejiang Sports History], No. 1, 1984, pp.8–11; and Bao Jiali, 'Qiu Jin and Women's Movement in the Late Qing', op. cit., pp. 371–2.

125. Zhu, Zhanqin, 'Datong shifan xuetang' [On Datong Normal College], in *Xinhai geming huiyi lu* [Recorded Recollections of the 1911 Revolution], Shanghai: Zhonghua shuju, 1962, p.142; CSHSPE, *Zhongguo jindai tiyu shi* [Modern Chinese Sports History], op. cit., pp.90–93; Liang, Guanggui, op. cit.

126. Ayscough, Florence, op. cit., p.167.

127. Zhu, Zhanqin, 'Datong shifan xuetang' [On Datong Normal College], op. cit., p.144.

128. Quoted in Qiu, Shixiong, 'Jianhu nuxia yu tiyu' [Qiu Jin and Exercise], *Tiyu bao* [Sports Daily], 10 March 1980; Zhu, Fangdong, op. cit., p.51; Yi Jiandong, op. cit., pp.113–14.

129. Qiu, Canzi (ed.), *Qiu Jin nuxia yiji* [Selected Works of Qiu Jin], op, cit., pp.57–8; also see Croll, E., *Feminism and Socialism in China*, op. cit., p.45.

130. See Tao, Chengzhang, 'Zhe an jilue' [The Record of Zhejiang Uprising], op. cit.; Feng, Ziyou, *Geming yishi* [Revolution History], op. cit., p.176.

131. Xu Zilin, (1873–1907) a revolutionary and a founder of Guangfuhui [The Restoration Society]. He was a teacher and subsquently the Principal of Shaoxin School from 1901 to 1904. He set up Zhejiang Sports Society in spring 1905 and opened Datong Normal College in autumn the same year. His aim was to gather together and train revolutionary forces to overthrow the Qing dynasty. When he went to Japan to study in February 1907, he recommended Qiu Jin as his successor. On his return he was appointed to Anqing, capital city of Anhui province, where he acted as assistant principal in a police academy. He and Qiu Jin felt that if they sowed the seeds in two places – Anhui and Zhejiang – revolutionary flowers would soon bloom in both places. So they decided on simultaneous uprisings on 19 July 1907. However, detailed plans for the armed revolt leaked out. The Governor of Anhui issued a command that all revolutionaries be seized. Pre-empting the situation, Xu therefore invited the Governor on 6 July to inspect a police drill at his academy. When the Governor arrived, Xu approached, gave a military salute in the European manner, and, drawing a revolver from his boot, fired at the Governor three times, inflicting mortal wounds. Xu then cried in a loud voice, 'I glory in belonging to the Revolutionary Party!' The Qing army besieged the academy and finally captured Xu, who was led before the dying Governor and then before a tribunal, where he frankly declared his revolutionary principles. The Vice-Governor pronounced the death sentence: Xu's body should be opened and his living heart removed. Xu died on 6 July 1907, but the news of Xu's execution

did not reach Qiu Jin until 9 July.

132. See Zhu, Zhanqin, op. cit.; Tao, Chengzhang, op. cit.; Fan, Wenlan, 'Nu Geming jia Qiu Jin' [Female Revolutionary Qiu Jin]; *Zhongguo funu* [China's Women], No. 8, 1956, p.11; De, Jiansi, 'Xinhai geiming zai Zhejiang' [the 1911 Revolution in Zhejiang]; Lu, Yueping, 'Huiyi xinhai geming de jijianshi he chuzhou guangfu jinguo' [Recollection of the 1911 Revolution in Zhejiang], in *Recollections of the 1911 Revolution*, op. cit., Vol. 4.

133. Zhu, Fangdong, 'Qiu Jin shi yi Datong tiyuhui nu jiaoyuan de zuimin beisha' [Qiu Jin was executed in her role of female physical educator of Datong Physical Education Society], *TWS*, No. 1, 1983, p.51.

134. Yiao, Tinghua, 'Zhenjiang de tiyuhui kao' [The Search for Sports Societies in Zhenjiang], *Zhejiang tiyu shiliao* [The Historical Material of Zhejiang Sports History], No. 3, 1986, pp.57–8.

135. Ayscough, Florence, op. cit., p.174.

136. Zhu, Fangdong, Qiu Jin shi yi Datong tiyuhui nu jiaoyuan de zuimin beisha' [Qiu Jin was executed in her role of female physical educator . . .], op. cit., p.52.

137. Bao, Jialin, 'Xinhai geming shiqi de funu sixiang' [Women's emancipation and the 1911 Revolution]; Lin, Weihong, 'Tongmenhui shidai nu geming zhishi de huodong' [Women Revolutionaries in the 1911 Revolution]; both articles are in Bao Jialin (ed.) *Zhongguo funu shi lunji* [Selected Works on Chinese Women's History], op. cit., pp.281–93 and 299–332.

138. Qiu, Jin, 'Jinwei xianshi' [Stones of the Jingwei Bird], in *Qiu Jin ji* [Collected Works of Qiu Jin], Shanghai: Zhonghua shuju, 1960, pp.126–27.

139. Qiu, Jin, 'Gei Wang Shizi de xin' [Letter to Wang Shizi], in *Qiu Jin ji* [Collected Works of Qiu Jin], op. cit., p.45.

140. Jian, Bozhan, op. cit., Vol.4, p.131.

141. See the report 'Wuhan gemin da fengyun' [Wuhan Revolutionary Storm], part 13, *Minli bao* [People's Independent Daily], 23 Oct. 1911.

142. This letter was published in *Minli bao* [People's Independent Daily], 31 Oct. 1911 entitled 'Wu Shuqin nushi tou jun wen' [Miss Wu Shuqin's Request to Join the Army].

143. This letter was published in *Shen bao* [Shanghai Daily], 13 Nov. 1911 entitled 'Shangxia nuxie daibiao Xue Shuzen shan Chendudu shu' [A Letter from Xue Shuzen to Governor Chen].

144. Chen Wanyan published the manifesto 'Nuzi beifadui xuanyan' [The Manifesto of the Women's Northern Expeditionary Regiment] in *Shi bao* [Times], 16 Jan. 1912.

145. Chen Hongbi, 'Guangfu shidai nujie huodong shi' [The History of Women's Activities in 1911 Revolution], *Shenzhou nubao* [China's Women], No. 1–2, Dec. 1912.

146. Wu Mulan published the manifesto 'Tongmeng nuzi jinzhan lianxidui xuanyan shu' [The Manifesto of the Women's Military Training Alliance] in *Minli bao* [People's Independent Daily], 12 Jan. 1912.

147. See the report 'Wu Mulan beibu qinxin xiangji' [The Details of Wu Mulan's Arrest], *Yaxiya bao* [The Eastern News], 15 April 1914. As this report indicates, Wu Mulan was later arrested for revolutionary activities in Yuan Shikai's period of office.

148. This comment was in the report 'Nu guominjun chuxan' [On the emergence of Women's Armies], *Shen bao* [Shanghai Daily], 16 Nov. 1911.

149. See the report 'Nuzi guominjun shiling Li Zhongxue qishi' [The Announcement of Li Zhongxue, the Commander of Zhejiang Women's Military Regiment], *Minli bao* [People's Independent Daily], 9 Jan. 1912.

150. See the report 'Sun Yat-sen yieshi nuzi guominjun beifadui' [Sun Yat-sen Visited the Women's Military Regiment], *Minli bao* [People's Independent Daily], 7 Jan. 1912.

151. Yun, Ruizhi, 'Ruizhi geming huiyilu' [The Autobiography of Yun Reizhi], *Minguang* [People's Light], No. 1, 10 Dec. 1946.

152. Maria was a woman fighter in the Italian popular movement; together with Garibaldi, she was honoured by revolutionaries in her day.

153. See the report 'Yun Weijun suidui gong Ning' [Yun Weijun, Leading her Troops, Fought Right in the Front Line of Nanjing], *Minli bao* [People's Independent Daily], 1 Dec. 1911.

154. See 'Nuzi junshi tuan jingao' [The Manifesto of the Women's Military Regiment], *Minli bao* [People's Independent Daily], 18 Nov. 1911 and the report 'Nu guomin jun chuxian' [The Emergence of the Women's Army], *Shen bao* [Shanghai Daily], 16 Nov. 1911.

155. The Society's original name was Nuzi chanzhen tongmenghui [The Alliance of Comrades for Women's Suffrage]. See 'Nuzi chanzhen tongmenghui guanggao' [The announcement of the Society of Comrades for Women's Suffrage], *Shenzhou ribao* [China's Daily], 30 Nov. 1911.

156. Lin Zhongsu went to Japan to study in 1903. She published her article in August 1903 in Shanghai Patriotic Girls' School Press. She became the President of the Society of Comrades for Women's Suffrage on 3 March 1912.

157. See 'Nuzi chanzheng tongmenhui caozhang' [The Regulations of The Alliance of Comrades for Women's Suffrage], *Shenzhou ribao* [China's Daily], 30 Nov. 1911.

158. See 'Nuzi chanzheng tongzhihui huiyuan Lin Zhongshu yuanyan' [The Announcement of Lin Zhongsu], *Tiantuo bao* [Tiantuo Daily], 23–24 Jan. 1912.

159. See 'Zhonghua minguo lianhehui fu linshi dazhongtong shu' [Letter for the Federation of the Republic to the Provisional President of the Republic of China], *Tongyidang ditichi baogao shu* [The First Report of the United Party, (n.d.). The 'certain woman' was, of course, Lin Zhongsu. The Federation of the Republic was the name for an alliance of the Revolutionary Alliance, the United Party and advocates of a constitutional monarchy. See Jian, Bozan, op. cit., pp.123–32.

160. 'Speech of Chang Taiyan to the First Congress of the Federation of the Republic of China', quoted in Rong, Tiesheng, op. cit., p.193.

161. 'Zhonghua minguo lianhehui fu lishi dazhongtong shu' [Letter from the Federation of the Republic to the Provisional President of the Republic of China], in *Tongyitang diyichi baogao shu* [The First Report of the United Party], 1912 (n.d.).

162. See 'Lishi dazhongtong zaifu Zhonghua minguo lianhehui shu' [The Reply from the Provisional President to the Federation of the Republic of China], in *Tongyitang diyichi baogao shu* [The First Report of the United Party], op. cit.

163. See 'Nuzi chanzheng tongzhihui huiyuan Lin Zhongsu yuanyan' [The Announcement of Lin Zhongsu], op. cit.

164. They included 'Zhonghua nuzi jingjin hui' [Chinese Women's Progressive Society] in February (advocated by Shao Hanying, the Society was founded in Shanghai. Its manifesto was published in *Shenzhou ribao* [China's Daily], 5 Jan. 1912 and *Tiantuo bao* [Tiantuo Daily], 3 Feb. 1912); 'Zhejiang nan nu pinquan weichi hui' [Zhejiang Equal Right Society] in February (see 'Zhejiang nan nu pinquan weichi hui zhangchen' [Regulations of the Zhejiang Equal Rights Society], *Tiantuo bao*, 16–23 March 1912; 'Zhejiang nan nu pinquan weichi hui faqi tonggao' [The Announcement of Zhejiang Equal Rights Society],

Tiantuo bao, 25 Feb. 1912; Chen, Peizheng, 'Nan nu pingquan hui yuanqi' [The Emergence of the Equal Rights Society], *Tiantuo bao*, 25 Feb. 1912; 'Zhonghua nuzi gonghe xiejin hui' [Chinese Women's United Society] in February (see 'Zhonghua nuzi gonghe xiejin hui jianzhang' [The Regulations of the Chinese Women's United Society], *Tiantuo bao*, 4–8 Feb. 1912; 'Zhonghua nuzi gonghe xiejin hui zhenqiu nuzi yijian shu' [Give your Opinions to the Chinese Women's United Society], *Mingli bao* [People's Independent Daily], 1 Nov. 1912; 'Hunan nu guomin hui' [Hunan Female Citizens Society] in March, (its manifesto was published in *Tiantuo bao*, 1 March 1912); 'Guangzhou nuquan yanjiu hui' [Guangzhou Women's Suffrage Research Society] in March found on 10 March 1912 with Chen Yuting as the chairman. The Society sent a telegram to SunYat-sen on the matter of women's right to vote. The details are in *Tiantuo bao* 10 March 1912).

165. The heroines of the 1911 Revolution such as Zhang Hanying, Tang Qunying, Zhang Zhaohan, Zhang Qunying and Wang Changguo, as we have mentioned earlier, devoted themselves and their families to the revolutionary cause. For more names see *Shi bao* [Times], 27 Feb. 1912.

166. The Petition was published in *Shi bao* [Times], Feb. 1912.

167. There is no record of any male radicals supporting the women's right to vote.

168. See 'Nuzi chanzhenhui shang Sun Yat-sen shu' [Letter of the Women's Suffrage Society to Sun Yat-sen], *Tiantuo bao* [Tiantuo Daily], 23 March 1912.

169. Ibid.

170. See the report 'Nuzi chanzhen tongmenghuo lizhen chanzhenquan' [The Alliance of Women's Suffrage is fighting for its Rights], *Shi bao* [Times], 23 March 1912.

171. Ibid.

172. See the report 'Nuzi chanzhen zhi jieying' [The Victory of Women's Suffrage], *Tiantuo bao* [Tiantuo Daily], 24 March 1912.

173. After the 1911 Revolution China still faced political, economic and military problems, especially with foreign powers and the conservative forces (made up of supporters of the defeated ruling house and warlords). Many Chinese still favoured a strong, central authority. Both the radicals and conservatives believed that the restoration of order required Yuan Shikai not Sun Yat-sen. Since 1906 Yuan Shikai had created China's modern Beiyang Army and was now a supreme military authority. During the Revolution he linked his Beijing base with the Beiyang Army and supported the Revolutionary Alliance and the Republican government. When the Revolution took place in Wuchang, Sun Yat-sen was in the United States, raising funds; he learned of the uprising from the American press. Hurrying home to China, he discovered the weakness of his position. The man with power was Yuan. Only Yuan could be president, and when Sun was elected by 16 out of the 17 provinces as provisional president, it was only on the explicit understanding – accepted by Sun himself – that he was simply to act as caretaker until Yuan could be elected later. For further details see Gray, J., op. cit., pp.144–5; Spence, Jonathan. D., *The Search for Modern China*, op. cit., pp.176–7; Hu, Sheng, op. cit., pp.1100–122; Jian, Bozhan, op. cit., pp.130–31.

174. Jian, Bozhan, op. cit., Vol. 4, p.177.

175. Ibid..

176. Peake, Cyrus H., op. cit., p.77.

177. Yuan, Shikai, 'Dazhongtong banding jiaoyu yaozi [The Aim of Education], Jan. 1915 in CSHI, *Jindai zhongguo tiyushi zhiliao ji* [Modern Chinese Sports History Reference], op. cit., pp.75–7.

178. Chen, Jinpan, op. cit., pp.226–7.
179. In 1915 the Minister of Education, Tang Hualong, published his speech entitled 'Guanyu zhengli jiaoyu fang'an' [On The Consolidation of Education] in which Tang insisted that the role of women's education must remain that of learning to be a virtuous wife and good mother. See 'Jiaoyu zhongzhang Tang Hualong tan nuzi jiaoyu' [Tang Hualong – the Minister of Education on Women's Education], in *Jiaoyu zazhi* [Education Journal], Vol. 6, No. 4, 1915, pp.2–3; Chen, Jinpan. op. cit., pp.229–30.
180. Wu, Yuzhang, *Wu Yuzhang huiyilu* [Reminiscences of Wu Yuzhang], Beijing: Zhongguo qingnian chubanshe [China's Youth Press], 1978, p.98.
181. Borthwick, Sally, 'Changing Concept of the Role of Women from the Late Qing to the May Fourth Period', in Pong, David, and Fung, Edmund S. K. (eds), *Ideal and Reality: Social and Political Change in Modern China 1860–1949*, Lanham: University Press of America, 1985, p.81; Jian, Bozhan, op. cit., p.141.
182. Chow, Tse-tung, *The May Fourth Movement: Intellectual Revolution in Modern China*, Cambridge: Harvard University Press, 1960, p.43.
183. Ono Kazuko, op. cit., p.89.
184. Wang Yuebo, a journalist working for *Minli bao* [People's Independent Daily], published an article entitled 'duiyu nuzi chanzhen zhi huiyi' [My Opinion of Women's Suffrage] opposing women's suffrage. He argued that women's physical weakness, women's educational weakness and women's emancipation would destroy family discipline and social order. The article was published in *Minli bao* on 28 Feb. 1912 and soon provoked an intense debate. His arguments were approved by some educated women, Zhang Renlan, for example, who had obtained her education in the United States, wrote an article to explain, according to her experience, that a woman's happiness came from helping her husband and nursing her children. Her article was published in *Minli bao* [People's Independent Daily], 9 March 1912.
185. See 'Gaodeng xiaoxuexiao tichao ke jiaoshou yaomu cao'an' [the Draft Solution of Gymnastics Teaching in Elementary Schools], Jan. 1916, It was published in *Jiaoyu gongbao* [Education Journal], No. 11, Jan. 1916, pp.12–15.
186. Widows, according to Confucian doctrine, should stay at home. See Rong, Tiesheng, op. cit., p.193.
187. For example, in Nanjing Women's Institute of Law and Politics in 1912, (see the report 'Chuangban nuzi fazheng xuetang gongqi' [The Announcement of the Opening of the Women's Institute of Law and Politics in Nanjing], *Dagong bao* [Dagong Daily], 2 April 1912); Nanjing Fuxin Women's School in 1912 (see the report 'Nanjing Fuxin nuxuexiao tebie guanggao' [The Announcement of the Nanjing Fuxin Women's School], *Minli bao* [People's Independent Daily], 16 March 1912); Women's Technology School in 1912 (see 'Zhongyang nuzi gongyi xuetang jianzhang' [The Regulations of the Women's Technology School], *Minli bao*, 7 April 1912); Suzhou Zuyin Women's College in 1912, (see the report 'Suzhou zuyin nuxiao zhuban nuzi guowen zhuxiuke yuanqi' [Brief History of the Suzhou Zuyin Women's College], *Minli bao*, 27 April 1912); Hubei Provincial Women's School in 1912 (see the report 'Hubei nuxue' [On Women's Education in Hubei Province], *Minli bao*, 21 May 1912); Beijing Women's Education Society in 1912, (see 'Beijing nuxue lianhehui yuanqi' [On the Establishment of the Beijing Women's Education Society], *Guomin gongbao* [Citizen's News], 9 May 1912); Jiangxi Provincial Women's Education Society in 1912 (see 'Zhuzhi nuzi jiaoyuhui' [On the Establishment of the Women's Education Society in Jiangxi], *Minsheng ribao* [People's Voice], 8 April 1912).
188. See 'Zhongyang nizi gongyi xuetang jianzhang' [The Regulations of the

Women's Technology School], *Minli bao* [People's Independent Daily], 7 April 1912; 'Suzhou zuyin nuxiao jianzhang' [The Curriculum of Suzhou Zuyin Women's College], *Minli bao* [People's Independent Daily], 27 April 1912; 'Jiaoyubu dindin xiaoxuexiao jiaozhe ji kechengbiao [The Rules and Curriculum of Primary Schools] issued by the Ministry of Education in Nov. 1912, *Jiaoyu zazhi* [Education Journal], Vol. 4, No. 10, Jan. 1913; 'Gaoteng xiaoxuexiao tichao ke jiaoshou yaomu chaoan' [The Draft Rules of the Teaching of Gymnastics and Physical Education Courses in Higher Primary Schools], *Jiaoyu gongbao* [Education Magazine], Vol. 2, No. 11, Jan. 1916, pp.2–4.

189. Yuan, Shikai, 'Jiaoyu zhi zhongzi' [The Aim of Education], op. cit.

190. The First National Games took place in Beijing between 18–22 October 1910; the second were in Beijing from 21–22 May 1914; the third were in Wuchang City, Hubei province from 22–24 May 1918.

191. The first Huabei Competition was held in Beijing on 24 May 1913; the second was in Beijing on 18–19 May 1914; the third was held in Tianjin in May 1915; the fourth was in Beijing on 19–20 May 1916; the fifth was in Tianjin on 20–21 April 1917; the sixth was held in Baoding, Hebei province in May 1918; the seventh was in Beijing 14–15 April 1919.

192. The first Far East Olympic Games was in the Philippines in Feb. 1913; the second was in Shanghai, China, in May 1915; the third was in Tokyo, Japan in May 1917; the fourth was in the Philippines in May 1919.

193. Wang, Chingwu (ed.), *Zhongguo jindai gongyunshi zhiliao* [The Archives of the History of the Workers' Movement in Modern China], Beijing: Kexue chubanshe, Vol. 2, p.1192; Rong, Tiesheng, op. cit., p.192.

FOUR

A New Woman for a New Age:
The May Fourth Era (1915–21)

꧁꧂

UNDER YUAN SHIKAI'S presidency the Women's Movement expired and the new Republic itself proved moribund. Yuan moved the capital of the Republic to Beijing – his power base in 1913, attempted to restore the feudal system and made plans to become emperor.[1] He outlawed the Nationalist Party and dissolved Parliament in 1914. Finally, in 1916, he set himself up as Emperor of China. His 'reign' was shortlived since he died in June 1916 and warlords plunged China into decades of turmoil.[2] The demise of the Republic and the subsequent political disarray led to a further critical re-evaluation of China's entire cultural heritage[3] in the form of two major movements – the New Culture Movement of 1915 and the May Fourth Movement of 1919. Both Movements comprise the May Fourth Era.

The New Culture Movement

By 1915 some intellectuals embraced anarchy, nationalism or socialism, while others espoused Mahatma Gandhi's passive resistance, Rabindranath Tagore's eastern ethics, Bertrand Russell's European idealism or John Dewey's American pragmatism.[4] A new generation, which included men like Chen Duxiu, Hu Shi, Wu Yu, Lu Xun and Li Dazhao, who had been educated both at home and abroad,[5] was coming of age. Its experience of the politics of their elders had been dispiriting. The actions of the older generation had revealed that China's ills were profoundly cultural and that meaningful political action would became possible only when these cultural ailments had been cured.[6] To this end the new men were ready to embrace new ideas. They made the journal of *Xin qingnian* [New Youth] a focus for fresh thought, and they had a fresh vision of

119

patriotism. The ideology of the old generation was viewed by them as blind and foolish. What China urgently needed, instead of unquestioning patriots, was nationalists who were capable of thinking clearly about relevant problems and who were conscious of the need to reject old solutions. Without this clarity of thought China would not become a healthy modern state. In their opinion, the task of the new generation was to devote itself to educational innovation and moral reform rather than political power.[7] Western concepts, especially 'science' and 'democracy', became their weapons with which to attack China's still influential feudal culture.[8] To mount this attack almost all the leading intellectuals gathered under the bold banner of *Xin qingnian* [New Youth].[9] Discussion in the journal centred on these concepts and led to the emergence of the New Culture Movement in 1915.[10]

The aims of the New Culture Movement were to introduce the positivism, equality, and democracy characteristic of Western culture to Chinese society, to alert the Chinese to the need for science and the scientific spirit, to inspire China with new hope and to build a new country.[11] In order to popularise the ideas and ideals of the New Culture Movement among the mass of the people the leaders of the Movement initiated a Literary Revolution.[12] It involved the use of the vernacular language instead of the traditional language of Chinese literature. Hu Shi stated that 'Chinese literature as it existed and still exists today is the literature for the minority . . . It is a literature of and for the intelligentsia. Any country that pretends and intends to be a democracy must provide for its citizens a medium of expression which will be easily comprehended by everyone.'[13] Chen Duxiu declared: 'First, we must overthrow the old aristocratic literature and establish a literature of the people. Second, we must overthrow the literature of the classics and establish a literature of realism. Third, we must overthrow the literature which is secluded from the world and establish a social literature. . . . For the old aristocratic literature is too dependent upon examples of ancestors, and hence we have lost our own spirit of independence and individuality.'[14] All leaders of the New Culture Movement now wrote articles in the vernacular and in 1918 Lu Xun published the first Chinese novel in 'the language of the people'. Most newspapers, journals and magazines were now published in the new written form.[15] The outcome of the New Culture Movement, as John Dewey once commented, was 'the manifestation of a new consciousness, an intellectual awakening in the young men and women who through their schooling had been aroused to the necessity of a new order of belief, a new method of thinking'. The Movement comprised a twentieth century Chinese Renaissance.[16] One Western observer stated: 'The renaissance of a quarter of the human family is occurring before our eyes and we have only to sit and watch the stage.'[17]

The New Culture Movement, however, in Mao Zedong's unflattering view, was composed of 'bourgeois intellectuals who unconditionally praised the outmoded individualist bourgeois culture of the West and advocated the servile imitation of capitalist Europe and America'.[18] Interestingly, Western scholars, such as D. W. Y. Kwok, Jerome Grieder and Benjamin Schwartz, agree with him, to the extent that in their view the New Culture Movement marked the 'high point' of Westernisation in modern China. Within the Movement, modern 'science' was explained in terms of its derivation from Western positivism,[19] modern 'democracy' in terms of its derivation from Western liberalism,[20] and the dovetailing conjunction of the two concepts in a Chinese context were seen as a direct and desirable legacy of the European Enlightenment, albeit modified somewhat to suit China's idiosyncratic social conditions.[21] Confucianism, those in the Movement argued yet again, was the past! 'The people of the twentieth century must devote themselves to the new; they cannot be satisfied to follow the old.'[22] Thus, 'overthrow Confucius and his sons' became a popular slogan.[23] Once again, an anti-Confucian movement arose, resulting in severe criticism of Confucian moral values, traditional relationships and old customs recently reintroduced by Yuan Shikai. The editor of the *Canton Times* wrote: 'Most of our people are slaves to precedent. Daily we witness efficiency sacrificed on the altar of custom and tradition. Precedent binds the race to the past. It curbs all efforts at progress. But a new emancipation has come to our people. It is not enough to say, 'China is not ready for modern things.' We must make her ready.' The new belief in democracy and equality brought China to the dawning of a new era. Critical reflection[24] led eventually to critical 'action' – the May Fourth Movement which began in Beijing on that day in 1919.[25]

The May Fourth Movement

The immediate spur to action, however, was spontaneous public anger. The occasion was the Treaty of Versailles signed at the end of the First World War. In 1914, Japan had seized the German concessions in Shandong province and a year later made the notorious 21 demands regarding special rights there.[26] The Chinese, who had sided with the Allies, had expected that after the War, in accordance with Wilson's Fourteen Points,[27] they would obtain greater independence and respect. They believed that at the very least the previous German and now Japanese-held concessions would be returned to China. However, the Allies had agreed that Japan should retain these privileges. During the Versailles Conference, the Chinese delegation was told that early in 1917, in return for Japanese naval assistance against the Germans, Great Britain and Italy had signed a secret treaty ensuring 'support [of] Japan's claims in regard to the disposal of Germany's rights in Shangdong after the War'.[28] The Japanese delegation also announced that they had come to their own secret agreement with the Chinese government in September 1918. The Chinese delegates seemed to have been genuinely unaware of this humiliating secret agreement. If that were not bad enough, the Treaty left the Japanese in control of Shandong. Other Chinese requests had not even been included on the Conference agenda, including the abolition of the infamous 21 demands, the abolition of German and Austria's special political and economic rights and the abolition of foreign countries' privileges in China.[29]

When news of all this reached Beijing, students refused to accept these humiliations – the failure to obtain equal international status and the Chinese government's weakness in accepting continued foreign encroachment on China's soil symbolised by an apparent readiness to sign the Treaty. On 4 May 1919 they demonstrated against the Treaty's omissions and commissions. The demonstration developed into a national movement for cultural and political rebirth. In addition, protest marches, demonstrations, strikes and a boycott of Japanese goods spread across the whole country. Finally, the government capitulated to the movement. The Versailles Conference ended without China's acceptance of the proposed conditions and without China signing the Treaty.

The movement was a major event in modern Chinese history. Jonathan Spence has observed that 'The term "May Fourth Movement" is both limited and broad in significance, depending on whether it is applied to the demonstrations that took place on that particular day or to the complex emotional, cultural and political developments that followed.'[30] Broadly, the New Culture and May

Fourth Movements have come to be known as the May Fourth Era, a term used to describe an era of attempts at intellectual, social and political reform covering the years 1915 to 1921.[31] The combination of patriotic fury and cultural introspection led to the Chinese people attempting yet another Sisyphean effort at change. China became a more dynamic nation: 'The glory of the May Fourth movement lies precisely in getting China to move.'[32] To employ another metaphor, the new generation now set out its second-hand stall – the goods were well-worn: the end of the feudal family, the denial of Confucianism, the introduction of democracy and the wholesale transformation of the traditional social system. By this circuitous route, once again supported by radical intellectuals, the Chinese Women's Movement was reborn and women moved centre stage as actresses in a new emancipatory drama.[33]

Rejection of the Feudal Family System

This time, the reincarnated Women's Movement dug deeply at once at the roots of its oppression – Chinese culture. With the assistance of radical writers, fresh efforts at emancipation started with an attack on the feudal family system – the core of sexual discrimination. Before continuing the chronology of the cultural attack by the Women's Movement and its allies on the feudal family, in view of its significance in Chinese history it is necessary briefly to reiterate its nature. The feudal family system, as mentioned earlier, was built upon the basis of the old Chinese theory adopted by philosophers of the Confucian school – the yin–yang doctrine. It will be recalled that yin represented the negative and inferior, and yang represented the positive and superior.[34] When this philosophy was applied to the Chinese feudal family system, yin became the female principle and yang the male principle. Since the system demanded unlimited subservience towards superiors, obedience, timidity, reticence and adaptability were held to be the main virtues of women.[35] Throughout her life a woman submitted to a linked series of authorities: her own family, her husband's family and, finally, her son.

Confucian philosophy not only provided an ideological justification for woman's low social position, but also underpinned woman's inferior legal status within the family system. Chinese women were virtually without property rights. When the family estate was divided,

123

all property was distributed among the males.[36] Within the family, only males – the grandfather, father, husband, or the older son – could dispose of money and property. This total absence of property rights is internationally and historically almost without parallel. To provide merely a handful of examples: in historic Babylon and Egypt, women of the upper classes enjoyed full property rights.[37] Under Hindu law, Indian women had certain qualified property rights, including the right to inherit.[38] In ancient Judea women had inheritance rights and both father and mother had estates.[39] In the Roman Republic, even when fathers and husbands had absolute legal power over them, women still gained the right to private property as early as the 2nd century BC and daughters and sisters could inherit their fathers' and brothers' estates.[40] Among the Germanic tribes in the early Middle Ages, the bridal price was handed over to the bride and remained her private property. In general, married women's property rights were subject to some restrictions, but few were imposed on widows.[41]

In contrast, Chinese women, historically, have been inferior domestically, economically and legally. Essentially, woman was the property of man. Young girls were sold by their fathers into slavery, concubinage, or prostitution. Husbands pawned or sold their wives into temporary marriages to other men.[42] This condition was all the more easily sustained by women's small bound feet, which kept them housebound – in the ownership of men. Footbinding not only restricted women's feet but women's physical power, individual freedom and human rights. As Olga Lang has pointed out, 'Women [elsewhere] won more rights, . . . because they played a greater role in production'.[43] Physical weakness, born of footbinding, stamped its imprint on the whole of a Chinese woman's life. It rationalised women's ideological, legal and economic inferiority and perpetuated the Chinese feudal family system.

The feudal family was not invented by Confucius and was not exclusively characteristic of China. Western civilisation too had family structures in which the man was dominant, and in which the woman was considered inferior. But there were two major differences between the Chinese patriarchal family system and the Western patriarchal family system. First, Confucianism tended to value the family more than Christianity. The Christian philosophers, like the Hebrew prophets who preceded them, stressed the importance of the family and respect for father and mother. But at the same time the Church interfered with family life and put its authority above that of the parents. Jesus promised that one who 'has left house, or parents, or brethren, or wife, or children, for the sake of the kingdom of God should receive manifold more in this present time, and in the world to come, life everlasting'.[44] This would not appeal to a Chinese person educated in the spirit of Confucianism. He or she would not enjoy any rewards either in this life or in the world to come if they had to forsake the family. Second, Confucianism saw no contradiction between the interests of the family and those of society, between family loyalty and community loyalty. The strengthening of the family was a means of strengthening the state. The family was 'the root of the state'. In consequence, as Francis L.K. Hsu has remarked: 'As far as overt behaviour is concerned, the first outstanding quality is an explicitly submissive attitude toward authority . . . There are very few uncertainties.'[45] The Confucian family system and its attendant morality, in short, laid the foundations for an authoritarian political structure which lasted for over two thousand years. Sexual discrimination lay at the very heart of this family system because a gender hierarchy was built into its structure and gender discrimination characterised its existence.[46] In essence, the Confucian family system was based on inequality, produced a people submissive towards authority, and women subjugated to men. It was for this latter reason, especially, that it was targeted by women in the May Fourth Era.

In the mid-nineteenth century, as we have seen, China began to change slowly from a feudal social system to a modern social system. The latter was instigated by individuals acting as independent units and its laws and ethics attempted to protect individual freedom and rights. Confucianism, in contrast, was based on a feudal society composed of family units. The individual was regarded as a dependent member of the family, and not as an independent unit within the society and state. Confucianism, in short, denied woman's individual rights in her capacity as a dependent member of the family. Consequently, the feudal family system was also considered inappropriate to the modern individualistic society as approved by intellectuals during the May Fourth Era.

In the early twentieth century women had not yet gained access to pre-eminent intellectual positions in Chinese liberal circles. For this reason it was male liberals who took up the public torch on behalf of women and argued their case in newspapers, journals and books. Cai

Chang, who was later a foremost communist ideologue, underlined this state of affairs when she wrote:

> By 1918 when my brother had entered the Higher Normal School, we were already influenced by the 'new thought', though this was a little before the May Fourth Movement. These two [Mao Zedong and Cai Heshen – Cai Chang's brother] organised the 'New People's Study Society'. My brother and I were good friends and I was the only girl permitted to join this society. Though my brother did not talk much to me on political questions, I learned a great deal from listening to conversations and participating in the society's activities.[47]

'When the New Culture Movement in 1915 challenged old ideas concerning women', Irene Dean has observed, 'the leaders were all men. They devoted much thought to women's problems, offered their own liberal solutions and translated relevant Western literature on the subject.'[48]

In publicly taking on the traditional family, intellectuals once more took up the cause of women's emancipation in China. They had no choice. The one led directly to the other. Arguments rehearsed earlier were heard yet again. A whole army of intellectuals went 'over the top'. Throughout the May Fourth Era they kept up the attack. Present and future political theorists and activists led the charge. Wu Yu (1871–1949),[49] a scholar who had studied law and political science in Japan, attacked the Confucian advocacy of social inequality between men and women.[50] Then Chen Duxiu (1880–1942),[51] the leader of the New Culture and May Fourth Movement, claimed, 'that to respect women's personality and rights is a practical need for social progress and we hope that they themselves will be completely aware of their duty to society'.[52] Xie Wuliang,[53] an historian, expressed the view that essentially men and women did not differ and women's talents were every bit the equal of men's.[54] Tao Menghe, a sociologist, in an article entitled 'Women's Problems' in Xin qingnian [New Youth] in January 1918, outlined the nature and history of the Western women's emancipation movement and asserted that, armed with this knowledge, the Chinese people would soon reject women's inferior position in the family and society and would ask for Chinese women's liberation.[55] Taking a lead from Tao, Zhou Zuoren (1885–1967),[56] a well-known novelist of the period, launched an attack on a fundamental element of feudal morality – female chastity. In May 1918 in an article 'On Chastity' in *Xin qingnian* [New Youth], he argued that chastity was not a moral concept. Morality involved those forms of behaviour considered right, proper, acceptable and applicable to all in society. But in China, he argued, chastity was only required of women. Society demanded that only women were chaste. Consequently, chastity was not a form of morality but a form of sexual discrimination.[57]

Zhou's logic had widespread repercussions. People reflected openly on sexual discrimination in the culture and on women's position in society.[58] Articles critical of woman's chastity, woman's filial piety and absence of individual rights appeared in journals and newspapers[59] and stimulated widespread discussion. Zhou's brother, Lu Xun (1881–1936),[60] China's 'Voltaire' of the New Culture and May Fourth Movement, with one exception, went further in his iconoclasm than Zhou. He savagely derided Confucianism as 'cannibalism'.[61] Nevertheless, he defended one aspect of Confucian family ethics on the grounds that it sustained a sensible cohesive continuity – chastity. He pointed out that female 'chastity' and 'virtuousness' were the ties that helped to hold the feudal family system together and thus maintained social cohesion. This, he asserted, was why in the Republican period (1911–16) a woman's 'chastity' was rewarded. However, he contemptuously rejected all other elements of Confucianism. Indoctrinated from childhood into Confucian ethics he stated, for centuries women had raised not a single protest about their lack of freedom and individualism within the family system. Discrimination had been completely internalised by them.[62] For Lu Xun, therefore, revolution was simple: if you wanted to change the society, you had to change the family system, and if you wanted to change the family system, you had to change women.

Others made essentially the same point in different words and ways. Liu Banlong, a progressive novelist and journalist, attacked the recent Yuan model of the ideal woman: good wife and virtuous mother. He described and criticised the boring life of the 'ideal woman' in 'Thoughts on Coming Back from the South'. 'Ideal women' lacked the spirit of independence. They were men's attachments. In his view, women's emancipation had no chance of success unless the mould in which women were shaped was not simply broken, but shattered.[63] Luo Jialun (1896–1969),[64] a well-known intellectual of the time, in an article entitled 'Women's Liberation' published in 1919 in *Xin chao* [The New Tide], made the same point that women must become persons in their own right and not remain as 'attachments to men'. The new society needed new women who shaped their own destinies.[65]

Hu Shi (1891–1962),[66] an American-educated scholar and a well-known leader of the New Culture and May Fourth Movements, claimed that lurking behind the issue of the model of the ideal woman, was the greater issue of Chinese attitudes toward their psychological inheritance.[67] In a speech delivered in the autumn of 1918 at the Beijing Women's Normal School, Hu Shi compared the relative positions of Western women and Chinese women in the twentieth century and argued that 'The major difference between Chinese women and Western women was that the latter possessed an independent spirit.' He continued, 'A good society certainly cannot be created by men and women like us who are unable to "stand alone" . . . The spirit of "independence" . . . is in fact an essential condition of a good society.'[68] It was Li Dazhao (1880–1927),[69] Professor of History and Librarian of Beijing University, a key figure in the New Culture and May Fourth Movements and the founder of the Chinese Communist Party, who spelt out the political implications of this philosophical position, when he pointed out that, 'True democracy can be only realised with the liberation of women. If women are not liberated, there can be no genuine democracy . . . There is a potential for transformation in all classes of society; it is only in the relationship between a man and a woman that a permanent barrier exists. Therefore democracy between the sexes is our first and foremost priority.'[70]

Darwinism, Nationalism and a New Femininity

Women's emancipation thus became an essential part of the New Culture and May Fourth Movements. 'Women's problems' were discussed throughout the whole country. Progressive students organised societies to discuss social reconstruction and reformation and tried to find ways to liberate women. Some journals were founded specifically to provoke women's consciousness of fitness, freedom and equality in this new era. Earlier ambitions were back on the ideological agenda. Nu bao [Women's Daily] had as its aims: to support, educate and strengthen women; the purpose of Nu jie zhong [Women's Bell] was to educate women in order that they may take part in the progress of society towards liberty and equality; *Xin nu xing* [New Women] had the objective of ensuring that women gave birth to a new society; *Funu zhi sheng* [The Voice of Women] was much concerned with the liberalising consequences of birth-control; *Xiandai funu* [The Modern Women] provided information on women's situation in the Western world; and *Jiefang huabao* [The Liberation Magazine] advocated individualism and encouraged women to live free lives. Almost all of the leading intellectuals joined in this discussion of women and their role in society and contributed articles to these journals. The issue of women's emancipation crossed sexual lines and evoked a profound depth of commitment in both sexes.

In 1919 *Xin qingnian*[New Youth] published a special issue on the Norwegian dramatist Henrik Ibsen. It included a translation of *A Doll's House*. Chinese interest focused not on Ibsen's critique of European middle-class society, but on Ibsen's conclusion: 'No social evil is greater than the destruction of the individual's individuality.'[71] 'Ibsenism' became an assault weapon pointed at the whole Confucian social structure, but especially at the family system. It was widely argued that democracy was impossible in a patriarchal state with a patriarchal family system where the individual had no place.[72] *A Doll's House*, was performed on stages all over the country. It made a tremendous impression on radical young women.[73] They saw Nora, the leading character in the drama who left her family, asserted her individuality and demanded her independence, as a symbol of a new international image of woman. Lines such as 'don't become a man's plaything', 'recognise individuality', and 'demand freedom' made a big impact. More and more young Chinese women imitated Nora and left their families in the quest for personal liberty.

A crucial question, of course, was what would happen to these 'Noras' after they left home? They needed economic security as well as personal independence in order to survive in society, otherwise, as Lu Xun pointed out, they would either sink hopelessly into depravity or return abjectly to their families.[74] The new society, he believed, needed a new woman mentally *and* physically equipped for her own survival as well as China's. In this context, women's bodies again attracted the intellectuals' attention, but it was not the late-nineteenth century revisited. This time, women's healthy bodies were not simply to ensure strong mothers for a strong nation, but to improve the quality of life of women themselves. The traditional aesthetics of femininity were newly challenged in this fresh period of

129

reform. From the viewpoint of traditional aesthetics, of course, the frail body was the acceptable symbol of femininity. A woman, too slim to withstand a gust of wind, with moth-eyebrows, cinnabar lips, pale complexion and three-inch feet, was the historic ideal of beauty. She would be desired by men and envied by women. In contrast, as Chinese culture had always looked down on manual labour, the robust body was the unacceptable symbol of the unenvied and undesirable female coolie.

Liberal men and women united again (as in the challenge to foot-binding) to cauterise an image of women deeply embedded in the traditional culture. Intellectuals expressed the optimistic belief that now that women's unbound feet were on the path of progress, the eradication of the evil features of women's treatment characteristic of the past was at last a distinct possibility.[75] Chen Duxiu reflected the views of many modernists where he explained that under Con-fucianism 'Chinese women's bodies and spirits couldn't develop'.[76] Traditional beauty denied women their humanity. Now women should develop those sound qualities of body and mind historically denied them.

How were women's bodies to be improved? Physical exercise, physical education and sport once again attracted attention – this time from those of the May Fourth Era. In October 1915, Chen Duxiu published an influential article entitled 'The Aim of Today's Educa-tion' advocating 'animalism'. It was social Darwinism – Chinese-style. From the viewpoint of evolution, he declared, the human species is an animal which can only survive if strong. Modern education, therefore, should teach the young generation of *both* sexes how to survive, physically and mentally.[77] He criticised feudal education which had educated the brain not the body. Youth had become feeble. The Chinese race had joined the lower order of the human species. Chen Duxiu practised what he preached. As an educationist in his early adulthood in Wuhu city, Anhui province, he established two schools in 1912: Anhui gongxue [Anhui Public School] and Huizhou gongxue [Huizhou Public School]. In both schools the students did gymnastics for up to six hours a week.[78] Sometime later in 'On the Problems of Physical Education for Youth' in Xin qingnian [New Youth], Chen stressed the significance of participation in physical exercise.[79] The evolutionary ball kept rolling. It was kicked by others. In 1915, for example, the second Far-East Asian Games took place in Shanghai, and Wang Zhenting (1882–1961),[80] the Chairman of the

130

Games Committee, wrote an article after the Games proclaiming that sport was the foundation of a self-reliant nation and that women's sport was as important as men's in this regard.[81]

A major player now entered this 'evolutionary' game. In June 1917 Mao Zedong (1893–1976) published his essay, 'On Physical Education and Exercise' in *Xin qingnian* [New Youth]. For the first time, Mao expressed his views on the subject. First, he defined physical education as a tool to develop physical health. Second, like the earlier revolutionary and feminist, Chen Jiefen, he was prepared to assert that of the three elements of education, moral training, intellectual development and physical well-being, the *latter* was the most important. A healthy body was the basis of moral and intellectual development. Third, Mao asserted that with regard to physical deterioration external causes were to be distinguished from internal causes. Physical fitness must be based on a positive mind. People must want to be healthy before they can be. Fourth, Mao revealed a completely dismissive attitude towards traditional cultural exercises regarding them as unscientific remnants of feudal values. He argued that modern exercises educated people to be tough, to struggle, to deny defeat, to be strong and to be self-reliant. He criticised traditional educationists' negative attitudes to physical education and many people's lack of awareness of its importance. Finally, in a telling phrase with later resonances, he declared that to participate in exercise was to participate in revolution.[82] Although Mao did not deal directly in his article with the relationship between exercise and women's emancipation, his later insistence on the importance of exercise for communist men *and* women in their revolutionary struggle clearly had its origin in these early reflections.[83]

Mao Zedong was not unique in his arguments about priorities. Some months earlier, in January 1917, Cai Yuanpei (1868–1940), a well-known educationist, had delivered a speech at Shanghai Patriotic Girls School. In his speech Cai reviewed the history of the development of modern exercise in China. He claimed that modern exercise had helped Chinese youth develop the mental and physical resolution to overthrow feudal society and the Qing government. Physical exercise for girls had served the purposes of revolution before 1911. Now, subsequent to the founding of the Republic of China, exercise for girls was still very important, because only when women had strong bodies could they became fully independent and participate effectively in social affairs. Women should develop themselves, therefore, morally, mentally and physically and of these physical development was the most important. Footbinding had seriously limited the potential for freedom. Now women in the Republic of China should have the right to release their bodies and liberate their minds and become full citizens of the new society. At the end of his speech he pleaded for women's participation in exercise in the interest of themselves and society.[84] It was a theme that remained popular. Yang Xianjiang (1895–1931), for example, a progressive educationist and editor of *Xuesheng zazhi* [Student's Journal],[85] also took it upon himself to explore the relationship between physical exercise and women's emancipation. In 'Self-awareness, Youth and Exercise' published in *Xuesheng zazhi* in 1923, he argued that exercise did not simply develop women's bodies, but also helped to develop women's individualism. The two elements were intrinsically linked.[86]

So the chorus sang the same tune and echoes of it could be heard everywhere among the urban radicals. Numerous articles appeared in journals and newspapers.[87] One journal *Tiyu zhoubao* [Physical Education Weekly],[88] published in Changsha city, Hunan province, was founded for the explicit purpose of introducing new ideas about women to wider society. Many of its articles stressed the importance of physical education for women. A 1920 article, for example, entitled 'The Reason for the Slow Progress of Chinese Physical Education', declared that the Yuan de-emphasis in the school and college curriculum of female physical education had inhibited the progress of Chinese physical education.[89] Women's deprivation was China's deprivation.

From Conservatism to Liberalism: Women, Education and Exercise

Under the pressing advocacy of these radicals and radical journalism, women themselves once more began to view participation in exercise as an integral part of their emancipation. Cai Chang was an early and influential case in point. Cai Chang (1900–91), who later became a communist leader and the Chairwoman of the All-China's Women's Federation in 1949, came from a lower middle class family. Her father treated her mother as a slave. Influenced by the 1911 Revolution and the ideals of women's emancipation, her mother, then 50 years old, determined to provide an education not only for her three children but for herself. She sold the clothes and silver and gold heirlooms of her dowry to realise money for them to go to school. When Cai

Chang's mother, with bound feet, first entered the school at Chasha, the capital of Hunan province, she was told compassionately that she did not need to take physical exercise classes. But she refused this offer and participated, even though her bound feet made this a tragic joke especially in dancing and athletics. After two years of study, Cai's mother graduated from the higher primary school and went back to her village and in 1913 opened up a school there. In *her* school, physical education was compulsory.

Cai Chang was a pupil at the school. She was keen on sport. Her father wanted to force her into an arranged marriage. Her mother resisted. She had no intention of submitting her daughter to out-moded social practices. She helped her daughter escape to Changsha where Cai entered the Zhounan Girls' School in 1914, a radical girls' school founded by students who had trained in Japan. Cai Chang trained to be a physical education teacher. When she graduated she taught the subject in the lower primary school attached to Zhounan Girls' School for four years before she went to France to pursue her revolutionary career. The motive behind the extraordinary efforts of Cai's mother to obtain an education for herself and for her children, as Cai herself later explained, lay in her mother's realisation that she had been exploited and oppressed by the old feudal family system and culture. She was obdurate that she and her children would escape through education.[90] In her view, and that of her daughter, physical education was a crucial part of the curriculum. The body had to be strong for the mind to be active. It was important to develop both. *Both* body and mind were symbols of freedom.[91] A further reason for her espousal of physical education, of course, lay in the fact that economic independence was part and parcel of successful personal liberation. School teaching was one way to achieve both.[92]

Meanwhile, in the wider field of education, influenced by the new ideals of 'democracy', 'science' and 'equality', attempts to overcome sexual discrimination continued.[93] Before 1919 there were no state universities for women in China.[94] In 1919, Deng Chunlan and Wanglan Xizhen, students of Beijing Girls' Normal School, sent letters to Cai Yuanpei, Chancellor of Beijing University, to request permission to study at the university. Cai Yanpei, as mentioned above, had already taken a personal interest in the Patriotic Girls' School in Shanghai and readily gave them permission to enrol. The following year, for the first time, Beijing University and Nanjing Normal University both formally permitted female students to register. On 12

May 1919, the Ministry of Education announced that females could register at all state universities.[95] This marked the first real opening of university doors to women students. In 1921 there were 651 female students studying in 31 Chinese-controlled universities.[96] Meanwhile, co-education in elementary schools had begun to be implemented throughout the country.[97] In 1906 there were 306 female pupils in the Chinese-controlled primary and middle schools, 180,949 in 1915 and 417,820 in 1922.[98] The objectives of female education changed as well. Before the May Fourth Era, as already discussed, the purpose of female education was to train women to be good wives and effective mothers. The curriculum included sewing, cooking, nursing and home economics. In the May Fourth Era women demanded change. They wanted professional training in order to survive successfully in society. Their demands were met. Male and female students now shared the same curriculum with educational institutions offering opportunities to students irrespective of their sex.[99] The pendulum was once more swinging from conservatism to liberalism, from regression to progression, from continuity to change.

On 1 November 1922, the Ministry of Education issued 'The Decree of the Reformation of the School System'.[100] This new school system drew heavily on American educational ideas and John Dewey's pragmatic education now dominated Chinese schools. Both the traditional Chinese education system and the regimented Japanese school system were anathema to the ideologues of a developing democratic society. The result was a complete transformation of Chinese education. The new school system emphasised that education must suit the needs of social evolution and pay attention to developing individualism in pupils. In 1923, the New Curriculum was issued and published in the *Education Journal*. The New Curriculum abolished military gymnastics in schools and 'Gymnastics' became known as 'Physical Education and Sport'. This course now included ball games, track and field, gymnastics, physiology and hygiene. The new system also made it clear that male and female had same right to participate in education, physical education and sport.[101] This 'Decree' was another important milestone on the long road of women's physical emancipation and it has not received the attention it deserves. Physical emancipation was as important in the context of the times to Chinese women as any other form of emancipation. The progressives' preoccupation with exercise was not an idle one. As argued above it had its cultural logic.

While an enlarged programme of physical education was now part of the reformed education system in China, there were considerable differences of opinion about the types and amount of exercise appropriate for pubescent girls, and an extended debate regarding the degree of compulsion and time to be devoted to it.[102] Nevertheless, a striking indication of the change in the attitudes of educators and the public to female exercise was the fact that some girls' schools and colleges now boasted excellent playing-fields and gymnasia.[103] One to two hours of exercise a day became common and female students took part in modern sports activities, such as basketball, volleyball, tennis, athletics and swimming.[104] When Grace Seton, a feminist writer, visited China in 1923, she found that 'The girls of today are indeed different from those of twenty years ago'. They were healthy. They enjoyed modern physical activities. They even joined athletic associations.[105] Lady Dorothea Hosie observed at about the same time: 'Oh, the lovely new Chinese girlhood! . . . The laughter of those girls at their sports, the memory of their free limbs and careless lithesomeness. Oh happy games . . . Chinese girls played with free hearts.'[106]

These developments once again urgently required professional female physical educationists.[107] New specialist physical education colleges, therefore, were opened to train female physical education teachers. Cai Yuanpei founded the Physical Education Institute attached to the Patriotic Girls' School in Shanghai in 1916, and Qin Xinhua, a female physical educationist, opened the Physical Education School of the North–South YMCA. Since the progressives believed that women's emancipation should start with physical liberation, more women's physical education training schools were enthusiastically founded.[108] These physical education institutes had one-year or two-year courses.[109] The students learned several subjects, including Chinese language and literature, English, history, education, psychology, physiology, gymnastics, athletics, dance, games, martial arts and swimming.[110] The aims of these physical education institutes were to provide women with opportunities for intellectual and physical development and to establish equal professional career opportunities with men. In the New Culture and May Fourth Movements female physical education teaching became a commonplace occupation.

These women physical educationists not only taught their female students how to exercise, but also attempted to convey to them 'the spirit of sport': self-respect, self-control, self-realisation.[111] For some students who assimilated this 'spirit', the consequent self-development

A women's volleyball match at the First Women's Championship in Beijing in 1923. (From Zhuang Bingsong, a female physical education teacher, a participant in the competition.)

was profound. Women's sport, which for years had been confined to a small, élite group and to an educational setting which insulated it from public view, came more to the front of the social stage. In 1916, Shanghai Patriotic Girls' School sent its basketball team to attend Jiangshu Provincial Competition Games in Yangzhou city.[112] In 1922, Beijing Women's Normal University held an open Internal Sports Competition, which included almost all of the traditional men's sports. The press next day reported, 'If you really want to know what equality means, go to the Sports Competition at the Beijing Women's Normal University'. It commented further that women had now demonstrated their ability to share the world with men.[113] In 1923, the First Women's Championship was held in Beijing.[114] In the same year, a Chinese Women's Volleyball Team attended the sixth Far East Asian Games in Japan. This was the first time that Chinese female athletes appeared on the international sports stage.[115] In 1924, when the third national Games took place in Wuchang, Hubei province, Chinese women athletes took part, for the first time, in the basketball, volleyball and softball competitions.[116]

The Missing Link! Bodies, Exercise and Emancipation

Female participation in physical exercise and competitive sport, it is suggested, had particular significance for women's emancipation and the May Fourth Era. Although studies of Chinese women[117] have observed that women challenged certain fundamental elements of the feudal system and culture – demanding marital reform, the freedom to love and to divorce, the right to vote and to education – not one of these commentators has pointed out the crucial relationship between exercise, women's bodies and women's emancipation in this period. Only Helen Snow's *Women in China* (1960)[118] and Bobby Siu's *Fifty Years of Struggle: the Development of the Women's Movements in China 1900–1949* (1975) have given the relationship a passing glance, and a superficial one at that.[119] They have all missed the essential point that the pursuit of physical freedom was an integral part of women's emancipation in China. The importance of the relationship between the New Culture and May Fourth Movements, women's physical freedom and women's emancipation has also been overlooked by more general historians.[120] They mention women's liberation in this period, but have wholly failed to do justice to the importance of female physical emancipation. In fact, they have mostly ignored it. Arguably, this fact says more about Western and Eastern intellectual traditions than it does about the actuality of Chinese history.

To say this is not to make a disproportionate but rather a proportionate claim for consideration of the relevance of physical freedom in the lives of Chinese women. It was not fortuitous that the Yuan regime proscribed girls' physical education in schools. It was a particularly unwelcome manifestation of undesirable femininity: modern, active, assertive. It denied old values, beliefs, norms. It proclaimed a new image that represented an unacceptable demeanour on *and* off the playing-fields. Its power was both its vitality and its visibility. It was dangerous on both counts. Here is its cultural significance. To understand fully its importance, we have to go back to where we began. The predicament of being born a woman in Chinese feudal society was specific. The ideal image of women's beauty prevented women's development, physically and mentally, and led to sustained domination by men. The oppression of women, through the mechanism of footbinding, came from imposed limitations on physical capacity. Consequently, the concepts of the fragile female, the weak body and 'handicapped biology' were formulated in a male-dominated culture. To have a chance of progress in their oppressive situation it was necessary for women to recognise both how domination had come about and how it had been maintained. There were social imperatives determining women's 'nature' to be recognised and rebutted. For this reason, arguments concerning the capabilities of women's bodies were at the analytical heart of women's liberation – and successful access to, and participation in physical exercise played a major part in the emancipation of the female body and mind. It provided incontrovertible evidence in support of change, it offered an instrument of rebuttal of gender mythologies, and it ensured a means to a new physical, psychological and cultural identity.

Of course, it was not all sweetness and light. Well into the twentieth century, women's involvement in exercise remained circumscribed by outworn social values and sanctions that reinforced a negative attitude to women by perpetuating myths about male superiority and female inferiority. But while exercise – or denial of access to it – could act as a potent idiom of conformity, it could also be a deviant activity, a channel for expressing hostility to social norms. In the May Fourth Era women's participation in exercise involved, consciously and unconsciously, affirmation of the rights of the individual woman and the general worth of the female sex. Participation in exercise, hedged about as it was by compromises with the social system, was symbolic both of active progress in the war of women's emancipation and of battles yet to be won. There was more than a chance relationship between women's acceptance on sports fields and in gymnasia *and* in other social situations. Exercise heightened women's consciousness of the capabilities of their own bodies, increased the level of their physical power, and provided a psychological confidence that spilt over into other areas of life. However, while these assertions are made with confidence, the limited nature of their applicability requires continual emphasis. They apply to only a favoured and fortunate few. The mass of women, especially in the rural areas, remained largely unaffected. It was the daughters of the urban privileged, for the most part, who constituted an emancipatory vanguard – sometimes, abruptly halted, occasionally in temporary retreat but eventually and inexorably moving forward – well in advance of the large army of peasant and worker women.

Conclusion

The New Culture and May Fourth Movements taught women about the concept of individual freedom. It provided a new climate, in which women could continue the attempt to free themselves from feudalism and gave them further opportunities to develop themselves physically and mentally. Women's participation in exercise, once again, presented them in non-traditional roles and provided important visible modifications to the feminine ideal: assertion, energy and action. Exercise brought women individual feelings of self-respect and self-awareness which were – in a wider context – the prevailing characteristics of the New Culture and May Fourth Movements. This consequence of individual participation in exercise for personal well-being rather than practical social purpose distinguished the women's emancipation movement of this period. In this way women's exercise had a special and specific cultural meaning for their emancipation in the May Fourth Era.

Notes

1. Jian, Bozan, op. cit., pp.177–8; Gray, Jack, op. cit., p.149.
2. Rodzinski, Witold, op. cit., p.269; Spence, Jonathan. D., *The Search for Modern China*, op. cit., pp.287–90; Moise, Edwin E., op. cit., pp.44–7.
3. Ye, Xiaoqin, 'Zhongguo chuantong wenhua zai jindai' [Chinese Traditional Culture in Modern Times], *Lishi yanjiu* [History Study], No. 1, 1986, pp.105–106.
4. Teng, Ssu-yu, 'Introduction: A Decade of Challenge', in Chan, F. Gilbert and Etzold, Thomas H. (eds), *China in the 1920s*, New York: New Viewpoints, 1976, p.1.
5. For a brief introduction see notes 49, 51, 60, 66, 69 of this chapter. Hu Shi went to the United States to study in 1910. In 1902, Chen Duxiu and Lu Xun went to Japan to study. Wu Yu went to Japan in 1905. Li Daozhao, coming from a poor peasant family, could not find the means to study abroad until 1913. Study abroad turned out to be a catalyst in their transformation into revolutionaries. In foreign countries young Chinese intellectuals experienced vibrant and prosperous nations – a vibrancy that heightened their awareness of China's cultural backwardness.
6. Schwartz, Benjamin I., 'Introduction', in Schwartz, Benjamin I. (ed.), *Reflections on the May Fourth Movement: A Symposium*, Cambridge, MA: East Asian Research Centre, Harvard University Press, 1972, p.7.
7. Lu Xun called the adoption of these values 'Nalai zhuyi' [Bring-it-here-ism]. Mabel Lee saw it as a symbol of the spirit of the May Fourth Movement. See Lee, Mabel. 'May Fourth: Symbol of the Spirit of Bring-it-here-ism for Chinese Intellectuals', *Far Eastern History* (Australia), Vol. 41, 1990, pp.77–96. Also see Lin, Yu-sheng, *The Crisis of Chinese Consciousness: Radical Anti-traditionalism*

    in the May Fourth Era, Madison: University of Wisconsin Press, 1979, p.156; Vera Schwarcz, *The Chinese Enlightenment*, op. cit., p.38.

8. Li, Kai, 'Guanyu Zhongguo jindai wenhuashi de jige wenti' [On the Question of Modern Chinese Culture], *Jingtu xuekan* [The Journal of Tianjing Universities], No. 1, Sept. 1983, p.121. And Jian, Bozan, op. cit., p.179.

9. *Xin qingnian* [New Youth] published in 15 September 1915. Its original name was *Qingnian* [The Youth]. It was renamed as *Xin qingnian* in 1916. Chen Duxiu was its founder and chief editor. It was the principal forum of the New Culture and the May Fourth Movements between 1915–19. After the Chinese Communist Party was founded in Shanghai in 1921, *Xin qingnian* became the mouthpiece of the Chinese Communist Party. It stopped in 1926.

10. The symbol of the beginning of the New Culture Movement was the publication of *Xin qingnian* [New Youth] in 1915. See Lo, R.Y., *China's Revolution from the Inside*, New York: The Abingdon Press, 1930, pp.50–6; Jian Buozan, op. cit., p.178.

11. Chen, Duxiu, 'Xianfa yu kongjiao' [Constitution and Confucianism], *Xin qingnian* [New Youth], Vol. 2, No. 3, Nov. 1917, pp.6–7.

12. Lo, R.Y. China's Revolution from the Inside, op. cit., pp.56–7.

13. Hu, Shi, 'Wenxue gaige chuyi' [My View On Literary Revolution], *Xin qingnian* [New Youth], Vol. 2, No. 5, Jan. 1917, pp.3–5.

14. Chen, Duxiu, 'Wenxue geming lun' [On Literary Revolution], *Xin qingnian* [New Youth], Vol. 2, No. 6, Feb. 1917, pp.1–3.

15. Lo, R.Y., op. cit., pp.58–9.

16. Hu, Sheng, op. cit, pp.1190–91; Jian, Buozhan, op. cit., p.180.

17. Quoted in Lo, R.Y., op. cit., p.59.

18. Mao, Zedong, 'Xin minzhu zhuyi lun' [On the New Democracy], in *Mao Zedong xuanji* [Selected Works of Mao Zedong], Beijing: Remin Chubanshe [People's Press], Vol. 2, 1963, p.704.

19. See Kwok, D.W.Y., *Scientism in Chinese Thought, 1900–1950*, New Haven: Yale University Press, 1965, *passim*.

20. See Grieder, Jerome, *Hu Shih and the Chinese Renaissance: Liberalism and the Chinese Revolution, 1917–1937*, Cambridge, MA: Harvard University Press, 1970, *passim*.

21. See Uberol, Patricia, '"Science", "Democracy" and the Cosmology of the May Fourth Movement', *China Report*, Vol. 23, No. 4 1987, p.378. Also see Schwartz, Benjamin, 'Chen Tu-hsiu and the Acceptance of the Modern West', *Journal of the History of Ideals*, Vol. 12, 1951, pp.16–74.

22. Chen, Duxiu, '1916 nian' [1916], *Xin qingnian* [New Youth], Vol. 1, No. 5, 1916, pp.3–5.

23. Chow, Tse-tsung, *The May Fourth Movement: Intellectual Revolution in Modern China*, op. cit., p.307.

24. Sun, Zhongshan [Sun Yat-sen or Sun Yatsen], 'Zhi haiwai guomindang tongzhi han', [A Message to the Overseas Comrades of Guomindong], in *Sun Zhongshan quanji* [Collected Works of Sun Zhongshan], Beijing: Renmin Chubanshe, Vol. 5, 1981, p.210.

25. Hu, Sheng, op. cit., pp.1188–203.

26. Twenty-one demands were issued by Japan in January 1915, in which it demanded economic rights for the Japanese in Manchuria, the right to station police and economic advisers in Manchuria, and major economic concessions in China proper. The demands were accepted by the government of Yuan Shikai in spite of popular Chinese protest.

27. Before the Peace Conference opened in Paris in January 1919, President Wilson

of the United States announced fourteen points which promised the creation of a new international order and the future protection of weak nations against the rapacity of the strong.

28. See Hu, Sheng, op. cit., pp.1194–95.
29. See Hu, Sheng, op. cit., pp.1196–97; Spence, Jonathan. D., *The Search for Modern China*, op. cit., p.293; Gray, Jack. op. cit., pp.198–9.
30. Spence, Jonathan. D., *The Search for Modern China*, op. cit., p.310.
31. Bernal, Martin, *Chinese Socialism to 1907*, Ithaca: Cornell University Press, 1976, p.6; see also Irene, Eber, 'Thoughts on Renaissance in Modern China: Problems of Definition', *Studia Asiatica*, No. 3, 1976, p.189.
32. Quoted in Schwarcz, Vera, *The Chinese Enlightenment*, op. cit., p.7.
33. Croll, E., *Feminism and Socialism in China*, op. cit., Ch. 5; Snow, Helen, *Women in Modern China*, op. cit., *passim*.
34. For further details of the yin–yang doctrine see the Prologue of this book.
35. See Croll, E., *Feminism and Socialism in China*, op. cit., p.12.
36. Kristeva, J., op. cit., pp.74–5.
37. Hobhouse, J., *Morals in Evolution*, New York: 1906. pp.179–80, 183 ff.; see also Lang, Olga, *Chinese Family and Society*, Archon Books, 1968, p.43.
38. 'Indian Law', in *Encyclopaedia Britannica* (14th ed.), xii, pp.231 ff. See Lang, Olga. ibid.
39. See the *Jewish Encyclopedia*, New York, 1903, V.338; see also Lang, Olga, ibid., p.44.
40. Goodsell, J., *A History of Marriage and the Family*, New York, 1934, pp.133–9.
41. Ibid., pp.205, 207, 208, 225; see also Lang, Olga, op. cit., p.44.
42. See Lang, Olga, ibid., pp.44–5.
43. Ibid., p.54.
44. Quoted in ibid., p.55.
45. Hsu, Francis L.K., *Under the Ancestors' Shadow*, New York: Columbia University Press, 1948, p.260.
46. Kriteva, J., op. cit., p.75.
47. Quoted in Snow, Helen, *Women in Modern China*, op. cit., p.235.
48. Dean, Irene, 'The Women's Movement in China', *The Chinese Recorder*, Vol. 58, No. 10, Oct. 1927, p.653.
49. Wu Yu (1871–1949) was born in Chengdu, Sichuan province. He went to Japan to study in 1905 and was influenced by Western liberal and democratic ideas there. His book, *Discussions of the Intellectual Trends in the Song and Yuan Dynasties*, was full of anti-Confucian ideas and was banned from sale by the Ministry of Education of the Qing government. In 1913 he edited the *Awaken-the-Masses Magazine* in Chengdu. This was also suppressed by the government because of its unconventional opinions. In 1906 Wu Yu was impressed by the anti-Confucian stand of *New Youth* and contacted Chen Duxiu. His anti-Confucian articles were published in *New Youth* from 1917 onwards. From 1919 to mid-1920, Wu Yu was invited to teach at Beijing University. Then he returned to Chengdu and taught at Chengdu University and the National Sichuan University. Among his published works are: *Wu Yu wenpinglu*, [Collected Essays of Wu Yu], Chengdu, 1936; *Wu Yu wenxulu* [Supplements], Chengdu, 1937; and a collection of poems, *Qiu shui ji* [The Autumn Water], Chengdu, 1913. Many of his essays were written in the vernacular.
50. Wu Yu, 'Jiating zhidu wei zhuanzhi zhuyi zhi genjudi' [The Family System is the Foundation of Authoritarianism], *Xin qingnian* [New Youth], Vol. 2, No. 6, Feb. 1916, pp.1–4.
51. Chen Duxiu (1880–1942) was born into a wealthy official family in Anhui

province. He was trained initially as a classical scholar but failed the province-level exams in 1897. He went to Japan to study in 1902. There he refused to join Sun Yat-sen's Revolutionary Alliance which he regarded as narrowly racist. Prominent in opposition to Yuan Shikai's imperial ambitions, he founded the journal *New Youth* in 1915 in Shanghai. In 1917 Cai Yuanpei, the Principal of the Beijing University, invited him to be a faculty dean at Beijing University. Meanwhile, as chief editor of *New Youth*, which rapidly became the most influential intellectual journal in China, he espoused bold theoretical investigation, a spirited attack on the past, and a highly moralistic approach to politics through the cleansing of the individual character. After the May Fourth student demonstration, Chen was jailed for three months by the Beijing authorities on a charge of distributing inflammatory literature. On his release, Chen left Beijing for Shanghai. He now became interested in Marxism and was eager for swift social change. In 1920 he was to become one of the first members of the new Chinese Communist Party and he was its first General-Secretary. In 1927, he was expelled from the Party because of his conservatism. He died in Jianjin county, Sichuan province in 1942.

52. Chen, Duxiu, 'Jin gao qingnian' [Call to Youth], *Qingnian* [The Youth], No. 1, Sept. 1915, p.2. English translation in Teng, Ssu-yu and Fairbank, John K., *China's Response to the West: A Documentary Survey, 1839–1923*, op. cit., pp.240–46.

53. Xie Wuliang was a prolific literary historian in the New Culture and May Fourth Movements. He joined the group of intellectuals centred around Chen Duxiu and *New Youth*. He published the first history of literature written by Chinese women in Shanghai in Oct. 1916. The book was entitled *Zhongguo funu wenxue shi* [A History of Chinese Women's Literature]. He was concerned with the social position of women, published several articles in *New Youth* and advocated women's emancipation in China.

54. Xie, Wuliang, *Zhongguo funu wenxie shi* [A History of Chinese Women's Literature], Shanghai, 1916, p.2.

55. Tao Menghe, 'Nuzi wenti' [Women's Problems], *Xin qingnian* [New Youth], Vol. 4, No. 1, Jan. 1918, pp.13–19.

56. Zhou Zuoren (1885–1967) was the brother of Lu Xun. He went to Japan to study in 1906 and married a Japanese wife. From 1917 he taught in Beijing University, Yanjing University and Beijing Women's Normal University respectively. He was famous for his essays, short stories and novels.

57. Zhou Zuoren, 'Zhenchao lun' [On Chastity], *Xin qingnian* [New Youth], Vol. 4, No. 5, May 1918, pp.2–6.

58. Su, Wu, 'Zhou Zuoren de funu jiefang guan' [Zhuo Zhuoren and his View of Women's Liberation], *Lishi yangiu* [History Study], No. 3, 1956, p.23.

59. After Zhou, Hu Shi published his 'Zhenchao wenti' [On Chastity], and Tang Yi, an influential journalist, published his 'Wo de jielie guang' [My View on Chastity] in *New Youth*. These articles stimulated a nationwide discussion about women's chastity in *Guomin rebao* [People's Daily] from 1918 and 1919.

60. Lu Xun, (1881–1936), whose real name was Zhou Shuren, was born in 1881 into a lower middle-class family in Shaoxing, Zhejiang province. His education combined the traditional with the modern. Confucian schooling was part of his childhood. In 1898, at the age of eighteen, he entered the Naval Academy in Nanjing, one of the new institutions teaching Western science and technology. In 1901, he was awarded a government scholarship for further study in Japan. At Kobun College, Tokyo, Lu Xun read voraciously in Western philosophy, political science and literature. In 1904 he went to Sendai to study medicine,

in the hope of popularising modern science (and avoiding in the future the inadequacies of traditional treatment which had killed his father).

However, in 1906 he saw a slide of the execution of a Chinese person during the Russo-Japanese War, and was staggered by the apathy of the Chinese onlookers. To cure disease now seemed less important than to arouse his fellow-countrymen; and he felt that literature was the best tool for this purpose. Thus from the start the aim of his writings was political: to awaken and enlighten the Chinese people. In 1918 he published his story, 'A Madman's Diary', in *New Youth*, an impassioned call to resist the Confucian 'man-eating culture'. He followed this with the essay, 'My Views on Chastity'. This was the real start of his literary career and when he began using the pen-name Lu Xun. In 1919 Lu Xun helped to launch the May Fourth Movement. One Chinese writer has remarked that 'Lu Xun's place in the May Fourth Movement of China was like Voltaire's in the French Enlightenment'.His *The True Story of Ah Kiu* was compared by a Western writer with Voltaire's *Candide*. Mao Zedong has called him ' The chief commander of China's cultural revolution . . . not only a great man of letters but a great thinker and revolutionary'; and elsewhere, 'the bravest and most correct, the firmest, the most loyal and the most ardent national hero, a hero without parallel in our history'. See Mao Zedong, 'Xinminzhu zhuyi lun' [On the New Democracy], in *Mao Zedong xuanji* [Selected Works of Mao Zedong], Beijing, op. cit, Vol. 1, p.78.

61. Lu, Xun, 'Kuangren riji' [A Madman's Diary], in Yang, Gladys (trans. and ed.), *Silent China : Selected Writings of Lu Xun*, London: Oxford University Press, 1973, pp.3–13.

62. Lu, Xun, 'Wode jielie guan' [My Views on Chastity], in Yang, Gladys, ibid., pp.137–47.

63. Liu, Balong. 'Nangui zagan' [Thoughts on Coming Back from the South], *Xin qingnian* [New Youth], Vol. 5, No. 2, Aug. 1918.

64. Luo Jialun (1896–1969) was an important figure in the May Fourth Movement, a leader of student demonstrations. He later became president of Qinghua University (1928–30) and then of the Nationalist Central University (1932–41). Before his death in Taiwan, he held the prominent post of Director of the National History Museum with special responsibility for the Nationalist Party archives.

65. Luo, Jialun. 'Lun funu jiefang' [On Women's Liberation], *Xin cao* [The New Tide], No. 3, 1917, pp.3–5.

66. Hu Shi (1891–1962), writer, philosopher and a leading figure of the New Culture and the May Fourth Movements. He came from a privileged family in Anhui province. In his childhood he had a Chinese classic education. Later, he studied in Westernised schools in Shanghai. In 1910, at the age of 19, he was awarded a scholarship to study in the United States. He took his BA in philosophy at Cornell University and then enrolled at Columbia University to study philosophy with, among others, John Dewey. He returned to China in 1917 and became a professor of philosophy at Beijing University. He later served as the Nationalist government's ambassador to the United States from 1938 to 1942.

67. Grieder, Jerome, op. cit., p.101.

68. Hu, Shi, 'Meiguo de furen' [American Women], *Xin qingnian* [New Youth], Vol. 5, No. 3, Sept. 1918, pp.4–6.

69. Li Dazhao (1889–1927) was an important figure of the May Fourth Movement. He was an early Chinese Marxist. He returned from Japan in 1908 as director of the Beijing University library and co-editor of *New Youth*. He was a mentor

and ally of radical students, who often held their meetings in his office. After the May Fourth events, Li soon became a founder of the Chinese Communist Party. He was captured and executed in Beijing by the warlord Zhang Zhuolin in 1927.

70. Li Dazhao, 'Funu jiefang yu minzu' [Women's Liberation and Democracy], *Shaonian zhongguo* [China's Youth], Vol. 1, No. 4, 1919, pp.27–8.

71. Hu, Shi, 'Yipushe zhuyi' [Ibsenism], *Xin qingnian* [New Youth], Vol. 4, No. 6, June, 1918, pp.2–6.

72. Eide, Elisabeth, 'Ibsen's Nora and Chinese Interpretation of Female Emancipation', in Malmgvist, Goran (ed.), *Literature and Its Social Context*, New York: Nobel Foundation and Plenum Press, 1978, p.141.

73. One of the best examples was Ding Ling. In 1922 she left home in Hunan and travelled first to Nanjing and Shanghai, and then to Beijing. There she lived an emancipated life with the aspiring poet Hu Yepin among a group of writers and artists, apparently the very model of a Nora who had successfully left home. See Spence, Jonathan D., *The Search for Modern China*, op. cit., p.411; Snow, Helen, *The Modern Chinese Women*, op. cit., pp.204–12.

74. Lu, Xun, 'Nora chuzho yihuo?' [What Happens after Nora Leaves Home?], in Yang, Gladys, op. cit., pp.137–47.

75. Ibid.

76. Chen, Duxiu, 'Kongzi yu xiandai shenhuo' [Confucian and Modern life], *Xin qingnian* [New Youth], Vol. 2, No. 12, Dec. 1916, pp.12–15.

77. Chen, Duxiu, 'Jinri zhi jiaoyu fangzheng' [The Aim of Today's Education], *Qingnian zazhi* [Journal of Youth], Vol. 1, No. 2. 15 Oct. 1915.

78. CSHSPE, *Zhongguo jindai tiyu shi* [Modern Chinese Sports History], op. cit., p.182.

79. Chen, Duxiu, 'Qinnian tiyu wenti' [On the Problems of Physical Education for Youth], *Xin qingnian* [New Youth], Vol. 7, No. 1, Jan. 1920, pp.3–4. In this article Chen advocated physical exercise for youth, but he disapproved of competitive sport.

80. Wang Zhenting, (1882–1961), educated in the United States, was a major figure in the Chinese YMCA who later became a key figure in Chinese politics and sports. He was the Foreign Minister of the Guomindang government. He approved of the development of modern physical education and sport in China. He was the first Chinese representative on the IOC (International Olympic Committee). He was the Chairman of the Chinese Olympic Committee for many years.

81. Wang, Zhenting, 'Direchi yuandong yundonghui zhi gangyan' [My View of the second Far-East Olympic Games], *Jinbu* [Progress], Vol. 8, No. 3, July 1915.

82. Mao, Zedong, 'Tiyu zhi yanjiu' [On Physical Education and Exercise], *Xin qingnian* [New Youth], Vol. 3, No. 4, April 1917, pp.5–12.

83. See Chapters 5 and 6 of this book; see also Witke, R., 'Mao Zse-tung [Mao Zedong], Women and Suicide in the May Fourth Era', *China Quarterly*, No. 31, July–Sept. 1967, pp.128–47; Ono Kazuko, op. cit., pp.100–101, 225; Han, Suyin, *The Morning Deluge: Mao Tsetung [Mao Zedong] and the Chinese Revolution, 1893–1954*, Boston: Little, Brown and Company, 1972, pp.51–2, 78–9.

84. Cai Yuanpei's speech was published in *Dongfan zazhi* [The East], Vol. 4, No. 1, Jan. 1917.

85. Yang Xianjiang (1895–1931) was a progressive educationalist and Chinese Communist Party member. He was the editor of several journals, such as *Shaonian shijie* [The World of Youth], *Xueshu shijie* [Academic World], *Laodong*

shijie [Labours' World], *Xuieshen zazhi* [Student's Journal] and *Zhongguo qingnian* [China's Youth]. He published many articles about education. His books included *Xin jiaoyu dagang* [Outline of Modern Education] and *Jiaoyu A.B.C.* [Education A.B.C.].

86. Yan, Xianjiang, 'Qingnian duiyu tiyu zhi zhijue' [The Self-awareness of Youth to Exercise], *Xuesheng zazhi* [Student's Journal], Vol. 10. No. 4, 1923, pp.1–6.

87. To name merely a few: 'On Women's Physical Education,' in *Chen bao* [Morning News] 28 March 1921; 'On Women's Physical Exercise', in *Xue deng* [Study Guide] June 1920; 'The Contribution of Women's Physical Educators', in *Funu pinglun* [Women's Review], 14 March 1922; 'My View Point of Women's Physical Education' in *Funu pinglun*, 9 May 1923; 'Real Beauty from Physical Exercise', in *Funu pinglun*, 14 May, 1923.

88. *Tiyu zhoubao* [Physical Education Weekly] was founded on 9 December 1918 by Huang Xin, a physical educator of Cuyi School in Changsha, and other progressive educationists in Hunan. Huang Xin was its editor. It was an influential journal. Some important figures of the May Fourth Movement such as Chen Duxiu, Cai Yuanpei, and radicals such as Mao Zedong, Yun Daiyin and educationists such as Xu Yibin wrote articles for this journal. It stopped publication on 25 October, 1920.

89. The original article has not been found. However, it re-appeared in *Xuiedeng – tiyu zhuanhao* [Knowledge – Physical Education, Special Issue], 25 Dec. 1922.

90. Cai Chang and her mother's story are both described in Snow, Helen, *Women in Modern China*, pp.233–6.

91. Ding Ling, a famous Chinese female writer, and her mother's story also reflected the changing image of women in this period. See Spence, Jonathan D., *The Gate of Heavenly Peace: the Chinese and their Revolution*, New York: the Viking Press, 1987, pp.163–217; Snow, Helen, *Women in Modern China*, op. cit., pp.198–257; see also note 73 above.

92. Chen, Dongyuan, *Zhongguo funu shenhuo shi* [History of the Life of Women in China], Shangwu yinshu guan [Commercial Press], 1937, p.396.

93. Ibid., p.388.

94. Chen Jinpan, op. cit., p.229.

95. See Cheng, Zhefan, *Zhongguo xiandai nuzi jiaoyu shi* [A History of Contemporary Women's Education in China], Shanghai: Zhonghua shuju, 1936, p.105.

96. Chen, Dongyuan, op. cit., p.389.

97. Co-education started in 1912, but wasn't popular in the country especially in the rural areas, because of the influence of Confucianism. After the May Fourth Movement, Confucianism was challenged and modern educational ideas were gradually accepted in rural areas. Consequently, co-education began to be practised throughout the whole country. Also see Chen, Dongyan, op. cit., p.388.

98. Chen, Jinpan, op. cit., p.305.

99. Shen, Shifu and Jian, Menglin, 'Jiaoyu zhongzhi yanju an' [The Aim of Education], April 1919, in *Diyichi Zhongguo jiaoyu nianjian* [The First Year Book of Chinese Education], Vol. 1, Oct. 1933, p.9; CSHI, *Zhongguo jindai tiyushi zhiliaoji* [Modern Chinese Sports History Reference], op. cit., pp.387–8.

100. CSHSPE, *Zhongguo jindai tiyu shi* [Modern Chinese Sports History], op. cit., pp.117–18.

101. Ibid.

102. Hao, Gengsheng, 'Shinian lai woguo zhi tiyu, 1917–1927' [On the Development of Physical Education in China, 1917–1927], *Tiyu* [Sport], Vol. 1, No. 2, 1927, pp.2–3.

103. For example, according to 'The Report of China's Physical Education and Sport, 1917–1927', Shanghai West-East Girls' School, Nanjing Women's University, Fuzhou Huanan Women's University and Beijing Yanjing Women's University had superb gymnasia and sports facilities. Ibid., p.4.

104. Yang, Zhikang, 'Wusi xin wenhua yundong he nuzi tiyu de fazan' [The May Fourth Movenment and Chinese Women's Emancipation', in CSHPES, *Lunwen ji* [Selected Works], op. cit, Vol. 3, 1986, p.96.

105. Seton, Grace Thompson, *Chinese Lanterns*, London: John Lane, The Bodley Head, 1924, pp.250–51.

106. Lady Dorothea Hosie, *Portrait of a Chinese Lady*, London: Hodder and Stoughton, 1929, pp.125–6.

107. Hao, Gengshen, 'Shinian lai woguo zhi tiyu, 1917–1927' [On the Development of Physical Education in China , 1917–1927], op. cit., p.5.

108. These included Dongya [East Asian] Women's Physical Education Institute (1916), The Republic Women's Gymnastic Institute (1916), Guangdong Women's Sport School (1917), Zhejiang Women's Gymnastic Institute attached Pucheng School (1917), Zheyang Women's Physical Education Institute (1920), Shanghai Liangjiang Woman's Physical Education College (1920), and the Sport Department Of Xinhua Arts School (1925).

109. See 'Tiyu shizhi zhi peiyang' [On Physical Educationists' Training], in *Di re ci zhongguo jiaoyu nianjian* [The Second Yearbook of Chinese Education], 1948, p.1320; also see CSHI, *Zhongguo jindai tiyushi zhiliaoji* [Modern Chinese Sports History Reference], op. cit., p.285.

110. CSHI, ibid., pp.308, 313, 317–21.

111. Xu, Yibin, 'Zhengdun tiyu shang jiaoyubu wen [Proposal to Consolidate Physical Education], *Tiyu zhazhi* [Sports Journal], No. 2, June 1914, p.1; Cai, Yuanpei, 'Tiyu wei xiu ji zhi ben' [Physical Exercise is the Foundation of Personal Development], in CSHSPE, *Zhongguo jidai tiyu wenxuan* [Selected Writings of Physical Education in Modern China], Beijing: Renmin tiyu chubanshe [People's Sport Press], 1992, pp.19–20.

112. Lin, Shitong, *Zhongguo tiyu wu qian nian* [Chinese Sports History], op. cit., p.187.

113. See the report 'Changuan nugaoshi dishichi zhounian jinian youyihui ji' [Beijing Women's Normal University holds an Internal Sports Competition], *Chenbao fukan* [Morning News], 16 Nov. 1922.

114. Zhuang Binshong, 'Beijing zaoqin de nuzi tiyu' [Recollections of Girls' Physical Activity in Beijing in the Early Twentieth Century], *TWS*, No. 1, 1983, p.49.

115. CSHPES, *Zhongguo jindai tiyu shi* [Modern Chinese Sports History], op. cit., p.156.

116. Ibid., p.148.

117. For example, Elisabeth Croll's brilliant monograph, *Feminism and Socialism in China* (1978); Chen Dongyan's *The History of Chinese Women's Life* (1938); F. Ayscough's *Chinese Women Yesterday and Today* (1938); Ono Kazuko's *Chinese Women in a Century of Revolution, 1850–1950* (1989), and other well-known works, such as Marilyn B. Young's *Women in China* (1973) and Margery Wolf and Roxane Witke's *Women in Chinese Society* (1974).

118. Helen Snow briefly mentioned it when she described Cai Chang and her mother's story. See Snow, Helen, *Women in Modern China*, op. cit., pp.198–203.

119. See Siu, Bobby, *Fifty Years of Struggle: the Development of the Women's Movements in China 1900–1949*, Hong Kong: Women's Publications Company, 1972, p.72.

120. For instance, Chow Tse-tsung, *The May Fourth Movement, Intellectual Revolution*

in Modern China, Cambridge, Harvard University Press, 1960; Vera Schwarcz, *The Chinese Enlightenment: Intellectuals and the Legacy of the May Fourth Movement of 1919*, Berkeley: University of California Press, 1986; Hu Sheng, *Cong yapian zhanzheng dao wusi yundong* [From the Opium War to the May Fourth Movement], Shanghai remin chubanshe, 1981.

FIVE

Iron Women of the Jiangxi Soviet (1929–34)

❧❦❧

BETWEEN 1929 AND 1934 the rural Soviets set up by the Chinese Communist Party initiated arguably the most radical social changes in modern Chinese history prior to 1949. Land was redistributed, new laws were implemented and society was reorganised; these actions constituted attempts at fundamental transformation. What happened to women in this upheaval? How did women react to the attempted changes? How did those changes relate to women's emancipation? Did exercise play a role in these changes? Specifically, did exercise contribute directly to female liberation? Such questions have not been asked before. To answer these questions we must first understand the progress of the Women's Movement under the leadership of the Communist Party in China.

Communist and Nationalist Policies and Attitudes towards the Women's Movement

The Chinese Communist Party (CCP)[1] was established in July 1921 in Shanghai. What were the Communist Party's policies concerning women? From its beginning, the CCP's attitude to women's emancipation was markedly different from the Nationalist Party founded in 1912.[2] The CCP made the emancipation of women one of the largest planks in its policy platform. By way of illustration, the Women's Department, which addressed women's issues, was created in 1922 when Xiang Jingyu, a female communist, returned from France.[3] The Party's first manifesto on the 'Resolution of the Women's Movement: the Current Situation in China', issued in the same year, made 'equal rights for men and women' and the 'freedom of women from feudal culture and society' major aims.[4] A year later the CCP formally recognised the right of women to vote, the need to protect female labour

149

from exploitation and the need to abolish all legislation restrictive to women.[5] By contrast, the Nationalist Party set its face against full equal rights for women.

Why did the CCP pay this close attention to women? One reason, as Mao Zedong(1883–1976), one of the founders of the CCP, explained in 1927, was that women were especially oppressed. As well as being dominated by three systems – political, clan and religious – a condition they shared with men, they were also dominated by men within the family. One of the goals of the peasant movement was to overthrow these four systems which represented the ideology and institution of patriarchal feudalism.[6] Xiang Jingyu (1895–1928), the first and most eminent leader of the Women's Department of the CCP, for her part, located the source of Communist concern in the fact that women had been harshly exploited and oppressed by the feudal social system and feudal culture of Confucianism for thousands of years. Women made up half the Chinese population – and were the most brutalised. They were, therefore, ideal recruits to the Communist revolution. They wanted revolution and they would support revolution.[7] In addition, as good Marxists, Chinese communists endorsed Marx's observation that 'the degree of the emancipation of women is the natural measure of general emancipation'.[8] However, although they emphasised the importance of women's emancipation, they never made this emancipation a top priority. In fact, the Chinese communists distanced themselves from the women's suffrage movement. They concentrated, in the tradition of Marx, Engels and Bebel,[9] on the economic foundations of the oppression and exploitation of women and linked the women's struggle to the wider issue of the proletariat struggle against the forces of capitalism.[10] Indeed, some Party members, such as Xiang Jingyu, strongly criticised the Women's Movement, feminist groups and emancipatory ideologies as inspirations of the Western bourgeois social and political system. They argued that a handful of vociferous, radical women participating in government could not bring about fundamental change. Women would still be exploited and oppressed by internal reactionaries and external imperialists and would remain without legal implementation of their rights. Women, they further asserted, could not hope to be effectively liberated until the whole oppressive social system was changed and all the oppressed were liberated. Therefore, the liberation of women was not an isolated issue and was not exclusively women's business, but belonged within the larger process of the liberation of the whole working class. In short, the Women's Movement in China was not an independent manifestation but part of the peasant and worker revolutionary liberation movement.[11]

After the Nationalist Party's coup of 12 April 1927,[12] the Communist Party split with the Nationalist Party. The Nationalist Party occupied the cities and the Communist Party retreated to rural bases. Its aim was to 'struggle for the masses by means of careful organisation, strikes, peasant activities and preparation for the establishment of Soviets'.[13] The Party also created a political arm of the Women's Movement by working out systematic procedures for recruiting and organising its members and by expanding the Movement in the rural areas.[14]

The Beginning of the Jiangxi Era and the Liberation of Women

There was a sea-change in Chinese history in the autumn of 1927. After opposing the Nationalist Party's coup, Zhu De,[15] a member of the CCP and the commander of the revolutionary army,[16] led the army to meet Mao Zedong's peasant army[17] at Jinggangshan, the border mountain area in Jiangxi province.[18] The two forces merged and became the Chinese Worker–Peasants' Red Army (known succinctly as the Red Army).[19] Zhu De was its Commander-in-Chief and Mao Zedong became its Political Commissar. They used this natural mountain stronghold to establish a soviet-style regime to further political revolution. The encirclement of the counter-revolutionary cities with revolutionary villages marked its beginning. Mao Zedong had said that 'a single spark can start a prairie fire'.[20] It proved to be true. By 1930 a total of 15 areas had expanded into provincial border-zones centred around Jiangxi province. Delegates from each of the soviets met to establish the Chinese Soviet Republic in Ruijin, Jiangxi, in November 1931. Mao was its first Chairman.[21] Although the word 'soviet' was borrowed from the Russian experience and language, the Chinese soviet differed from the Russian in that it did not centre on the proletariat in the urban areas. A Chinese soviet was any area controlled by the Chinese Communist Party. In fact, the Chinese soviets were mostly rural military base areas.[22]

When the soviets were established, women's rights were set down in several policy documents of the Party. In 'The Guiding Principle of Labour Women's Struggle', issued by the Central Executive Committee of the Party on 8 November 1930, a major ideological state-ment, the CCP insisted that in liberated areas its soviets must establish laws protecting and emancipating women. In these areas men and women were equal. Women over the age of 16 were to have the right to vote. They were to be eligible for political office. They were to have rights to land and choice in marriage. They were to be equal to men in politics, law, education and the economy.[23] The 1931 Constitution of Jiangxi Soviet set those principles in law.[24] The Labour Code of the same year granted, in Article 29, equal pay for equal work for both women and adolescent girls.[25] The Land Law of 1931, in Article 1, stated that 'Hired farm hands, coolies and toiling labourers shall enjoy equal rights to land allotments, irrespective of sex'.[26]

These innovations gave women the foundations in law necessary for economic emancipation. The marriage laws, for their part, brought women greater personal and social freedom. The first set of marriage laws, The Marriage Regulations, were included in the 1931 Constitution. They were based on Soviet Russia's Legal Code of 1926, with local Chinese circumstances taken into account and they were China's first modern marriage laws.[27] The second set of marriage laws were introduced in April 1934[28] and were the most radical to be passed by the Communist Party.[29] Although they were subsequently watered down[30] – the right to divorce and to choose a husband were eventually withdrawn – the right to dispose of property and to have control of the marriage children were retained.[31] These early laws – even in diluted form – fundamentally changed women's legal status for the better.

The significance of the marriage laws for women's emancipation needs to be emphasised. In the 1920s, despite various earlier political reforms, urban women's emancipation had its ups and downs. However, rural women's lives had still remained much the same as before. Sexual discrimination, of course, was a fundamental part of the patriarchal structure of family control that underpinned the feudal autocratic order. Nothing in this regard essentially changed in the vast rural areas in the first quarter of the twentieth century, despite several politically motivated movements.[32] Most women's lives followed a common pattern. In hard times peasant families were forced to sell their daughters as slave girls or to give them in adoption as 'tong-yang-xi' (little daughters-in-law).[33] Little daughters-in-law were frequently older than the boys for whom they were intended so that the groom's family could get at least some useful labour from the girl before marriage. Thus, prior to marriage 'child brides' worked hard, endured the dominance of future mothers-in-law, and were often nursemaids to their infant husbands.[34] However, for girls not sold as adopted daughters-in-law, conditions were not much more palatable. Their marriages were always arranged by the parents and they were treated, in the marriage, not as human beings but as things; machines for producing sons and sources of labour. Marriage still meant total servility: 'If a woman marries a chicken, she should obey the chicken; if she marries a dog, she should obey the dog.'[35] A woman in marriage had absolutely no freedom and escape from the marriage came only by being driven out of the home or by death.

The CCP and the Red Army, as they moved through the rural areas, spread heretical ideas about such subjugated women, made frequent use of propaganda which pointed to their bitter lives, gave them liberty and established marriage laws to protect them in the future. Chou Shu-nu, a child bride who joined the Red Army, recalled that when the CCP and the Red Army arrived at her village, they told people that it was wrong to have child brides. It was time for change. Women should have the right to personal freedom. 'It seemed', Chou Shu-nu remembered, 'that what those people had to say fitted exactly my idea of justice and truth, especially the part about freedom of marriage and child brides.'[36]

Other changes in women's lives were also advocated by the CCP, in particular, participation in evening and day school to learn to read and write in order to motivate 'the masses of women to rise up in order to overcome the actions of those who would ridicule women who would go to school.'[37] This emphasis on education remained strong in the Jiangxi era. In 1934 Agnes Smedley wrote of the CCP soviets that 'Great cultural progress has taken place. Thousands of schools, night schools, clubs, and classes for the eradication of illiteracy have been founded.'[38]

There were marked differences between the CCP's and the Nationalist Party's policies on women's emancipation. The CCP forbade child brides, whereas the Nationalist government only allowed the child bride to break her betrothal;[39] the Communists explicitly forbade both concubinage and bigamy, while the Nationalists, in effect, only opposed bigamy;[40] the Communists instituted a marriage age of 20 for men and 18 for women, in contrast to the Nationalist Party's 18 and 16 respectively. While the Nationalist regulations allowed women to divorce, the Communists went further by institutionalising a woman's right to child custody if she wished to raise the child.[41] The Communists also went further with regard to the principle of marital freedom of choice; they attacked 'the arranged feudal marriage system'- a system based on the legal, economic and political inequality of the sexes.[42] In addition, the Communists established marriage registration, thus giving them more control over marriage than any previous Chinese regime.

Although the CCP paid careful attention to women's emancipation, it was not sympathetic to feminism. It had 'grander' objectives. Its purpose, as Mao declared, was to save the Chinese people from destruction and to promote and lead the anti-imperialist movement. In short, the agenda was 'not only the freeing of 450 million Chinese people, but taking a step toward the freeing of the whole suppressed peoples of the world'.[43] The Party's attitude towards the Women's Movement was not to free women to concentrate on women's issues, as feminists demanded. They wanted to free women from the feudal culture and family in order for women to attend to the economic, social and political struggle side by side with men. The fight against both a strong Nationalist Army and powerful provincial warlords required men and women to join forces at the front and in the village. As the Party insisted: 'we must encourage women . . . to substitute for men. In the work behind the front, we need many women. We must implement the law to protect and emancipate women. We should lead and stimulate women's participation in revolutionary war. Women's emancipation must be associated with revolution'.[44] The Party, therefore, took the Women's Movement under its wing to develop it as part of the wider communist political movement.[45]

From 1928 to 1931 the Communists had two major goals: to expand the soviet areas and to develop and strengthen a regular revolutionary army – the Red Army. The Red Army was the most pressing ambition. It grew from less than 10,000 in 1928 to 70,000 by April 1930.[46] The ultimate goal was 100,000 soldiers.[47] While the Jiangxi period (1928–1934) was a time of formulating Party ideals and groping for effective governmental forms, the expansion of the Red Army was the dominant priority due to the urgent requirement of military survival.[48] The soviets were frequently under attack from National forces and provincial militia. National armies under Chiang Kai-shek,[49] supported by the foreign powers, attacked the Jiangxi Soviets five times in three years.[50] Survival in the border areas depended – purely and simply – upon the ability to fight. 'An independent regime must be an armed one', Mao wrote at the time, 'wherever there are no armed forces, or the armed forces are inadequate, or the tactics for dealing with the enemy are wrong, the enemy will immediately triumph!'[51] The need for complete military competence shaped the structure of the soviets. Women, therefore, were encouraged to take up military activities and the consequent militant image of the women of the Chinese soviets helped in no small way to bury historic stereotypes of quiescent femininity.

The Red Sports Movement

The Communist soviets revived the Taiping Rebellion's concept of liberated women warriors[52] and structured the community around the idea of Darwinian survival through war. To realise both ambitions they created a formal system of physical exercise for women which for the first time permeated all levels of society. The physical freedoms of the privileged urban few of earlier years now also became the freedoms of the poverty-stricken rural many. Women of every background exercised with a single purpose – military survival. The emancipatory ideal of the female liberated body, both physiologically and psychologically, became the property of the ideologically committed of all classes. Curiously the process was both circular and unilinear: the return to old Taiping ideological idealism and the creation of a new Communist pattern of action.

Military activities and military training were firmly based on exercise, physical education and sport in the Jiangxi Soviet period. The soviet areas, from 1927–34, saw a systematic attempt to promote physical exercise in armies, schools, factories, peasant and youth organisations, counties and villages. This effort was called the 'Red Sports Movement'. The name 'Red Sports Movement' (referred to hereafter as the RSM) was adopted officially in 1932,[53] but it originated in 1929 after the Party's Gutian Conference.[54] In the Resolution of the Gutian Conference, the Party decided to establish in each company of the Red Army a physical training programme and a club system.[55] These were years of struggle for survival. Fitness, toughness and stamina meant surviving and winning the war. In the view of the Party, sport was one of the best ways to unite the masses into a disciplined, patriotic, successful, martial force. In 1929, therefore, the Party advocated the introduction of the RSM throughout the soviet areas. By 1933, there were 1,917 clubs in the soviet villages (there were 2,932 villages in the soviet areas at that time).[56] Additional sports clubs and organisations existed in urban schools and factories.[57] Mao stated in the Report of the Second All-Chinese Soviet Congress of 1934 that 'A Red Sports Movement has been developing rapidly. Even remote villages have held track and field events and sports fields have been made in many places.'[58] As the responsibility of the Educational Committee of the Soviet Republic and the Red Sports Society,[59] the RSM, then, became a mass movement in which exercise was considered a fundamental aspect of the physical, cultural and military training of people in soviet areas. It was a method of enabling the masses to develop fitness, build up *esprit de corps*, and develop endurance. More than this, it was a means of binding the bulk of the workers and peasants to the Party, Soviet and Red Army, and of drawing them into political activity. Exercise was an inseparable part of political education.

In essence, then, in the words of the Party, the aims of the RSM were 'to cultivate worker–peasant class team spirit and to make strong bodies to suit the needs of the class struggle' and 'to train the worker–peasant class to be an iron force in order to defeat all its enemies'.[60] Exercise was therefore to be a means of achieving fitness, of cultivating loyalty, of assisting military training and of encouraging political involvement.[61] Its adoption for these purposes, of course, was not exclusive to 'Red China' but was a common practice in the twentieth century construction of new nations, new identities and new ideologies.[62] The activities of the RSM included athletics, football, basketball. tennis, gymnastics and military activities such as unarmed combat, shooting and bayonet drill.[63] Competitive sport was strongly encouraged by its leaders.[64] Competitive activities would be especially valuable, they believed, in drawing men and women into exercise; they could also be used to raise skill levels, for example, for developing hand/eye co-ordination. Above all, competitive sport, the Party asserted, was an effective instrument by which the masses could be trained to be aggressive.[65] The full significance of access to competitive games on the part of women – a major emancipatory step – will be discussed more fully in a later chapter.[66]

In concentrating attention here on the evolution of exercise in the soviets there is, of course, a danger of exaggerating its relative importance in Soviet society – and indeed in Chinese soviet policy-making. However, as an element of overall culture, exercise was certainly assigned a specific and important role in the Chinese soviet strategy for the creation and survival of a new ideology, a new identity and a new society during the Jiangxi period.

The Red Sports Movement and the Red Army: Women Soldiers of Iron

The RSM, as mentioned above, was the brain-child of the Red Army. Sport was to create 'a new Chinese' – strong, disciplined and patriotic – able to fight and thus to ensure the solidarity, stability and success of the Chinese Soviet Republic.

The organisation of sport was through the club[67] and Lenin rooms.[68] Every division of the Red Army had a club and every company of the Red Army had a Lenin room. In April 1934, the Educational Committee of the Chinese Soviet Republic issued the 'Resolution of the Organisation and Work of Clubs and Lenin Rooms in the Red Army' to strengthen the structure of sport in the army. According to this Resolution, the aim of the Clubs and the Lenin Rooms was 'to foster the Red Army soldiers' active spirit and lifestyle, to help them to give up their bad habits, to improve their educational level, to use sport as an instrument for building an "iron" Red Army in order to achieve the complete victory of revolution in China.'[69] The Resolution recommended that every division of the Red Army should set up a club. Its administration was to be in the hands of a director and a management team. The director, who was usually appointed by the political department of the Red Army division, was to be in charge of the management team. The management team was to consist of the director from each Lenin room in each company of the Red Army division. The responsibility of both the director and the management team was to plan and implement the Lenin room's programme of work. There were five sections in the club: performance, art, wall-newspaper, education and sport. The aim of the sports section was to plan and implement a physical exercise programme and to supervise sports activities and competitions in each company of the division.

Each Red Army company's Lenin room was under the control of the club. The structure of the Lenin room was similar to the club. Each Lenin room had a director. The director was elected by a general meeting of the company. He was advised by the political instructor of his company and supervised by the club of his division. There were six sections in a Lenin room: variety show (including acrobatics and magic shows); performance (including comedy, music and singing); wall-newspaper (reporting and editing the news); education (learning to read and write); sport (athletics, ball games and military exercise) and a youth group.

Since in the main the Red Army, mostly from the families of poor workers and peasants, had never had an opportunity for schooling,[70] clubs and Lenin rooms were regarded as its schools. In these 'schools', as one Red Army soldier Xiuan Jintang recalled, 'There was a performance every Saturday night. The wall-newspaper changed twice a week. In the morning and evening, we participated in military exercise and physical activities, such as boxing, bayonet drill, high jump, long jump, tug-of-war, bars, climbing the walls of the city, obstacle race, vaulting horse and throwing hand grenades.'[71] Li Zhaobin, another soldier, recalled that 'the Red Army soldiers greatly enjoyed sport. If they seized basketballs and volleyballs from the enemy they were as excited as if they had found treasure.' 'Although we lived under very harsh conditions', he wrote, 'we still had a sport movement in our company. At the end of the day's march, sport relaxed us. We enjoyed it.'[72] 'Football was the soldiers' favourite pastime'. Other members of the Red Army like Hu Yimeng and Hu Yuanfa remembered,

> We kicked the ball up into the sky and pushed each other to get at it. We really loved the game. We also played basketball and volleyball. High jump and long jump were popular and common activities because they didn't need complex facilities. We would simply soften the ground and cut a square, then put in some sand – if possible, or put a bamboo pole between two benches or stones, and then we would enjoy ourselves.[73]

Commanders, officers and rankers of the Red Army all participated enthusiastically in physical activities. Smedley observed that 'the whole Army took part in athletic exercise, competing in every kind of sport'.[74] Many Party and Army leaders' reminiscences certainly include sporting anecdotes. For instance, Mao Zedong, Commissar of the First Front Red Army, liked to swim and climb. On occasion, he volunteered to referee basketball matches. Nie Rongzhen, a Red Army commander, enjoyed long-distance running; Den Fa, the Head of the Security Council of the government, Zhang Aiping, the Chief of the Young Pioneers and the Youth League, and Yang Yong, another Red

Army commander, preferred to play basketball, volleyball and football. Zhu De, the Commander-in-Chief of the First Front Red Army, who had been a sports instructor, allegedly spent time with his colleagues discussing how to win battles against the Nationalists in order to obtain basketballs or footballs from the Nationalist cities for competitions in the soviet areas![75] He was also the sporting star of the soviet areas. His skill at long jump, high jump, and especially the pole jump were greatly admired. Any basketball match in which he took part attracted a large audience including his wife, Kang Keqing, overall commander of the Red Army women soldiers, who brought her troops to watch.[76]

Women soldiers were not only spectators but participants on battlefields and in sport grounds. There were about 100 women soldiers in the Red Army when it was founded in Jinggangshan in 1927.[77] After several years the number increased although there are no precise figures available. In addition to the famous Kang Keqing, the 'girl commander', as the men of the Red Army called her, less celebrated Red Army women played an active part in battle. Wei Xiuying, for example, was present at some 100 battles and spent half a lifetime in the military. She was a classic communist revolutionary. Sold by her parents at the age of five as a child bride, as she grew up she worked in the fields like a slave and she was often beaten and had little food. When the Red Army arrived at her village she cut off her long hair and joined it. 'The Woman Wei', Harrison Salisbury commented, 'was one of tens of thousands who joined the Red Army from the "model county" of the red zone. A division was formed of recruits from Bingo. Its population was 240,000, and 80,000 impoverished peasants like the woman Wei joined the Party and the Red Army.'[78] There were almost two thousand women with the Fourth Front Army. Zhao Lan, a woman soldier, described the value of exercise to them,

> In the morning, we got up very early. We did our physical exercise in the fog. After breakfast, we practised grenade throwing, marksmanship, bayonet-drill . . . We participated in sport activities, such as high jump, long jump and horizontal bars everyday. We also had a long distance running competition everyday. We liked all sport events, especially long distance running, because all of these activities would help us when we were in battle.[79]

Old people, who live in Jianguo county, the soviet area in the border between Sichuan and Shanxi provinces,[80] can still remember the heady days of the Red Army. It set up a soviet government in every county and built playgrounds in every village. There were more than 100 playgrounds in the area. The playgrounds were called Red playgrounds or military-training fields. They had facilities, such as horizontal bars, a wooden horse and a jumping pit. At Jianmen village, 'Every morning and afternoon, there were male and female soldiers doing their physical training. And every evening, after supper, a team of women soldiers, carrying their swords on their backs, took part in horseback racing. Their confident bearing impressed all who saw them. These women soldiers belonged to the women's regiment of two thousand.'[81]

Women soldiers not only served in the regiments, they also attended the Red Army schools and academies. There are no precise details of the numbers of women soldier students in these schools. Nevertheless, fragmentary information from those years reveals their presence. In early 1932, for example, Kang Keqing, the commander of the Red Army women soldiers, and 200 women from the division of Women Volunteers went to the Red Army Academy to study for six months. Afterwards, ambitious to become a general of the Red Army, Kang stayed on and became a full-time student. She described men's and women's training in the academy as exactly the same.[82] The structure of the Academy as well as the Army's other schools were similar to an army company. There were clubs and Lenin rooms to promote the RSM and to assist the Party's political and physical education programme. Like the company, the Academy used sports activities and competitions to train the students to become efficient Red Army cadres.[83] Some women also studied in the Red Army's School of Medicine. This school also held sports competitions, for example, at its opening and graduation ceremonies. The purpose was to publicise and promote the RSM in order to ensure the health and fitness of both the Red Army and the masses.[84] On 24 July 1933, for example, the School of Medicine held a typical sports competition. It included 100-, 200- and 400-metre races, high jump, long jump, table-tennis, basketball and tennis. Women students took part in the running events.[85]

Women soldiers' participation in sport improved their health, emphasised their equality and changed their public image. In time, they gained equality of image on both battle-field and playing field. Smedley quotes a Red Army man speaking of Kang's troops in 1930: 'The Women's Volunteer Corps under the woman commander Kang fought furiously and without fear, as if to show that they were the equal of the best of our Red Army units.'[86] In the *Stories of the Revolutionary Struggle of Jiangxi Women* published in 1963, the women were described as protecting their regime, land and the fruits of victory which they had gained. It seems certain that they, with the men, fought strongly and often showed incomparable bravery. More than this, when the Red Army opposed the Nationalists' invasions of the soviets, the women not only fought but provided medical assistance, worked in transport units and formed entertainment units. They marched with the army, encountered the enemy and in the front line saved and aided the wounded.[87] Harrison Salisbury notes that in the Red army sexual difference was ignored.[88] Women were not considered the weaker and inferior sex and early on they had earned equal status. Liu Yin, a woman cadre of the First Front Army,[89] remembered that on the Long March in 1935, the Red Army soldiers had to walk great distances each day. There was quarrelling between the sexes; the men complained that the women were better treated than they were and didn't carry their fair share of the rice bags. As a result, the women were placed in a separate unit, with Liu Yin as captain and Li Bozhao in charge of the commissary. Now they could not expect preferential treatment.[90] This imposed sexual equality made women soldiers' lives arduous, but they coped. As Woman Wei concluded: ' Everyday we were in difficulties. Every day we had a hard time.'[91] The women's regiment within the Fourth Front Army crossed the Grasslands and Great Snow Mountain three times and spent eight months wandering over the Tibetan plateau.[92] Equality demanded by men, required women to be fitter. In the long term, compulsory physical training helped them both to obtain and maintain this fitness.

Women and the Party

Some women joined the Red Army, while many more participated in various mass organisations in the soviet areas. These organisations included children, adolescents and adult female and male peasants and workers. The most important were the Handicraft Industry Union, the Farmhand Union, The Poor Peasants Association, the Red Vanguards, the Young Pioneers, the Children's Corps and the Women's Association. In short, they covered virtually all occupations, all ages and both sexes. They were an integral part of the soviets. As Kim noted: 'The structure of the soviet government in Jiangxi . . . was highly centralised in the sense that all institutions were centrally created and all policies centrally controlled and supervised through the mechanism of the party . . . through the conferences at each level of government, and by the reporting and inspecting system.'[93] The government endorsed the organisations and the organisations in turn supported the government at the grass roots level. This was their basic purpose. In late 1931, the Women's Association, however, was abolished by the government. It feared their growing independence. Women were compelled to participate in the other mass organisations according to their age, education and occupation. On 26 March 1931, the government declared that the Women's Association, which had been formed in accordance with the party's policy in 1927, was to be abolished. Other organisations should now set up women's working sections to integrate women's work. Women were pressed to join them.[94] On 10 September 1931, the 'Resolution of Women's Work in Xiang-Gang (Hunan and Jiangxi provinces) Border Soviet Area' declared that all women's independent organisations were to be abolished.[95] The Resolution argued that the soviet government was the representative of the worker–peasant class. This class embraced both sexes. There was, therefore, no need for an independent organisation exclusively for women. However, two women's agencies – the Women's Life Improvement Committee and the Working Women's Congress – were set up by the government to study women's issues and to promote women's work within the soviet region. The task of the Women's Life Improvement Committee was to investigate the situation of women in the soviet, to consider women's problems and to make recommendations regarding women's issues to the soviet government. The aim of the Working Women's Congress was also to concern itself with women's problems and to offer suggestions for their solution. In addition, they concerned themselves with the education and mobilisation of worker–peasant women.[96] These two agencies were not women's mass organisations. The first was a government advisory body – actually it was a department of the government; the second appears to have been a kind of worker–peasant women's 'parliament'.[97]

This dramatic change of soviet policy exposed fears that large-scale exclusive women's organisations might separate in time from other soviet institutions and become instruments of autonomous feminism which, it was believed, meant placing women's interests above peasant and worker interests. This danger was perceived to come from female students – élite women intellectuals – who were acutely sensitive to historical inequality, family oppression and sexual exploitation, which were more readily accepted by worker–peasant women. It was believed that these students would insist on bringing up the issue of women's rights in family and society. This would challenge male power both in the family and community and bring about confrontation between the sexes. Such a diffusion of energy was not to be tolerated. Energy was to be used, by all, to bring about revolutionary class change. Furthermore the Communists were realists. The attitude of peasants concerning women would not change overnight. The Communists knew this only too well. A peasant revolt did not mean that peasants themselves would immediately change their negative attitude to women which had been deeply rooted in feudal culture for over a thousand years. The cry of communist women for freedom was more often than not ignored by communist father, brother and husband.[98] In this situation, any radical change in sex roles would have aroused deep antagonisms and stimulated confrontation. The Communist Revolution was a peasant-focused revolution which required male and female peasants to unite to fight against Nationalists and Imperialists. The Communists never allowed feminism to interfere with this purpose. The Women's Movement was always subordinate to the orthodox objectives of social change, economic reform and military victory over the Nationalists and, later on, the Japanese.[99]

Nevertheless, despite the fact that the Communist Party never allowed the Women's Movement independence, it far from ignored women. As already pointed out, they constituted half the population and were filled with revolutionary spirit. They had most to gain and least to lose![100] They were, therefore, invaluable as the Party had to be careful to keep a balance between women's demands and men's prejudices, retaining the support of both women and men while pursuing a seamless party. For this reason the Chinese Communist Party never shifted in its casuistic attitude towards the Women's Movement. Salaff and Stacey charge that the Party operated on the basis of expediency rather than principle with regard to women.[101] Frenier has also argued that 'the Party's policies towards women were largely based on expediency – that is when women were needed they were appealed to on the basis of their low position in society but when they were not, their concerns were ignored'.[102] However, it could be equally argued that, based on a fuller reading of the archival records of the Party[103] and a fuller understanding of recent Chinese history, the essence of the Party's attitude and policy towards women's liberation was not expediency but consistency.

First, the Communist Party advocated women's freedom aggressively, always attached importance to women's work and never ignored women's emancipation. Second, the Party never put women's emancipation at the top of its agenda. The CCP was not a feminist party but a 'unisex' party. Its goal was to overthrow imperialist and reactionary rule, to liberate all oppressed people – male and female, and to build a communist China. In this sense, the Women's Movement was to be involved in the politics of a class struggle rather than a sex war. The Women's Movement was not subordinated to the authority of men, as Julia Kristena simplistically states,[104] but subordinated to the Party's aims. These were more than simply gender driven. This explains why the Party, on the one hand, pushed women's liberation forward, and on the other, restricted its pace. In this way, open conflict between the sexes was avoided and concessions were made which would at least partly accommodate traditional male peasant attitudes. To avoid women's too overtly aggressive assertion, therefore, women were forced to join 'unisex' organisations. In this way women's emancipatory ambitions could be swallowed up in wider political imperatives. In essence, therefore, the aims of reorganisation were to distract women from exclusive feminism, to encourage them to support class struggle and to focus their efforts on the defeat of the Nationalists and Imperialists. To these ends, women's activities were now subsumed within general mass organisations.

Exercise, sport and military training for women were a feature of all these organisations and women were strongly encouraged to be involved in the RSM.[105] Generally speaking, males and females between the ages of 23–50 joined the Red Vanguards,[106] between the ages of 16–23 joined the Young Pioneers,[107] and between the ages of 8–15 joined the Children's Corps.[108] The older adults joined the Poor Peasants Union, the Handicrafts Union and other mass organisations. As in the army, in these organisations, exercise, games, athletics and drill were de rigueur. For one good reason – everyone in the soviet was considered a potential soldier. In her book, *China's Red Army Marches*, Agnes Smedley observed that the Red Vanguards were made up of both armed and trained men and women who 'guarded the villages and towns and all the paths in the Soviet regions'.[109] Mao was still more specific. In 'The Investigation of Xinguo County', he stated that women in the county were an integral part of the Vanguards and groups of 40 to 50 females aged between 23 to 50 constituted a team. They did the same training as male Vanguards, including military drill for three hours each month.[110] In 'The Model of Soviet Work in Changgang Village', Mao described the RSM and the 'cultural movement' in a Chinese communist model village.[111] He wrote that:

> the Changgang village as a whole was made up of four smaller hamlets. Each hamlet had a Club, there were Sport, Wall-newspaper, and Performance committees within the Club. Men and women participated in activities organised by those committees. Women in the hamlet were Vanguards. They drilled twice for 5 hours every month in their hamlet and took part in the military drill competition in the local town once a month.[112]

Mao was so pleased with Changgang village's athletic, cultural and educational work that he asked that every Soviet village learn from it.[113]

The Young Pioneers

Girls and young women in the soviet areas, aged between 15 and 23, were encouraged to join the Young Pioneers. It vigorously promoted the RSM. According to the 'Resolution of the Present Work of the Young Pioneers in the Soviet Area' (28 April 1931), the main objectives of the organisation were to extend and improve the Young Pioneers' military and athletic activities.[114] To achieve these objectives the Central Committee of the Young Pioneers established a Sports and Physical Exercise Committee. It had large ambitions. It attempted to promote the RSM in every branch of the Young Pioneers. On 13 June 1932 the Headquarters of the Young Pioneers issued an order which requested that clubs be set up in all branches to promote sport.[115] On 27 November 1932, Zhang Aiping, the Chief-commander of the Young Pioneers, provided the Young Pioneers with teaching materials which were intended to serve as inspirational literature.[116] In 1934, to facilitate the development of the RSM throughout the Young Pioneers, the Headquarters of the Young Pioneers edited and published two instructional books, *Games for Young Pioneers* and *Gymnastics for Young Pioneers*. Both were approved by Zhou Enlai[117] and Zhang Aiping.[118] Later, the Central Committee for the People's Education used them as text books in both the Children's Corps and the Lenin Schools.[119] They were the first primary-school physical education textbooks in the Soviet areas.[120]

From 1933 onwards, Zhang Aiping, attempting to lead from the front, wrote a number of articles advocating the RSM. One prosaically entitled 'Developing the Red Sports Movement',[121] published in the *Qingnian Shihua* [True Words of Youth], provided a blueprint for the growth of the Movement. He insisted that it was necessary to encourage working class youth to participate in the Movement because the class struggle needed the physically strong. He criticised the lack of a realisation of the importance of participation in sport by leaders of the Young Pioneers. He demanded that sport be made available in every branch and suggested how this was to be done. It was necessary to build playgrounds. Every village should have one right in its centre – and it should include facilities for running, jumping, swimming, basketball and football, and a specific area for Young Pioneers to train. To fund construction every village should gather contributions. He also recommended a programme of exercise: gymnastics in the morning and evening three times a week throughout the year, camping in spring and autumn, swimming in summer and gymnastics competitions between teams, villages, towns, counties and provinces.

As an indication of his own enthusiasm Zhang wrote a song called 'The Gymnastic Song of the Young Pioneers'. If its lyrics were banal, its message was clear.

> Young Pioneers come to develop their bodies,
> They are doing gymnastics, playing games.
> They are strong, active and good at military skills.
> Young Pioneers come to develop their bodies.
> They are playing war games.
> They are fighting against the white dogs. [the Nationalist armies]
> They are the reserve forces of the Red Army.
> Young Pioneers come to develop their bodies,
> They defend the Soviet.
> They are young, but strong.
> They are the great heroes and heroines.[122]

As the song makes abundantly clear, exercise in its various forms was intended to inculcate in the young duty, discipline and strength. This view was communicated unrelentingly by the Party and government leaders. It was conscientiously supported by them too. For example, on 30 May 1932, the Young Pioneers of Fujian province held a provincial sports meeting called 'The View of Young Pioneers of Fujian Province'. The Commander-in-Chief of the Red Army, Zhu De, was its organising Chairman. At the Athletic Competition of the Young Pioneers of the Soviet Area in September 1932, Zhou Enlai, Xiang Ying, Liu Bocheng, Ren Boshi and Zhang Aiping were the referees – 21 teams and 688 athletes participated in five events: high jump, long jump, obstacle race, the 1600-metres race and swimming.

Although there are no statistics available from this period to show precisely how many girl Pioneers participated in such competitions, they certainly took part in the RSM. It was part of every-day life. *Hongshe zhonghua* [Red China], the Party's periodical, reported that in Huken, Tanhu and Zipu villages the Pioneers, boys and girls, had their Lenin rooms and did physical training every day.[123] Mao observed that in Xingguo county almost every village had a branch of the Young Pioneers, and that in addition to daily exercise these boys and girls performed military drill twice a month.[124] Agnes Smedley recalled a strong, happy girl with shingled hair and a frank, healthy face smiling from the ranks of the Young Pioneers as she watched them at their drill.[125]

Children's Corps

The minds and body of the young are especially important to revolutionaries. The young knows no past, it only has a future. It is the true believer of tomorrow. Consequently, girls and boys between the ages of eight to 14 were encouraged to join the Communist Labour Children's Corps.[126] Its aim was to teach boys and girls the basic principles of communism and to train them to be the reserve force of the Young Pioneers. The Young Pioneers, in turn, as mentioned above, were the reserve forces of the Red Army. Exercise played an important role in the Children's Corps. The Party advocated the use of sport to attract boys and girls. In January 1932, the First Jiangxi Provincial Congress issued 'The Resolution of the Work of Children's Corps in the Soviet Area'. It demanded that every village should build playgrounds for modern ball games and traditional folk games.[127] Children's Corps in every village were now required to do physical exercise and military drill. Mao was pleased with the Children's Corps' work in Xingguo county. In particular, he considered the fact that these children did military drill three times a week most impressive.[128] On 1 April 1933, 'A View of Communist Children's Corps of Centre Soviet Area' – a big sports meeting – was held in Ruijin, the capital of the Chinese Soviet Republic. Zhang Aiping's article, entitled 'Our Happy Festival', vividly described how the girls and boys of the Children's Corps enthusiastically prepared for this important event:

> April 1st is our festival. We are going to celebrate it. Brothers and sisters, let's review our achievements – study and exercise. Let's encourage our fathers and brothers to join the Red Army. Let's continue our 'Saturday helpers activity' to help Red Army soldiers' families and let's participate in all kind of exercise. We will tell the world that we are happy, lively and healthy children in the Red Soviet.[129]

Physical Education in School

Exercise, military training and the RSM not only suffused the Red Army, the mass adult organisations and the mass children's organisations, it also permeated the soviet formal educational system. In the soviet areas, many children (girls and boys) aged 7–15 received free education. They attended the Lenin school set up in every village by the local government. In 1934 there were 3,052 Lenin primary schools in 2,232 villages and counties' in soviet areas. There were 89,716 students studying in these schools[130] and at least one-third were girls.[131] In school, girls and boys were equal. The curriculum was the same for both sexes. The aim of education was to train 'the builders of Communism in the future, and the new generation now for the class struggle'.[132] Correspondingly the purpose of the school was to educate the students to be politically aware, to acquire basic knowledge and to possess strong bodies.

To achieve the latter goal, the Central Committee for the People's Education issued several decrees stressing the need for physical education courses in schools. In October 1933, for example, a decree dealing with the curriculum of the primary school ordered that every pupil should attend physical education classes.[133] In February 1934, Zhang Wentian,[134] the Chairman of the Government, issued a decree that instructed every school to establish a sports field.[135] A more detailed decree dictating educational priorities was issued by the Central Committee for People's Education in April 1934. It stated that the curriculum should be as follows:

1. Lower primary schools (three years): there were three subjects to be taught. Each week there was to be Chinese language – four hours; mathematics – four hours; games and physical exercise – eight hours.
2. Higher primary schools (two years): there were four subjects to be taught. Each week there was to be Chinese language and literature – six hours; mathematics – six hours; social science – two or three hours; physical education and games – eight hours.

A closer examination of the curriculum throws even further light on the militaristic and muscular ethos of the Jiangxi Soviet era. Physical education was an obligatory course, a fundamental component of the curriculum. It was supported and reinforced by school clubs which promoted the RSM. The primary purpose of this considerable effort to improve standards of fitness in the young was to train boys and girls to be ready to join their older brothers and sisters on the battlefield.[136]

Sport, Duty, War

'Sport was the best way to inculcate energy, resolution, enterprise, application, self-control and single-minded devotion to duty.'[137] This positive view of sport propounded by Zhu De was popularised by the whole machinery of formal and informal propaganda. The Red Army, the Party and the Government used sport as an instrument to prepare for war, to wage war, to create and to popularise military mythical heroes and heroines. Sports fields were successfully linked to battlefields. When the Third Red Army Regiment obtained the championship in the Jiangxi Provincial Ball-games Competition in May 1933, *Qingnian shihua* [True Words of Youth][138] commented: 'The Red Army soldiers are brave and strong on the playground. They will show these qualities on the battlefield. For this reason the Nationalist army has always been defeated by the Red Army.'[139] When the Red Army of

Fujian Division held a sports competition in July 1933, the champion regiment was praised as 'ever-victorious both on the sports and battle-field'.[140] Mao told his soldiers, 'You must do physical training and physical exercise. Only when you strengthen your body will you be able to fight well against our enemies.'[141] In short, sport was a pre-requisite of a strong revolutionary fighting force.

Ideological, political and athletic activities were melded into one. Inter-army matches and sports meetings took place on every impor-tant commemorative day, such as Labour Day (1 May); Party Day (1 September) and Army Day (1 August). On 1 May 1933, for example, the First Division of the Red Army held a Sports Competition in Yong Feng county. Two hundred Red Army athletes attended the competi-tion. The events included high jump, long jump, 100-metre, 200-metre and 500-metre races, basketball, football and military exercises (shooting, hand-grenade throwing and crossing a swing-bridge). Zhu De, the Commander-in-Chief, and Mao, the Political Commissar, were at the opening ceremony and then watched the whole competition.[142] Later, on 1 August 1933, the First Regiment of the Red Army held a Red Sports Meeting in Ruijin to celebrate Army Day. The soldiers participated in 100-metre and 500-metre races, hurdles, pole vault and football.[143] The First Front Red Army in Yongfeng also held its sports meeting to celebrate Army Day. Xiao Hua, then a Red Army soldier, described the scene with enthusiasm:

> The exciting sports meeting had lasted from morning to night. When the moon was rising above the top of the mountain, Zhu De, the Commander-in-Chief, announced that the competition was now finished. He awarded medals to the champions. Then the sports meeting came to an end with the shouted slogan 'We will recruit 1,000,000 iron Red Army soldiers in order to fight against Imperialism and the Nationalists and build a Soviet China.[144]

The evidence speaks for itself. Exercise – the basis of active, strong, aggressive action – formed an important part of the training of the Red Army soldier. As one officer put it: 'We must develop a sports movement to train our bodies to be strong and healthy. Education is necessary, but physical education is more necessary. Sport is action. Soldiers are trained for action. We should spread the ideal of developing a sports movement in order to train soldiers who not only have class consciousness but also masculine bodies.'[145] Zhu De, the

Commander-in-Chief, was more specific, 'To win the war, we need to recruit 1,000,000 iron Red Army soldiers. Therefore, we need to develop a sports movement among the masses which will provide soldiers who are strong – with iron muscle and steel bone.'[146]

Precept became practice. Sports competitions became a functional fashion. From 1931 to 1934 they spread through the whole soviet area. Inter-organisation, inter-county and inter-provincial events took place everywhere.[147] Ideologically speaking, the most significant of all the sports meetings was the Red Sports Meeting of the Whole Soviet Area which took place in Ruijin, the capital of the Soviet Republic, on 30 May 1933. On 5 May the Chinese Soviet Republic had issued a decree covering the whole country – including the Nationalists areas. It declared:

> For the purpose of breaking the Fourth Attack of the Nationalists and Imperialists, we must develop The Red Sports Movement to train the workers and peasants to have the collective spirit and strong bodies to meet the needs of the class struggle. This is urgent and necessary. Consequently, the Soviet government has decided to have a formal athletic meeting of the whole Soviet area in the red capital of the Soviet on May 30th 1933. This Red Sports Meeting is to test the physique of the workers and peasants and to act as a demonstration to our enemies.[148]

The opening ceremony of this famous 'Sports Meeting of the Chinese Soviet Republic' began at six o'clock in the evening. Its slogan was 'to train the iron muscle and steel bone of the worker–peasant class in order to defeat the enemy'. Communist Party and Army leaders, such as Bo Gu, Wang Shengyong, Xiang Ying, Zhang Aiping, He Changgong, Yang Shangqun and Den Yinchao constituted the organising committee. Bo Gu was the chief referee. Loupu (Zhang Wentian), Den Yinchao, Kai Feng (He Keqiuan), Mao Zedong, Xiang Ying, Yang Shangqun, Chen Yun and He Changgong were the referees. Over 160 selected athletes from the Red Army, the schools and the mass organisations of the whole Soviet area participated.

Activities included ball games – basketball, football, volleyball, tennis, table-tennis and athletics – high jump, long jump, pole vault, discus, shot, javelin and obstacle, 50-metre, 100-metre, 200-metre and 400-metre races. The meeting lasted for three days. At the closing ceremony, the first sports society in the soviet area was established. It was called the Red Sports Society of the Chinese Soviet Republic. Its aim was to consolidate the RSM throughout the soviet area. Xiang Yin, Wang Shenyong, Deng Fa, Zhang Aiping and Shi Bicheng were elected as members of the Society. The Red Sports Society's ambition was to join the International Association of Red Sports and Gymnastics Associations (better known as Red Sports International – RSI). [149] This decision was approved by the 180 competing athletes who represented thousands of peasants and workers. The Society agreed that under the leadership of the RSI, the Communist Chinese Red Sports Association – a branch of the RSI – would oppose the Lucerne Sports International (LSI), a branch of the Bureau of the Socialist International,[150] and promote the RSM among the working classes of the world.[151] In August Fujian and Jiangxi branches were also founded.[152]

Women's Participation in Sports Competition

Where did women fit into this revolutionary plan for the national and international promotion of competitive sport? The Party, of course, had always appreciated that sport, suitably controlled, was a powerful means for realising women's emancipation.[153] Women therefore, were encouraged to attend sports competitions. At the 30 May Sports Meeting Zhang Aiping pointed out bluntly that one of its short-comings was that there were no women athletes involved and he demanded their future participation.[154] His was an influential speech with positive consequences for women. Subsequently, women athletes took part in the Fujian Provincial Red Sports Meeting (2 August 1933)[155] and the Jiangxi Provincial Red Sports Meeting (3 August 1933).[156]

On 17 December 1933, *Qinnian shihua* [The True Words of Youth], reported that the women's Marx–Communist University's basketball team was successfully established. It further announced that:

> For the purposes of the development of the Red Sports Movement and for the women in the soviet area to advance the struggle, female athletes ask for the women in the whole soviet area to exercise and to train to become stronger for participation in the struggle. The women's basketball teams are the pioneers of their day.
>
> What do you think, girls and women in the Soviet University,

Red Army Academy and every college, school and mass organisation? How about you? Would you like to support the women's basketball players? Then organise your sports teams as soon as possible! Do exercise! Welcome the Second All Chinese Soviet Congress with your strong bodies and fighting spirit.[157]

According to a 1934 inquiry,[158] there were several universities, colleges and institutes set up by the government in Jiangxi to train communist cadres of both sexes, such as the Marx–Communist University, the Bank Special Training School, the College of Education, the Red Army Academy, the Drama School and the Agrarian Culture School. In addition, Smedley observed that there were many other normal schools and other institutions for the training of women.[159] In the universities and schools, women attended physical education classes. They also did a great deal of physical exercise after school. In the Soviet University in Ruijing, for example, in which there were 2,000 men and women in training,[160] the women students participated in basketball, table-tennis, gymnastics, running and walking.

However, women's participation in competitive sport, especially at public sports meetings, was not as extensive as men's. This was too much to expect. Women were eventually encouraged to participate but participation was relatively slow to gather momentum. Tradition was still the obstacle which barred the way. Competitive sport posed problems. This was true in both Communist and Nationalist areas, as will be described in due course. Chinese culture never approved of women appearing in public to show off either their athletic ability or their physical form. In patriarchal culture, female sexuality and physicality had come to be defined as synonymous. A culture which defined women in these terms was ill-disposed to see a reformation of sensual physicality or the adoption of 'masculine' forms of physicality. In the final analysis, this meant that women were either still to be excluded from the practices and institutions of sport or, when they did participate, it was in a way that was acceptable to traditionalists. The Party officially acknowledged that the problem which affected women in sport was peasant and worker resistance to unacceptable social and cultural change, especially men's resistance to change in women's status and image.[161] The Party consequently moved gradually on the issue, as we have seen, including involvement in competitive sport. To a degree it was calculatedly and deliberately Janus-headed. Nevertheless, competitive sport with its emphasis on aggression, conquest and self-assertion – traditionally masculine rather than feminine virtues – was now made available to women in the Party's interest. Political survival was essential and women, through fitness training of every kind, were to be prepared physiologically and psychologically to help that survival.

Conclusion

The Jiangxi Era ended in October 1934 when the Nationalists were successful in their fifth attempt at encirclement. The majority of the Communists left the rural soviets and began the celebrated Long March which took them to Shanxi in late 1935. There the mistakes of the Jiangxi Era were scrutinised. From 1937 the United Front with the Nationalist Party resulted in new policies.[162] The Communists compromised their principles in the attempt to ensure national unity to resist Japanese aggression. As a result of these policies in the Border Areas (also called the Liberated Areas), the Red Sports Movement and the Women's Movement advanced to new positions in their steady march towards cultural change.

In the context of the history of modern China and from the perspective of the Women's Movement, the Jiangxi period is prototypical. In addition to legal advances, land reform and mobilisation, which have received due attention,[163] changes in women's physical image through exercise – achieved in no small measure – foreshadowed the future. These changes were slow, but they were real and they were the foundation of future social developments. Arguably one of the most significant cultural innovations of the Jiangxi Era was the RSM and to date its emancipatory role has not been adequately recorded. It played a not inconsiderable role in the gradual replacement of patriarchal values and was, therefore, instrumental in the eventual rejection of those values. The RSM created new opportunities for women's development – mentally and physically. It challenged the patriarchal culture, it contributed to the redefinition of the image of women and it produced radical female role-models. While few in number their influence was marked. Depictions of Jiangxi women who undertook strenuous physical exercise and intensive military training and fought with the Communist armies are still used today to ensure there will be no return to traditional attitudes and to underline the duties,

174

responsibilities and possibilities of contemporary Chinese women under Communism. Even more to the point, the RSM was the means of transforming female exercise from a prerogative of the privileged into a pragmatic tool of the 'proletariat' – a process that once established was to continue in the Yan'an period of Communist reconstruction. This ensured that physical freedom – with all its cultural implications – was increasingly in the hands of more and more women.

Notes

1. It was called in Chinese, Zhongguo Gongchandang and was founded in July 1921 in Shanghai. Thirteen Chinese delegates, who represented the approximately 60 CCP members in China, and Maring, a Comintern agent attended. Their decision on party role and organisation took a conventional Leninist line. Chen Duxiu, the leader of the New Culture and May Fourth Movements was elected Secretary-General of the CCP in absentia. Mao Zedong was one of the delegates representing Hunan province – his home province. The CCP remained a tiny force on the national scene. By 1922 it counted around 200 members all told, not including those overseas. For details of the establishment of the Party see North, Robert C., *Chinese Communism*, London: World University Library, 1966, pp.28–30; and his *Moscow and Chinese Communists*, Stanford: Stanford University Press, 1967, p.58. Also see Chen, Jerome, *Mao and the Chinese Revolution*, London: Oxford University Press, 1965, pp.75–88; Moise, Edwin E., *Modern China: A History*, op. cit., pp.48–53; Spence, J. D., *The Search for Modern China*. op. cit., pp.310–24; Hu, Sheng, op. cit., pp.1192–1201.

2. With the Qing dynasty at an end in 1911, Sun Yat-sen directed that the Revolutionary Alliance transform itself into a centralised, democratic political party that would run candidates for office in the December 1912 election. The Party was now renamed Guomindang, the Nationalist Party. For details of the creation and development of the Nationalist Party, see Rankin, Mary B., *Early Chinese Revolutionaries: Radical Intellectuals in Shanghai and Chekiang, 1902–1911*, Cambridge, MA: Harvard University, 1972; Spence, J. D., *The Search for Modern China*, op. cit., pp. 342, 345, 356; Hu, Sheng, *From the Opium War to the May Fourth Movement*, op. cit., pp. 872–934, 978–98, 1103–1108; Schiffrin, Harold Z., 'The Enigma of Sun Yat-sen', in Wright, Mary Clabaugh (ed.), *China in Revolution: The First Phase, 1900–1913*, op. cit., pp. 443–6; Lu, Zhou, *Zhongguo guomindang shigao* [Draft History of the Nationalist Party], Taibei: Shangwu yinshuguan, 1970.

3. Xiang Jingyu (1895–1928) was a leader of the Communist women's movement and a close friend of Mao Zedong. She was a feminist before she went to France to study in late 1919, having graduated in 1915 from the Zhounan school, the most progressive girls' school in Changsha, Hunan province. She established its first co-educational primary school where she instilled in her students a sense of patriotism, a responsibility to awaken the masses, respect for sexual equality, and contempt for the degrading customs of ear piercing and

footbinding. In the May Fourth Movement she was in the vanguard of Changsha's massive student movement. When she went to France to study, Xiang financed her studies by working part-time in a rubber plant and textile mill, experiences which brought her into direct contact with the French proletariat. By the time the Socialist Youth Corps and the Youth China Communist Party were founded in France in 1921, she and her husband, a close friend of Mao Zedong, had joined the Communist Party. On returning to China in 1922, she criticised Chinese feminism and proved particularly adept at organising working-class women. She thus brought a new dimension to the Party's activities and identified another important source of party support.

The Second Party Congress appointed her as the first woman member of the Central Committee, and made her the first head of the Women's Department. During the next three years all decisions on women taken by the Central Committee were initiated by her. She was captured by the Nationalist Party in the late spring of 1928. She defended herself in the name of the French revolutionary goals of liberty, equality and fraternity, and against the imperialism which was enslaving the Chinese people. She was executed in May 1928. For further details of Xiang's life, see Li, Li-san, 'Tao Xiang Jingyu tongzhi' [Mourning Comrade Xiang Jingyu] written in Moscow in 1935 and reprinted in *Hongqi piaopiao* [The Red Flag Waves], Beijing, Vol. 2, 1957, pp.28–32; Witke, Roxane, 'Women as Politicians in China of the 1920s', and Leith, Suzette, 'Chinese Women in the Early Communist Movement', both in Young, Marilyn B. (ed.), *Women in China: Studies in Social Changes and Feminism*, op. cit., pp.41–3, 50–1, and Snow, Helen. *Women in Modern China*, op. cit., pp.244–49.

4. The Second Congress of the CCP: 'The Resolution of Women's Movement', July 1922; see also the CCP's first manifesto 'On the Current Situation in China' issued in July 1921, in Brandt, Conrad., Schwartz, Benjamin, and Fairbank, John K., *A Documentary History of Chinese Communism*, London: George Allen & Unwin, 1952, p.63.

5. For the Third Congress of the CCP an updated document also called 'The Resolution of Women's Movement', was issued in June 1923.

6. Mao, Zedong. 'Hunan longmin yundong kaocha baogao' [The Report on an Investigation into the Peasant Movement of Hunan], which was first published in 1927 in the *CCP Weekly* and *Chinese Correspondence*. See Chen, Jerome, *Mao and the Chinese Revolution*, op. cit., p.111. This article is now in *Mao Zedong xuanji* [Selected Works of Mao Zedong], Beijing: Renmin chubanshe, Vol. 1, 1991, pp.1–17.

7. See Wang, Yizhi, 'A Great Woman Revolutionary', *China Reconstructs*, March 1965; pp.5–8; Witke, R., 'Women as Politicians in China of 1920s', op. cit., 41–3.

8. Marx, K., *The Holy Family* (Chinese translation), Beijing: Renmin chubanshe, 1976, p.56.

9. Ferdinand August Bebel (1840–1913), German socialist, born at Cologne, went to Leipzig in 1860, where four years later he established himself as a master turner (expert gymnast). As a member of the Reichstag he was an influential representative of socialism, and his several terms of imprisonment only increased his popularity. From 1875 onwards he was a leader of the German Social Democratic party, along with Wilhelm Liebknecht, and represented the Marxist wing of the party as against the followers of Lassalle. He wrote much on the Socialist movement, on the peasants' war, on the status of women and on Sunday labour. His book *Women and Socialism* (1879) was a standard reference work for the CCP's women's movement.

10. Marx and Engels in the *Communist Manifesto* (1848) first expounded socialist views on 'the women's question'. Subsequently Bebel in his *Women and Socialism* (1879) and Engels in his *The Origin of Family, Private and the State* (1884) developed the argument that the solution to the problem of sexual inequality lay in the abolition of capitalism. The phenomena of oppression and exploitation were seen as an essential reflection of the economic base of capitalist society. It was thus inevitable that in a society based on property women would be oppressed. With the overthrow of capitalism and the establishment of socialist production, human relationships would be freed from economic oppression, all exploitation would cease and women would be emancipated.

11. Croll, E., *Feminism and Socialism in China*, op. cit., p.121; Wang, Yizhi, op. cit., pp.25–6; Witke, R., 'Women as Politicians in China of the 1920s', op. cit., p.43.

12. The Nationalist party advocated the Three Principles of the People: anti-imperialist nationalism, democracy and socialism. In 1923, Sun, unable to deal with the warlord government in the North and disillusioned with the Western powers refusal to help, turned to the Soviet Union and the new Communist Party for an alliance to fight the warlords. The first United Front with the Communist Party was set up. Sun died in 1925 and Chiang Kai-shek moved to take command of the Nationalist Party which was a curious mixture of patriots, merchants and bankers. For some considerable time Chiang Kai-shek had seen that the alliance of a landlord and merchant party with Communist revolution was unlikely to endure. In April 1927, at a meeting in Nanjing, the Nationalist Party leaders associated with Chiang decreed the establishment of a national government and proscribed the CCP. The CCP was virtually destroyed. Some leaders went into exile and a few went underground in the cities of the coast. Little was heard of those tattered little groups of Communists who sought refuge in the hills and more backward parts of the countryside. Survivors withdrew deep into the countryside. For details of this split, see Moise, Edwin E., op. cit., pp.63–6; Robottom, John, *Modern China*, London: Longman, 1971, p.27; Reason, Joyce, *Chiang Kai-shek and the Unity of China*, Edinburgh: Edinburgh House Press, 1943, pp.28, 33–4, 43; North, R.C., *Chinese Communism*, op. cit., p.104; Isaacs, H., *The Tragedy of the Chinese Revolution*, Stanford: Stanford University Press, 1951, p.37; Fitzgerald, C.P., *The Birth of Communist China*, Harmondsworth: Penguin, 1964, p.67.

13. North, R.C., *Chinese Communism*, op. cit., p.107.

14. 'Zhongguo gongchandang di liu shi daibiao dahui funu yundong jieyi an' [The Resolution of Women's Movement at the CCP's Sixth Congress] (10 July 1928), in CWF, op. cit., Vol. 2, 1991, pp.16–18.

15. Zhu De (1886–1976) was born in Yinong county, Sichuan province. He studied at Yunnan Military Academy in 1909 and became a member of Sun's Revolutionary Alliance in the same year. He participated in the 1911 Revolution. Later he went to Germany to study and joined the CCP there in 1922. In 1928, when the split in nationalist ranks occurred, he was the director of a military school in Nanchang, Jiangxi province. He commanded a disaffected column of the Nationalist army which fought its way to western Jiangxi where his troop united with Mao's peasant army. The two forces merged to form the Red Army. He was the Commander-in-Chief of the Red Army in 1930s and the Commander-in-Chief of the Chinese Liberation Army from the 1940s to 1970s. For details of his life, see his biography written by Smedley, Agnes, *The Great Road: The Life and Times of Chu Teh [Zhu De]*, London: John Calder, 1958 and

177

her *Battle Hymn of China*, London: Victor Gollancz, 1944, pp.119–21.

16. Carlson, E. F., *The Chinese Army: Its Organization and Military Efficiency*, New York: Institute of Pacific Relations, 1940, pp.15–16.

17. When in 1927 the Nationalist Party proscribed the CCP in all major cities, Mao Zedong went back to his hometown, Hunan, to organise resistance. Since it began in September 1927, it was called the Autumn Harvest Uprising. After the failure of the uprising, Mao Zedong and his peasant troops, almost a thousand men, went to Jinggangshan where they met Zhu De's troops.

18. Jinggangshan is a spiny-backed outcrop, rising four to five thousand feet, which separates Mao's home province Hunan from Jiangxi. There are few more remote places in China. Positioned along the border, spilling over the edge of each province, roadless and heavily wooded, Jinggangshan had for centuries been a preserve of outlaws. No authority exerted much effort to find out what was going on in this wilderness. It was a most suitable place for Mao to establish his revolutionary state. Harrison E. Salisbury has a vivid description of Jinggangshan in his book, *The Long March*, London: Macmillan, 1985, pp.22–8.

19. Agnes Smedley suggests that the colour of red in Chinese culture means life and happiness so it was chosen as the symbol of the new army. In contrast, the colour of white means death so the Red Army soldiers called the Nationalist Army, the White Army. See Smedley, Agnes, *China's Red Army Marches*, London: Lawrence and Wishart, 1936, p.92. It should not be overlooked, however, that the Soviet Union used red as a symbol of the blood of the revolutionary masses shed as the price of their national independence and freedom. The Soviet Union's army was also called the Red Army.

20. Mao's article 'Xingxing zhihuo heyi liaoyuan' [A single spark can start a prairie fire] is in *Mao Zedong xuanji* [Mao Zedong's Select Works], Beijing: Renmin chubanshe, Vol. 1, 1991, pp.97–108.

21. Snow, Edgar, *Red Star Over China*, Harmondsworth: Penguin, 1972, pp.207–208, (first published in 1938 by New York: Grove Press Inc.); North, R.C., *Chinese Communism*, op. cit., pp.122–3.

22. Waller, Derek J., *The Kiangsi Soviet Republic: Mao and the National Congress of 1931 and 1934*, Berkeley: Centre for Chinese Studies, China Research Monographs No. 10, University of California, 1973.

23. CWF, op. cit., Vol. 2, pp.73–7.

24. This Constitution besides granting women equality included the statement: 'all workers, peasants, Red Army men and all toilers and their families, without distinction of sex, religion or nationality . . . . shall while on Soviet territory, be equal before the law and shall be citizens of the Soviet Republic.' In Article 4 the Constitution granted to all adults above the age of sixteen the right to vote and to be elected to soviet positions. For details, see Yakantoff, Victor A., *The Chinese Soviets*, New York: Coward-McCann, Inc., 1934, pp.148–9.

25. Ibid., p.227.

26. Brand, C. et al., *A Documentary History of Chinese Communism*, op. cit., pp.224–5.

27. The Marriage Regulations were issued on 28 November 1931 by Mao Zedong, the Chairman of the Chinese Soviet Republic, and Xiang Yin and Zhang Guotao, the Vice-Chairmen. The document is in CWF, *The Historical Archival of Chinese Women's Movement*, op. cit., Vol. 2, pp.151–4. The English translation is available in Meijer, M.J., *Marriage Law and Policy in the Chinese People's Republic*, Hong Kong: Hong Kong University Press, 1971, pp.281–2. See also Davin, Delia, *Women–Work: Women and the Party in Revolutionary China*,

Oxford: The Clarendon Press, 1976, pp.28–30; Johnson, Ann, *Women, the Family and Peasant Revolution in China*, Chicago: University of Chicago Press, 1983, pp.51–62.

28. The document is in CWF, op. cit., pp.373–4. For an English translation see Johnson, Ann, op. cit., pp.115–37.

29. Hu, Chi-hsi, 'The Sexual Revolution in the Kiangsi Soviet', *The China Quarterly*, Vol. 59, 1974, pp.477–90; Ono Kazuko, op. cit., p.152; David, Delia, *Women–Work*, op. cit., p.28.

30. Ibid., pp.29–30. The reason for this situation lay in the fact that the whole period was marked by a desperate fight for survival by serious tension and struggles within the Party leadership and economic and social policies were unevenly and imperfectly carried out. The strength of conservative attitudes towards women took immense efforts and long periods of time to overcome.

31. The Marriage Laws of 1931 ultimately developed into the Chinese Soviet Marriage Law promulgated on 8 April 1934, and finally evolved into the Marriage Law of the People's Republic of China in 1950. See Davin, Delia, 'Women in the Liberated Areas', in Young, Marilyn B., op. cit., p.74; Ono Kazuko, op. cit., pp.152–3; Hu, Chi-hsi, op. cit.

32. For example, the One Hundred Day Reform (1898), the 1911 Revolution, the New Culture Movement and the May Fourth Movement (1915–1921). All of these political movements had an important impact on urban women's lives but had little influence on rural women.

33. A custom in rural areas: a bride could be provided cheaply for a son by adopting a future daughter-in-law while she was still a child.

34. For details of the custom of adopting daughters-in-law and the rural marriage situation, see Ono Kazuko, op. cit., pp.142–5.

35. Ibid., p.145.

36. Hinton, John, 'Story of A Red Army Woman', *China Reconstructs*, November 1963, pp.34–5.

37. Gongnong xian funu shenghuo gaishan weiyuanhui [Gongnong county women's life improvement committee], 'Gongnong xian diyichi funu shenghuo gaishan weiyuanhui chujin lianxi huiyi jueyian' [Resolution of the First Chairperson's League Conference of Gongnong County Women's Life Improvement Committee] (1931), in *Shi Sou Collection* on Microfilm, Reel 4 (from the Hoover Institute Library, Stanford). In October 1934, when the Nationalists were successful in their fifth attempt at encirclement, the Communists had to leave their Jiangxi Soviet in a hurry and left many documents behind. Chen Cheng (his pen name was Shi Sou), a General of the Nationalist Army, collected these documents. It was known as the *Si Sou Collection* or *Chen Cheng Collection*.

38. Smedley, Agnes, *China's Red Army Marches*. op. cit., p.xviii. The author was one of three women journalists from the Western world. The others were Anna Louise Strong (see note 43) and Helen Foster Snow (see Chapter 6, note 3). Their writings about the era of the Jiangxi Soviet and Yan'an were generally agreed to be reasonably accurate. Agnes Smedley was born in 1892 and grew up in rural Missouri. She arrived in China in 1929 and interviewed veterans of the Long March in 1935. She went to Yan'an, the Communists' capital, in 1937. There she formed good relationships with Communist leaders like Mao Zedong and Zhu De. She never became a CCP member but she did join the Communist 8th Route Army in 1937 – wearing army fatigues and cropping her hair – and travelled hundreds of miles on foot. Her works included *Chinese Destinies* (1933), *China's Red Army Marches* (1934), *China Fights Back: An American Woman with the Eighth Route Army* (1938), *Battle Hymn of China*

(1943), *The Great Road: The Life and Times of Chu Teh* (1956).

39. Van der Valk, M.H., *Conservatism in Modern Chinese Family Law*, Leiden: E.J. Brill, 1956, p.50.

40. Ibid., p.47.

41. Meijer, M.J., *Marriage Law and Policy in the People's Republic*, op. cit., 1971, p.281.

42. Ibid., p.43.

43. Strong, Anna Louise, *The Chinese Conquer China*, New York: Doubleday, 1949, p.409. The author was born in 1885. She came to China in the 1930s. Her first account of China was her *China's Millions* (1928). *Dawn out of China* was based on her experience in China, from July 1940 to July 1947, and *The Chinese Conquer China* (1949) detailed her travels in Communist China. Her most famous piece was her 1946 interview with Mao Zedong then in Yan'an. Her accounts of women constitute the most comprehensive account of Communist attempts to organise rural women during the late 1920s and of the Party's relationship with Chinese women.

44. 'Linshi zhongyang zhengfu wengao, Renmin weiyuanhui xunling (No. 6): Guanyu baohu funu quanli yu jianli funu shenghuo gaishan weiyuanhui de zhuzhi he gongzhuo' [The Decree of Central Government (No. 6): On Protecting Women's Rights and Establishment of Women's Life Improvement Committee], 20 June 1932, *Hongse zhonghua* [Red China], No. 26, 1932.

45. Witke, R., 'Woman as Politician in China of the 1920s', in Young, Marilyn B., op. cit., p.43.

46. North, R.C., *Chinese Communism*, op. cit., p.106.

47. See *Qingnian shihua* [True Words of the Youth], Vol. 2, No. 17, Sept. 1933.

48. The Red Army was the most important of the three elements of Communist rule: army, party and government. The Party exercised civil authority through the Central Bureau for Soviet Areas, but while Party control was extensive over both the soviet areas and the Red Army, it was never complete. As to government, according to Ilpyong J. Kim, the early Jiangxi Soviet government was merely a mass organisation of workers and peasants supporting the Red Army. See Kim, Ilpyong J., *The Politics of Chinese Communism: Kiangsi [Jiangxi] under the Soviets*, Berkeley: University of California, 1973.

49. Chiang Kai-shek (1887–1975), the Commander-in-Chief of the Nationalist army and the President of the National Party. He was born into a family of comfortably off merchants and landlords. Like many young Chinese he bitterly resented the low esteem in which China was held by other countries. He trained at military academies in both China and Japan. He greatly admired Sun Yat-sen who led the Nationalist Party and became Sun's military adviser. He became convinced that the Nationalist Party would only succeed in unifying China if it built up an army of its own and could act independently of the warlords. He thus requested advice and assistance from military experts. Sun sent Chiang to the USSR to see how the Communists had built up their Red Army. With Russian advisers Chiang returned to China and set up the Huangpu Military Academy at which both the National Party and the Communist Party's officers received training before 1927. Thus Chiang knew Communist leaders such as Zhou Enlai but he himself never became a Communist. He was more interested in restoring national prestige and uniting the whole country under one government. When Sun died in 1925, Chiang was able to use his position as army leader to take over control of the Nationalist Party. Chiang acted with the Communists to destroy the power of the northern warlords in the Northern Expedition of 1927. But, fearing the consequences of the great

social changes which the Communists were encouraging among the workers and peasants, he decided that the CCP must be destroyed. After the Nationalist Party's coup of 12 April 1927, Chiang set up a Nationalist government in Nanjing and fought for the next 20 years against warlords, the Japanese and the Communists for the control of China. After the CCP took over Mainland China, Chiang became President of the Guomindang government on Taiwan from 1949 until his death 26 years later.

50. As the influence of the Communists spread in the Jiangxi, Sichuan and Fujian border areas, Chiang Kai-shek decided that the new Soviet Republic was a serious threat to China's future. He decided that all the 'red bandits', as he called the Communists, must be destroyed. Between December 1930 and October 1933 he mounted four unsuccessful campaigns against the Jiangxi Soviet area. Then, with advice from Nazi military advisers, he began his fifth 'extermination' campaign. About 1,000,000 civilians and Red Army soldiers were starved to death or killed. For details of Chiang's campaigns, see Strong, Anne Louise, *China's Millions*, London, 1936, pp.396–411.

51. Quoted in North, R. C., *Chinese Communism*, op. cit., p.108.

52. Whether this was conscious or unconscious is not clear, but there can be no doubt that the liberated women of the Taiping Army had much in common with the liberated women in the Red Army.

53. The name 'Red Sports Movement' first appeared in *Gongnong duben* [Workers and Peasants textbooks], 1932, No. 3, Lesson 77. It stated: 'The Red Sports Movement can strengthen the body and stimulate a revolutionary spirit. Every worker and peasant should participate. The form of the Red Sports Movement includes athletics, ball games, competition and performance.' In 1933 the term was used widely by the Party and media. In March 1933 Zhang Aiping, the Chief-Commander of the Young Pioneers, published an article entitled 'Developing the Red Sports Movement'. In April 1933 *Qingnian shihua* [True Words of the Youth], the periodical of the Youth League, the Party's organisation for youth aged 18 to 25, proposed the creation of a Red Sports Society to develop the Red Sports Movement in the Red area. In October, a Jiangxi Provincial Red Sports Meeting took place. In November *Qingnian shihua* introduced a special column entitled 'Red Sport'. In December, the editor of *Qingnian shihua*, published an article entitled 'The Red Sports Movement and Youth'.

54. In December 1929 the Fourth Division Red Army, led by Zhu De and Mao Zedong, held a Conference in Gutian county, Fujian province. At this Conference Zhu and Mao established the basic principles of the Red Army.

55. Mao, Zedong, 'Zhongguo gongchandang hongjun di si jun di jiu shi daibiao dahui jueyi an' [The Resolution of the Ninth Congress of the Fourth Division Red Army], October 1929, in *Mao Zedong xuanji*, [Mao Zedong's Selected Works], Dongbei Press, 1948, pp.3–7.

56. Gu, Shiquan, 'Shuqu shiqi Julebu he Leninshi de tiyu' [The Club and the Lenin Room's Sports Activities in the Soviet Area], *TWS*, No. 5, 1986, p.32.

57. Gu, Shiquan, ibid.

58. The Second All-Chinese Soviet Congress was held at Ruijin, the capital city of the Chinese Soviet Republic, in January 1934. During the Congress Mao, whose influence had been increasing within the Chinese revolutionary movement, made a speech. He called for a Red Army of a million men, the enlargement of the Red Guard and other reserve forces, and the boosting of agriculture and industrial production. His speech was entitled 'rechi quanguo suweiai daibiao dahui baogao' [The Report of the Chinese Soviet Republic Central Committee and People's Committee to the Second All-Chinese Soviet Congress]

and it was published in *Hongse zhonghua* [Red China], No. 3, 26 Jan. 1934. For details of this Conference, see Strong, Anne Louise, *China's Millions*, op. cit., pp.406–408.

59. Gu, Shiquan, 'Shuqu shiqi Julebu he Leninshi de tiyu' [The Club and the Lenin Room's Sports Activities in the Soviet Area], op. cit., pp.31–2.

60. CSHSPES, *Zhongguo jindai tiyu shi* [Modern Chinese Sports History], op. cit., p.367.

61. 'Zhuzhi laoku qingnian de tiyu yundong' [On the Promotion of Peasant and Worker's Physical Exercise], *Qingnian shihua* [True Words of Youth], Vol. 2, No. 8, March 1933; 'Ben bao faqi chishe zhuzhi' [We Promote the Red Sports Movement], *Qingnian shihua* [True Words of Youth], Vol. 2, No. 11, April 1933.

62. Mangan, J.A., 'The Social Construction of Victorian Femininity: Emancipation, Education and Exercise', op. cit., p.1; Gerry, Finn, 'Sporting Symbols, Sporting Identities: Soccer and Intergroup Conflict in Scotland and Northern Ireland', in Wood, I.S. (ed.), *Scotland and Ulster*, Edinburgh: The Mercat Press, 1994, pp.31–46.

63. 'Chishe tiyu yungong' [The Red Sports Movement], in *Gongnong duben* [Worker and Peasant's Text Books], No. 3, Lesson 77, 1932 (n.p.).

64. The leaders of the Army, the Party and the Government were present at, participated in, and referees at almost every competitive sports meeting. On such occasions they would instruct the spectators and the athletes on the value of sport.

65. Xiao Hua, who was then a young Red Army soldier, became a General of the Chinese Navy after 1949. In an article, 'Huoxian shang de qingnian wanhui' [Youth Competition at the Front] in 1933, he wrote that Zhu De, the Commander-in-Chief of the Army was the chief referee of the competition. Zhu De made a speech in which he emphasised that the aims of sports competitions were to attract the masses, train their collective spirit and their military skills. This view was repeated and re-emphasised on several later occasions. This article was also published in *Qingnian shihua* [True Words of Youth], Vol. 2, No. 24, Aug. 1933.

66. See Chapter Six.

67. Agnes Smedley said of the club system that 'there was a Club in each regiment to direct the political, cultural, and recreational activities of all the men in the ranks. There were four committees under the Club's direction – athletics, cultural work, wall-newspapers and evening meeting.' See *China's Red Army Marches*, op. cit., pp.199–200. Jonathan Kolatch also mentioned the club system in his book, *Sport Politics and Ideology in China*, op. cit. Both descriptions were simple, as well as inaccurate. These inaccuracies will be considered later.

68. Vladimir Ilyich Lenin (1870–1924), the Russian revolutionary, was the founder of the Bolshevik Party and the Soviet state. The Chinese communists named their educational and cultural centres after him. There was always a portrait of Lenin on a wall in each centre.

69. 'Hongjun zhong Julebu Leninshi de zhuzhi gongzuo' [Resolution of the Organisation and Work of Club and Lenin Room in the Red Army], April 1934, in Cheng, Yuanhui (ed.), *Laojiefangqu jiaoyu zhiliao* [Educational Archives of Soviets and Liberated Areas], Beijing: Jiaoyu kexue chubanshe, 1981, pp.27–9.

70. Kang Keqing recalled that in 1926 when she was 15 and before the Red Army arrived at her village, she could neither read and write. Many Red Army soldiers like her were from very poor backgrounds. See Nym Wales (Helen Snow's pseudonym), *Red Dust*, Westport: Connecticut, 1972, p.212.

71. Xiuan, Jintang, 'Huiyi gang dongbei sheng hongjun pengyang junzheng

xuexiao' [Recollections of Pengyang Military and Political School], in Zeng, Biao, *Suqu tiyu ziliao xuanbian* [Selected Sources of Physical Education of the Jiangxi Soviet Area], 1985, p.51 (n.p.).

72. Li, Zhaobin, 'Hongjun shiqi de wenhua shenghuo diandi' [Recollections of the Cultural life in the Red Army: The Red Army's School-Club], *Jiefangjun wenyi* [Journal of People's Liberation Army's Literature], No. 8, 1952, pp.21–3.

73. Hu, Yimeng, and Hu, Yuanfa, 'Huiyi hongjun zai huangpo de tiyu huodong' [The Recollections of the Red Army's Sports in Huangpo Village], in Zeng, Biao, *Suqu tiyu ziliao xuanbian* [Selected Sources of Physical Education of the Jiangxi Soviet Area], op. cit., p.56.

74. Smedley, Agnes, *China's Red Army Marches*, op. cit., p.200.

75. Liu, Lian, 'Zhu zong shiling chanjia de lanqiu sai' [Zhu De and Basketball Competitions], in Zeng, Biao, *Suqu tiyu ziliao xuanbian* [Selected Sources of Education of the Jiangxi Soviet Area], op. cit., pp.59–60.

76. Zeng, Biao, 'Zhu zong shiling he yichang lanqiusai' [Zhu De and a Basketball Match], *TWS*, No. 3, 1986, pp.27–8.

77. Snow, Helen, *Red Dust*, op. cit., p.214.

78. Salisbury, Harrison E., op. cit., 1985, p.32.

79. Du, Zhong, and Huang, Yao, 'Chuanshan genjudi de gongnong tiyu huodong' [Worker–Peasant's Sports Activities in Sichuan–Shanxi Border Red Area], *TWS*, No. 4, 1983, p.45.

80. The Red areas expanded rapidly from the Jiangxi–Hunan–Fjuian border to Shanxi–Sichuan and Jiangxi–Anhui border areas. The Fourth Front Army was in the Shanxi–Sichuan border area and the Second Front Army was in the Jiangxi–Anhui borders. In 1934 the Communists controlled an area of 100,000 square miles with a population of roughly 36 million.

81. Jie, Jinin, 'Hongjun zai jiange de tiyu huodong' [The Red Army's Sports Activities in Jiange County], *TWS*, No. 6, 1986, p.4.

82. Snow, Helen, *Red Dust*, op. cit., p.216.

83. See 'Gongnong hongjun xuexiao shengda de yundonghui' [The Report on the Big Competition of the Worker–Peasant Red Academy], *Hongse zhonghua* [Red China], No. 32, 6 Sept. 1932.

84. 'Weisheng xuexiao tiyu dahui' [The Report of the Competition of the Red Army's School of Medicine], *Qingnian shihua* [True Words of Youth], Vol. 3, No. 4, 17 Dec. 1933.

85. 'Hongjun weisheng xuexiao tiyu yundong hui' [The Report of the Sports Meeting of the Red Army's School of Medicine], *Qingnian shihua* [True Words of Youth], Vol. 2, No. 7, 12 March 1933.

86. Smedley, Agnes, *China's Red Army Marches*, op. cit., p.176.

87. Jiangxi sheng funu lianhehui [The Jiangxi Women's Association] (ed.), *Jiangxi funu geming douzheng gushi* [Stories of Jiangxi Women's Revolutionary Struggle], Beijing: Zhongguo funu chubanshe [Chinese Women's Press], 1963, p.2.

88. Salisbury, Harrison E., op. cit., p.81.

89. There were 30 women cadres marching with the First Front Army and they were mentally and physically tough. After the year-long march, they reached Yan'an safely.

90. Salisbury, Harrison E., op. cit., p.88.

91. Ibid.

92. The leader of the Fourth Front Army, Zhang Guotao (1897–1979) was one of the founders of the CCP and the Vice-President of the Chinese Soviet Republic in the Jiangxi Era. During the Long March, Zhang's troops and Mao's troops

met in North Sichuan in June 1935. After weeks of discussion the two leaders could only agree to disagree, Mao insisting on the need to drive yet farther north and east to Shanxi or Ningxia, Zhang wishing to build an isolated and defensible soviet in the Sichuan–Xikang border region. Mao wanted to form a 'united national defence government' when he reached his new base area, so that all Chinese could join forces against Japanese aggression. Mao's intention, in fact, coincided with the Comintern's recent decisions in Moscow. It is not clear if Mao was in touch with them or simply thinking along parallel lines. Zhang sought independence from the Comintern for the CCP and was unhappy with this arrangement. While Mao's troops continued towards the north, Zhang's troops took the reverse route south. Mao's troop arrived in Shanxi in October 1935 and set up a Communist base there. Zhang's plan to establish a Communist base in the Sichuan–Xikang border region failed. His troops were badly mauled in heavy fighting with regional warlords and the Nationalist army. They had to head north. Over the course of the following year, 1936, surviving troops from Zhang's army slowly straggled into Shanxi.

93. Kim, Ilpyong J., op. cit., p.53.
94. See 'Jiangxi shengzhengfu tonggao diyihao: guanyu chexiao funu gongzuo weiyuanhui wenti' [No. 1 Announcement of Jiangxi Provincial Government: on the Issue of Abolishing the Women's Work Committee], 26 March 1931, in CWF, op. cit. Vol. 2, pp.161–2.
95. See 'Xiang-Gang-Bian suqu funu gongzuo jueyi an' [The Resolution of Women's Work in Hunan–Jiangxi Border Soviet Area], 10 Sept. 1931, in CWF, ibid., Vol. 2, pp.157–60.
96. Ibid.
97. Both Davin, op. cit., and Kim, op. cit., neglect these women's agencies. Frenier criticised Davin and Kim for this omission. She argued that the two institutes were women's mass organisations. In fact, they were government agencies. See Frenier's dissertation, op. cit., p.57.
98. Kristeva, Julia, op. cit., p.114.
99. Ibid.
100. 'The Announcement of Hunan Provincial Committee of CCP (No. 14) On the Current Situation of Hunan Women and the Principle of Our Work', 25 Nov. 1927, in CWF, op. cit., Vol. 2, p.8.
101. Salatt, Janet Weitzner, and Merkle, Judith, 'Women in Revolution: the Lessons of the Soviet Union and China', Socialist Revolution, 1970, Vol. 1, No. 6, pp.59–62.
102. Frenier, Mariam Darce, op. cit., p.3.
103. See CWF, Zhongguo funu yundong lishi zhiliao [The Historical Archives of Chinese Women's Movement], four volumes, published by the Chinese Women's Press in 1988 and the Chen Cheng Collection, op. cit..
104. Kristeva, Julia, op. cit., p.114.
105. Simultaneously, the Party sought to impose its ban on footbinding – some men still, even at this late date, prevented women from unbinding their feet in the belief that they were prettier when bound. The Jiangxi Soviet Executive Committee told its cadres in no uncertain terms: 'The soviet of each level must do its best to enforce the Unbinding Feet Movement and . . . to make it possible for women with unbound feet to learn to work.' This attitude and its consequences created favourable conditions for participation in the Red Sports Movement among those oppressed physically by feudal customs. See Jiangxi Provincial Soviet Executive Committee, 'Concerning working women's special benefits', 22 Jan. 1934, in Chen Cheng Collection, Reel 6.

106. The Red Vanguards were a military youth organisation (between the ages of 23–25) in the soviet area. It was a reserve force of the Red Army. It was supervised by the government, the Youth League and the Army.

107. The Young Pioneers was a youth organisation (between the ages of 13–16) in the soviet area. It comprised a reserve force of the Red Army. It was supervised by the Youth League and the Party.

108. The Children's Corps was the organisation of children (between the ages of 8–15). It was a reserve force of the Young Pioneers. It was supervised by the Young Pioneers and the Youth League.

109. Smedley, Agnes, *China's Red Army Marches*, op. cit., p.206.

110. Mao, Zedong. 'Xingguo diaocha' [The Investigation of Xingguo County], in *Mao Zedong xuanji* [Selected Works of Mao Zedong], Dongbei shudian [Dongbei Press], op. cit., pp.75–81.

111. Mao, Zedong. 'Xiangsu gongzuo de muofan – Changgang xiang' [The Model of Soviet Work in Changgang Village].This document is in the Gangxian Museum, Jiangxi province, China.

112. Ibid.

113. Ibid.

114. C.Y. Suqu zhongyangju [The Soviet Central Committee of the Youth League], 'Muqian Suweiai quyu shaonian Xianfengdui gongzuo dagang' [The Outline of the Present Work of the Young Pioneers in the Soviet Area], 4 Jan. 1932, in *Zhongguo qingnian yundong lishi zhiliao* [Historical Archive of the Chinese Youth Movement], edited and published by Zhongguo qingnian tuan zhongyang weiyuanhui [The Central Committee of the Chinese Youth League], 1957, pp.5–7.

115. Shaonian xianfengdui zhongyang zhongduibu [The Headquarters of the Young Pioneers], 'Shaonian xianfengdui zhongyang zhongbu xunli' [The Order of the Headquarters of the Young Pioneers], 13 June 1932, in Chen, Yuanhui, op. cit., pp.23–4.

116. Zhang, Aiping. 'Shaonian xianfengdui zhongyang zhongduibu de xin: wei jianli wenhua jiaoyu yu tiyu yundong de muofanqu de gongzhuo' [Letter from the Headquarters of the Young Pioneers: Setting up Model Branches of Education and Sports Movement], *Qingnian shihua* [True Words of Youth], No. 21, 27 Nov. 1932.

117. Zhou Enlai (1898–1976) was at this time the Commissar of the Young Pioneers. After 1949, he served as Chinese Premier and was influential in Chinese foreign policy for three decades.

118. See 'Zhongyang zhongduibu minling di si hao' [The No. 4 Order of The Headquarters of the Young Pioneers] issued by Zhang Aiping, the Chief, and Zhou Enlai, the Commissar of the Young Pioneers on 8 April 1934. The original document is in Ruijin xian geming lishi bowuguan [Ruijin county's Revolutionary History Museum], Jiangxi province, China.

119. The Central Committee for People's Education [Zhongyang jiaoyu renmin weiyuanhui] approved these two books in March 1934. The original document of approval is in Ruijin Revolutionary History Museum, Jiangxi province, China.

120. Gu, Shiquan, 'Zhongyang suqu shiqi Lenin xiaoxue Ertongtuan he Shaoxiangdui de tiyu' [Sports Activities of Lenin Schools and the Young Pioneers in the Soviet Period], *TWS*, No. 6, 1986, p.29.

121. Zhang, Aipin. 'Fazhan hongshe tiyu yundong' [Developing the Red Sports Movement], *Qingnian Shihua* [True Words of Youth], Vol. 2, No. 9, 26 March 1933.

122. Zeng, Biao, 'Zhang Aiping yu tiyu' [Zhang Aiping and Sports], *Xin Tiyu* [The New Sport], No. 4, 1982, pp.13–15.
123. See the report, 'Muofanyun de Lenin shi gongzuo' [The Model Work of Lenin Rooms], *Hongse zhonghua* [Red China], No. 166, 24 March, 1934.
124. Mao, Zedong, 'Xingguo Diaocha' [The Investigation of Xingguo County], op. cit.
125. Smedley, Agnes, *China's Red Army Marches*, op. cit., p.206.
126. See the document of the Central Committee of the Youth League, 'Tuan zhongyang guanyu retong yundong jueyi an' [The Central Committee of the Youth League' Resolution about the Children's Corps Movement], 17 June 1931, in Zhongguo qingniantuan zhongyang weiyuanhui [The Central Committee of the Chinese Youth League], op. cit., p.86.
127. See 'Xiang-Gang suqu retongtuan gongzuo jueyi'an' [The Resolution of the Work of the Children's Corps in the Soviet Area], Jan. 1932. (This document is in Jiangxi Provincial Museum, China).
128. Mao, Zedong, 'Xingguo diaocha' [The Investigation of Xingguo County], op. cit.
129. Zhang, Aiping, 'Women de jieri' [Our Happy Festival], *Qingnian shihua* [True Words of Youth], Vol. 2, No. 6, 5 March 1933.
130. See the report, 'Di erchi quanguo suweiai daibiao dahui de baogao' [The Report of the Chinese Soviet republic Central Committee and People's Committee to the Second All-China Soviets Congress], op. cit.
131. There are no numbers available to show how many girl students enrolled in these schools, but according to Mao's investigation of Xingguo county, there were 12,806 students in Lenin primary school of which boys numbered 8,825, and girls 3,981. Girl students thus comprised more than one third of the student numbers. This, however, reveals that conservative views still had to be overcome.
132. See 'Xiaoxue kecheng yu jiaozhe caoan' [A Draft Resolution of the Curriculum] issued by the Centre Committee for the People's Education in Oct. 1933. This document is in *Suqu jiaoyu ziliao xuanbia* [Selected Archives of Education in the Soviet Areas] edited and published by Jiangxi renmin chubanshe [Jiangxi People's Press], 1981, pp.12–14.
133. Ibid.
134. Zhang Wentian (1900–76) joined the CCP in 1925. He was the head of the Propaganda Department and the Chairman of the Government from 1933 to 1934.
135. See 'Zhonghua suweiai gongheguo xiaoxuexiao zhidu zhanxin tiaolin [Draft Decree of Primary Schools System in the Chinese Soviet Republic], 16 Feb. 1934. This Decree is in *Suweiai jiaoyu fagui* [The Law of Education in the Soviets Period] edited and published by Jiangxi renmin chubanshe [Jiangxi People's Press], 1956, pp.66–7.
136. Zhang, Aiping, 'Women de Jieri' [Our Happy Festival], op. cit.
137. See Zhu De's speech, quoted in Liu Lian, 'Zhu zhong shiling chanjia de lanqiu sai' [Zhu De and the Basketball Competitions], op. cit.; Xiao, Hua, 'Huoxianshang de qingnian wanhui' [The Youth Competition at the Front], op. cit.
138. *Qingnian shihua* [True Words of Youth] was the periodical of the Central Bureau of the Young Pioneers and the Youth League. The Youth League supervised by the CCP, was, and still is, the reserve force of the CCP. People between the ages of 18 and 25 can apply to join it. It recommends outstanding members to the CCP.
139. See the article entitled 'Jiangxi wuyi qiunei dabisai' [Jiangxi Provincial Ball

Games Competition], *Qingnian shihua* [True Words of Youth], Vol. 2, No. 15, 14 May 1933.

140. Gu, Runmin, 'Fujian junqu yundong dahui shengkuang' [The Report of the Sports Competition of Fujian Red Army Division], *Hongse zhonghua* [Red China], No. 92, 8 July 1933.

141. Quoted in CSHSPE, *Zhongguo jindai tiyu shi* [Modern Chinese], op. cit., p.366.

142. Zeng, Biao, 'Hongse tiyu zai douzhen zhong fazhan' [The Development of the Red Sports through Struggle], in CSHSPE, *Lunwei ji* [Selected Works], op. cit., Vol. 1, 1984, pp.35–40; Wang Wenjin, 'Hongjun tiyu bisai jiangzhang' [The Medals of the Red Sports Competitions], *Xin tiyu* [The New Sport], No. 11, 1981, p.5.

143. This newspaper report was published in *Hong xing bao* [Red Star News], No. 7. The report is in the Ruijin county museum, Jiangxi province.

144. Xiao, Hua, 'Bayi qianfang junshi jishu bishai' [The Front Military Competition of the First of August], *Qingnian shihua* [True Words of Youth], Vol. 2, No. 27, 3 Sept. 1933.

145. Ou, Yangqing, 'Wei xuexi he tigao junshi jishu re douzhen' [Studying and Improving Our Military Skill], *Hongse zhonghua* [Red China], No. 97, 29 July 1933.

146. Quoted in Xiao Hua's article [Huoxian shang de qingnian wanghui' [The Youth Competition at the Front], op. cit.

147. This ubiquity may be illustrated by events in 1933.
    January: Red Academy Revolutionary Competition (2 Jan.).
    February: Yudu County Guerrilla Sports and Military Meeting (5 Feb.).
    March: Civil Service Basketball Competition (19 March).
    April: The Third Regiment – Jiangxi Provincial Civil Service Competition (16 April); a match between the team of the Bureau of the Soviet Political Security and the Red Army's School (23 April).
    May: The First Red Army Front Inter-Army Match. (1 May); Ruijin County Basketball and Football Competition (1 May); Jiangxi Provincial Clubs' Ball Games Competition (1 May); The Chinese Soviet Republic's May 30th Sports Meeting (30 May).
    June: Fujian Red Army Division's Sports Meeting (16 June), (mass organisations and schools were invited to join the competition which included 19 events); The Red Army Medicine School's Inter-School Match (24 June); The Red Army's Supplementary Regiment's Sports Competition (29 June).
    July: The First Ruijin County Sports Competition (19 July); The First Red Sports Meeting of Dindong County (20 July).
    August: The First Red Army Front's Military and Sports Competition (1 Aug.); The First Red Army Regiment's Red Sports Meeting (1 Aug.); The Fujian Provincial Red Sports Meeting (2 Aug.) – at the end of the Sports Meeting the Fujian Branch of the Red Sports Society was established; The Jiangxi Provincial Red Sports Meeting (3 Aug.) – the athletes came from the Red Army troops, the Young Pioneers, Civil Service and the mass organisations of ten counties. At the end of the Sports Meeting, the Jiangxi Branch of the Red Sports Society was founded.
    November: Sports Meeting in Jiangxi province to celebrate the Russian Soviet Day (7 Nov.);The Ruijin County Inter-club Sports Meeting (29 Nov.).
    December: The Xijiang County's Inter-Schools' Match (3 Dec.); The Red Army's Medicine School's Sports Meeting. (3 Dec.); The Students Sports Meeting of the Wenxi town, Xinguo County (15 Dec.); Fujian Provincial Performance and Sports Meeting (27 Dec.) – this competition was held by the Fujian Provincial

Education Department to celebrate the Second Congress of the Soviet Republic. All of the competitions were reported by *Qingnian shihua* [True Words of Youth] and *Hongse zhonghua* [The Red China] in 1933.

148. This decree was entitled 'Wusa juxin chishe yundonghui' [Red Sports Meeting Will Take Place on 30 May] and it was published in *Hongse zhonghua* [Red China], No. 77, 8 May 1933.

149. A post-war phenomenon was the mounting division between socialists and communists over the leadership and aims of the workers' sports movement. There were two major international sports organisations: The International Association of Red Sports and Gymnastics Association (RSI) and the Lucerne Sports International (LSI). The RSI was a branch of the Communist International or Comintern. The LSI was a branch of the Bureau of the Socialist International. The two workers' sports organisations were hostile right from the start. The Communist RSI wished to build an international sports movement that would be a political vehicle of the class struggle. The socialist LSI was not concerned with the sports movement as an active revolutionary force, instead, it was to be a strong, independent movement within capitalist society ready, after the revolution, to implement a fully developed system of physical culture. Eventually, the LSI banned all RSI members from its activities and all contacts with the USSR. For more details see Riordan, J., *Sport, Politics and Communism*, op. cit., pp.36–7. The Red Sports Society in Jiangxi declared that it was a member of the RSI. Therefore, the Red Sports Movement in Jiangxi could be seen as a part of the international workers' sports movement and the international communist movement.

150. Ibid.

151. Zhang, Aiping, 'Wusa chise yundong dahui de zhongjie' [Report on the Significance of 30 May Sports Meeting], *Qingnian shihua* [True Words of Youth], Vol. 2, No. 18, 11 June 1933.

152. See Bi Chen's report 'Jianxisheng chise tiyu yundonghui zhongjie' [Report on the Significance of the Jiangxi Provincial Sports Meeting], in *Qingnian shihua* [True Words of the Youth], Vol. 2, No. 25, 20 Aug. 1933, and Tang Jian's report, 'Bayi Fujian quansheng chise tiyu yundong dahui de zhongjie' [Report on the Significance of the 1 August Fujian Provincial Red Sports Meeting], in *Qingnian shihua* [True Words of Youth], Vol. 2, No. 25, 20 Aug. 1933.

153. See 'Xiang-e-gang sheng gong nong bin suweiai di yi chi daibiao dahui wenhua wenti jueyi an' [The Resolution of Culture and Education of the First Congress of Xinag-e-gang Soviet Area] 23 Sept. 1931; 'Di re chi min-zhe-gang sheng su dahui wenhua gongzuo jueyi an' [The Resolution of Culture and Education of the Congress of Min-zhe-gang Soviet Area] autumn 1932; and 'Yongxin xian jiaoyu wenti jueyi an' [The Resolution of Culture and Education of Yongxin County] 3 June 1932. These documents are in Jiangxi danganguan [Jiangxi Provincial Archives], China.

154. Zhang, Aiping, 'Wusa chise yundong dahui de zhongjie' [Report on the Significance of the 30 May Sports Meeting], op. cit.

155. Bi, Chen, 'Jianxisheng chise tiyu yundonghui zhongjie' [The Significance of the Jiangxi Provincial Sports Meeting], op. cit..

156. Tang, Jian, 'Bayi Fujian quansheng chise tiyu yundong dahui de zhongjie' [Report on the Significance of the 1 August Fujian Provincial Red Sports Meeting], op. cit.

157. Bi, Chen, 'Nuzi lanqiudui de chuxian' [The Emergence of Women's Basketball Teams], *Qingnia shihua* [True Words of Youth], Vol. 3, No. 4, 17 Dec. 1933.

158. The statistics are in *Hongse zhonghua* [Red China], No. 239, 29 Sept. 1934.

159. Smedley, Agnes, *China's Red Army Marches*, op. cit., p.xviii.
160. Ibid., p.xviii.
161. 'Minxi suweiai zhengfu tonggao di qi hao: muqian funu gongzhuo zhongxin gongzuo' [No. 7 Announcement of Minxi Soviet Government: Present Aims and Works of the Women's Movement] 6 Dec. 1930, in CWF, op. cit., Vol. 2, p.97.
162. See Chapter Six.
163. Davin, D., op. cit.; Frenier, M., op. cit., pp.37–81.

SIX

Freedom Without Feminism:
The Yan'an Women
(1935–49)

꒰ঌ৴৹৴ঌ৴꒱

T HE LONG MARCH ended in October, 1935.[1] Eight thousand Party members and Red Army survivors arrived in the northwest – one of the most remote and impoverished areas of the country – to join groups of Communists who had established base area governments in northern Shanxi in the early 1930s.[2] The CCP gradually expanded its territory and in July 1936 a base was established where Shanxi, Gansu and Ningxia provinces intersect. It was called the 'Sha-Gan-Ning Border Area' or 'Border Area' or simply the Liberated Area. Its capital city was Yan'an.[3] In 1936 the population under Communist control was less than one million. From this inauspicious beginning the CCP spread across north China and back into south and east China. In about 15 years it controlled the whole mainland of China.[4]

Historians have already noticed the importance of the Japanese invasion in bringing about the CCP's victory.[5] The invasion transformed the Civil War into a National War and the Communists and Nationalists formed a United Front – arguably the result of the 1936 Xi'an kidnapping of Chiang Kai-shek.[6] However, the two parties remained distinct and in control of different parts of China. The Communist-held area around Yan'an was formed into a 'special border region', which was never invaded by the Japanese. Consequently, it experienced a time of relative tranquillity compared with the period of the Jiangxi Soviet.

This partial peace and the associated stability in the Border Area for the next eight years provided the CCP with an opportunity for creative reconstruction unprecedented in its stormy history. During the years of war with Japan the strategy and tactics of the Communist movement in China matured to become a viable revolutionary programme.[7] One of the ingredients of the CCP's success was the committed advocacy of women's emancipation. The Communist Women's Movement, of course, was born in the early 1920s and evolved steadily in the Jiangxi Soviet period, but it achieved sharp theoretical and practical definition in the Yan'an period. The policies and procedures worked out in Jiangxi, but honed in Yan'an, became the model for the Women's Emancipation Movement in other areas.[8] Many of these policies and procedures remain important to the thinking of the Party today.

Consolidation rather than Destruction – A New Start

To the extent that women were of service to the Party it claimed to, and indeed did liberate them from feudal authoritarianism, cultural and sexual oppression. It believed that not only would women, as an especially oppressed group, make good revolutionaries, but that once granted equality, women would have gained so much that in appreciation they would remain strong supporters of the Party's causes. This belief in the pragmatic political value of women's liberation characterised the Yan'an period, but the methods employed to achieve realisation of this liberation were determined to a great extent by local conditions. CCP policies governing the form and content of women's emancipation reflected an awareness by the CCP of the peculiar conditions in the Shan-Gan-Ning Border Area. In effect, it was forced to start all over again – and sow fresh seeds of selective freedom in far stonier social ground than Jiangxi.

The Border Area, particularly northern Shanxi, was one of the poorest regions of China. Its fertile loess soil was subject to marginal and unpredictable rainfall. Remote and inaccessible, even in 1936, it was largely untouched by modern influence. In the recent past its population had suffered from harsh warlordism, ever-worsening peasant indebtedness, ever accelerating rates of land tenancy, rising rates of absentee landlordism, heavy taxes and famine. Mark Selden has summed up the grim condition of the peasantry as especially intolerable even for China.[9] Peter J. Seybolt has pointed out it was an area with a 60 per cent infant mortality rate and a one per cent literacy rate.[10]

The remoteness and poverty of the area shored up conservative attitudes towards women. This conservatism was manifested in the continued use of footbinding, which had largely died out elsewhere in

China, wife-beating, concubinage, poor female health and the sale of women and children during the great famines of the early 1930s.[11] According to Delia Davin, the Confucian ideal that women should remain secure in their home was more prevalent here than Jiangxi, 'perhaps because it was a frontier area with a long history of border raids'.[12] But it can be argued equally that this area had been a centre of feudal Chinese culture for a long time.[13] Old sayings such as 'Officials depend on seals; tigers depend on mountains; women depend on their husbands', 'If I buy a horse, I can beat it; if I marry a wife, I can do as I like with her',[14] were subscribed to not only by men but also by women themselves. Chen Boda, the foremost interpreter of the thought of Mao Zedong, stated that women were seen as men's appendages. The husband was the wife's owner, the wife was the husband's serf. Marriage was a slave system.[15] Jack Belden noticed that women in this area thought so little of their position in society that often they wished to be reborn as dogs so that they might wander where they chose, instead of being shut up inside their husband's home day and night without freedom.[16] Deng Yingchao,[17] the leader of Communist Women's Movement, pointed out that in this area the fight to overcome the idea that women should be concerned with nothing but household affairs was particularly difficult. 'Our job wasn't easy: giving them a sense of their importance and an awareness of what we wanted our country to be.'[18]

During the Yan'an period, as noted above, the CCP, the party of worker and peasant, allied itself with the Nationalist Party, the party of the bourgeoisie and landlord, in order to unite to fight the Japanese imperialists.[19] Because of this alliance the overt Communist aims became: to support the Nationalist government in the plans to hasten peaceful unification under Chiang Kai-shek, to realise bourgeois democracy, and to organise the whole nation to oppose Japan.[20] In this situation radical policies could not be undertaken because that would destroy the United Front. The Party's policy toward a peasant revolution was different, therefore, from the Jiangxi Era. It has been characterised as necessary retrenchment.[21]

This retrenchment influenced CCP policy on a wide range of issues including women's emancipation. The Party had to tread even more cautiously than in Jiangxi. It tried to find a way to liberate women without provoking resentment on all sides: rich and poor, progressives and conservatives, communists and nationalists. As Jack Belden stated, not only 'Chinese society in general, but even the structure of the state, from the village at the bottom to the throne at the top, was definitely influenced by the status of women as slaves, private property . . . and producers of sons for the ruling class . . . Any all-out attempt to free women could only result in the upheaval of the whole social pyramid and a tremendous change in the correlation of forces struggling for power.'[22]

The liberation of women, therefore, was still something to be achieved warily, pragmatically and certainly more gradually than hitherto, rather than by idealistic, quick and complete implementation. The CCP began with the introduction of laws similar to those instituted in the Jiangxi Soviet. It declared that women were equal in society, government, economy, education and the family. But the Party was fully aware that economic independence and social transformation involving women would not be accepted easily. In such a remote area with widespread illiteracy and restricted communications, it was appreciated that it would take a long time to make the new laws universally effective and to translate the movement's principles into permanent practices.[23] The new marriage law, for example, incorporating the principle of free choice was widely publicised, but 'free marriage' was presented only as the ideal. Instead of encouraging free choice and divorce, the Party emphasised 'togetherness' based on compatibility of political views! Women were mobilised for production in order to obtain economic freedom *for* their families, not *from* their families. In short, once again the emphasis of the Party's policy was on sexual cohesion not confrontation.

In Yan'an, as in Jiangxi, therefore, the Party liberated women only up to a point and once again with its own priorities firmly in mind. Women were encouraged to change their view of themselves but not to the extent of becoming a threat to family solidarity or Party unity.[24] The Party recognised that raising the status of women should start in the family because the status of women was most intimately related to its structure, and the family still had a basic significance for women's lives. However, the central feature of traditional Chinese society as a whole was that the individual's loyalty toward the family transcended all other social obligations. The family was of paramount importance in the pattern of social organisation. As the majority of families based on traditional marriages continued to operate mostly according to traditional principles a sudden change in women's status, which would have a disruptive influence on family unity and harmony, would pose a serious threat to the stability of the Communist base.[25]

194

For practical reasons, then, the Party felt the need to bring about both women's liberation and to maintain general social cohesion. To cope with this two-pronged problem, the Party argued that: 'Our slogan is not "emancipate women from the family", because it will not work at present.'[26] It advocated instead a new family concept which was intended to be 'constructive' rather than 'destructive'. Its aim was 'to establish a harmonious family'.[27] The main methods were to educate male peasants and mothers-in-law to train daughters, wives and daughters-in-law in family equality; and to educate women to abandon their old inferior image and be counted in the family as a real member – a human being.[28] Women's essential role was still confined to being a virtuous wife, good mother, filial daughter and daughter-in-law, but with an added new meaning and dignity: they were to be active, important, and respected in the community![29]

The Party's attitude and policy towards women, however, were attacked by feminists. When Westernised women intellectuals from urban areas like Shanghai and Beijing came to Yan'an, they brought with them ideas of women's emancipation influenced by feminist values developed in the May Fourth Era. They favoured an all-out attack on the feudal family sytem. The great clash between them and the Party came in 1942 when Ding Ling,[30] a feminist who is now an important communist writer, wrote her 'Thoughts on March 8' (International Women's Day)[31] in *Jiefang ribao* [Liberation Daily], the party's official organ. She criticised the party's policy towards women and stated that the traditional view of womanhood was still prevalent in Yan'an. She argued that the Party leadership was using the slogans of national resistance and party solidarity to undermine the recently hard-won rights of women. The Party counter-attacked her views as 'narrowly feminist'[32] and, as Ding Ling told the journalist Gunther Stein, she and others were severely criticised. They were told that full sexual equality had already been established and that their feminism was outdated and harmful.[33]

Bourgeois feminism in the style of a Miss Sophie (the heroine of Ding Ling's novel *The Diary of Miss Sophie*) was regarded as pointless. The Party put forward, as an alternative to the 'Feminist Woman', the 'Yan'an Woman'. In theory, she was equal to man (by communist proclamation) but she was to remain a model wife, a good mother and a filial daughter-in-law. She was now to embrace with satisfaction these newly 'equal' social roles rather than have them imposed upon her. In short, the traditional sexual division of responsibilities

195

remained in place. The rhetoric of equality was a politically prudent innovation. It permitted family and party peace. It allowed the party to establish and maintain its control over this staunchly conservative area. It accomodated radicalism and conservatism. It was a sober piece of social engineering carefully attuned to a particular place at a particular time. The consistency of Communism with regard to the emancipation of Chinese women still lay in the consistency of its admirable principles and in its less admirable practices, and finally in its determination to ensure that liberation was seen in social class not sexual terms.[34]

Since women could not obtain total freedom – politically, economically or socially – as feminists requested, the Party sought to distract them from these uncomfortable realities by stressing the 'special oppression' of women and the party's determination to eradicate it. This 'special oppression' referred to women's physical suffering. Women's tortured bodies, once again, became the focus of the emancipatory effort and a calculcated distraction by the Communists from wider and in their view, more dangerous political emancipatory ambitions.

Shan-Gan-Ning Border Area, as mentioned earlier, was substantially more conservative than Jiangxi. History specified masculinity and femininity in a traditional way: girls were sold as brides, husbands had the customary right to beat and berate their wives and to keep them indoors. Even the poorest peasants did not allow women out to work where they would meet strangers.[35] Women stayed at home keeping house and bearing and raising children. Women were men's attachments, slaves and possessions. Juilet Mitchell has observed that 'The language of reciprocity and equality is meaningless in this world divided into subject and object'.[36]

In feudal China man created submissive woman. Footbinding, of course, was the ultimate tool to deny women the physical expression of freedom. And the physical victim was often effectively 'brainwashed'. More often than not she accepted her own physical 'castration', acknowledged herself as inferior and accepted the negative roles of femininity. Footbinding was, therefore, the pre-eminent symbol of sexual oppression. When the anti-footbinding campaigns began in China late in the nineteenth century they were rejected in Yan'an. When Helen Snow visited Yan'an in 1939 she noticed that nearly all women in this area, including peasants, still had bound feet.[37] The official CCP attitude that women were equal to men was here declared in a socio-cultural setting far more traditional and conservative than any the Party had encountered in Jiangxi. Nevertheless, the circumscribed emancipation of women remained consistently one of the Party's goals – for the most practical of reasons, as already discussed: namely, that without women's participation in the revolution, the revolution could not succeed.[38]

Li Chunchen, the head of the Women's Department of the CCP at that time, stated: 'In the past in Jiangxi and Sichuan[39] women joined the fighting during the partisan period, and were busy disrupting the enemy and disarming enemy outposts . . . . Here in the Northwest women are physically weaker. They have bound feet, so they couldn't attempt strenuous work like that.'[40] During the Yan'an period, the proscription of footbinding was necessary, in particular, to remove the obstruction to women's participation in manual labour. This was important to the revolutionary cause – so important that during the Yan'an period, women were discouraged from joining the army and encouraged to participate in manual work: 'With the able-bodied men at the front, women's responsibility for the economy became especially important: without the active participation of the broad masses of women the Border Areas' economic plans could not be completed.'[41]

The abolition of footbinding in Yan'an, therefore, became the CCP's first priority. In May 1938, Deng Yinchao, a leader of the Communist Women's Movement, reported that Anti-footbinding Committees had been set up in every Women's Association in the Border Area to bring about the end of the despicable and ancient custom.[42] In August 1939, Shan-Gan-Ning Area Consultation Assemblies issued a directive entitled 'Directive for the Prohibition of Footbinding in Shan-Gan-Ning Area'. It proclaimed that the tradition of footbinding must stop. Women in the Border Area, under the age of eighteen, were forbidden to bind their feet. If any did so, their parents would be sentenced to one year in prison. Women with bound feet, under the age of 40, were ordered to unbind their feet or their parents or parents-in-law or husbands would spend half a year in prison. Women with bound feet, above the age of 40, were advised to unbind their feet. Every local government and mass organisation had to take action and work to implement this directive.[43]

In December 1940, the Second Congress of Women's Association of Shan-Gan-Ning Border Area stated that the campaign against footbinding had become one of the most important activities of the women's associations. It forbade the binding of girls' feet, encouraged adolescents and advised mature women to unbind their feet. It was its ambition to ensure that by the end of 1941 the feet of all young women in the Border Area were unbound.[44]

Hair as well as feet symbolised past and present. Bound feet and long hair were both considered decadent – symbols of oppressive custom. Modernity was represented by freed feet and short (bobbed) hair. For the Chinese, hair was irrevocably associated with revolution[45] and the Party made much of natural feet and cut hair. It was at pains to label them as fundamental manifestations of an escape from physical oppression. It had carefully chosen its limited emancipatory targets and its means of distraction from the more extreme and unacceptable emancipatory aims favoured by radical feminists.

As noted earlier, there was a practical purpose behind its apparent political altruism – usefulness to the Communist movement. Physical liberation took women out into the world to share in the work outside the home, a world until then dominated by men – politically, economically and culturally.[46] Women were now to share this world with men, but as 'Yan'an women' – mobile, strong, healthy *and* still acquiescent.

Women's Physical Education

Release from footbinding was only the first, albeit major, step in the female emancipation programme in Yan'an. Women were now spared physical mutilation but their bodies were weak. The Communists now followed the well-worn path of the earlier Christian missionaries. To physical freedom was added physical exercise. In both cases the broad purpose was the same – to create a new woman for a new society. The Jiangxi period had set a precedent and the Yan'an period of the CCP was to see a further development in women's physical and mental freedom, both in theory and practice. The development happened at several levels in part-time, full-time and higher education for women.

There was no tradition of education for women and girls in the Border Area. Now girls were encouraged to study with boys in primary and middle schools. Some districts even set up girls' schools. The number of female pupils increased[47] and girls and boys studied the same curriculum. Before 1941 the curriculum of the Border Area was almost a replica of that of the Jiangxi period. According to Shan-Gan-Ning Border Area Primary Schools' Regulations (August 1939), the primary school's curriculum included: Chinese language, mathematics, general science, drawing, singing and physical education. Due to an acute fear of Japanese attack,[48] every primary school had to have a physical education programme which concentrated on military training[49] and every primary school had a sports ground.

The comparative calm of the Yan'an period led the Party to overhaul its education policy. In Febuary 1941 the Border Educational Committee issued a new Decree which added a new course to the school syllabus: health education.[50] The combined aims of physical and health education were to nurture new citizens: active, strong, fit, ready to fight the enemy, politically sound and able to build a new society. Physical education courses now included: drill, martial arts, basketball, football table-tennis, gymnastics, running races, high jump and long jump. Girls fully participated in all these activities.[51] Under Communism, a new generation of girls grew up who had no desire to have bound feet, who enjoyed their natural physical development, and who experienced a new degree of equality from birth.

However, there was a special difficulty in setting up a school system in the Border Area – a severe shortage of teachers. Traditional education above the primary school level had been concentrated in the towns. The Border Area had never had easy access to the distant cities which were the centres of university education, and between 1939 and 1945 it was cut off even from the smaller towns with middle schools. Earlier in the 1930s there was an inflow of students from both the Nationalist and the Japanese-occupied areas, but by the end of 1938 the Nationalist Party had stopped the free movement of students into the 'Liberated Border Area' and after 1939 it became increasingly difficult for students to cross the Japanese lines.[52] Therefore, in the border region of Shan-Gan-Ning the percentage of educated people was extremely small and the region faced an acute shortage of qualified teachers. Thus teacher-training colleges were opened and teacher-training programmes were established as a matter of some urgency.[53]

In 1939 the First Teacher-Training College of the Border Area was set up.[54] In the spring of 1940 the Second and Third Teacher-Training Colleges were opened, followed by Guan Teacher-Training College and Longdong Academy. These colleges trained teachers and educational administrators[55] and they were open to women.

Eventually, they contained hundreds of female students. In the Second and the Third Teacher-Training Colleges there were distinct women's divisions.[56]

For reasons already fully outlined above, physical education was compulsory in these training institutes.[57] The students attended two hours of physical education and two hours of military training every week. However, there was one substantial difference between the Yan'an period and Jiangxi period institutes. In the Yan'an colleges physical education was separate from military training. Arguably, this separation benefited women. They now had a greater opportunity to develop their bodies not only in support of the war effort, but in the interests of their personal well-being.

Besides teacher-training colleges there were over 20 full-time cadre training institutes in Yan'an city by 1942.[58] Female students had access to all these schools and institutes and took part in their compulsory physical exercise programmes.[59] As Wu Jiangpin, a Communist cadre, remembered, in these institutions and schools women had their daily morning exercise, and in addition, took part in basketball, volleyball, table-tennis, athletics and mountain climbing in the afternoon and on public holidays. A model institute was the North Shanxi Public School – a cadre training centre. By 1938 it had 3,000 students, and some one sixth were women ranging in age from 17 to 40.[60] As Xinhua ribao [New China Daily][61] proudly reported, women appeared to participate fully and enthusiastically in the available physical and military exercises.[62]

These women not only enjoyed their new-found physical opportunities in the colleges and schools. More importantly, they later became teachers, educationists and cadres. They were sent to various parts of China to mobilise and educate rural women.[63] In this way they spread the idea of physical recreation and healthcare throughout the Border Area and beyond. Claire and William Band also noted in the late 1930s that many women in the Border Area attended night schools, noon schools and literacy groups in their effort to learn to read.[64] In 1938 there were 619 winter schools of this kind with 1,470 female students. By the end of July 1939 there were 418 women students in night schools, 2,340 women in part-time schools and 10,053 in 5,513 literacy groups.[65] These highly motivated students achieved substantial progress. Anna Louise Strong stated that prior to the Communist Party take-over 90 per cent of the village women were illiterate.[66] By 1946 about half of Yan'an's women could read

Female students of the Anti-Japanese Military and Political University in Yan'an. (From the Chinese Revolutionary History Museum.)

simplified newspapers. The teachers and cadres not only taught rural women to read but also, as Li Chun-chen, the Head of the Women's Department observed, stressed the value of physical exercise, with the result that 'now most young girls here take exercise every day and are healthier. Previously this was considered unladylike.'[67]

While most women were educated only to lower or middle school level, some aspired to go to university. At the Chinese People's Anti-Japanese Military and Political University, the Women's University and the Yan'an University, physical education was an integral part of their student life. The Chinese Anti-Japanese Military and Political University was the spiritual successor to the Red Army Academy in Jiangxi. It was founded in June 1936.[68] It soon became the Party's premier educational institution. Its aim was to train high-ranking Communist military and political cadres. The student population grew rapidly: from about 200 in 1936 to nearly 5,000 in 1938 and to 8,000 in 1939.[69] The students, male and female, came from 27 provinces of China. Women students took the same courses as men – academic and athletic. The university was famous for its physical training which took place largely through the Salvation room. The Salvation room was the successor to the Lenin room in the Jiangxi period. It changed its name in accord with the wartime priority – national salvation. During the Yan'an period, schools, mass organisations, army units and peasant villages were encouraged, and indeed, in most cases required to have a cultural and educational centre – the Salvation room. The university, as in so many other aspects of education and culture, led the way in the early years of the war. And the organisation, function and activities of the Salvation room provided a model for others to emulate.

The label had been changed but it was old wine in a new bottle. The organisation and purpose of the Salvation room and the Lenin room were identical. Exercise was a basic ingredient. The Physical Education Committee promoted ball games, track and field competitions, mountain climbing, basketball, volleyball, table-tennis, football and other forms of physical exercise including 'political games' on such themes as 'killing traitors and smashing Japanese imperialism'.[70] One commentator on the university and its ethic of muscularity, vividly described its programme of physical exercise in 1938:

> Evening is the set time for physical exercise here. Men, women, the young, the old, teachers, students, administrators and the

staff come out to the playground. Some are playing football, some are playing table-tennis, some are involved in their volley-ball matches, some are doing high jump and long jump, some are running, some are playing military games. In this athletic atmosphere, with smiles on their faces, they train their bodies to iron muscle and steel bone for the Anti-Japanese War. . . . Our sport is a new sport. We don't need professional athletes. We advocate a mass sport movement. We don't want the weakling stereotype cherished by some Chinese scholars. We want the healthy body–healthy mind ethos to be completely triumphant.[71]

These university women personified an élite – the new women of Yan'an, equal in spirit, effort and opportunity to men. In military manoeuvres they marched and fought side by side with men.[72] They engaged in virtually every physical activity. They organised women's basketball teams and volleyball teams and attended competitions inside and outside the university. Furthermore, they learned to swim in the Yan'an river. This action greatly challenged feudal tradition which forbade the female body to be revealed in public. But the university prized them as healthy, modern women depicting the new image of a new era.[73] They were the vanguard of an 'emancipatory regiment of women'.

Such women not only had access to the leading higher education institute, they had their own institution. The Women's University was opened at the suggestion of Mao Zedong and approved by the Central Committee of the CCP on Women's Day, 8 March 1939 expressly for the purpose of training women cadres to promote female emancipation.[74] Wang Min (1904–74), the General Secretary of the CCP from 1930 to 1934, the first President of the Women's University, in his opening-day speech, explained carefully the significance for the Women's Movement of the founding of the Women's University. Wang stressed that creating a special school for women was not a step forward in the struggle for equal rights for women because women in the Border Region already had equal rights! However, they did have special needs after years of exploitation under feudalism. Many women were still unwilling to socialise with men to whom they were not closely related, and some, particularly in the backward northwest, remained dominated by tradition and continued to bind the feet of their young daughters. The Women's University was founded because it was recognised that women cadres would take upon themselves, with fervour and commitment, the difficult and delicate task of communicating effectively with these peasant women in order to free them in time from their oppressed condition, restricted mentalities and outmoded ideas.[75] In the Women's University, therefore, the rhetoric to placate the radical coexisted with the structure to produce the liberated.

During, the wartime period of the United Front Strategy, when the Party was deliberately holding in check the land aspirations of the peasants, as discussed earlier, it could not afford to alienate the peasant by liberating women. However, the fury of China's unleashed women was potentially a tremendous revolutionary force. Mao Zedong stated: 'The day when women of all China stand up, will be the time of the achievement of the Chinese revolutionary victory.'[76] The CCP in Jiangxi, but most especially in Yan'an, had to keep a balance, on the one hand to retain the support of male peasants and on the other to promote the emancipation of the female peasants. How this was attempted has been outlined above. The result was that women were like square pegs trying to fit into the round hole of the Communist Yan'an culture – a calculated combination of the feudal and modern. The CCP ideal of the Yan'an woman needed exceptional qualities – emotional, mental and physical. She was required to be a worker who could provide food for her children, a virtuous mother who could teach her son to be loyal soldier, a good wife who could help her husband to fight the enemy at the front, and a filial daughter who could go to battle instead of her old father.[77] To carry off these roles successfully she needed health, fitness and strength. Women's cadres were trained to be models for future generations. They set both tone and pace. For this reason physical exercise was heavily emphasised at the Women's University.

The emphasis on exercise was continuous. There was a club to promote women's physical activity and a student in charge of the physical exercise programme in every class.[78] There was morning exercise every day and a spare-time physical training teaching programme. There was evening basketball, volleyball, tennis, athletics and gymnastics, swimming in summer, skating in winter, and sports competitions. Many Yan'an people still remember the Women's Sports Meeting held by the Women's University to celebrate International Women's Day on 8 March 1940. Yang Lie, a woman cadre, who was in charge of the club, led 100 women students who performed an impressive athletic dance before thousands of spectators. Male comrades proudly recalled, 'Our women comrades loved physical activity . . .They were new women who had the physical strength to be valued members of family and society.'[79] The women themselves found that they were increasingly more confident in themselves. They were sure that if the Party and society gave them the opportunity they would be able to achieve all their emancipatory ambitions.[80]

The CCP created dovetailing programmes of exercise within the education system for the young at primary, secondary and tertiary educational levels, within the wider framework of an educational structure which attempted to provide for physical, economic, military and political survival and success. In theory, this system was classless and available to all. Limitations imposed upon it were those of unburied prejudices, restricted resources and watchful political pragmatism. In the sum total of human experience, and more especially of female experience in China, however, the removal of many, if not all, barriers to physical liberty with the eventual wider psychological, social and economic ramifications, deserves to be both recorded and applauded. Without any doubt, it thrust forward the cause of female emancipation – even if it was still far short of the finishing-post.

Women's Role in the Physical Culture

New developments were apparent in all spheres of Yan'an life. The exercise cult was no exception. The pronounced emphasis on military training typical of the Jiangxi period gave way in the early years in Yan'an to a new emphasis. A fresh start was made by a new organisation, the Yan'an Physical Education and Sports Committee, which was founded on 4 May 1940. Li Fuchun was its honorary Chairman.[81] Its aim was to develop a New Sports Movement – a mass physical exercise movement – in Yan'an. Then in January 1942 the New Sports Society, a research centre, was established on the recommendation of educationists. Its major concern was to develop the New Sports Movement under scientific direction. It concentrated on promoting research, introducing the latest theories of physical education and publishing physical education textbooks. Simultaneously, the first Physical Education Department under the Communist regime was founded at Yan'an University. Its purpose was to provide qualified instructors to service the Movement.[82]

'Exercise the Body to Fight the Japanese' – Mao Zedong's words in *Xinhua ribao* [New China Daily], 9 September 1942.

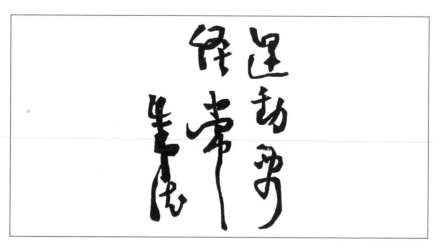

'Exercise regularly' – Zhu De's Words in *Xinhua ribao* [New China Daily], 9 September 1942.

Basically, these were the years of physical culture rather than competitive sport. Competitive sport bred, in some censorious minds, attitudes alien to communist society. Competitive sport, it was alleged, led to narrow specialisation and diverted attention away from the basic aim of providing healthy exercise for the masses. It turned them into passive spectators. Such were the views of influential authorities, such as Zhu De, Deng Fa, Li Fuchun and Zhang Yuan,[83] who dominated the thinking on physical education during the 1940s. Exercise, as Mao Zedong commented, was not art for arts sake. It was a utilitarian process for producing physical fitness, military skills and collectivist attitudes.[84] The Physical Education and Sports Committee therefore advocated a New Sports Movement in which physical exercise and sports activities were to be used to reform the quality of people's bodies in order to help them reform, in turn, the nature of society. The slogan now, in consequence, was 'Everybody is to do exercise'.[85]

Throughout the liberated areas, the Committee directed and approved physical education programmes for clubs and groups, ratified the regulations of sports organisations, drew up a calendar of sporting events and ensured that the calendar was completed. This put an end to any schemes for organisational or regional autonomy. The New Sports Society's task, on the other hand, was to devise exercise programmes to help secure the goals of the revolutionary state. The classic example of this was the startling innovation of mass physical culture – the ten minutes' daily exercise programme for all, in an attempt to get everyone into the habit of doing at least a ten-minutes exercise every morning before breakfast or every evening after supper.[86]

With exercise smoothly integrated in the educational system, the Party turned its attention to the integration of exercise into the wider social system. Adult women, among others, became the focus of political attention, as was made clear shortly after the founding of the Sports Committee, by Zhang Yuan, the second Chairman of the Sports Committee and the Head of the New Sports Society. Zhang wrote an article strongly advocating women's physical exercise. He further recommended that it should adopt Charles H. McCloy's theory of women's physical education,[87] which had been enthusiastically embraced in the Nationalist area[88] and will be discussed later when the Nationalists receive close attention. For the moment it should be simply noted that it concerned women and the kinds of exercise appropriate to them. Refugees from the Nationalist areas such as Zhang Yuan brought McCloy's theory to the Red area.

Zhang argued that China should learn from the West that exercise was a habit for life.[89] His argument was endorsed by Yang Lie,[90] a female physical educationist and Chairman of the Sports Committee. In an article entitled 'On Women Comrades' Physical Education and Exercise' in the *Jiefang ribao* [Liberation Daily], the periodical of the CCP, in September 1942, Yang asserted that women were well aware of the social significance of sport for them, but they needed to know how to exercise effectively. She recommended that women should participate in dance, gymnastics, swimming, skating, volleyball and table-tennis. She appealed for the local authorities to take a leading role in the promotion of women's exercise.[91] It was a clear political hint and provided the clearest evidence, of the CCP's intense pre-occupation with exercise in the community.

This preoccupation was revealed in other ways. For example, although competitive sport was criticised as a bourgeois activity which could lead to the separation of sport from other more cohesive social activities, and criticised by McCloy as unsuitable to women's physio-logy and psychology,[92] it was never wholly rejected by the Com-munists. Zhu De made it clear that competition could, indeed, should, serve, as a means of involving the masses aggressively in the fight against the enemy and in building a new socialist country.[93] During the Yan'an period, as mentioned above, sports competitions therefore took place in regiments, schools, factories, villages and civil service departments. The value both of competitive sport and the associated grand sports festivals was clearly understood by the Party. It was recognised as a means of uniting classes, occupations and sexes under Communism and as a means of inculcating appropriately aggressive attitudes to military success on the part of men and women.

No better illustration of competitive sport as an instrument to cohesion and aggression can be found than the Sports Meeting held in Yan'an, the capital of Red China between 1–6 September 1942.[94] On this occasion, the major figures of Party, Army and Government were present and *Jiefang ribao* [Liberation Daily] included an article written by the editor entitled 'Promote the Sport Movement'. Nearly 2,000 male and female athletes participated. The events included athletics, swimming, volleyball, basketball, shooting, climbing, wrestling, weightlifting, horsemanship, martial arts, diving, water-polo, tennis, baseball and football. Women athletes participated in all the events

Mao Zedong playing table-tennis in Yan'an in 1946. (From China Sports Museum.)

except the military exercises. Six women's basketball teams, four women's volleyball teams, seven women's athletics teams and five women's swimming teams attended and they attracted a big crowd.[95] Women athletes were regularly 'big news' in the papers.[96] *Jiefang ribao* [Liberation Daily] commented accurately that their athletic image had helped them to overcome both traditional passivity and prejudice.

Women athletes at the 1 September 1942 Yan'an Sports Meeting. (From Wang Zengming et al. (eds). *Hongxing yao titan* [Red Star Over the Sports Field]. Xi'an: Shanxi renmin meisu chubanshe, 1990.)

Women not only attended mixed competitions. They also organised their own event in March 1940, known as the Yan'an Women's Sports Meeting – held to celebrate International Women's Day. It was not simply a sports competition, but was heavy with political meaning. The leaders of the Party, such as Mao Zedong, Wang Min and Wu Yuzhang, attended to demonstrate their support for women's exercise. Six hundred women participated in gymnastics, folk dancing and bayonet charges.[97] The event lasted two days. Interestingly, it ended with a loudly shouted slogan from the audience, 'Long live women's emancipation'.[98] The link between physical freedom and women's emancipation was asserted in this moment. Another metaphorical milestone on the long road of emancipatory struggle had been passed.

The sports meetings of Yan'an made a profound impression upon both sexes, but upon women in particular, among whom there was still residual inhibition, passivity and conservatism as a result of crushing custom. Sport offered a basic freedom to women – that of their bodies in action and it revolutionised the social definition of the legitimate female body. It invoked a new confidently assertive attitude – a way of thinking and feeling – about what it was now to be 'feminine' which became internalised and hence 'real'. The Yan'an Women's Sports Meeting in March 1940 may be considered a significant as well as metaphorical milestone in Chinese women's emancipation. It was a proof of progress. In the Liberated Area, exercise played a notable part in changing the consciousness of women about their bodies, helped them to develop their personalities and change their identities for the better. They were now parents, workers and athletes – and in some cases, soldiers.[99] In the most conservative of cultural settings they had become more equal. In short, they were Yan'an Women – but those with the fullest freedom were still a small if *classless* élite.[100]

Women's Hygiene and Health Education

It should be stressed again that Yan'an emancipation fell well short of feminist ambitions. The Party, as already mentioned, wanted women simultaneously to subordinate their interests to the revolution and to liberate themselves as women. This liberation, of course, was a multi-faceted phenomenon. Access to sports was only one of its facets. There was a pressing need to improve health standards, eliminate disease and epidemics, reduce infant mortality and the overall mortality rate, and to make women aware of the importance of hygiene, personal and social, as well as individual fitness. Throughout rural China, and particularly in the poverty-stricken northwest, poor health was a major obstacle to progress of any sort. The Communists were keenly aware of the problem. Long-standing customs and habits had to be changed. Concentration on these worthy ambitions, of course, also served usefully to distract radical emancipationists from more controversial and unwelcome reforms.

Consequently, cadre-training schools and teachers' schools now offered hygiene and health-care courses. The students learned physiology, anatomy, hygiene and sound health practices. Seybolt noted at the time that in some institutions like the Anti-Japanese Political and Military University students were issued with only two or three suits of clothing annually and luxuries like soap were almost non-existent, but they were expected to keep themselves and their living and working areas neat and clean. Students were regularly inspected, and indeed 'inspected' each others' appearance and cleanliness.[101] A Health Committee was added to every Salvation room to educate students and the masses in more sensible, and hygienic practices. Health care as well as physical education became vehicles of political reform and emancipatory freedom, in the new Yan'an.

Health education was seen as a special need and responsibility of women due to their harsh lifestyles which involved multiple births, births employing insanitary midwifery, multiple children, and endless labour. The lifestyle of the Chinese peasant meant frequent illness and premature aging. Smedley observed in the 1930s that 'in China, people still think of a woman of thirty as old'.[102]

It was impossible, for the cultural reasons already discussed, to have every woman immediately participate in exercise, so it was all the more important to promote health education. This symbolised rationality, progress and modernity. It was regarded by the Party as one of the most popular, suitable and effective instruments for implementing its political reforms. A resolution passed in 1940 by the Congress of Women's Associations of the Border Area required that each geographic area should open health training classes run by cadres specially trained to deal with women's health problems.[103] Women should be told how to take good care of themselves since they were to play an important role in the reformed family and society. Village cadres began to investigate households to locate pregnant and sick women in order to tell them of the general, pre- and post-natal health services available. Cadres also called the village women together to hear lectures on health care. Traditional midwives were also educated in new midwifery methods.[104]

A major health problem of women was childbearing. Joshua Horn commented on traditional childbirth customs: 'Many harmful super-stitions were associated with childbirth. In some areas women had to give birth unaided in a shed or out-house; in others, mother and child were kept in a darkened room for several weeks after delivery . . . and the practice of biting through the umbilical cord and applying cow-dung to the stump caused many babies to die of tetanus.'[105] However, the trained cadres with their 'new' ideas were educated women inexperienced in childbirth practice and inexperienced also in pre- and post-natal care. Traditional midwives had this experience and were thus trained to use the new sanitary midwifery methods which included scientific birth instruction, the use of clean implements, washed hands and the rejection of bad superstitious practices.

Childcare was seen as an important aspect of the new health care. It was designated of special benefit for women, in accordance with the traditional view that women were most involved in the raising of children. It was now to be a state responsibility. This would benefit both mothers and children: mothers could work and children would be better educated.[106] The Party claimed that 'Public raising of children must be actively proclaimed . . . to allow professional women to work with peaceful hearts and to permit worker–peasant women to participate more in production.'[107] Children, of course, brought up by the State would be carefully socialised into its requirements. Public childcare was more talked about than realised during the Jiangxi era. However, during the period of the Liberated Area some nurseries and kindergartens were established. When Clare and William Band visited Yan'an in October 1943[108] they noted of one of the kindergartens:

There were 260 children, between the ages of one and six. There were forty teachers, several cooks and laundrymen. Children were from busy parents all over North china, many on war duties at the front. Modern psychological methods of discipline by kindness were being practised; the teachers evidently were in love with their work and the children. . . . Director of the children's home, Lin Hua, had been trained in child education at Moscow.[109]

Although not nearly enough institutions were available to take care of all children, there was a steady rise in the number of childcare centres in the late 1930s. By 1945, in the Communist areas, there were 26,700 childcare institutions taking care of 1,250,000 children in cities and 6,000,000 children were said to have been organised in childcare institutions in rural areas.[110] The most famous, and possibly the largest, was Yan'an Nursery. It was founded in October 1938. Over 900 children – boys and girls – had passed through by 1949. About 290 children were there at any time. Children, between the ages of two months and seven years , were divided into three classes. Modern educational and psychological methods of discipline by kindness were practised. Toys and teaching resources were made by the teachers. Boys and girls did their morning exercise, played games and sang nursery rhymes. The motto of the nursery was: 'loved, neat, brave and lively'.[111]

Conclusion

Under strict Communist direction, as in the Jiangxi period, the Women's Movement in the Yan'an period was not an independent feminist movement. It served the Party in its wider revolutionary ambitions. To the credit of the CCP, against considerable conservative odds and in a severely reactionary environment, the 'Yan'an woman' was successfully created: freed from footbinding, allowed schooling, able to exercise, trained for careers as well as promoted as 'modern' wife, mother and daughter-in-law. It was also a classless 'rebirth', extended to an ever-increasing number of women in both urban and rural communities in all sections of the Liberated Area as it expanded.

It may be asked, however, whether women freed from one form of social bondage were not falling prey to another. Women as historical square pegs were being forced into a contemporary round hole of Communist culture. Nevertheless, what is discernible from the Yan'an period is the *tendency* toward greater sexual equality. Changes in the political, social, educational and economic status of women were inimical to the traditional family system and did help to develop a new system more in harmony with feminist concepts of women's proper role and status. While the reconstruction of femininity was firmly linked to the Communist culture and women were bombarded with fresh but selective images of femininity that were impossible to ignore and difficult to oppose, Helen Snow observed when she visited Yan'an in 1938 that the women working in the factories sparkled with vitality and cheerfulness and health. They had been given a measure of freedom, dignity, and confidence. The Yan'an Woman was a reality.[112]

In concentrating attention on the emancipation of the female body, there is clearly an obvious danger of exaggerating its relative importance in Communist society and in Communist policy-making. However, there is an equal danger in neglecting the body as an important dimension of female emancipation. As an adjunct of overall Communist culture, and as an instrument of general Communist purpose, women's physical emancipation through the anti-footbinding campaign, physical education and sport and health education was certainly assigned a specific and significant role during the Yan'an period. It is not to be marginalised. It should be recorded. It was a positive harbinger of things yet to come, but patience on the part of women was still required before their fuller coming after 1949 in the People's Republic of China.

Notes

1. The Long March, the 6,000-mile journey from central China through south and southwest China, then over the high snow mountains and torrential rivers of the Tibetan grasslands, started in October 1934 and ended in October 1935. Of the 35,000 who started the march, only some 8,000 finished. It was a great test of human courage, endurance and strength. For the Chinese it became a symbol of a new beginning when, against all the odds, Chinese Communism survived to become the core around which China could become a single united country. Among those who have written about the Long March was Edgar Snow who had first-hand experience of China in the 1920s and 1930s. Another American, Agnes Smedley, wrote an account of the Long March as told to her by Zhu De, the Chief-Commander of the Red Army. In 1984 the historian Harrison Salisbury was able to retrace the route of the Long March and published his book, *The Long March, the Untold Story*. In recent years several memoirs of leaders and generals who took part in the Long March have been published.
   The Long March, as Mao Zedong claimed, 'is the first of its kind in the annals of history. It is a manifesto, a propaganda force, a seeding-machine . . . It has proclaimed to the world that the Red Army is an Army of heroes, while the imperialists and their running dogs, Chiang Kai-shek and his like, are impotent.' (See Mao Zedong, *Mao Zedong xuanji* [Selected Works of Mao Zedong], 5 Vols, Beijing: Renmin chubanshe, 1991, Vol. 1, p.160.) However, these brave words could not hide the fact that the CCP lost virtually its entire structure of southern and eastern bases. Eight years of endeavour appeared to

have been almost completely swept away, and rebuilding the shattered edifice would be profoundly difficult.

2. In 1931 Liu Zhidan and Gao Gang, in the local garrison at Yan'an, organised a mutiny against the feudal authorities, founded the Shanxi People's Red Army and set up a soviet government at Yan'an. It was Liu Zhidan and Gao Gang's soviet that welcomed Mao's Communists at the end of their Long March. See Claire and William Band, *Two Years with the Chinese Communists*, New Haven: Yale University Press, 1948, p.237.

3. The Yan'an period lasted from the end of December 1936 to the end of the Second World War in 1945 but, as a general term, the Yan'an period refers to the era from the end of the Long March in 1935 until the Communist seizure of power on 1 October 1949. See Helen Snow, *Inside Red China*, Dacapo, 1979, p.xiii. The author is an American, born in 1907. She studied at Yenjing University in Beijing from 1934 to 1935. In 1937 she made a trip to Yan'an. While in Yan'an, she wrote biographical sketches of Communist leaders, among them two women, Kang Keqing and Cai Chang. She was never a Communist but wrote sympathetically about the Communist cause and revolution. Her work is sound and detailed and is especially interesting in regard to women workers and to the working conditions of women in the Liberated Areas during the Sino-Japanese War. Her books on China include *Inside Red China* (1939), *The Chinese Labor Movement* (1945), *Red Dust* (1952), *My Yenan Notebooks* (1962) and *Women in Modern China* (1967). She also compiled the *Nym Wales* [her pseudonym] *Collection* housed at the Hoover University, USA.

4. The Party membership grew from a little over 20,000 members in 1936 to nearly 1,250,000 members at the Seventh Party Congress in April 1945, and the Red Army swelled to over one million men by 1945. This new political and military framework formed the structural backbone which enabled the Communists to come to power four years later. See Dorries, Carl E., 'Peasant Mobilization in North China and the Origins of Yenan Communism', *China Quarterly*, Vol. 68, Dec. 1976, p.697.

5. Chalmers Johnson in *Peasant Nationalism and Communist Power* (Stanford: Stanford University Press, 1962) was the first to focus on the forces of nationalism generated in the conflict as the prime motive forces in providing the Chinese Communists with a mass base sufficient to win the Chinese civil war. Carl E. Dorries then pointed out that 'Seemingly overnight the Communist Party made rapid new gains in strength and territory.' From a small, isolated soviet in the isolation of northwest China on the Shanxi–Gansu border in 1935, the Communist Party enlarged its territories. By the end of the Anti-Japanese War Communist-backed resistance governments ruled huge portions of north and central China. See Dorris, Carl E., op. cit., pp.697–719.

6. After the Japanese army's invasion of China in 1931 anti-Japanese sentiment grew throughout the country. By 1937, Japanese troops occupied the entire Tianjin and Beijing region. The Japanese military and civilian leaders were eager for further gains to match those in north and central China. Chinese people of all classes and political creeds became more and more categorical in their demands on the Nationalist Government to stop the civil war and to establish a genuinely democratic United Front embracing the Nationalist Party, the Communists, and all liberal elements in resistance against Japan. A strong national movement resulted, the Communists' underground agitation contributed to its rise. The Manchurian troops commanded by Zhang Xueliang, the young marshal, that were supposed to fight the Communists became part of the movement. They entered into agreement with the Communists and Chiang

Kai-shek, suspecting that all was not well, flew to Xi'an the capital city of Shanxi province to see for himself. He was taken prisoner by his own generals, Zhang Xueliang and Yang Huchen, in December 1936. They demanded that Chiang listen to the Communist proposals for joint action against Japan. Chiang finally agreed to stop the civil war and to establish a United Front to fight against the Japanese. The Communists agreed to accept the authority of Chiang's government and put their forces under his supreme command. The Red Army was now known as the Eighth Route Army although it remained Communist. Another Communist army, the New Fourth Army, was founded a year later. See Stein, Gunther, *The Challenge of Red China*. London: Pilot Press, 1945, pp. 12–15.

7. Seybolt, Peter Jordan, *Yenan Education and the Chinese Revolution, 1937–1945*, unpublished Ph.D. thesis, Harvard University, 1969, p.1.
8. The principal Liberated Areas in northern China were Shanxi-Gansu-Ningxia, Shanxi-Chahar-Hebei, Shanxi-Hebei-Henan, Hebei-Shandong-Henan, Shanxi-Suiyan and Shandong.
9. Selden, Mark, *The Yenan Way in Revolutionary China*, Cambridge, MA: Harvard University Press, 1971, p.15.
10. Seybolt, Peter Jordan, op. cit., p.200.
11. Stacey, Judith, 'When Patriarchy Kowtows: the Significance of the Chinese Family Revolution for Feminist Theory', *Feminist Studies*, Vol. 2, 1975, p.67.
12. Davin, Delia, *Women-Work*, op. cit., p.34.
13. Lu, Yuanzheng, 'Huanghe wenhua he tiyu de qiyuan' [the Yellow River and the Origin of Physical Education], *Tiyu bao* [Sports Daily], 4 May 1989.
14. Quoted in Belden, Jack, *China Shakes the World*, Pelican, 1973, p.416, first published in 1949 in New York by Harper & Bros. The author was an American journalist present in North China in the 1940s.
15. Chen, Boda, 'Xin funu de jinshen guan' [The New Women's New Spirit], *Funu yundong wenxian* [The Material of the Women's Movement], Harbin, 1948, p.108.
16. Belden, Jack, op. cit., p.416.
17. Deng Yingchao (1903–92). Her revolutionary career started in the 1919 May Fourth Movement in Tianjin. She became Zhou Enlai's wife in August 1925. She was an important leader of the Communist Women's Movement. She became the Chairman of the Chinese People's Political Consultative Conference in 1988. Her early life story is told in Helen Snow's book, *Women in Modern China*, op.cit., pp.254–7.
18. Cusack, D., *Chinese Women Speak*, London: Routledge & Kegan Paul, 1959, p.198.
19. Snow, Helen, 'Interview with Mao Zedong', in her book, *My Yenan Notebooks*, Madison: Conn, 1961, p.128; Snow, Edgar, *Red Star Over China*, Pelican, 1973, p.459, first published in 1938 in New York by Grove Press Inc.
20. Snow, Edgar, op. cit., p.460.
21. Forman, Harrison, *Report from Red China*, New York: Henry Holt, 1945, pp.178–9. The author travelled to Yan'an and spoke with Mao Zedong. Mao admitted that according to the agreement with the Nationalist Party and government on 22 September 1937, the Party gave up its land reform policy. Now it would not take the land from the landlord, as in the Jiangxi era. Instead, the Party persuaded landlords to reduce their rents to a reasonable figure, while assuring them that these lowered rents would be paid regularly by the tenants. Areas under the CCP control had a government which was called democratic, which included landlords, merchants and capitalists, as well as

peasants and workers. The policy of retrenchment gave the CCP a national role of changed status in Chinese society.

22. Belden, Jack, op. cit., p.413.

23. Yang, C.K., *Chinese Communist Society: the Family and the Village*, Cambridge, MA: MIT Press, 1959, p.135.

24. Chen Ruoguang, 'Zhonggong shandong fenju guanyu sandong funu gongzhuo de zonjie yu jinhou funu yundong de xin renwu' [The CCP Shandong Committee on Women's Work and New Tasks], in CWF, op. cit., Vol. 3, pp.396–7. The author was then the General Secretary of the CCP's Shandong Women's Committee. Also see Stein, Gunther. *The Challenge of Red China*. London: Pilot Press, 1945, p.198; Selden, Mark, op. cit., pp.115–16.

25. Yang, C.K., op. cit., p.135.

26. The Central Women's Committee of the CCP, 'Kangri gangzheng shiqi Zhongguo funu yundong de chubu zhongjie he jinhuo funu gongzou de yijian' [The Conclusion of the Period of the Chinese Women's Movement and a Proposal for the Women's Work during the Anti-Japanese War], 1945, in CWF, op. cit., Vol. 3, pp.768–9.

27. The Central Women's Committee of the CCP, 'Zhonggong zhongyang fuwei guanyu muqian funu yundong de fangzhen he renwu de zhisixin' [A Letter on the Direction and Work of Present Women's Movement from the Central Women's Committee of the CCP], 3 March 1939, in CWF, ibid., pp.138–43.

28. Tian, Xiujiuan, '1943 nian qian Jing-Cha-Yi nongchun funu gongzhou de chubu guji' [An Account of Women's Work in Jing-Cha-Yi Rural Areas before 1943], in CWF, ibid., p.804. The author was then the General Secretary of the Women's Committee of the North Communist Party Bureau.

29. Zhou, Enlai, 'Lun xianqi liangmu yu muzi' [On the Virtuous Wife and the Good Mother and their Responsibilities], *Xinhua ribao* [New China Daily], 17 Sept. 1942.

30. Ding, Ling, (1904–86), born into a gentry family in Hunan, had been educated in a modern school in Changsha, Hunan. She and her mother had both been caught up in the dreams for a new China that lay at the heart of the May Fourth Movement. In 1927 she published her first novel, a feminist story, *The Diary of Miss Sophie* in 1927 which made her famous. Ding Ling joined the CCP in 1931. In 1936 she was held under house arrest in Nanjing by the Nationalist Party, but managed to escape and reach Yan'an. In Yan'an she began to write stories that criticised CCP cadres for insensitivity to women workers, and for enforcing an ideological outlook that destroyed individual initiative and opinion. She was criticised in the Rectification Campaign in 1942. Later, Ding Ling made up for her alleged errors of judgement in Yan'an by writing a thoroughly favourable evaluation of land reform during the civil-war period in her novel, *The Sun Shines over the Sangan River* (1948), which was awarded the Stalin prize for literature in 1951. In the anti-rightist Campaign in 1958 Ding Ling was criticised once again for her Yan'an articles and was subsequently purged as an inveterate 'anti-Party element'. She was sent to the countryside to be re-educated for more than 20 years. After 1979 Ding Ling was rehabilitated and was elected a member of the Executive Committee of the Chinese Literature Association. For more details about Ding Ling's life and works see Spence, Jonathan D., *The Gate of Heavenly Peace*, op. cit., pp.328–30; and Feuerwerker, Yi-tsi Mei, *Ding Ling's Fiction: Ideology and Narrative in Modern Chinese Literature*, Cambridge, MA: Harvard University Press, 1982, pp.101–102; Snow, Helen, *Women in Modern China*, op. cit., pp.198–205.

31. An English translation is Berton, Gregor. 'The Yenan Literary Opposition', *New*

Left Review , Vol. 92, July–August 1975, pp.102–105.

32. Berton, Gregor, 'The Yenan Literary Opposition', ibid., p.94; McDougall, Bonnie, *Mao Zedong's Talk at the Yenan Conference on Literature and Art: A Translation of the 1943 Text with Commentary*, Ann Arbor: University of Michigan Press, 1980, pp.69–70.

33. Stein, Gunther, op. cit., p.206.

34. For a thorough historians' analysis of the women's movement in the Yan'an period, see Croll, E., *Feminism and Socialism in China*, op. cit., pp.198–222; Davin, Delia, *Women-Work*, op. cit.; Frenier, Mariam Darce, op. cit., pp.140–183.

35. J.L. Buck's survey showed that women supplied only 16.4 per cent of all the farming labour. See Buck, John L., *Land Utilization in China*, New York: Council on Economic and Cultural Affairs, 1956, pp.301–303, (first published in 1937), see also Young, C. K., op. cit., p.139.

36. Mitchell, Juliet, *Psychoanalysis and Feminism*, New York: Pantheon Books, 1974, p.307.

37. Snow, Helen, *Inside Red China*, op. cit., p.192.

38. Brandt, *et al.*, *A Documentary History of Chinese Communism*, op. cit., p.326. The emancipation of women was important to the Marxist conception of the proletariat revolution.

39. When the Fourth Front of the Red Army arrived in Sichuan province in 1932 many women joined up. There was a regiment of 2,000 women solders when the Red Army left Sichuan in 1935, but on the Long March many were killed or captured by the Nationalist Army and local warlords. Only 800 arrived at the Border Area. Helen Snow mentioned the famous women's regiment in her book: *Inside Red China*, op. cit., p.195; and also see Ono Kazuko's book *Chinese Women in a Century of Revolution, 1850–1950*, op. cit., pp.160–61; see also 'Dongzhen huiyi lu' [Red Army Soldiers' Recollection], in *Hongqi piaopiao* [The Red Flag Waves], Vol. 3, op. cit., pp.11–19.

40. Quoted in Snow, Helen, *Inside Red China*, op. cit., p.196.

41. Cai, Chang, 'Yijie funu gongzuo de xin fangxiang' [On A New Task of Women's Work], *Jiefang ribao* [Liberation Daily], 8 March 1943.

42. Deng, Yinchao, and Meng, Qingshi, 'Shan-Gan-Ning Bianqu funu yundong gaikuang' [The General Situation of the Women's Movement in Shan-Gan-Ning Border Area], *Xinhua ribao* [New China Daily], 10 June 1938.

43. This directive is in *Shan-Gan-Ning geming genjudi shiliao xuanji* [The Historical Material of Shan-Gan-Ning Border Area], Beijing: Renming chubanshe, No. 1, 1958.

44. See 'Shan-Gan-Ning bianqu fulianhui di re chi kuaida zhiweihui dahui jieyi' [The Resolution of the Second Women's Congress of Shan-Gan-Ning Border area], 20 Dec. 1940, *Zhongguo funu* [Chinese Women], Vol. 2, No. 9. 1940.

45. Bobbed hair was the symbol of revolution in the 1920s. In 1927 when the National Party split with the CCP, girls with bobbed hair were subject to execution as Communists. See Snow, Helen *Inside Red China*, op. cit., p.170.

46. When the custom of footbinding finally died out after 1949, the association of bobbed hair with revolution continued. During the Cultural Revolution bobbed hair became a special symbol of revolution. Most women had to cut their hair short to show their revolutionary consciousness.

47. For example, in Ning Xian County, there were only two girls in primary school in 1938, but some 200 girls attended primary schools in 1939. In the Border Area as a whole by 1939 there were 883 primary and middle schools with 20,400 pupils. Among them there were 3,400 girls. See Yun, 'Shan-Gan-Ning

bianqu tufei mengjin de nuzi jiaoyu' [On the Rapid Development of Women's Education in the Border Areas], *Zhongguo funu* [Chinese Women], Vol. 1, No. 8, 16 Dec. 1939. (Yun was the pen name of a leading woman Party member).

48. On 6 March 1938, the Educational Committee of the Border Area claimed that primary schools should strengthen military training in order to prepare strong soldiers for the Anti-Japanese War. It demanded that students should be organised as an army. Students should climb mountains at least once a day and learn how to fight in the mountain areas. See 'Shan-Gan-Ning bianqu kangzhan shiqi xiaoxue yingai zhuyi de jige gongzou de tonggao' [The Work of Primary Schools of Shan-Gan-Ning Border Area during Anti-Japanese War], issued by the Educational Committee. (This document is in Shanxi Provincial Archives, Xi'an, Shanxi province, China.)

49. 'Shan-Gan-Ning bianqu xiaoxue guichen' [The Regulation of Primary Schools of Shan-Gan-Ning Border Area], issued by the Education Committee, on 15 Aug. 1939, in 'Shan-Gan-Ning bianqu difang jiaoyu danxin fali' [Educational Decrees of Shan-Gan-Ning Border Area]. (This document is in Shanxi Provincial Archive Institute, Xi'an, Shanxi province, China.)

50. See 'Shan-Gan-Ning bianqu xiaoxue quicheng' [The Curriculum of Primary Schools in the Border Area], in *Kangri genjudi zhenche tiaoli huiji* [The Collection of Policies and Decrees in the Border Area], published in Yan'an, 1943. Health education included personal hygiene, public health, and environmental sanitation.

51. Zhao, Feng, 'Zhandou zhong de bianqu retong' [Boys and Girls in Our Border Areas], *Xinhua ribao* [New China Daily], 4 Jan. 1944.

52. In 1931 the Japanese invaded Manchuria and set up Manchukuo there. In 1937 the Japanese troops invaded north China. By 1938, the Japanese occupied central China and some major cities such as Beijing, Shanghai, Wuhan and Nanjing, the capital of the Nationalist Party. The Nationalists had to flee to Sichuan and set up a new capital in Chongqing. China was divided into three parts: the Communists in Yan'an, the Nationalists in Chongqing and the various Japanese puppet regimes.

53. Lindsay, Michael, *Notes on Educational Problems in Communust China, 1941–1947*, New York: Greenwood Press, 1978, pp.35–6.

54. Yun, op. cit.

55. Besides the great shortage of teachers there was a great demand for educated personnel. The Border Area governments had, in many districts, to built up an almost completely new social service, and they needed a fairly large staff because they were trying to administer a great deal more than the old-style Chinese local government. The organisation of the mass-movement associations also required a large number of workers. In the broadest sense this was educational work but it competed with the school system for the services of educated personnel. The same is true of the Army Political Department, which included army education among its duties. See Lindsay, Michael, *Notes on Educational Problem in Communist China*. op. cit., p.36.

56. Liu, Duanfen, 'Dire shifan fazan jianshi' [A Brief History of the Second Teacher-Training College], Feb.–March 1943; Liu, Ti, 'Biaqu zhongden jiaoyu fazan qingkwang' [The Development of Elementary Education in the Border Area], 1943. (These two documents are in Shanxi Provincial Archives, Xi'an, Shanxi province, China.)

57. See 'Shan-Gan-Ning bianqu zhanxin shifan xuexiao guicheng chaoan' [The Draft Regulation of Teachers' Training Institutes in the Border Area of 1942]. (This document is in Shanxi Provincial Archives, Xi'an, Shanxi province,

China, no date available.)

58. These included the North Shanxi Public School, the Border Region Party School, the Central Party School, the Marxist-Leninist Academy, Zedong Youth Cadre Training School, the Border Region Vocational School, the Minorities School and the Administrative Academy. In addition, other specialist institutes were set up such as the Lu Xun Academy of Arts, the Natural Science Research Institute, Yan'an Medical School and Yan'an Agricultural School.

59. Wang, Zengmin *et al.*, *Shan-Gan-Ning bianqu tiyu shi* [Sport History of The Border Area], Xian: Shanxi renmin chubanshe [Shanxi People's Press], 1990, pp.20–21. These educational institutions were included.

60. Seybolt, Peter Jordan, op. cit., p.154.

61. *Xinhua ribao* was the CCP's newspaper during the Yan'an period.

62. Gu, Min, 'Chong douzhen zhong xunlian yu xuexi' [Physical Training and Study for Struggle], *Xinhua ribao* [New China Daily], 26 May 1938.

63. Stein Gunther described winter schools, night schools, part-time schools and women's literate groups in the Liberated Areas. See Stein, Gunther, op. cit., pp.262–3.

64. Band, Claire and William, *The Two Years with the Communists*. New Haven: Yale University Press, 1948, p.129.

65. The Border Area consisted of 19 counties. The above statistics are in Yun's article, 'On the Rapid Development of Women's Education in the Border Area', op. cit.

66. Strong, Anna Louise, *The Chinese Conquer China*, op. cit., p.59.

67. Quoted in Snow, Helen, *Inside Red China*, op. cit., pp.173, 193.

68. The Red Army's University was stopped when the Long March began in 1935, and no comparable institution was established until 1 June 1936. Lin Biao and Lo Ruiqing (President of the School and Dean of Studies respectively) established the Anti-Japanese Red Army University in the caves outside Bao An, Shanxi. The new name reflected the fact that the Communists had already declared war on the Japanese, and since 1935 had been promoting the idea of a popular front to resist fascism. This replaced the previous emphasis on class struggle. Accordingly, the Workers' and Peasants' Red Army became the Anti-Japanese Red Army and the same change was made in the name of its cadre-training institution. Following the Xi'an Incident in December 1936 (see note 6 above), the Communists moved their headquarters from Bao An south to Yan'an and dropped titular references to their ideology. The Red Army became the Eighth Route army under the nominal command of Chiang Kai-shek, and its school changed its name to the Chinese People's Anti-Japanese Military and Political University. For further details, see Seybolt, Peter Jordan, op. cit., pp.31–68.

69. Seybolt, Peter Jordan, ibid., pp.32, 39, 42.

70. Dongyuan she (a students' society of the university), 'Tiyu' [Physical Education and Sport], *Kangda dongtai* [Newsletter of the Anti-Japanese Military and Political University], 1938, pp.132.

71. Ibid., pp.133–4.

72. Xie, Hanwen, 'Kangda xueyuan de yeitun yanxi' [The Students' Military Manoeuvre], *Xinhua ribao* [New China Daily], 19 Sept, 1938.

73. Dongyuan she, 'Da shidai de xin nuxing [A New Image of a New Era], *Kangda dongtai* [Newsletter of the Anti-Japanese Military and Political University], 1938, p.53.

74. Mao Zedong and Wang Min both made speeches at the opening ceremony. Their speeches were both entitled 'Zai Yan'an zhongguo nuzi daxue kaixue

dianli shang de jianghua' [The Speech at the Opening Ceremony of the Yan'an Chinese Women's University]. Mao's speech was published in *Xin zhonghua bao* [New China News], 25 July 1939, and Wang Min's speech was published in *Zhongguo funu* [Chinese Women], Vol. 1, No. 1, 1939.

75. Wang, Min, op. cit.

76. Mao, Zedong, 'The Speech of the Opening Ceremony of the Women's University', op. cit..

77. Wang, Min, 'The Speech at the Opening Ceremony of the Women's University'. op. cit.

78. Wang, Zengmin, op. cit., p.49.

79. Wu, Jianping, 'Yi Yan'an' [Recollections of Yan'an], *Xin Tiyu* [New Sport], No. 2, 3, 1957, pp.3–5, 11–15.

80. Certainly, when the opportunity arose women were able to advance their cause. For example, after the War, during the land reform campaign, women's emancipation was promoted. Hinton and Snow both stated that Chinese women became a tremendous revolutionary force. See Snow, Helen, *Inside Red China*, op. cit., p.184; Hinton, William, *Fanshen: A Documentary of Revolution in a Chinese Village*, New York: Vintage Books, 1966. Hinton was an American who worked with the Communists in North China during the land reforms in the late 1940s.

81. Li Fuchun (1900–75), born in Changsha, Hunan, joined the CCP in 1923. He was the Director of the Political Work Department of the Red Army in 1930s and General Secretary of the Central Committee of the CCP in 1940s. After 1949 he became Minister of Finance and Vice-Prime Minister of the Chinese government.

82. Zhang, Yuan, 'Yan'an tiyu shenghuo pianduan' [Recollections of Yan'an's Physical Culture], *Xin tiyu* [New Sport], No. 7, 1957, pp.5–7.

83. For information on Zhu De, the Commander-in-Chief of the Red Army, see note 15, Chapter 5. For information on Li Fuchun, General Secretary of the Central Committee of the CCP, see note 81 above. Deng Fa (1906–46), an important leader of the Communist Workers' Movement, was the Director of the Security Bureau of Jiangxi Soviet Government in 1930s and Principal of the Communist Cadres' Training Institute in Yan'an in 1940s. Zhang Yuang, a refugee from the Nationalist areas, was the second Chairman of Yan'an Physical Education and Sports Committee, Director of the New Sports Society and the Head of Physical Education Department of Yan'an University from 1940 to 1943. All four were board members of the New Sports Society and Yan'an Physical Education and Sports Committee.

84. Ma, Haide, 'Yi Yan'an shiqi tiyu shenghuo' [The Recollections of Physical Exercise in Yan'an], *Xin Tiyu* [New Sport], No. 8, 1980, pp.10–12. The author's English name is George Hatem. Ma Haide is his Chinese name. He was born in Buffalo, New York, in 1910. He studied at the American University in Beirut and the University of Geneva. In 1933 he and two young American doctors decided to practise in Shanghai, specialising in venereal disease; but the other two gave up and returned home. He met Agnes Smedley who introduced him to a Communist engineer named Liu Ting. This man told him of the desperate need for doctors in the Red areas, so instead of returning to the States as he had intended, he went to Yan'an in the autumn of 1936. He worked at the International Peace Hospital in Yan'an. After 1949 he decided to stay and he is still in China, now aged 85.

85. Zhang, Yuan, 'Ruhe tuidong jianshen yundong' [How to Promote Physical Education and Sport], *Jiefang ribao* [Liberation Daily], 21 March 1942.

86. On 5 February 1942, the Sports Committee and the Liberation Daily advocated 'ten minutes' physical exercise every day. On 15 March the *Liberation Daily* reported that it had become a popular movement. Yan'an Physical Education and Sports Committee sent its message to every workplace and school to encourage people to exercise regularly. See 'Yan'an tiyuhui jianyi ge jiguan xuexiao jiaqian tiyu' [The Suggestion of Strengthening Physical Exercise in Every Workplace and School], *Jiefang ribao* [Liberation Daily], 23 June 1942.

87. Charles Harold McCloy (1886–1959) was an American physical educationist. For details about him see Chapter Eight.

88. See Chapters Seven and Eight.

89. Zhang, Yuan, 'Kaizhan tiyu yundong' [On the Development of Physical Exercise], and 'Ruhe tuidong jiansheng yundong' [How to Promote Physical Exercise]. Both articles were published in *Jiefang ribao* [Liberation Daily], 20 Feb. 1942 and 21 March 1942.

90. Yang Lie (1914–91) was a female physical educationist. She graduated from Shanghai Liangjiang Women's Physical Education Institute in 1933. She went to Japan to study in 1935. She arrived in Yan'an in October 1939 and joined the CCP in 1941. She taught physical education in Yan'an University and became a major figure in the promotion of women's physical exercise in Yan'an. She was the third Chairman of the Yan'an Physical Education and Sports Committee. After 1949 she became the Director of the Physical Education Department of the Ministry of Sport and then the Director of the Research Committee of Shanghai and Guangzhou physical education institutions.

91. Yang's article was published in *Liberation Daily* on 19 Sept. 1942.

92. See Chapter Eight.

93. Zhu, De, 'Zhu Jiuyue yundong dahui' [For the September Sports Meeting], *Jiefang ribao* [Liberation Daily], 2 Sept. 1942.

94. There were competitions and matches in Yan'an almost every weekend. There were more than 200 competitions taking place in the Yan'an period inside and outside schools, colleges, armies and mass organisations. The big ones included Yan'an May Sports Meeting (1–5 May 1937); The Border Area Anti-Japanese Sports Meeting (1–6 August 1937);Yan'an Youth Sports Meeting (6–8 May 1939); Yan'an Women's Sports Meeting (16–17 March 1940), Jia Xian Students Sports Competition (the spring of 1943) and Yan'an Skating Competition (Feb. 1943). Girls and women attended these sports meetings. For further details see Wang Zengmin, op. cit., pp.114–32. and CSHSPE, *Zhongguo jindai tiyu shi* [Modern Chinese Sports History], op. cit., pp.398–9.

95. The details of this Sports Meeting are in *Jiefang ribao* [Liberation Daily], 15 Sept. 1942.

96. From the first day of the Sports Meeting, woman athletes became popular news in the newpapers. *Jiefang ribao* reported their competitions including basketball, volleyball, athletics and swimming on the front page. See *Jiefang ribao* [Liberation Daily], 1, 2, 3, 4, 5, 7, 9, 15, 19 Sepember 1942.

97. Xue, Ning, 'Yan'an di yi chi funu yundong daibiao dahui' [The Yan'an Women's Sports Meeting], *TWS*, No. 6, 1991, p.41.

98. Yu, Min, 'Sanba yundong dahui shuxie' [The Report of the Women's Sports Meeting], *Xin zhonghua bao* [New China News], 29 March 1940.

99. See 'Yan'an gejie funu xiangyin sulian funu haozhao fan faxishi dahui gao quanguo quan bianqu zimai shu' [Yan'an Women's Manifesto: A Response to the Soviet Russian Women], *Jiefang ribao* [Liberation Daily], 14 Oct. 1941.

100. Dong, Fangmin, 'Muqin yundongyuan' [Mother-Athletes]. *Jiefang ribao*

[Liberation Daily], 5 Sept. 1942; Wang, Jialin, 'Women de yundong dahui' [On our Sports Meeting], *Jiefang ribao* [Liberation Daily], 5 Sept. 1942.
101. Seybolt, P.J., op. cit., p.61.
102. Smedley, Agnes, *Chinese Destinies: Sketches of Present-Day China*, New York: The Vanguard Press, 1933, p.11.
103. See 'Shan-Gan-ning bianqu fulianhui di re kuoda zhiweihui dahui jieyi' [The Resolution of the Second Women's Congress of the Shan-Gan-Ning Border Areas], 20 Dec. 1940, *Zhongguo funu* [Chinese Women], Vol. 2, No. 9, 1940.
104. Ibid.
105. Horn, Joshua S., *Away with All Pests: An English Surgeon in People's China 1945–1969*, New York: Monthly Review Press, 1960, p.125.
106. See 'Zhanshi retong baoyuhui Shan-Gan-Ning bianqu fenhui chengli jinguo jiqi zhuijin gongzhuo baogao' [The Report of Shan-Gan-Ning Border Areas' Childcare Committee], *Xinhua rebao* [New China's News], 27 August, 1938.
107. Ibid.
108. The Bands taught in Beijing 1930–40. They had to escape from Beijing after Pearl Harbor. Their book, *Two Years with the Chinese Communists*, resulted from wartime experiences beginning in 1941 when they hid from the Japanese in the highlands of Hobei, and their trip to Yan'an. They were among the very few non-Chinese observing Chinese Communists during the Second World War.
109. Band, Claire and William, op. cit., pp.257–8.
110. Muo, Chi, 'Tuoreshuo de yi tian' [A Day in a Nursery], *shidai funu* [Modern Women], Vol. 1, No. 2, 1946, p.44.
111. Yang, Lie, 'Yan'an baoyuyang de tiyu' [Physical Education in Yan'an Nursery], *TWS*, No. 1, 1989, p.42,
112. Snow, Helen, *Inside Red China*, op. cit., p.197.

SEVEN

One Step Backward and One Step Forward: Emancipation and Exercise in the Nationalist Area (1928–49)

そっぺのぺと

E XERCISE IS AN important location for publicly presenting and dramatising the body as a cultural artefact. A history of the body at exercise is a history of aesthetic, cultural and political investment in the body. A history of exercise in modern China, therefore, comprises an important chapter of the history of the body. However, virtually all scholars of Chinese studies still largely disregard the historical role of exercise in efforts to improve the status of women and mostly ignore the significance of exercise in women's emancipation. Nevertheless, because exercise is directly connected with the body, the most conspicuous symbol of women's oppression and a fundamental fact of women's exploitation, for Chinese women its availability represented a new and important dimension in their lives.

In the 1930s this was as true for the Nationalist area as the Communist area. There were clear similarities in the femininity demanded of Nationalist and Communist women. Both endorsed a femininity that was a blend of past and present – for different reasons: Nationalists because of a sincere commitment to tradition; Communists because of an insincere commitment to tradition. Essentially, Nationalists wished to strengthen cultural roots while Communists wished to sever them. Practicality ensured that Nationalists embraced modernity and practicality determined that Communists embraced history. Both needed healthy, fit, skilled women as efficient mothers, wives and workers. The constraints of past and present encumbered them both and produced a similarity of practice if not principle. In essence, Nationalists reinstated Confucianism, in part, and Communists retained it, in part, but both for very different purposes.

After the Communists had been defeated in 1927 and desperately tried to find places to survive in the rural countryside, the Nationalists, led by Chiang Kai-shek,[1] the Commander-in-Chief of the National Revolutionary Army and Sun Yat-sen's successor (who died on 12 March 1925) continued their task of unifying China under one-party rule. They already held the long stretch along the lower Yangzi River, the richest and most developed area in China. This power base enabled the Nationalists to overcome local warlords elsewhere. By 1928, they had extended their territory north to the former capital of China – Beijing. From there their influence stretched on into Manchuria. The warlords in those areas were either destroyed or allied themselves with the Nationalists. In April 1927 Chiang and his supporters set up their own Nationalist government in Nanjing.[2] Chiang became its President and the Commander-in-Chief of the Nationalist armed forces. The history of China now split into two interlinked but separate narratives: the history of the Communist soviets in Jiangxi and Yan'an and the history of the Nationalist government in Nanjing.[3] Earlier chapters dealt with the former, this and the next chapter deal with the latter.

From 1928 to 1949, while challenging Western imperialist intrusion, facing up to Japanese aggression from the outside and waging war against the Chinese Communists from the inside, the Nationalist government controlled about two-thirds of China's population and the greater part of China.[4] The warlords' era was ended and much of the country was unified. Sun Yat-sen's Three Principles of the People – anti-imperialist nationalism, democracy, and socialism – were declared the official ideology.[5] The country was modernised – roads, telegraph lines and railways were built and modern industry was expanded. The government was supported by the landed, industrial and commercial classes, and recognised by many foreign governments as the legitimate government of China. The ambition of the Nationalists was to unify the whole country. Military force was used ruthlessly in an attempt to control or annihilate warlords and to destroy both communists and dissidents;[6] Confucianism was used once again to promote national morality in order to maintain general order and social stability.

As discussed in earlier chapters,[7] the principal concept of Confucianism, was 'hierarchy'. This gave every man and woman a definite place in society and defined his or her relationships with others. Confucius believed that if every man or woman knew his or her place and acted in accordance with his or her position, social order would be ensured.[8] This concept was endorsed by Chiang and his Party and they immediately put it into practise after they established the Nationalist government.

The Nationalists restored the Women's Movement but defined feminism in their own image by 'rescuing' it from the 'immoral' influences of both Communist ideology and Western civilisation.[9] They had seen young girls' eager adoption of Western culture: English high-heeled shoes, Parisian perfumes, American silk stockings, the high-slit flowing gowns, the one-piece female bathing-suits, and the 'abuses' of free love and divorce.[10] They warned that this immoral behaviour would destroy family life and bring social unrest. Moreover, there was the greater danger that those young girls without appropriate 'education' might be attracted by Western democratic ideas or Communist revolutionary theories which would shake the foundations of the Nanjing government. The Nationalist Party and government, together with compliant feminists, therefore, took the Women's Movement in a somewhat idiosyncratic direction.

At first the Nationalist government seemed prepared to give women 'freedom'. The *China Critic* reported in 1928 that the Nationalist party 'intend to ensure the emancipation of women's rights in China on the principle of equality between men and women in law, in economics, in education and society'.[11] Soumay Cheng, a woman lawyer, was appointed to the Commission with responsibility for drafting the new 'Code of China'.[12] The new Civil Code was finally issued in December 1930. It asserted that women were entitled to choose their own husbands, and to divorce; their rights became more symmetrical with those of men. Daughters, both married and single, were granted the same legal rights as sons regarding property inheritance and rights of ownership. The following year a new Factory Law ensured that equal work brought equal pay for both men and women workers. At the same time, the penal law was revised to acknowledge that *both* husband and wife had a mutual obligation to be faithful. Although the ideal of women's equality was not always carried through with absolute consistency, the new laws, in theory, if not always in practise, greatly improved the legal status of women in the Nationalist area.[13]

The Nationalist Party, however, had little truck with assertive feminism. Since in the view of the Party the new laws signalled the realisation of all the goals of the Women's Movement, its continued existence was not necessary. Militancy was condemned and political action was suppressed. These improvements in women's rights in law appeared to mollify many feminists – and to draw their sting. A leading feminist now stated: 'The meaning of the Women's Movement is not to annihilate . . . men's valour, nor is it to put an end to the grace of women's nature or evade the function of motherhood. . . . The Women's Movement must cut out, root and branch, the attitude of antagonism between the sexes.'[14]

Most of the leading feminists at this time, like the pioneering women emancipationists at the turn of the century, were from wealthy families and well educated in the fields of either education, law or medicine. But they were different from the pioneers: they eschewed confrontational thought and action. They disregarded the struggle of previous decades and were prepared to credit the emancipation of women to the liberality of the Nationalist government. Since this government had acknowledged their rights in law, they now chose to believe that women at last had rid themselves of the old conventions and institutions and had achieved what Western women had achieved: the right to education, a profession and suffrage.[15] In their view it was now time for Nationalist feminists to construct a new conciliatory path for women to tread.

Influential voices in society called to women to follow them along this path.[16] Zeng Baosun, the Principal of Ai-Fang Girls' School in Changsha, Hunan province, pointed out that there were now three choices for women: 1. Reversion; 2. Westernisation; 3. Amalgamation (of the best of Chinese culture with the best from the West). 'The Third one', Zeng said:

> is . . . what we want. To achieve this it is necessary for the modern Chinese woman . . . to have a thorough knowledge of the culture and civilisation of her own country . . . For then, and not until then, will she be able to re-evaluate and make the best use of those desirable old Chinese ideals such as maternal love and wifely devotion. With a foundation like this she can build a superstructure of Western training in the arts, science and philosophy, or anything else she chooses. Therefore, for the modern Chinese women, let her freedom be restrained by self-control, her self-realisation be coupled with self-sacrifice, and her individualism be circumscribed by family duty. Such is our new ideal of womanhood.[17]

Wu Yifang, President of Ginling College for Women in Nanjing, also made it clear that future generations of women would combine the rich heritage of Confucian virtues with the advantages of a modern vocational education.[18] 'Feminism' became a mixture of the new Western values and the old Eastern beliefs. Emancipation was expressed in terms of personal development, job opportunities, maternal love and wifely devotion.[19] A composite ideal of womanhood was proclaimed and social harmony was expected to be achieved. The Nationalist woman was to be as much concerned with past as present image. Simultaneously, and significantly, the influential magazines for women, *Funu gongming* [The Voice of Women] and *Jiezhi yuekan* [The Domestic Management Monthly],[20] which earlier had promulgated an aggressive emancipatory view of women in China, now changed their tune. Their emphasis now was on education and domesticity. Many of the articles dealt with home management, because women would always be the makers of the home no matter what social changes took place in the future.[21] In short, the Nationalist ideal of womanhood was a combination of Occidental modernity and Oriental tradition.

Feminism, Education and the Law of Sport

Education was the key to realising the ideal of the new woman and achieving the goal of social harmony. The Song sisters were perfect models. They had been brought up in a Christian home, educated in America and married respectively the present and future political leaders of China.[22] The middle class now believed that education for a girl was the means of securing a high-status husband or if she was not happy with the idea of marriage, a career for herself. One father of three daughters told Lady Dorothea Hosie, an emancipationist from the West, that the Chinese girls' future lay with education: 'I shall have no money to leave them: I must earnestly wish, therefore, to give them a good education. If they marry, they will then wish to marry sensible men, not fools or knaves. If they do not marry, they will know how to support themselves.'[23] The women's magazine *Nusheng* [Women's Voice] was started in 1932, with the aim of giving advice to young girls on education and marriage in order to better their lives. It was the ambition of the editor, Wang Yiwei, a graduate in journalism from Fudan University, to see her magazine in every girls' school and every home in China.[24]

In the Nationalist area, from 1928 to 1949, middle-class girls, Song Qingling, the wife of Sun Yat-sen, recalled, were free to go to primary, middle school and college.[25] Influenced by patriotism and liberalism, they embraced the aims of the Nationalist system of schooling with enthusiasm. Now an important part of a girl's education was to ensure her health. Lin Yutang, a widely read writer of the time, stated that the modern ideas from the West must be taken as liberalising influences working for the good of Chinese womanhood and for the Chinese race. Restraints on the body must end. Women should be fit to work for the good of the nation. Therefore the first priority of Nationalist womanhood was health. 'Let women be proud of their own sex, and let them enjoy a healthy body' was a popular catch phrase of the time.[26]

As a consequence, in the Nationalist controlled area of China between 1928 and 1949 women's exercise expanded rapidly. Middle-class women enjoyed radical forms of physical freedom. Even conservatives encouraged women's participation in exercise – for the purpose of producing healthy mothers. Women's exercise, paradoxically, partially denied women's traditional image and partially confirmed their traditional responsibilities. Women's exercise, as well as the Women's Movement, therefore, constituted one step forward and one step backward on the road to liberation. This stilted progress stemmed not only from men's conservatism, but from women's confusion. They were ambivalent and contradictory about their new roles. To understand why it is necessary to consider their education in some detail.

In December 1927 a National Physical Education and Sports Committee was established under the Education Ministry of the Nationalist government.[27] It was the first time that the Chinese had an official national body to supervise exercise throughout the country. In May 1928, the first 'national' education conference under the new regime took place in Nanjing. Seventy-seven delegates attended. A 'physico-military' education system, modelled on Imperial Germany to educate boys in the spirit and practise of militarism, was agreed upon. Military drill and training for boys became compulsory in schools and summer camps. Girls, for their part, were now encouraged to participate in gymnastics, physical education and sport. It was the belief of the conference that physical education was the most effective way to inculcate obedience, responsibility, hygiene, enthusiasm for physical activity and, above all, a spirit of service to the nation.[28] Exercise was to be the responsibility of *both* sexes. It was the effective link between the Chinese body and patriotism and patriotism was the motive force behind the nationalist espousal of exercise. At the conference a motion was passed that all teaching materials in the primary and middle schools should emphasise the humiliating experiences suffered at the hands of Western and Eastern imperialism during the last century in order to arouse among the pupils a deep patriotic consciousness.[29] The country needed to be unified, the nation wanted to be powerful and the people should be made aware of their patriotic responsibilities. A *Digest of Textbooks* used in schools stated that Chinese citizens should 'love to serve their country. Their duty is first to serve their country second to attend to their private affairs'. Cyrus Peake in his book *Nationalism and Modern Education in China* described a picture of the period illustrating a lesson of unity and duty. A Chinese man and a woman bend under the weight of the world, on which a map of China is outlined, and in the background a crowd of people, both young and old, rush forward to help them.[30] China was not to fall to the ground. It was believed that a healthy and strong physique was – for both men and women – a most potent way to serve China.[31]

To promote exercise the government issued the Law of Sport for Citizens on 16 April 1929. It was the first sports law in Chinese history. It laid a foundation for the systematic organisation of exercise throughout Nationalist China. It stated:

1. Boys and girls must take part in physical education and sport. Their parents and guardians are responsible for their supervision;
2. The aim of physical education and sport is to develop men and women's bodies for the good of the country;
3. Every male and female should participate in physical activity in which scientific sports methods are applied;
4. Old customs which present an obstacle to the physical fitness of men and women must be banned by the local authority;
5. Every town, city and region must have public sports stadiums;
6. Physical education should be an obligatory course in middle schools and colleges. Students will not be allowed to graduate unless they pass their physical education test.
9. Physical education teachers and instructors should be qualified.[32]

The Law was revised in 1941 but retained much of its original content. It re-emphasised that every man and woman must exercise and that central and local government must take a role in controlling, administering and financing sport.[33] To accompany these two laws, the central government also issued regulations for implementation.[34] There were more than 40 laws and regulations issued between 1927 and 1949, covering sport, sports administration, physical education in schools and sport in society.[35] All made the same point: men and women were equal in terms of rights of access to exercise, and women were to participate in exercise, not only for themselves but for the race – for China's tomorrow.

This was not token legislation. Women's participation was not only required in law but in practice. It was now commonplace for girls in schools to take part in physical education. Physical education was considered the nation's highest educational priority[36] – a crucial tool for promoting both national unification, health and identity. This view went unaltered throughout the period of the Nanjing government. During these years of educational experimentation, the aim of female physical exercise remained consistent: to awaken girls and women to a consciousness of their duty to the nation, not only in mind but in body, not only mentally but physically.

For their part, professional educators did their 'bit' to improve Chinese girls' physical condition. Most of them obtained qualifications abroad. When they returned they became leading educationists or physical educators and some eventually became major figures in the Ministry of Education and on the National Physical Education Committee of the Ministry of Education,[37] including Wang Zheng-ting,[38] Wu Yunrui,[39] Yuan Dunli,[40] Hao Gensheng,[41] Zhang Huilan.[42] They created a system of physical education complete with modern professional ideals, they edited texts, planned curricula and improved teaching methods. Between 1931 and 1940, under their supervision, the Nationalist government issued five physical education decrees covering primary and middle school, college and university curricula.[43] According to these decrees, female pupils and students at *all* levels, were to attend physical education classes and participate in physical activities.

Some idea of the influence of these decrees may be gauged from the fact that in May 1933 *Tiyu zhoubao* [Physical Education Weekly][44] reported that the Shanxi Provincial Women's College of Education in Xi'an had a fixed morning and afternoon exercise time every day, in addition to physical education classes of ten hours a week. Six hundred girl students in the attached primary school had comprehensive physical exercise facilities and physical education classes. These primary school pupils also received supervision from physical educators after classes. The journal also reported that the Elementary School of Shanghai likewise aimed to popularise physical exercise. Girls, in addition to their physical education classes, had compulsory morning and afternoon exercises. They also attended gymnastics, athletics and swimming sessions.. They had a physical exercise examination once a month.[45] Even in Gansu, an isolated province in western China, the Provincial Educational Council strenuously promoted physical education and issued instructions regarding compulsory exercise in schools. The Council demanded *inter alia* that every school and every county should hold a sports meeting each May to demonstrate the beneficial results of their physical education programme.[46]

Schools, of course, catered for the middle classes. However, the value of physical education for the masses was emphasised with equal zeal. The official view was that physical activity could help female adults fulfil their duties and functions as citizens of the new Republic. Female adult exercise programmes, therefore, under the supervision of a newly formed special administrative unit called the 'Women and Children's Department' were established in Public Stadiums which were created in most cities and towns in order to comply with the Laws on Sports for Citizens.[47] There were 1,139 public stadiums in 1929. The figure had increased to 2,826 by 1938.[48] Public stadiums units organised athletic competitions, supervised mass physical exercise and encouraged women and children to exercise.

Furthermore, in September 1932, the Ministry of Education started a Model District Sports Movement. The Ministry requested that every county and province select one district or town as a model of sports progress to stimulate others. One of the criteria for selection was the level of women's involvement in exercise, and their consequent healthy condition.[49] The Model District Sports Movement was to be found throughout the country, but it was especially well organised in Guanggong, Jiangsu, Zhejiang, Anhui and Shandong.[50] There were 109 counties in Shangdong province. Every county had its sports stadium. The slogans of the province were 'popularise sports activity and let the masses play' and 'there are no classes in sports stadia, let's play together'.[51] Zhejiang province was particularly successful at stimulating female participation in exercise. In one month alone, February 1937, some 5,363 women played basketball, volley-ball, cycling, table-tennis and athletics in the provincial stadium.[52]

Between 1928 to 1949, the Nationalist government developed a complete national physical training system for both men and women. The government was wholly committed to the long-standing view that the only way to restore the nation was through the promotion of the spirit of nationalism and the creation of strong bodies. The government made a special effort to encourage women's participation. They proclaimed again and again that only through adequate exercise could women efficiently fulfil their duties in the domestic and in the public domain.[53] However, the nature of the Nationalists' conservative and somewhat narrow interpretation of this equality of involvement was nicely demonstrated by Gao Zi,[54] a female physical educationist, who stated that women with healthy bodies would be strong mothers of the nation. This was the essential Nationalists interpretation of equality: women could help and serve the country in their special biological way – not as soldiers but as the strong mothers of strong soldiers.[55] Nationalist women, in short, were defined in public discourse by reference to the performance of their traditional duties as 'wives' and 'mothers'. In this Nationalist context, and on the crest of a wave of patriotism, national identity was considered more important than gender identity. In contrast to Europe both earlier and at this time, exercise, was therefore not predominantly a 'male preserve'.[56] It did not play such an important part in the education of élite males as it did in the West.[57] Exercise was perceived by the Nationalists as a tool to strengthen the whole nation – men and women for *disparate* roles in order to restore the country to its former greatness.

Exercise reshaped masculinity in the Anglo-Saxon world in the late nineteenth century.[58] Exercise reshaped femininity in China in the early twentieth century. The growth of English 'athleticism' was associated in part with the preparation of upper-class boys for service on the frontiers of the British empire.[59] The evolution of a Chinese 'athleticism' was associated in part with the preparation of women to serve as the mothers of a martial China. In short, the Anglo-Saxon world emphasised men's biological destiny; exercise became a symbol of distinction between the sexes characterised to a considerable extent by male inclusion and female exclusion.[60] By contrast, the Chinese Nationalist world concentrated equally on men's and women's biological destinies. Exercise was a symbol of unity between the sexes disparately engaged in a common enterprise – the revival of the nation. Even conservatives, like Lin Yutang, who, as already mentioned, strongly approved of traditional ideals of female morality came to claim that the *first* priority of modern education should be to develop women's physical qualities.[61] The new femininity constituted a modern body and an ancient morality. Both, in harness, would ensure that women would fulfil their patriotic mission.

The New Life Movement and Women's Exercise: A Class Gap

In February 1934, Chiang Kai-shek launched the New Life Movement from his Nanchang headquarters, Jiangxi province, where he served as Commander-in-Chief of the military operations for the suppression of communism. The leadership of the Nationalist Party held the view that the material and spiritual 'degeneration' of the people was responsible for China's continuing crisis. This was considered to be the direct consequence of communist and imperialist influence. It was time to launch an indigenous moral crusade to revitalise the country. The crusade was to signal the start of a new phase of Chinese history, one that was to be both *conservative* and *liberal* – embracing the modern without abandoning the ancient: 'The movement was conservative, but conservative in a very specific sense: far from being a reaffirmation of traditional Chinese political conceptions, it was fashioned by and in response to the twentieth-century Chinese revolution. Its underlying spirit had greater affinity with modern counter-revolutionary movements than with political attitudes inherited from China's past.'[62] It was, in short, not a backward-looking but a forward-looking response to modern problems. For want of a better term, it may be referred to as radical conservatism.

The New Life Movement was remarkable for the exaggerated argument of its proponents that the key to China's national salvation lay in hygienic activities to purge the unhealthy habits of body and mind of the Chinese people. Chinese life at that time, according to Chiang, could be summarised in a few unattractive epithets: 'filthiness', 'laziness' and 'degeneracy'. The purpose of the Movement was to transform this old life-style into one characterised by the attractive epithets: 'cleanliness', 'energy' and 'discipline'. This would constitute the first step towards achieving a 'New Life'.[63] Reform would lead to the moral regeneration of the Chinese people and enhance a public awareness of, and concern for China's problems. As one zealot argued: 'If we want to change men's hearts, we must stress training to mould good personalities; to reform everyday lives and nourish good habits.'[64] Chiang's aim was nothing less than to rebuild China from its moral foundations.[65]

Underpinning the aims of the Movement 'to revive native morality', according to Chiang, was the revival of Confucianism to maintain social stability through national discipline. Chiang claimed:

> The New Life Movement aims at the promotion of a regular life guided by the four virtues 'li', 'yi', 'lian', 'chi' [propriety, righteousness, integrity and a sense of shame]. These virtues must be applied to ordinary matters, such as food, clothing, shelter, action. The four virtues are the essential principles for the promotion of morality. From these rules one learns how to deal with men and matters, how to develop oneself, and how to adjust oneself to one's surroundings. Whoever violates these rules is bound to fail; and a nation which neglects them will not survive.[66]

Hence, to achieve a satisfactory life-style meant not only embracing modern practicality but also reviving 'past ethics'.[67] In Chiang's uncomplicated view the Movement was characterised by simple principles, honest behaviour, physical soundness and spiritual regeneration. Equally, in his view, the Movement was not one of naive neo-Confucian revivalism but a sophisticated response to the modern problems of China. It was the Nationalist Party's version of the much later 'Cultural Revolution'.[68]

Chiang's call for a Chinese New Life in February 1934, was followed by an immediate response by the population that exceeded his expectations. Within a matter of weeks, the Movement had spread 'like wildfire' over most of China, encouraging some to believe that China's long-promised 'rebirth' was close at hand.[69] Through March and April, New Life Promotional Associations were established in nine provinces as well as three municipal centres. By the first anniversary of the Movement in February 1935, 15 provinces, three municipalities, and nine railway centres had New Life organisations. As of the end of 1935, organisations had spread to 19 provinces, five municipalities, 12 railway centres, and ten overseas Chinese communities. At the lower administrative level, the organisation had been extended to 1,132 counties by 1935.[70]

What was the influence of the New Life Movement on the Women's

Movement, and what was the relationship between the Movement, the Women's Movement and women's physical liberation? Studies of Chinese women have touched on the first question,[71] but not the second. While the New Life Movement had negative consequences for the Women's Movement politically,[72] it gave women an enhanced opportunity to free their bodies further through exercise – with serendipitous consequences for a more progressive view of femininity in society.

The New Life Movement and the Women's Movement established a symbiotic relationship. They were linked though Chiang's wife Song Meiling, by this time the Head of both the Chinese Women's Movement and the New Life Movement. In February 1936 Song Meiling established the Women's Department of the New Life Movement. In her view the purpose of the Movement was 'to help the people, to train them to take their rightful place in society and enable them to become useful citizens in a modern democracy'.[73] What (and where) was women's rightful place? Song Meiling believed it was at *home* as a virtuous wife, because there was one fundamental principle which the traditional code of ethics had laid down for women and that time would never change: 'virtue is more important than learning.' She said, 'To my mind, if one has to choose between virtue and learning, virtue is the more to be cherished.'[74]

Girls' education, according to Song Meiling, should emphasise sexual differences and prevent the unreflective appropriation of male standards of thought. She insisted that 'boys and girls needed separate training with a view to the development of their respective talents'. Girls should be instructed in sewing, hosiery, embroidery, weaving, flower-arrangement, toy-making and rattan work.[75] In response, Zen Baosun, the Pricipal of Ai-Fang Girls' School in Changsha, argued that girls' education was not intended to match the male standard of thought and life. It was not to turn girls into pseudo-males. Girls' education should be a thorough preparation of girls' requirements in life – needlework, cookery, domestic science and home management.[76]

In addition to fulfilling myriad domestic roles, middle-class women were also encouraged to play appropriate and limited social and economic public roles. At least while they were young and single, they should obtain professional qualifications and enter employment. Social work was advocated for the leisured. Some women's organisations and branches of the National New Life Movement Promotion

Committee urged that the Women's Movement should concentrate on child welfare, home reform, mothers' training and charity work.[77] However, little was said about careers continuing after marriage or women's participation in the workforce. Rather, these middle class women were encouraged to recognise that care of the household and children was their primary duty. A traditional relationship between the sexes was again sanctioned by the New Life Movement. Nationalist concern, in theory, embraced all women; in practice it concentrated largely on middle-class women in the urban communities. For urban working-class women, the question of how to achieve 'true motherhood' was academic; survival was the top priority.

Modern industrial capitalism in twentieth century China, as in England and the United States a century earlier, was built on the intersection of textile manufacture and female and child labour. For instance, a study of 29 cities in nine provinces in 1930 showed that women constituted 46.7 per cent of the labour force, men, 46.4 per cent and children, 6.9 per cent. Another study of 23 cities, carried out three years later, give the startling figure of 56 per cent for women workers.[78] According to a study of 28 cities in nine provinces (Jiangsu, Zhejiang, Anhui, Jiangxi, Hubei, Shangdong, Guangdong, Guangxi and Fujian) in 1930, most of the women workers were to be found in occupations categorised under 'textile industry' – a total of 337,546 out of 363,610.[79] In Shanghai, China's largest industrial centre prior to 1949, cotton was king and the majority of mill-workers were women. Including those employed in the silk and tobacco factories, women accounted for almost two-thirds of the total industrial work force in Shanghai.[80] The wages that these women received were amazingly low. On average, women working in the cotton textile industry received Chinese $7.5 a month in the 1920s and $12 a month in the 1940s.[81] At the same time, the cost of living was roughly Chinese $12–20 for a single worker and Chinese $21–35 for a worker with a family of five per month.[82] It is obvious from the figures on women's wages and the cost of living that it was almost impossible for a woman worker to support herself. As a result, these women had barely enough food and few other basic necessities. A study of the housing and living conditions in a slum area in Nanchang city in the 1930s vividly illustrates the common experience of poor working-class women: 'With the exception of a few houses, most of the homes of the slum area of Nanchang city are cheaply made huts. They are small, damp and poorly ventilated. With exception of one bed, one table and one chair, all worn out and filthy, there is hardly anything left. As for kitchen utensils, they have only one stove, several bowls and several pairs of chop-sticks.'[83]

Hours were long, cotton textile workers in Shanghai working roughly 12 hours a day, and some even working more than 15 hours.[84] Some of these women also worked the night shift. With hardly any breaks during their working hours, not even for meals, they had to eat while they were working. A lucky few had 15- to 30-minute meal breaks.[85] Holiday were at a minimum. A study of 31 factories in Tianjin in 1927 shows that most of these factory women workers had one rest day every seven days. In Shanghai, however, most women had only two rest days a month.[86] Many workers suffered from tuberculosis, ulcers and malnutrition. Consequently, the death rate in cotton textile factories was high. In the Yufeng Cotton Mill in Shanghai, 30 per cent of the workers died within three years of starting work there and the majority of those who did not die were chronically sick.[87] The poor working conditions, long hours of work, low wages, plus other means of exploitation and maltreatment, resulted in a sub-human form of existence. Women suffered both continual physical and psychological illness.

Peasant women in the Nationalist area suffered as much as working-class women. Military attacks and interventions from the foreign powers and warlords continually destroyed traditional Chinese peasants' lives. As the peasants rapidly became poorer, women became more and more peripheral to the family economy, and were, in ever-increasing numbers, sold to landlords as servants or child-brides. One way to escape from rural destruction was to migrate to the cities in search of a job.[88] In many cases, peasant girls and women were 'sold' to factory owners to work for a number of years without pay.[89] A song at that time described their pitiful condition:

Living in the countryside was full of hardship,
Trying one's best still left the stomach empty
No other choice but to
Come all the way to find jobs,
Letting people know that we can bear hardship . . .
There are more than ten hours of work everyday,
Work until the head aches and the waist gets sore,
Eyes become red and swollen . . . [90]

The idea of educating and emancipating working-class and peasant women was not suggested until the late 1920s and early 1930s when female radicals came to the conclusion that the women's movement in the Nationalist area was too middle class.[91] On the creation of the New Life Movement, Jiang Yixiao, a woman reporter, requested that, in view of the fact that only 1 per cent of Chinese women were literate,[92] 'The Women's Movement should not be only a middle-class movement, but should educate and awake working-class and peasant women.'[93] In response, the New Life Movement certainly tried to improve the living conditions of working-class and peasant women, but its efforts were unimpressive. A number of middle-class girls were trained and then sent to factories and countryside to educate and mobilise their poorer counterparts.[94] Literacy classes were set up, childcare centres were opened, health education was provided, recreations such as singing and games were introduced.[95] However, the effort of these few well-intentioned proselytisers had little influence on working-class and peasant women's lives. They were too many and their basic concerns remained 'survival' issues such as food, clothing and shelter. Even when the New Life Movement intensified in the late 1930s consideration of working-class and peasant women remained minimal. Since educated, articulate and literate women had little contact with their underprivileged counterparts, they had difficulty articulating their experiences, and although they may have recognised the importance of educating and mobilising these women, they did not know how to do it. These privileged women did not understand their counterparts. When they spoke of 'women', they actually meant middle-class women.[96] It is no wonder that the Women's Movement in the Nationalist area was largely restricted to the middle class.

The death knell of an independent Women's Movement came in May 1938 with a conference called at Lushan, Jiangxi province by Song Meiling.[97] It decided that the Chinese Women's Advisory Committee of the New Life Movement (of which, of course, Song Meiling was the President) would from henceforth be the agency through which *all* women's activities were to function.[98] The various autonomous elements of the Women's Movement was now taken over by the New Life Movement. 'Work in the women's movement', Song Meiling said, 'should be concerned with general education, vocational training, women's service and welfare and family problems.'[99] Girls and women were pressed to improve their housekeeping as part of the Women's Movement and the New Life

Movement. Along with her husband, Chiang Kai-shek, Song Meiling travelled to many parts of China to explain the principles of both Movements and to encourage orderliness, cleanliness, simplicity and frugality – in an attempt to reform domestic habits. Her purpose in life now appeared to be the re-establishment of traditionalism!

How did the New Life Movement influence Chinese women's lives? Han Suyin, an independent-minded, foreign-trained doctor recalled, in a vivid account, her reaction to the fixed and rigid rules of behaviour advocated by the Movement.[100] On her marriage, her husband, one of Chiang Kai-shek's staff in Chongqing, was determined to eradicate 'the foreigner' in her and to reintroduce her to Confucian feudal domestic traditions in order to turn her back into a true Chinese woman. She recalled how the traditional ideology strongly affected her thoughts and behaviour. She was full of zeal, ardour and a willingness to comply with it. She began to have feelings of shame about her 'foreignness' and to develop both a belief in the immorality of the ideas of freedom and equality for women and a willingness to accept double standards for men and women.

The past had once again become the present. Men and women had different duties in the society. Historic platitudes regained their currency: 'Let men earn the bread to feed the family and let the women bear children . . . Of all the rights of women, the greatest is to be a mother . . . A curly headed child is her triumph and her delight, more surprising than the greatest book she has ever written and saturating her with more real satisfaction than the moment of her greatest triumph on the stage . . . so nature has ordained, so let men and women live.'[101] Modern, as ancient, Chinese womanhood was represented by the 'wise, gentle and firm mother'. The well-known Song sisters became icons of tradition. They were continually paraded as representatives of past and present ideals: educated women, devoted wives, and, in the case of Song Qingling, a devoted widow, and Song Ailing, a devoted mother: 'Even the smallest child in China is well aware that Madams Kong, Sun and Chiang are excellent wives and helpmates.'[102]

The more equal position of women in the Communist areas during this period was attacked by the New Life Movement as one of sexual immorality and 'unnatural behaviour'.[103] Some nationalist women may have felt envy when they read reports from the Border Area: 'They had women in the Red armies, girls dressed as boys and carried guns! They encouraged slave girls and concubines to revolt against their masters! Their widows remarried! They did not insist on 'chastity'! They incited the peasant women to stand up and denounce their husbands' misdeeds!'.[104] Nevertheless, the strict political control within the Nationalist Party areas did not allow for the expression of alternative viewpoints and positions on 'the women's question'. Song Meiling insisted, 'Women have to assist in sustaining the morale of the nation in its gravest trial, in obeying implicitly the orders of the Government.'[105] The order of the government for women was to embrace marriage and motherhood which were glorified and praised publicly in the New Life Movement.

Exercise and Nationalism

The New Life Movement, as noted earlier, was to create 'new citizens' including 'new women'. The 'new women' were to be a composite of ancient and modern qualities: domestic and public. The former took women back into the home, the latter allowed women outside – if only for a time. Since the Movement was a mixture of conservative and liberal ideas – the present rooted in the past – 'the new women' could not escape contradictions in their lives. But one facet of the Movement was uncomplicated. Health was at the top of the agenda: 'A healthy mind resides in a healthy body' went the well-aired slogan. Healthy bodies were not only the source of a vital spirit but also, through the latter, the source of national salvation. Health, strength and nationhood were indivisible:

> In order to become a healthy modern citizen, it is necessary first to have strong and robust bodies; having a strong body, one then has a strong spirit; having a strong spirit, one can then acquire all the abilities to strengthen the nation; having all kinds of abilities to strengthen the nation, one can naturally defend the state and glorify the nation, help our state and country to forever accord with the world and never again suffer from the aggression and oppression of foreign countries or receive disdain and insults.[106]

The key to a healthy body, predictably and logically, was exercise. As Chen Lifu, the leader of the Nationalist Party, wrote in *Qinfen tiyu yuebao* [Qinfen Sports Monthly][107] in October 1934: 'Physical educa-tion is the only way to strengthen the body. With a healthy body one can achieve the fulfilment of intellect and morals.'[108] Simultaneously, Zhou Fuhai, the Director of Jiangsu Provincial Educational Council, wrote an article to explain the triangular relationship between exercise, body and the New Life Movement. Tired clichés were penned. Exercise was part of education. It promoted a healthy body as well as a healthy spirit. Both would lead to the fulfilment of the mission of the New Life Movement.[109]

Chiang Kai-shek himself wrote an open letter to the nation entitled 'Promotion of Sport and Exercise' on 2 March 1935 demanding the rigorous implementation of physical activity programmes:

> We must have a mass physical exercise campaign. From now on all the students and teachers of primary and middle schools, all staff of Party offices, social services and the army must participate in physical activity. They must choose one event as their regular exercise and have their daily exercise time fixed between five to six o'clock every day without exception. They are encouraged to do outdoor activities but they can do some indoor exercise if the weather is not good. Physical training must be constant. The principals of schools, the heads of government office and army officers must supervise and discipline their pupils and staff and report to their superior.[110]

On 19 April 1935 Chiang wrote a further letter to the public along the same lines to ensure the implementation of his demands.[111]

Chiang made inspirational demands; Shao Rugan,[112] a physical educationist, made practical suggestions. In *Qinfen tiyu yuebao* [Qinfen Sports Monthly] in May 1935, in 'How to Promote a Mass Physical Exercise Campaign,' he advocated the opening up of school playgrounds to ordinary people, the training of more physical educationists and general participation in physical exercise, if necessary, enforced by police supervision![113]

As a consequence of this intense political pressure an additional measure was introduced – a Physical Education and Sports Department was founded by the New Life Promotion Committee in 1935. Famous physical educationists, such as Yuan Dunli[114] and Dong Shouyi,[115] were invited to be its members. At the same time, the National Educational Council gave orders to every provincial educational council to set up a Sports Council to promote the sports campaign. By the end of July, 19 provinces and large cities had sports councils.[116] These sports councils and the Physical Education and

Sports Department of the New Life Promotion Committee were responsible for the training of physical educators and for organising mass physical activities such as swimming, hill-walking, cross-country running, basketball and volleyball.[117]

Encouraging girls and women to participate in physical exercise, as noted above, was one of the main tasks of the New Life Movement. The Director of Jiangsu Provincial Educational Council, Zhou Fuhai, called it the New Mission of Chinese Sports in October 1934.[118] Liu Shengcen,[119] the Director of Physical Education in Sichuan Provincial Education Council, claimed in May 1935 that one purpose of the New Life Movement was the cultivation of women's social commitment through sport.[120] Chinese women, he asserted, were traditionally myopic in perception. They considered only themselves and their families, and had little awareness of, or concern for, the larger society and the nation. Social commitment through sport would help them contribute to national survival by stimulating awareness of the nation and building up a spirit of responsibility and sacrifice. Playing fields were the ideal place for them to learn to work together, to develop a corporate sense of unity and to strengthen their bodies.

Zhu Xiaochu, an experienced physical educator, made the relationship between the New Life Movement and women's bodies explicit in his article 'On the Problem of Chinese Women's Health' in May 1936. 'The essence of the New Life Movement', he stated, 'is to transform old habits into new ones. Chinese women's poor physical ability is one of the old problems which should be changed by the Movement.' He continued: 'Generally speaking Chinese women seldom participate in physical exercise and have no knowledge of hygiene. The modern girls like fashion but have no sense of beauty. They bind their chests and feel shame about their menstruation. Men still think the beauty of femininity is small feet, small waist, fragility and passivity. Physical activity is regarded as unladylike by both men and women themselves.' It was, a dangerous situation, he warned, when girls were ashamed to put on sports wear for physical education and married women seldom exercised. Women were half the population and an important force for the salvation of China. Physical exercise, he argued, could bring women good health, could ensure endurance for every kind of labour and the most demanding tasks. 'Women's physical recreation', he concluded, 'will bring China a new hope. That is the goal of the New Life Movement.'[121]

Civil authorities, educationists and feminists mobilised women to join the New Life Movement. Most physical activities, in institutionalised form, occurred within the education system. Girls attended physical education classes in primary and middle schools and went on camping holidays.[122] Uniforms, the cropped hair, the 'wholesome' military discipline and physical activities were part of a physical recreation 'package' for girls.[123] Female students in colleges and universities, for their part, were encouraged to do physical exercise. According to the Report of the Education Ministry in September, 1935 Yanjing University, Women's Wenyou College, Chaoyang College, Minguo College, Women's Normal College, Hebei Medical College and Henan University set the pace.[124] The programme of Yanjing University was particularly outstanding. There were 300 women students in Yanjing University. A Women's Physical Education Committee had been set up with responsibility for female student health and exercise. Women had their own sports facilities including one gymnasium, one croquet court, one ring-tennis court, one badminton court, one archery range, one playground, one swimming pool. one basketball court, two volleyball courts and seven tennis courts.[125] The Committee organised several activities, such as play day, sports day, health week, posture week, gymnastic performances and sports competitions.[126]

While girls' physical education was steadily becoming an integral and important aspect of curricula in schools and institutions, increasing numbers of sports and leisure pursuits were becoming available to women outside the formal education system. One educationist called for women not to forget their physical exercise after they left school.[127] Zhang Yifeng, a female physical educationist, introduced women to 'Chinese' women's gymnastics, a mixture of Swedish, German and Danish gymnastics, suited to the Chinese women's physique.[128] Professional women and housewives were encouraged to go to the gymnasium and playground in their spare time. In Wuchang, the capital city of Hubei province, for example, educators organised a women's sports association.[129] Song Meiling made it clear that the health of a nation's (middle-class) women was a measure of 'civilisation' and that women should engage in public exercise 'consistent with those duties that embrace the care of their homes and our country'.[130] Physical education was established as a fundamental aspect of education – the source of self-discipline, moral standards and 'ladylike' behaviour.[131]

If one event symbolises the change in attitude to women's bodies in the Communist area – the Yan'an Women's Sports Meeting, in the Nationalist area, the same could be said of the First Jiangxi Women's Sports Meeting. In the spirit of the New Life Movement, the First Jiangxi Women's Sports Meeting was held on 14 October 1934 in Nanchang, the capital city of Jiangxi province. All women students in the city were asked to be present. Fourteen famous women athletes, including Qian Xingsu,[132] a national champion, were invited to attend. The Meeting was intended to be a show case of recent achievements in the promotion of women's physical strength and fitness, and a stimulus to women to exercise.[133] Whatever the nostalgia of some Confucian Nationalists for inert femininity there was to be no total return to the past.

Conclusion

While Communists looked more to the future, Nationalists looked more to the past. They embraced old certainties and old standards – including the ideal of traditional femininity. Nevertheless, they could not escape the present – its political humiliations, its military threats, its moral confusion. If there was to be national regeneration the past could not be recreated. It had to be adapted. Nowhere was this more true than of the image, behaviour and expectations of women. The basic source of efficient regeneration was health, with the concomitants of fitness, strength and endurance. For this reason the Nationalists, like the Communists, supported the selective emancipation of women, and gave priority to the reconstruction of their bodies. The motive, as with the Communists, was fundamentally political – China's rebirth – not, however, to replace, as in the case of the Communists, but to recreate the Old Order. The reality is that the physical liberation of women had its limitations under the Nationalists as well as the Communists. It was only after 1949 and the rise to power of the CCP that a more complete physical liberation became a possibility. It will be briefly mentioned in the epilogue. However, the full story of that achievement is the basis for additional research and is beyond the scope of this current book.

Nevertheless, the momentum for female emancipation was maintained in the Nationalist as well as in the Communist areas. In one aspect of liberalisation, however, Nationalist ideological fixations underpinned by twentieth-century scientific argument constrained women in their attempts to fulfil themselves through their bodies – that is, in competitive sport. However, even in the face of implacable conservative resistance and authoritative scientific argument, advances were eventually made here as well as we shall now discover.

Notes

1. See Chapter Five, note 49.
2. Before Chiang's government there was a formal nationalist government called the 'Guomin' government which was set up by Sun Yat-sen's followers in 1925 in Canton. In January 1927 the Guomin government was moved from Canton to Wuhan city. Chiang Kai-shek and his supporters became disaffected with the radicalism of the Guomin government, because of its collaboration with the communists. They therefore set up their own Nationalist government in Nanjing in April 1927. These two governments were later merged in 1928 and the subsequent government at Nanjing evolved as the common government. For details, see Ch'ien, Tuan-sheng, *The Government and Politics of China 1912–1949*, Stanford: Stanford University Press, 1950, pp.91–3.
3. Gray, Jack, op. cit., p.232.
4. Moise, Edwin E., op. cit., p.69.
5. Spence, Jonathan D., *The Search for Modern China*, op. cit., p.338.
6. Chiang and his government believed that the nation needed a single supreme leader, a one-party dictatorship and military domination to keep the country unified. See Moise, Edwin E., op. cit., p.69; Rodzinski, Witold, op. cit., p.322.
7. See Prologue, Chapters One and Three.
8. Lin, Yutang, *My Country and My People*, op. cit., pp.169–70.
9. Strong, Anna Louise, *China's Millions*, op. cit., p.17; Croll, E., *Feminism and Socialism in China*, op. cit., p.154.
10. Lin Yutang, a famous writer at the time, described the Chinese girls' love of Western luxury and their loss of domestic virtues. A foreign observer reported that many of the women leaders worried about Chinese women's misunderstanding of their new legal rights and new freedoms. See Lin Yutang's book, *My Country and My People*, op. cit., pp.162–3; Green, O.M., *China's Struggle with the Dictators*, London: Hutchinson, 1941, pp.107–108.
11. Pye, E.M., 'The Women's Movement in China', *Asiatic Review*, Vol. 25, 1929, p.217.
12. She was very excited and thought her dream had come true. She felt it symbolised the progress of China and she worked to embody within the civil code the principle of absolute equality for women. See Wei, Tao-ming, *My Revolutionary Years*, New York: Charles Scribner, 1943, pp.168–70.
13. Croll, E., *Feminism and Socialism in China*, op. cit., pp.155–6.
14. Pye, E.M., op. cit., p.214.
15. Dr Zeng Baosun, Founder and Principal of Ai-Fang Girls' School in Changsha claimed that the emancipation of Chinese women had been achieved. Compared with the women of the West who had to fight hard for their educational rights, employment and suffrage, the Chinese women gained theirs at very little cost. See Tseng Pao-swen, 'The Chinese Women Past and Present', in Chen, Sophia H. (ed.), *Symposium on Chinese Culture*, Shanghai: China Institute

of Pacific Relations, 1931, p.288.

16. See Chen, Sophia H., *The Chinese Woman and Four Other Essays*, Beijing, 1934 (n.p.).

17. Tseng, Pao-swen, 'The Chinese Women Past and Present', op. cit., p.292.

18. See Tang, Leang-li, *The New Social Order in China*, London: East and West Ltd., 1936, p19.

19. Pye, E.M., op. cit., pp.214–17.

20. *Jiezhi yukan* [The Domestic Management Monthly] was founded in the spring of 1921. It was, in the beginning, a quarterly. In 1926 it became a monthly. It dealt with the problems of drinking, smoking and domestic harmony. *Funu gongming* [The Voice of Women] was issued at first as a bi-weekly and published in Shanghai in 1925. It changed to a monthly and was published in Nanjing in 1934. It dealt with the making and amending of laws pertaining to women. Women legislators took a keen interest in it. See Liu, Herman C.E., 'The Chinese Women's Movement and Magazines', *Chinese Recorder*, Feb. 1934, p.86.

21. Ibid.

22. Song Eiling (Soong Ailing) was the eldest of the three Song sisters who married Kong Xiangxi, a recognised descendant of Confucius and later chief financial adviser to the Nationalist government. Song Qingling (Soong Chingling) was the middle Song sister who became the wife of Sun Yat-sen in 1914. After his death, she supported the alliance of the left wing of the Nationalist Party and the CCP. Song Qingling remained in China after 1949 and was appointed to several nominal positions within the Communist government. Song Meiling (Soong May-ling) was the youngest of the Song sisters and wife of Chiang Kai-shek. An American-educated Methodist, Song Meiling played an active part in politics in the 1930s and 1940s, sponsoring refugee relief efforts and women's organisations as well as acting as spokeswoman in the West for her husband's cause. For details, see Hahn, E., *The Soong Sisters*, New York (n.p.), 1945.

23. Hosie, Lady Dorothea, *Portrait of A Chinese Lady*, London: Hodder and Stoughton, 1929, p.150.

24. The regular contributors to this magazine were professional women. They included Wu Luyin who received her higher education in Beijing and worked in the S.M.C. Girls' School in Shanghai; Su Xueling, who was educated abroad and worked in Wuhan University; Chen Linyi who was also educated abroad was Dean of Women at the Chinese University. They believed that Chinese women had secured practically all their rights in principle, but that very few women were as yet able to make use of them. The important thing was to teach them how to use their rights correctly. See Liu, Herman C.E., op. cit.

25. Soong Ching-ling, 'Women's Liberation', in Young, Marilyn B., *Women in China*, op. cit., p.202.

26. Lin, Yutang, *My Country and My People*, op. cit., p.163.

27. CSHSPE, *Zhongguo jindai tiyu shi* [Modern Chinese Sports History], op. cit., p.302.

28. Peake, Cyrus H., op. cit., pp.93–4.

29. Da xueyuan [The University Council], *Qiuanguo jiaoyu huiyi baogao* [National Educational Conference Report], 1928, p.586.

30. See Peake, Cyrus H., op. cit., p.161.

31. In 1929 the Nationalist government issued 'The Aims of Education'. This document stated that mass education and formal education should pay attention to the development of sports because they could strengthen people's bodies, raise their spirits and develop discipline. See *Di yi chi Zhongguo jiaoyu nianjia* [The

First Chinese Educational Annual Book], No. 1, Oct. 1933, p.16.

32. 'Guomin tiyu fa' [The Law for Sports for Citizens] 18 April 1929, in *Diyichi Zhongguo jiaoyu nianjian* [The First Chinese Educational Annual Book], No. 1, Oct. 1933, pp.897–9.

33. 'Guomin tiyu xiuzhen fa' [The Revised Law of Sports for Citizens], 9 Sept. 1941, issued by the Nationalist government, in *Direchi zhongguo jiaoyu nianjian* [The Second Chinese Annual Educational Book], Dec. 1948, p.1279.

34. For example, 'The Implementation of the Law of Sports for Citizens' (Sept. 1932), 'The Enforcement of the Revised Law of Sports for Citizens' (Dec. 1941), 'The Plan of Enforcement of the Revised Law of Sports for Citizens' (Aug. 1945). These regulations are in CSHI, *Zhongguo jindai tiyushi zhiliao ji* [Modern Chinese Sports History Reference], op. cit., pp.90–95.

35. Tan, Hua, 'Jiu zhongguo de tiyu lifa huodong' [Physical Exercise Legislation in Modern China], *TWS*, No. 2, 1989, pp.14–15.

36. Chiang, Kai-shek, 'Tichang tiyu tongdian' [On the Promotion of Physical Exercise], *Qin Fen*, Vol. 2, No. 7, April 1934; pp.1–2; see also Chiang's speech, 'Zai sanmin zhuyi qingnian tuan gongzuo huiyi xunchi [The Speech at the Nationalist Youth League's Conference], *Guomin tiyu jikan* [Citizen's Sports Quarterly], No. 1, Sept. 1941, pp.2–3.

37. A brief history of the Nationalist government's control over physical education and sport is as follows: first, a 'Quanguo tiyu zidao huiyuanhui' [National Committee for Physical Education] was established in December 1927. It was composed of well-known athletes and specialists in physical education. Its aim was to promote physical culture on a large scale. In May 1928, the First National Educational Conference took place. It emphasised physical training. Second, in April 1929 the government issued Guomin tiyu fa [the Law for Sports for Citizens]. It stands out as the highlight of the first year of Nationalist government rule in the area of physical exercise and sport. Third, in October 1932, the 'Jiaoyubu tiyu weiyuanhui' [the Physical Education Committee of the Ministry of Education] was established. It replaced the old National Committee for Physical Education and became a department of the Ministry of Education. Its activities included the creation of plans for the national development of physical education, the formation of a strong academic physical education programme and the creation of a national physical education bureaucracy and budgetary apparatus. In 1940, its name changed to Guomin tiyu weiyuanhui [the Chinese Physical Education Committee]. However, it was still under the leadership of the Ministry of Education and its tasks remained almost the same. At the same time the Physical Education Committee of the Ministry of Education co-operated with another non-governmental sports organisation, 'Zhonghua tiyu xiejin hui' [the China Amateur Athletic Federation]. For details of the latter see Chapter Eight, note 58.

38. For information on Wang Zhenting, see Chapter Four, note 80.

39. Wu Yunrui (1892–1976) obtained a Masters Degree at Columbia University, USA in 1927. When he returned to China he became the Professor and Director of the Department of Physical Education, Nanjing National University.

40. Yuan Dunli (1895–1968) went to the United States in 1923 and obtained his BA and MA degrees at Columbia University. He returned to China in 1927 and became Professor and Director of Beijing Normal University. He then took up the same positions in Zhejiang University. Finally, he became the President of Beijing Normal University in the 1940s.

41. Hao Gengshen (1899–1976) graduated from Springfield College, USA in 1923. After he returned to China he was a professor in several Chinese universities

and the first Physical Education Consultant to the Ministry of Education in 1933.

42. Zhang Huilan (born in 1898) studied in several universities in the United States and obtained two masters degrees and one doctoral degree. She was Professor and Director of several women's physical education departments including Ginling Women's University and the National University.

43. See 'Lower-middle School Physical Education Curriculum' and 'Upper-middle School Physical Education Curriculum', (July 1931); 'Primary School Physical Education Curriculum', (Oct. 1932); 'Draft Curriculum of Physical Education for Colleges and Universities', (Feb. 1936); 'Physical Education Curricula for Primary and Middle Schools, Colleges and Universities', (March 1940).

44. *Tiyu zhoubao* [Physical Educational Weekly]. An influential journal, it was founded in February 1932 in Tianjin. The journal ceased in 1937 as a result of the Japanese invasion. Its aim was to promote physical education and exercise throughout north China.

45. See *Tiyu zhoubao*, Vol. 2, No. 13, May, 1933, pp.17, 22.

46. See the report in *Tiyu zhoubao*, Vol. 2, No. 19, June 1933, p.3.

47. See CSHSPE, *Zhongguo jindai tiyu shi* [Modern Chinese Sports History], op. cit., p.244.

48. Ibid.

49. See *Diyichi zhongguo jaoyu nianjian* [The First Chinese Annual Education Book], op. cit., pp.897–901.

50. CSHSPE, *Zhongguo jindai tiyu shi* [Modern Chinese Sports History], op. cit., pp.245–6. For political reasons this book failed to give the Sports Model District Movement a fair hearing. It took a wholly negative view of the Movement.

51. See the report in *Tiyu zhoubao*, Vol. 2, No. 25, July 1933, p.51.

52. See the statistics of the number of participants in the Zhejiang Provincial Sports Stadium, in *Zhejiang tiyu* [The Zhejiang Physical Education Monthly], Vol. 4, No. 7, March 1937.

53. Gao, Zi, 'Zhongguo nuzi tiyu wenti' [On the Problems of Chinese Women's Exercise], *Jiao yu xue* [Teaching and Learning], Vol. 2, No. 7, Jan. 1937, p.243.

54. Gao Zi was born in Nantong, Jiangsu province in 1902. She graduated from the Physical Education College of the YWCA in Shanghai in 1919, and then graduated from the Physical Education Department, Wisconsin University, USA in 1923. Before 1949 she was the Dean of the Physical Education Department of Beijing Normal University, Professor at Shandong University and the National Central Government University and Principal of Wende Girls' School in Shandong province.

55. Gao Zi, 'Zhongguo nuzi tiyu wenti' [On the Problems of Chinese Women's Exercise], op. cit., p.240.

56. In Europe, the bourgeoisie attempted ideologically to separate men from women by defining gender differences in terms of character rather than by roles and their associated duties. The former polarization between the sexes in essential economic and reproductive processes shifted into the realm of symbol, generating an 'essentialised' notion of gender. Sports played an important role in defining and reinforcing gender differences in these periods and this continued into the twentieth century. See Hausen, Karin, 'Family and Role-Division: the Polarisation of Sexual Stereotypes in the Nineteenth Century – an Aspect of the Dissociation of Work and Family Life', in *The German Family: Essays on the Social History of the Family in Nineteenth- and Twentieth-Century Germany*, New Jersey: Barnes and Noble Books, 1981, pp.51–83; Mangan and Park, op. cit., p.3.

57. See Mangan, J.A., *Athleticism*, op. cit., p.106. Professor Mangan describes the part that sports played in shaping masculinity in the Anglo-Saxon world.
58. Ibid.
59. Ibid., p.106.
60. See Vertinsky, P., *Eternal Wounded Woman*, op. cit.; Dunning, Eric, 'Sport as a Male Preserve: Notes on the Social Sources of Masculine Identity and its Transformations', in *Elias and Dounning*, op. cit., pp.267–83.
61. Lin, Yutang, *My Country and My People*, op. cit., p.163.
62. Dirlik, Arif, 'The Ideological Foundation of the New Life Movement: A Study in Counterrevolution', *Journal of Asian Studies*, Vol. XXXIV, No. 4, Aug. 1975, p.945.
63. Chiang, Kai-shek, 'Xin shenghuo yundong zhi yaoyi' [The Aim of the New Life Movement], in Pei, Qinghua (ed.), *Xin shenghuo luncong* [Selected Works on the New Life Movement], Shanghai: Zhonghua shujiu, 1936, p.112.
64. Zu, Shicheng, *Xin shenghuo yu jiu shehui* [The New Life Movement and the Old Habits], Nanjing (n.p.), 1935, p.50.
65. Chen, Walter Hanming (ed.), *The New Life Movement*, Information Bulletin, Council of International Relations, Nanjing, December 1936, p.189.
66. Chiang, Kai-shek, 'The Outline of the New Life Movement', In Chen, ibid., p.225.
67. Chiang, Kai-shek, 'Xin shenghuo yaoyi' [The Aim of the New Life Movement], op. cit., p.6.
68. Dirlik, Arif, op. cit., p.945.
69. Chen, W.H., *The New Life Movement*, op. cit., pp.191–2.
70. Chen, W.H., ibid., p.200.
71. Diamond, Norma, 'Women under Kuomintang Rule: Variations of the Feminine Mystique', *Modern China*, Vol. 1, No. 1, Jan. 1975, pp.8–13.
72. See Croll, E., *Feminism and Socialism in China*, op. cit., p.180; Dalmond, Norma, ibid., pp.8–9.
73. Song, Meiling, *We Chinese Women*, New York: International Secretariat, Institute of Pacific Relations, 1943, p.111.
74. Mme Chiang Kai-shek (Song Meiling), *China Shall Rise Again*, London: Routledge and Kegan Paul, 1941, p.52.
75. Song, Meiling, *Madame Chiang's Message in Peace and War*, Hankou: China Information Committee.
76. Tseng, Pao-swen, op. cit., p.289.
77. See the report of Wu Jufang, the Director of Guangdong Women's Branch of the National New Life Movement Promotion Committee, 'Guangdongsheng xinshenghuo yundong cujinhui funu gongzuo weiyuanhui yinian gongzuo zhongjie' [The Report of Work of Guangdong Provincial New Life Movement Committee], *Guangdong Funu*, Jan. 1941, pp.2–7; see also the report of Jiangxi Women's Committee in *Jiangxi funu di sinian* [The Report of the Work of the Fourth Year of Jiangxi Women], edited and published by Jiangxi Women's Committee, 1941; Mei, H.C., 'The Role Women's Clubs Play in the Social Reconstruction of China', *Chinese Recorder*, Vol. 67, No. 12, 1936, p.751.
78. Chen, Chongguang, 'The Changing Status of Women in the Early Republic', MA thesis, Zhongguo wenhua xueyuan shixue yanjiusuo [The History Institute of Wenhua University], 1972, pp.65–9.
79. Li, Wang Limeng, *The Chinese Women's Movement*, Shanghai: Shangwu yinshuguan, 1934, p.60; Guo, Zhenyi, 'The Great Shanghai Plan Should Note a Few Issues on Women', *Dongfang zazhi* [The East], Vol. 31, No. 5, March 1934, section on 'women', pp.1–4; Bi, Yun, 'Xiandai zhiyi funu zhi buxin' [The

Misfortunes of Contemporary Career Women], *Dongfang zazhi* [The East], Vol. 33, No. 15, Aug. 1936, pp.112–17.

80. See Honig, Emily, *Sisters and Strangers – Women in the Shanghai Cotton Mills, 1919–1949*, Stanford: Stanford University Press, 1986, pp.1, 53.

81. Sources from Gu, Bingyuan, 'Shanghai nugong de weiti' [The Issue of Women Workers in Shanghai], *Qingnian funu* [Young Women] Vol. 8, No. 5, May 1929, pp.4–10; Shanghai Bureau of Social Affairs, *Wages and Hours of Labour, Greater Shanghai, 1929*, Shanghai, 1929; Shanghai shehuiju, *Shanghai gongchang laogong tongji* [The Investigation of Shanghai Labour], Shanghai: Zhonghua shuju, 1946.

82. See Hunug, Junlue, 'The Wage System of China', *Dongfang zazhi* [The East], Vol. 24, No. 18, Sept. 1927, pp.44–5.

83. Jie, Yu, 'Nanchang chenlei pinminku zhong de funu' [The Women of the Slum in Nanchang City], *Jiangxi Funu* [Jiangxi Women], Vol. 1, No. 1, Jan. 1937, p.36.

84. Gong, Du. 'Nugong weiti' [The Issue of Chinese Women Workers], *Funu zazhi* [Women's Magazine], Vol. 15, No. 6, Sept. 1929.

85. Ibid.

86. See the report in *Nu qingnian* [Young Women], Vol. X, No. ii, Feb. 1931, p.56.

87. Shi, Jingxiang, 'Baoshen gong' [Indentured Workers], in Li, Yuqing (ed.), *Nugong de zhailan* [The Calamity of Old Women], Xianggang: Zhaoyang chubanshe, 1971, pp.22–8.

88. Chow, Tse-tung, op. cit., pp.381–3; Peng, Zeyi, *Zhongguo jindai shougongye ziliao 1840–1949* [Materials on the Modern Chinese Handicraft Industry 1840–1949], Beijing: Zanlian shuju, 1957, Vol. 2, pp.233–5, 258–60.

89. Shi, Jingxiang, op. cit.

90. Quoted in Siu, Bobby, *Women of China: Imperialism and Women's Resistance 1900–1949*, op. cit., p.92.

91. De, En. 'Puji woguo funu de zhongxue jiaoyu he zhiyie xunlian' [Elementary Education and Training and Women of our Country], *Funu zazhi*, [Women's Magazine], Vol. 15, No. 1, Jan. 1929, pp.12–15; Liu, Chengfu, 'Zhongguo jiaoyu xunlian he funu de zhiyie' [Elementary Education and Training and Women's Occupation], *Funu zazhi*, ibid., pp.26–9; Zhu, Yingmei, 'Gaijin nugong shenghuo de tujin' [The Ways to Improve the Livelihood of Working-class women], *Funu zazhi*, Vol., 17, No. 6, Jan. 1931, pp.9–12.

92. Buck, J.L., op. cit., pp.373–9.

93. Ji, Hong, 'Jizhe fangwei ji' [An Interview with Jiang Yixiao, a Woman Reporter], *Funu zazhi*, Vol. 6, No. 2, Feb. 1937, pp.37–42.

94. Ao, Yunzhang, 'Ruhe zhuzhi longmin funu yundong' [How to Organise the Peasant Women's Movement?], *Funu gongming* [Women Citizens], Vol. 6, No. 3, May 1942, pp.21–2.

95. Jiangxi Provincial Women's Committee, 'Jiangxi funu gongzou di si nian' [The Report on Jiangxi Women's Work], in CWF, op. cit., Vol. 3, pp.540–57.

96. Siu, Bobby, *Women of China*, op. cit., p.112.

97. Song, Meiling, 'Lushan funu tanhuahui faimo ci' [The Speech at the Opening Ceremony of the Women's Conference at Lushan], *Funu shenghuo* [Women's Lives], Vol. 6, No. 3, May 1938, pp.1–3.

98. Ibid.; see also 'Lushan funu tanhuahui fabu dongyuan funu canjia jianguo gongzuo dagang' [The Outline of Women's Work – Lushan Women's Conference], *Funu shenghuo* [Women's Lives], Vol. 6, No. 7, May 1938, pp.4–7.

99. Song, Meiling, *We Chinese Women*, op. cit., p.111.

100. Han, Suyin, *Birdless Summer*, London: Jonathan Cape, 1968, pp.132–56.

101. Lin, Yutang, *My Country and My People*, op. cit., p.146.
102. Hahn, E., op. cit., p.xvii.
103. It was reported that in July 1934, the wife of an official in Wuchang was arrested for immoral behaviour. She had been sleeping outdoors wearing short trousers because of the heat. She died in prison a few days later. See Lin, Yutang, *My Country and My People*, op. cit., p.189.
104. Han, Suyin, *Birdless Summer*, op. cit., p.147.
105. Song, Meiling, *Madame Chiang's Message in Peace and War*, op. cit., p.117.
106. Chiang Kai-shek. 'Lun xin shenghuo' [On the New Life Movement], in Pei, Qinghua, op. cit., p.18.
107. *Qin Fen tiyu yuebao* [Qin Fen Sports Monthly] (hereafter *Qin Fen*), one of the most influential physical education and sports journals in modern China, was founded in October 1933 but stopped in July 1937 as the result of the Japanese invasion. Its manager was Ma Chongjin, Director of the Shanghai Educational Council, and its editors were Shao Rugan and Ruan Weichun, well-known physical educationists. Its aim was to promote physical exercise and sport for the restoration of China. Many influential politicians, educationists, physical educationists and athletes contributed to this journal.
108. In *Qin Fen*, Vol. 2, No. 1, Oct. 1934, p.12.
109. Zhou, Fuhai, 'Zhongguo tiyu zhi zhuixin shimin' [The New Mission of Chinese Physical Education], *Qin Fen*, Vol. 2, No. 1, Oct. 1934, p.12.
110. Chiang, Kai-shek, 'Tichang tiyu tongdian' [On the Promotion of Physical Exercise and Sports], op. cit.
111. Cited in Shao, Rugan, 'Ruhe tichang quanmin tiyu' [How to Develop Mass Physical Activity], *Qin Fen*, Vol. 2, No. 8, May 1935, p.53.
112. Shao Rugan (1890–1982) graduated from the Physical Education Department, Nanjing Normal University in 1918. He was the Principal of Nanjing Physical Education Institute, the Editor of *Qin Fen*, the Director of Physical Education in Shanghai Educational Council and the Director of Shanghai Stadium before 1949.
113. Shao, Rugan, 'Ruhe tichang quanmin tiyu' [How to Develop Mass Physical Activity], op. cit.
114. See note 40 of this chapter.
115. Dong Shouyi (1895–1978) studied in the Springfield College, Massachusetts, USA from1923 to 1925. After his return to China he became a Professor at Beijing Normal University. He then taught in several universities. He was a member of the IOC in 1947.
116. See the report in *Qin Fen*, Vol. 3 No. 10, July 1936, p.47.
117. CSHSPE, *Zhongguo jindai tiyu shi* [Modern Chinese Sports History], op. cit., p.247.
118. Zhou, Fuhai. 'Zhongguo tiyu de zuixin shiming' [The New Mission of Chinese Sports], *Qin Fen*, Vol. 3, No. 1, Oct. 1934, pp.11–12.
119. Liu Shengcen (born in 1902) graduated from Zhejiang Physical Education Institute in 1923. He founded the South-west Physical Education Institute in 1926 and also set up Wanxian city sports stadium in 1926. He became the Editor of *China Daily* in 1935 and he was also appointed as the Director of Physical Education in Sichuan Provincial Education Council in 1935. He published many articles on the revolution in Chinese physical education.
120. Liu, Shengcen, 'Tiyu jiuguo lun' [On the Salvation of China through Physical Exercise], *Qin Fen*, Vol. 2, No. 8, May 1935, pp.19–22; Vol. 2, No. 11, Aug. 1935, pp.13–17.
121. Zhu, Xiaochu, 'Zhongguo funu de jiankang wenti' [On the Problem of Chinese

Women's Health], *Qin Fen*, Vol. 3, No. 8, May 1936, p.12.

122. Zhang, Yifeng, 'Tongzijun dajianyue yundi shenghuo jishi' [Our Camping Holidays], *Qin Fen*, Vol. 4, No. 3, Dec. 1936, pp.48–9.

123. Ibid.

124. The report of the investigation carried by the Education Ministry was published in *Qin Fen*, Vol. 2, No. 11, Sept. 1935, pp.35–9.

125. Zhang, Yinfeng, 'Yanjing da xue nusheng tiyubu gaikuang' [The Yanjing Female Students' Physical Education Committee and Women's Sports Facilities], *Tiyu yanjiu yu tongxun* [Physical Education Research and Information], Vol. 2, No. 4, June 1935, pp.151–7.

126. Tei, Yin, 'Nusheng kangjianzhou de yiyi he zhuzhi' [Women's Physical Exercise and Healthy Week], *Tiyu yanjiu yu tongxun*, ibid., pp.96–9.

127. Ting, 'Qin funumen buyao fangqiliao xuesheng shidai de yundong' [Don't Forget Physical Exercise after You Leave School], *Tiyu yuekan* [Sports Monthly], No. 2, Nov. 1934, pp.3–4.

128. Zhang, Yinfen, 'Zhongguo nuzi jianshencao wenti' [On the Chinese Women's Keep Fit Movement], *Tiyu yanjiu yu tongxun* [Physical Education Research and Information], Vol. 3, No. 1, Sept. 1935, pp.11–17.

129. See the report in *Qin Fen*, Vol. 1, No. 8, May 1934, p.65.

130. Quoted in Diamond, Norma, op. cit., p.13.

131. Din, Xueqin, 'Tiyu xunlian shang de lianxin wenti' [The Different Sexes and Different Physical Exercises], *Tiyu yanjiu yu tongxun*, Vol. 4, No. 1, 1936, pp.1–2.

132. Qian Xingsu (born in 1913), a student of Dongya Physical Education Institute 1933–35, was an athletics champion at the Fifth and Sixth National Sports Meetings in 1933 and 1935 and a member of the Chinese Team at the Far East Championship Games in 1933. For details see Yue, 'Yundong nujie' [Athletic Heroine], *Qin Fen*, Vol. 1, No. 1, Oct. 1933, p.59.

133. A report entitled 'Jiangxi shoujei nuzi yundonghuo zilue' [The Overview of the First Jiangxi Provincial Women's Sports Meeting] was published in *Qin Fen*, Vol. 2, No. 2, Dec. 1934. (page number unavailable).

EIGHT

Towards Full Equality:
Seeking Competitive Success
(1928–49)

࢟࠻࠼࠰࠻࠼

IS A WOMAN made by nature or culture? The question lies at the
heart of this study.[1] Of course, the body is simultaneously part of
nature and part of culture. Nevertheless, a woman is born in nature
and reborn in culture. In a real sense, her body is transferred from
nature to culture by society. And patriarchy as a social system
requires man's authority over woman. Thus, within patriarchy, a
woman's body 'is situated in the context of a political struggle which
seek to regulate human beings within an administered society'.[2]
Within patriarchal societies her body is defined as a consequence of
the social control which results from social domination – a symptom
of man's exploitation of woman – in the seemingly arrogant words of
Max Weber, 'because of the normal superiority of the physical and
intellectual energies of the male'.[3] In the history of China women's
exercise is part of an actual and ideological struggle against forms of
patriarchal authority, and an attempt to transfer the body to a non-
patriarchal community. This transference in China, as we have seen,
was a long drawn-out process.

Prior to 1949 the symbolic high point of this struggle, it is
suggested here, was the acceptance of women by both Communists
and Nationalists into the world of *competitive sport*. It was a significant
capitulation. Resistance to the denial of traditional femininity explicit
in this acceptance was lengthy and sustained – not only in the East
but in the West. Guttmann has pointed out that in the West, the
exclusion of women from contests as distinct from play 'has lasted
longer than the exclusion of blacks'.[4] Women in the West, while
participating in competitive activities in schools and colleges, were
officially banned from major official competition in some sports until
the first quarter of the twentieth century. In 1929, a contributor to

School and Society caught the mood of the times when he wrote that while competition was natural to males, 'in women it is pro-foundly unnatural'.[5] He, like countless others, was opposed to the 'masculinisation' of womanhood explicit and implicit in competition. He added, for good measure, that 'feminine health and attractiveness, whether physical, emotional or social, certainly are impaired if not destroyed by the belligerent attitudes and competitive spirit . . . which intense athletics inevitably fosters'.[6] As late as 1930 the Women's Division of the National American Athletic Federation of the USA asked that women be omitted from the 1932 Olympics on the grounds that 'strenuous athletic contests were physically and psychologically unhealthy'.[7] Competitive sport, in short, was a bastion of Fortress Masculinity. To breach the walls of this bastion was to go a long way in razing the old defences of patriarchal sport. In both West and East, they were eventually breached.

Access to competitive sport in both the West and the East, is arguably the shining symbol of the physical emancipation of women's bodies – and a fitting theme with which to conclude this study of the physical emancipation of Chinese womanhood.

McCloy and the YMCA

In early twentieth-century China, denial of access to competitive physical activities on the part of conservative elements in society was the consequence of both ancient Chinese conceptions and modern Western theories of female psychology and physiology.[8] In Europe and North America, in the late nineteenth century, there were influential figures of authority who adopted an intractable scientific viewpoint about women's 'fixed' and inferior biological natures, and there were numerous publications which served to sustain the notorious female conservation of energy thesis right into the first three decades of the twentieth century.[9] For many years Western doctors and educationists considered that women were victims of their biology.[10] As in feudal China it was believed that man and woman were complementary opposites; two aspects of one essence, but that women were biologically inferior to men.[11] The Western belief in the fundamental biological difference between the sexes in the specific context of exercise was brought to China by the American physical educationist Charles Harold McCloy (1886–1959). He reinforced Eastern philosophical prejudice with Western 'medical' argument.

McCloy studied philosophy, biology and physical education in various American universities between 1906 and 1913.[12] Subsequently he was sent to China by the North American YMCA to help train Chinese physical educationists. He arrived in China in the autumn of 1913 and returned briefly to the United States in the spring of 1919. He returned to China again in 1920 and finally left China for good in 1924. During his years in China he contributed to physical education courses in various parts of the country,[13] became Dean of the Physical Education Department of Nanjing Normal University in 1915, the General-Secretary of the Sports Department of the Chinese National YMCA from 1917 to 1919, the Dean of the Physical Education Department of the Southern-eastern University, the General-Secretary of the National Amateur Sports Association, and the Chairman of Jiangsu Provincial Society of Physical Education and the National Research Society of Physical Education from 1921 to 1924. There were other educationists from the YMCA who made their distinguished contribution to the development of Chinese physical education, such as Max J. Exner[14] and A. H. Swan,[15] YMCA Physical Directors, who established physical education training programmes in China. However, it was, McCloy who brought Western medical theories directly to bear on Chinese women's exercise. These views heavily but not exclusively influenced Chinese women's physical education in the early decades of the twentieth century.

When McCloy returned to China in 1920 he became increasingly concerned with propagating his own physical education theories. He incorporated his ideas into the programme at the South-eastern University where he was the Head of the Physical Education Department. In order to promote his ideas as widely as possible, McCloy founded a journal called *Tiyu jikan* [Physical Education Quarterly] in May 1922. It became the official journal of the National Physical Education Research Association in March 1923. The name was changed to *Tiyu yu weisheng* [Physical Education and Health] in 1924.[16] It was a professional journal, its articles dealing with teaching methods, applied theories of biology and psychology and physical development. As McCloy stated, the journal 'did a good deal to advance physical education in the YMCA as well as in the schools',[17] and 'served as a guidepost in the field of research work in physical education'.[18]

Female physical and mental growth was one of McCloy's academic interests. In 1923 he published 'The Difference between the Sexes in Physical Exercise' in *Tiyu jikan*, in which he argued that women differed from men in terms of physiology and psychology. Their physical activities must be based on these differences. He asserted confidently that:

1. Women could not cope with intensive training because their hearts and lungs were small;
2. Women could not take part in long-distance running, because their feet were small (70 yards was their maximum distance);
3. Women were not good at rings and jumps, because they had broad hips;
4. Women should not participate in violent physical activities, such as races and jumps. These would damage their soft and fragile womb – the important organ of reproduction;
5. Women should not exercise during their menstruation period because the loss of blood would exhaust their bodies.

McCloy also asserted that from the psychological point of view women were more emotional and less competitive and individualistic than men so they should be treated differently from men in their physical training classes. Competitive events were contrary to female nature and female exercise should aim not for aggression but for grace.[19]

After consulting with two American leading female physical educationists, Ethel Perrin and Florence D. Alder, McCloy was reinforced in his convictions. In another article, 'On Women's Competitive Sports', in *Tiyu jikan* in early 1924 he repeated his well-rehearsed arguments and then stated that there was a causal consequence to the different physiological characteristics of men and women. They resulted in differing mental, psychological and behavioural reactions. For example, the female vasomotor system was unstable and highly sensitive to stimuli, causing girls to be mentally and physically more irritable than men. This fact meant that strenuous activities such as competitive sports were unsuitable for them. They needed their own restricted physical programmes. He recommended his physical education programme for girls in primary schools and middle schools. Finally, he warned that while exercise was necessary for a woman's physical development, educationists had to be aware that a woman's frame was 'feminine'. Her body was not that of a strong man but a delicate woman.[20]

In pursuit of evidence to support his assertions McCloy began to collect data related to the physical abilities, skills, and physiques of Chinese boys and girls in Shanghai, Nanjing, Suzhou and other coastal cities. He tabulated, computed and analysed this data. Finally, a complete set of physical ability tests for girls and boys was published for the first time in China, along with performance tables, based on sex, age, height and weight. McCloy's research demonstrated to his satisfaction that women needed exercise to improve their physical condition, but intensive, aggressive exercise would damage their natural organs. Their physical education should therefore differ from men's. It should be recreational rather than competitive.

McCloy was considered by many Chinese to be intelligently conservative in his views on women's physical exercise. His views on the necessity of restricted female physical exercise met the demands of the Nationalists. Theories which appeared to marry Western modern theory and Chinese traditional belief regarding women's physical inferiority were easily accepted by Chinese society and were widely acknowledged as sound by many Chinese educationists. He emerged as the leader of physical education theory and practise in China between 1921 to 1926.[21] The programmes that he worked out during the 1920s for girls and boys were used by the Nationalist Chinese schools until the end of the 1940s. However, his was not the only voice to be heard. As a result, the reality of female exercise was not quite as McCloy advocated, as will shortly become clear.

McCloy, therefore, found a ready Nationalist audience. In the 1920s and 1930s more and more educationists were beginning to advise women to exercise, but many agreed with McCloy that activity had to be suitable to women's nature and should cease during a woman's menstrual period. For example, in 1934, Zhu Shifang, a professor at the Chinese Women's Physical Education Institute, who had more than ten years' experience teaching female physical education, argued in 'On Girls' Athletic Training in Middle Schools' in *Qin Fen tiyu yuebao* [Qin Fen Sports Monthly], with seemingly simplistic and wishful reductionism, that

> evolution has shown that men and women had different responsibilities. Men had to hunt for food in a wild environment. They had to be tough, strong and powerful. Women always

259

stayed at home to look after the family and produce children. They were gentle and refined. These were the unchangeable natural characteristics of men and women. So, psychologically women don't like intensive physical exercise. If teachers force them to do it they will feel depressed. And physiologically, because women's hearts and lungs are weaker than men's, women should avoid aggressive exercises. . . . Women should stop all exercise during their menstruation.[22]

Precept was followed by parable. Two years later in the same journal, a lecturer of the Physical Education Department of Ginling Women's University in Nanjing, Shun Shuqian, graphically described the awful consequences of participation by women in exercise without any knowledge of their special physical liabilities. She recounted that she had a friend who loved exercise very much. She did physical training two hours every day in the sun, rain and snow. When she had her first menstruation at the age of eighteen she was advised not to exercise during her period. She laughed at the advice. She continued her routine. Two years later she was very ill. The doctor told her that her womb had been damaged due to irresponsible physical exercise. She wept. But it was too late. She had lost her child-bearing capacity for ever. She came to regret her athletic life. 'This story tells us', Shun said, 'that girls and women must not do any physical exercise during their periods in case they make irredeemable mistakes in their lives.'[23]

The relentless proselytising had its success: the message was widely received. When the girls' basketball teams from Tianjin Number Ten School played in public in April 1933, *Tiyu zhoukan* [Sports Weekly] argued that such competitions should be discouraged because they used male rules which made the game too aggressive. The periodical expressed concern for the girls because they had no knowledge of their bodies and their capacities. It called for the authorities to take the matter seriously because this kind of competition would certainly damage girls' internal organs.[24] In another article, wholly typical of the climate of the time, entitled 'The Problem of the Sexes in Physical Exercise', the author, Din Xueqin, a physical education teacher at the Dinyi Girls' School in Suzhou, Zhejiang province, claimed,

> In the modern society a woman's physical health is as important as a man's. Women have the responsibility to produce healthy

children for the sake of the reformation of the nation, and for its economic independence. All of these needs require physical strength. This physical strength can only come from physical exercise. However, because of the biological differences between the sexes women's physical ability is inferior to men's. So women should avoid participation in aggressive physical activity especially in menstruation and pregnancy periods.[25]

Unrelenting pressure of this kind in the specialist and popular press clearly defined physical opportunities for women, culturally pre-scribed gender roles, and defined the biological capacities of the respective sexes. Women's physical freedom was certainly advocated and women gradually obtained the same opportunities to participate in physical exercise as men. However, participation in the *same* physical activities as men was not favoured by Nationalist conserva-tive opinion – for reasons directly to do with the physiology of the female body and the procreative functions specific to women, as well as the longevity of traditional images of femininity. Many Nationalist physical educationists re-socialised women into an acceptance of, and belief in, the notion of their biological inferiority. In this way scientific radicalism sustained cultural conservatism, but ultimately this con-servatism did not prevail.

Consideration has already been given to the gradual involvement of women in competitive physical activities in the Communist area[26] in the face of resistance on the part of peasant conservatism, which remained influential despite Communists idealism and its supporting rhetoric. Attention has been drawn also to the cautious approval of women's involvement in competitive exercise by the Communist Party in the interests of producing healthy, fit, vigorous women to ensure economic and military survival. Attention will now focus on similar conflicting patterns of conservatism and liberalism in the Nationalist area, characteristic respectively of 'neo-Confucian'[27] *nostalgiens* and Nationalist pragmatists, and stimulated respectively by an atavistic desire for past femininity on the part of the 'neo-Confucians', and the need for strong women for national survival on the part of the Nationalist authorities – despite their enthusiastic espousal of Confucian rhetoric. Developments, therefore, regarding the gradual participation by women in competitive physical activities in both Communist and Nationalist areas were, in some crucial respects, strikingly similar – and in both instances denoted a significant actual and symbolic breakthrough by women into new roles, new images and new possibilities.

In both areas an important psychological transition occurred through exercise. A fit female body assumed a new individual significance. A healthy body became a vehicle of self-belief. As Nietzsche argued: 'The determination of what is healthy for your body depends on your goal, your horizon, your energies, your impulses, . . . and above all on the ideals and phantasms of your soul.'[28] In the China of the 1930s exercise ensured a new female personality type which sociologists have referred to as 'the performing self'. This new personality required validation from audiences through successful performances of the self. The new self was a visible self and the body, suitably presented, came to symbolise the status of the personal self. This new self was epitomised by the successful *sportswoman*. Women were not satisfied with recreational playgrounds. They wanted to enjoy the prestige, the pleasure and the prospects of the public competitive sports field – the male-oriented domain. Here, the ultimate emancipatory physical dramas were enacted.

'Bodies: past and present.' (Cartoon in *Qin Fen tiyu yuebao* [Qin Fen Sports Monthly], October 1935.)

Modern competitive sport was not a native Chinese phenomenon. Its confrontational spirit and aggressive emphasis were contrary to the Chinese philosophical tradition of harmony. As noted earlier,[29] competitive sport in educational institutions came in the nineteenth century from the West, initially with missionaries, and subsequently by way of Chinese students returning from Europe and the United States. In the wider community Western traders, sailors and soldiers also played an early role. In the 1760s Western merchants had sporadic rowing competitions on the Pearl River but the first rowing club – Canton Rowing Club – was founded on 21 June 1837.[30] The British organised football matches in Hong Kong in 1897 and football then spread from Hong Kong to the mainland to places like Shanghai, Nanjing and Beijing. The first Chinese football association was founded in Hong Kong in 1908. Later, other competitive games arrived – the products of American cultural imperialism: baseball was brought to China by Chinese students on their return from Yale University in 1887; while basketball came to China through the YMCA in Tianjin in 1896.[31] The first efforts of the Chinese were picturesque. The wife of the director of YMCA recalled that when the Chinese students played basketball they wore long gowns and long pigtails.[32]

Volleyball came to China later than basketball. It was played in Hong Kong, Guangdong (Canton) and Shanghai at the first decade of the twentieth century. However, in the First Far Eastern Asian Games in 1913 the Chinese delegation had no volleyball team. They had to gather some football players and athletes together to compete against the Japanese and the Philippines. The following year, volleyball became a formal event at the Chinese National Athletic Meeting.[33] Table-tennis came to China by chance and stayed! An owner of a stationery shop in Shanghai brought back some bats and balls from Japan, but nobody showed any interest. He had to press people to come and see how the game was played. Gradually table-tennis become popular. Today, along with volleyball, it is a national game.

When modern competitive sport came to China, it was mostly a male-frequented domain. The first three National Athletic Meetings between 1911 to 1924,[34] and the first six Far Eastern Championship Games (FECG)[35] between 1913 to 1923,[36] for example, took place without women athletes. Some oddly lay the blame at the door of the missionaries. Susan Brownell has stated: 'Because Western sports were introduced into China through Western-run schools, and especially by the YMCA, the Western bias against women in sports was reflected in the limited participation of Chinese women from the turn of the century until the 1930s.'[37] However, the truth is that the missionaries, and to a lesser extent the YMCA (and the YWCA), brought the idea of women's physical liberation to China, advocated Chinese women's emancipation from feudal culture both spiritually, mentally and physically, and encouraged physical activities including competitive sports for girls in schools, universities and society. Limited participation was more the product of indigenous cultural resistance. Brownell's assertion, flying in the face of the evidence, constitutes a myth in the making.

In the context of exogenous stimulus to change and indigenous resistance to it, the history of the YWCA is illuminating. The YWCA of China was founded in 1896.[38] In August 1915 the YWCA Physical Education Institute was established in Shanghai. Its aim was to train qualified female physical education teachers for schools, colleges *and* clubs. Its curriculum included anatomy, physiology, psychology, pedagogical theory and methodology, athletics, gymnastics, basketball, volleyball, tennis, table-tennis and games. After two years' study, students became qualified teachers and instructors. Between 1915 and 1925, 150 graduates from the institute became pioneers of Chinese women's competitive sport.[39] At the same time, in order to improve Chinese women's health, various branches of the YWCA organised a range of physical activities including competitive activities in schools and cities.[40]

In June 1921 when the Fifth Far Eastern Championship Games were held in Shanghai, 1,000 Chinese girls, led by Vera Barger,[41] National Director of Physical Education for the YWCA of China, gave an impressive exhibition of physical activities in the stadium on the second day of the Games. The main purpose was to demonstrate a variety of games and sports – of both a competitive and non-competitive nature – which could be adopted for popular use. It was filmed with the intention of eventual distribution to cities and towns where exercise for girls was still poorly developed.[42]

The missionary schools, the YWCA and the YMCA had a powerful influence on Chinese women's competitive sport. When these agencies started their work in China, physical competition was a modern phenomenon little known and little understood. Through their work in the early period, girls and women, in school and after school, were set on a path which cut through traditional bias – but progress along the path was slow.

The reason for the slow progress of women's involvement of competitive sport, of course, was traditional culture. It had denied women's abilities for over a thousand years. The influence of historical culture was clearly evident from the reactionary attitudes of both conservatives and liberals in the early years of the twentieth century (see Chapter Four). Girls' schools only appeared after 1840 and co-education only started in the early twentieth century. For years physical education was mostly limited to the school system and there were only small numbers of girls in schools (six per cent in primary school and three per cent in middle school between 1922 and 1923),[43] As discussed above, girls' physical education in schools was based on prevailing socio-medical arguments. In such conditions, women's competitive sport could not fail to mature slowly. It needed time to become accepted and established. The sports field was not predominantly a 'male preserve' to the extent that it was in the West, especially in the Communist area (see Chapters Six and Seven). However, while women enjoyed relatively liberated bodies, they were simultaneously under cultural pressure to constrain them to meet the prevailing image of femininity. Competitive sport with its stress on instrumentality, power, product, rationality and control[44] portrayed an essentially masculine image. Competitive sport, in fact, whatever the emancipatory ideals aired, or political requirements asserted, in both Communist and Nationalist areas remained for many fundamentally an institution to generate, strengthen and celebrate the role of men and the values of masculinity.[45]

By the 1920s, after more than 60 years' experience of legitimately engaging in exercise, women confronted a dilemma. In the interests of cutting an appropriate feminine figure they might deny themselves the opportunity for full physical fulfilment, or they might be tempted to enter and merge with their male counterparts into a rationalised, organised, aggressive world of competitive sport. This was the conundrum. Competitive sport offered the opportunity for full physical freedom, creating new and meaningful opportunities for women. Some women now accepted, or if necessary demanded, that offer.

Athletes and the State

The first time that Chinese women athletes appeared on a notable competitive sport's stage was at an international competition: the Sixth Far Eastern Championship Games in 1923. Between 1913 and 1921, five FECGs had taken place without women's participation.[46] In 1923, influenced by Olympic idealism and the New Culture and May Fourth Movements, the Games organisers introduced exhibition matches in volleyball and tennis for women for the first time. China sent volleyball and tennis teams and the Chinese volleyball team defeated the Japanese team, amazing the world with this single feat.[47]

They then successfully took part in the seventh, eighth, ninth and tenth FECGs in 1925, 1927, 1930 and 1934 respectively.[48] The events included volleyball, tennis, athletics and swimming. The Chinese volleyball team won again in 1927, 1930 and 1934,[49] and Chinese women won all swimming events at the Tenth Games in 1934.[50]

Inspired by the 1923 FECG, in May 1924, the Second Central China Sectional Athletic Competition organised by the Central China Sports Association included women's volleyball as an event.[51] Four volleyball teams from the provinces of Jiangxi, Anhui, Hunan and Hubei competed. The Hunan team became champions. This was the first time that Chinese women athletes participated at a national sports meeting. Subsequently, the North China Sport Association decided to introduce women's events into the programme of its sectional competitions, commencing in 1929 with the Eighth North China Sectional Athletic Competition.[52]

In April 1930, when the Fourth National Games took place, they included 498 woman athletes. They competed in athletics, volleyball, basketball and tennis.[53] Another exciting scene took place on the track when there was a dispute in the final of the 200-metre relay. The last leg runners of Guangdong and Harbin, crossed the finishing-line at the same time, but the officials arbitrarily gave the title to the Guangdong team. The Harbin team protested against the decision. After deliberation, the Organising Committee awarded joint titles to both teams. It was a symbolic moment. Women were now willing to assert themselves.[54] The image of passive acquiescence was moribund. Women athletes attended the fifth (1933), sixth (1935) and seventh (1948) national athletic meetings. Their events were extended to include swimming, softball, martial arts, table-tennis and archery.[55]

Tradition, in the shape of Confucianism, driven backwards by the political imperatives outlined above, was in retreat. Modernity, in the form of McCloy, was increasingly ignored. In the National area women now participated in sport competitions at all levels as a matter of course in national, provincial, inter-city, inter-college and inter-school events.[56] Chinese women also participated in the Olympic Games in 1936 in Berlin and in 1948 in London.[57]

How had all this happened in the face of such contrary ideological pressures? The plain fact is that the struggle for fulfilment in women's lives through competitive sport, despite the retrogressive demands associated with femininity of the neo-Confucians, was neither ignored

Women hurdlers at the Fifth National Games in the Nationalist area in 1933 in Shanghai. (From the China Sports Museum, Beijing.)

nor rejected by the Nationalist government. It saw the new sports-women, despite its diplomatic endorsement of the rhetoric of atavistic femininity, as instruments of social inspiration and national salvation – models for a new patriotic womanhood.

In 1924 the Nationalist governing body of sport, the China National Amateur Athletic Federation was founded in Nanjin, the capital city.[58] The aim of the Association was to supervise and organise all national and international athletic competitions. It was also the official national representative organisation in all inter-national athletic organisations, such as the IOC. The Federation was strongly supported by the Nationalist government. The government, which had always concentrated on physical education in schools, now also supported athletic competitions, seeing them as important stimulants to patriotic feeling. When the Fourth National Games, took place in Hangzhou, Zhenjiang province in 1930, the local govern-ment gave financial support and Chiang Kai-shek was the honorary Chairman of the Meeting. He attended the opening ceremony and made a now-famous speech:

> A healthy body contains a healthy spirit. A healthy citizenship constitutes a healthy nation. A healthy nation produces a healthy culture. Looking at history, weak people and weak

nations have never survived. Our Republic's Central Government understands that Chinese sport needs to be promoted so as to restore our culture and save our country. So we support the National Games. . . . If we want our country to be as strong and great as the Western countries we must develop sport. It is the foundation. From now on we must have sports meetings in cities and schools and villages. We must educate every family to take part in sport. Sport can train a fit body and a healthy spirit. Strong parents will give us strong sons, race and nation. A strong nation will be capable of competing with other nations in the world . . . So develop our sport for our country's sake.[59]

Chiang Kai-shek's speech inspired those who heard it and it was quoted everywhere in the Nationalist areas. He passed the torch to others. After the Fourth National Athletic Meeting, the National government, recognising the educational function of sports meetings, took steps to put these meetings under the control of the Ministry of Education. The Ministry set up an organising committee to finance and supervise national sports meetings. The following fifth, sixth and seventh national athletic meetings were run by the Nationalist government.[60]

Kong Xiangxi,[61] Minister of Finance in the Nationalist government, at the Sixth National Athletic Meeting, following the lead of Chiang Kai-shek, expressed the government's view of the value of the meeting at the opening ceremony: 'Today our nation and our people face a time more crucial than ever before. We need intelligent people and strong soldiers to save our country. If we don't have . . . strong bodies our country will cease to exist. An athletics meeting is the best place to train and test the quality of physique and spirit of our nation.'[62]

Chiang Kai-shek sent a supportive telegram to the meeting. Rehearsed arguments were reiterated: 'The aim of the athlete today is to contribute towards the strengthening of the country and the race. An athletics meeting is the place to fortify the country and the race. Every citizen, man *and* woman [emphasis added], must be strong and healthy so that they can with greater advantage share the responsibility of overcoming the national crisis (the Communists and the Japanese).' Chiang emphasised that he had advocated a sports movement a long time ago and that he had made many speeches on how to promote sport. He hoped that his colleagues and his people would remember them and put his ideas into practise. Finally, he claimed: 'An athletics meeting can stimulate people's competitive spirit and build the foundation for restoring our nation.' Sport, in short, was not play, but an instrument of education, a tool to construct the nation's unity and a weapon to save China.

Wang Jingwei,[63] another member of the Nationalist government, in a speech at the Sixth National Athletic Meeting in 1935, asserted: 'A healthy mind always dwells in a healthy body. With a sound body, one can carry on any struggle to the finish, and not give up midway, but a weak spirit in an unhealthy body cannot lead us to ultimate victory. In this lies the significance of athletics.'[64] At about the same time, the chairman of the Nanjing government Lin Shen stated: 'Our government advocates sport because it links health and physical strength and our country's future.'[65] Sports meetings under the Nationalists had become an examination of the quality of Chinese bodies, a stage on which to display the unity of the country and a showcase of national spirit and fitness.[66]

Women's participation in competitive sport in both Communist and Nationalist China then had a political importance. The simple truth of the matter was that not every Nationalist held to the domesticated image of femininity of Song Meiling. One Nationalist article in 1932, entitled 'The Relationship between the Promotion of Women's Sport and the Restoration of Our Nation', pointed out that women's participation in physical activity did not only mean equality with men but also the sharing of responsibility for the country's well-being. Only if women had strong bodies could they play their part at home as healthy mothers of their children and in society as citizens, to work for the good of country. In this way, and with the employment of these arguments, women's competitive sport, directly and indirectly, helped extend the foundations of women's increasing physical liberation.[67] Once again, influential figures beat the drums of patriotism. Wang Jianwu, the Director of the Department of Physical Education, Henan University, stated, in 1935, that 'Chinese women should take part in more athletics meetings. This would change their public image and give them confidence so that they could become real citizens and serve their country.'[68] Shen Shiliang, the General-Secretary of the China National Athletic Association, for his part, argued in 1935, 'Women's participation in competition will change their image not only within China but in the world. Westerners know all about Chinese women's low social position. If we show that our women are liberated and as strong as theirs, they will no longer look down our nation.'[69]

Cheng Dengke,[70] Professor of the National University and an influential physical educationist, went further and demanded that:

> Women should be involved in sport not only in school physical programmes but also in public competition. Women's sport is not a means of entertainment and a source of health but a lamp of the restoration of the nation. Women athletes have a special responsibility. They have to represent Chinese women on international stages. They are soldiers on different battle fields. They have to win so that the world will know that the Chinese are unbeatable.[71]

In 1932 Wang La in 'The Direction of Women's Sport' also argued that girls' school sports programmes should be encouraged and that local training programmes and meetings should be organised to attract the female population to participate in exercise so that they would have healthy bodies, the confidence to liberate themselves and be able to work effectively for the good of the country.[72] In this way, supported by authority and promoted by experts, women's competitive sport entered into its golden age, in the *relatively* tranquil years before China was caught up in the horrific maelstrom of the Japanese War (1937–45), the Second World War (1939–45) and the Civil War (1945–49).

Sportswomen and their Success

Before any successful participation there had to be a structure for learning how to participate. Progressively, more and more physical education departments were founded in Nationalist universities and teacher training colleges and more physical education institutes were established. They increased from 12 in 1928 to more than 80 in 1948. Women students steadily gained access to almost every physical education department and institute in Nationalist China. Opportunities for study became available[73] and in these departments and institutes, women prepared to enter the physical education profession. The curriculum, according to the decrees of the Ministry of Education in 1934[74] and 1942,[75] included history, language, geography, physics, chemistry, music, psychology, physiology, anatomy, hygiene, sports theory, sports administration, sports statistics, gymnastics, athletics, swimming, ball activities, military drill, martial arts, education theory and pedagogy.

Women graduates from these institutes and universities mostly became physical educators in schools and colleges. Lu Lihua, the principal of Liangjiang Women's Sport Institute declared that the graduates from her institute all taught in schools and colleges.[76] *Qin Fen tiyu yuebao* [Qin Fen Sports Monthly] in September 1933 reported that the graduates of 1934 from Dongnan Women's Physical Education Institute had all found jobs in universities or schools. Outstanding athletes got the better jobs.[77] These athletes created athletes. Their students were competitors at the Fifth National Athletic Meeting in 1933 and other events – regional, national and international.

Thus, physical education departments and institutes were not only the matrix of the physical education profession, but also the source of successful athletes. A major purpose of these institutes was to train outstanding sportswomen and almost all leading female athletes came from these establishments. The most successful were the Department of Physical Education at Ginlin Women's University,[78] the Physical Education Division of Shanghai Patriotic Women's College,[79] Dongya Physical Education Institute[80] and Lianjiang Women's Physical Education Institute.[81] They had basketball, volleyball, tennis, table-tennis, track and field teams. In Liangjiang Institute there was even a women's football team.[82] Female athletes were trained by professional coaches at a fixed time every day. Consequently, it is no surprise that women champions at this time frequently came from these places.[83] The Liangjiang women's basketball team, for example, represented Shanghai and won the championship at the Fifth National Athletic Meeting in 1933.[84]

In the wake of international successes the image of women in Nationalist China was certainly reconstructed. In April 1931 the Liangjiang women's basketball team from Liangjiang Women's Physical Education Institute was invited to visit Japan and Korea. It was the first time that a Chinese women's team had gone abroad. It won in Korea and beat the Japanese teams nine times out of ten.[85] This was at a time when relations between China and Japan were tense. Japanese imperialist intentions were growing more and more pronounced (Japanese troops invaded Manchuria in September 1931).[86] The Chinese women's victories made a great impact in Japan and China,[87] boosting the confidence of China and Chinese women. In 1935 the women's basketball team was invited by the Over-seas Chinese Sport Association of Manila, to attend a basketball competition in the Philippines. The team, led by Lu Lihua, attended the competition and then visited 14 cities in South-east Asia including Rangoon, Saigon, Kuala Lumpur and Singapore. The team competed 40 times with local teams, competing with male teams if there were no women's teams available. They won 35 games, including victories over several men's teams.[88]

In 1935 the women's athletics and basketball teams of Dongya Physical Education Institute also visited South-east Asian cities including Singapore, Saigon, Kuala Lumpur and Manila. Their aim was to promote women's sport among overseas Chinese in order to link them with their motherland. These Chinese were greatly impressed by the women athletes' performance and decided to raise a fund to support the Institute. They hoped that it would train ever more women athletes and change the image of 'weak Chinese' in the world.[89] These institutes with their successful emphasis on competitive sport enabled women successfully to enter into a hitherto male world of competitive physical activity. They participated with confidence and enjoyment and gradually won acceptance in their newly assertive social roles.

Women's Sport and Women's Emancipation: Case-study

Competitive sport, then, which had been viewed down the years as essentially, if not exclusively, a male preserve was now seriously participated in by both girls and women who increasingly gained public acceptance as athletes. These athletes competed with ever reducing criticism and enjoyed widespread public applause for their victories. They were healthier, fitter and happier than their inhibited predecessors. Furthermore, their new sense of self-worth reduced their traditional cultural dependence. Achieving a sense of control over the body was fundamental to the acquisition of control over the personality and the environment. Chen Yimin, a student of Liangjiang Women's Physical Education Institute, a champion at the Fifth National Athletic Meeting, in 'My Athletic Life' in the *Qin Fen tiyu yuebao* [Qin Fen Sports Monthly] in 1934 informed her female readership how sport had liberated her body and mind and brought her into a new world. She recounted how she had been born in the countryside of Sichuan province, how she had gone to a city school and learned sport, and how, after she had became a famous athlete in the city, families came to propose marriage. But more than anything, she wanted to become a national champion, so she refused marriage and

The Chinese Women's Swimming Team at the Tenth Far East Athletic Championship Games, 1931. (From the China Sports Museum.)

Chinese women participants at the Olympic Games, 1936. The second from the left was Li Sen. (From The Archives of Chinese Sports Culture and History, Beijing.)

left home for Shanghai thousands of miles from her hometown. She became a student in Liangjiang Women's Physical Education Institute where she trained hard. In 1933 her ambition was realised when she became a national champion. Sport had given her a fit body, a measure of success and the confidence to make decisions for herself. Chen expressed the hope that women who read her article would follow her example and achieve their own liberation.[90] She set herself up as a self-proclaimed role model.

Wu Tang was another who described how sport had provided her with a fuller vision of life than traditional domesticity. Wu Tang was born in 1925 in Beijing. She was addicted to sport and in 1941, when she was sixteen she competed in the North China Athletic Championship and came first in the high jump and the sprints. At the subsequent North China Championship in 1942 she broke regional records and won three titles. When she graduated from middle school she could have easily chosen a respectable husband because she was famous. However, she chose not to because she wanted to continue her sports career, to become a top athlete, to win gold medals at the Olympics for China, and to be independent. To this end, in 1942 she became a student in the Department of Physical Education, Beijing Normal University. Although the Second World War denied her the chance of Olympic success, she later asserted that sport had taught her to be self-reliant and self-confident, and had provided her with the opportunity to be economically independent. She worked as a physical educator for most of her life and recalled proudly that sport broadened her life to the benefit, not only of herself, but her country.[91]

Yet another sportswoman who demanded and worked for freedom of choice was Li Sen. Li Sen was born in Changsha, the capital city of Hunan province in central China. When she was at a middle school, like Wu Tang, she was obsessed with sport. Her dream was to became a top athlete for the greater glory of China. After she graduated from secondary school, she went on to a physical education institute to train and study. She became a national athletics champion at the Sixth National Athletic Meeting in 1935, and represented China at the Berlin Olympic Games in 1936. After she became successful, the head of Hunan province, General He Shen wanted her as a concubine. At that time not many women could deny such a powerful man. However, Li Sen refused the General. She had her own career. She went to Chengdu, the capital city of Sichuan province, and became a teacher in a girls' school.[92]

Many of the graduates from physical education institutes were able to live independent lives. Furthermore, their experience of sport gave them a sense of their own worth and an appreciation of their capabilities. Excellence at competitive sport was a celebration of their bodies' strength and competence. It was a source of self-esteem, personal autonomy and social success. Graduates from the Department of Physical Education, Ginling University will serve to illustrate the point. They became physical educators in schools, colleges and sports associations.[93] In their autobiographies these women leave the reader in no doubt that sport gave them opportunities, physically, mentally and morally, to shape their own lives. Lu Lihua, an influential female physical educationist, the founder and, as mentioned above, Principal of Liangjiang Women's Physical Education Institute from 1922 to 1940, asserted that the first priority of women's emancipation was to encourage women to take exercise, to be confident both in body and spirit. In her view, and in the views of others, the sports field was the best place to train Chinese women to be 'new women' – fit, free and assured.[94]

A New Sexuality with Emancipatory Overtones

Sportswomen now caught the Chinese erotic imagination. Their pictures and stories filled newspapers and magazines. They were called 'sports queens'.[95] They became newly favoured icons of desirable sexuality. The Chinese began to turn their backs on the old type of beauty. They wanted a modern depiction which the sportswoman provided. The outstanding example was the 'Chinese mermaid', Yang Xiuqiong, a swimmer from Hong Kong. Yang was the swimming champion of Hong Kong in 1931 and was invited by Sydney Sport Association, Australia to compete there in 1932.[96] She won all individual titles both in the women's swimming events at the Fifth National Athletic meeting in 1933[97] and the events of the Tenth Far East Asian Championship Games in 1934. She also broke records at the Sixth National Athletic Meeting in 1935[98] and she was a member of the Chinese team at the 1936 Berlin Olympic Games. Her outstanding performances made the Chinese proud, while her beauty and her gentle demeanour made her a focus of desire. Yang was the perfect image of modern femininity for Nationalist China. She was considered to be one of four perfect Chinese women. (The other three

'The New Beauty'. (Cartoon in *Qin Fen tiyu yuebao* [Qin Fen Sports Monthly], January 1936.)

were artist He Xiangning, writer Din Lin and Song Meiling, the wife of Chiang Kai-shek.) When the New Life Movement was promoted in Nanchang in 1934, the capital city of Jiangxi province, Yang was invited to compete there. It was reported that when she was swimming 'the whole city was empty' because everyone had gone to see her![99] When she did not appear at the Sixth National Athletic Meeting, spectators asked for a refund.[100]

Women athletes' photographs filled newspapers, magazines, posters and illustrations. They offered a comparison of two types of women: the 'old' – fragile and frail, and the 'new' – strong and robust. Underneath the photographs there was invariably the caption: new beauty and new femininity.[101] Female athletes had established new norms of womanhood with their supreme physicality which were radically different from the past. The new femininity was widely accepted by society. A general impression of some force gained ground that sportswomen were 'new women' – liberated models of new femininity. So much so, that when word circulated in Beijing in 1933 that Wang Yuan, a famous woman athlete, was to be a concubine of the Chinese Ambassador to Japan, a feeling of anger resulted. The general view was that any woman was obliged to be a concubine of a rich and respectful man, except a sportswoman.[102] Articles in newspapers criticised Wang Yuan heavily.[103] It was widely agreed that she had sullied the honour of the woman athlete.[104]

Why did these sportswomen became models for Chinese women? The answer is simple: they were educated, healthy, independent in mind and pocket. Certainly few in number, nevertheless, they were significant role models. They refused to compromise their enthusiasm for competitive sport simply because certain societal pressures dictated a more genteel, passive approach to exercise. They paved the way for

楊秀泳後之各種神態

Icon of the New Femininity: the swimming champion Yang Xiuqiong. (From the China Sports Museum, Beijing.)

today's sportswomen, just as present athletes' achievements are laying down stepping-stones for future generations. The Nationalist sportswomen were heroines of the women's emancipation movement. Although not all sportswomen were feminists, virtually all of them were in favour of women's liberation. Their success in sport helped to construct a new sexual identity. This created a new dimension for the Women's Movement. Sportswomen had become the icons of emancipation, a fact which seems to have escaped the notice of social historians. These women had their counterparts, as related in earlier chapters,[105] in the Communist area of China.

The physical emancipatory process was inexorable and to a substantial degree, beyond the control of political ideological principle – past or present. The process was driven by the powerful and practical requirements of Nationalist – and Communist – survival in the face of considerable internal and external threats to their existence. More than anything else, events in Nationalist and Communist territories, formed a barrier to past peasant prejudices against women and past bourgeois traditions concerning women. These events ensured that those women who took advantage of new political circumstances did so with a measure of success – and thus took their physical liberation a step further. This time it was a hugely symbolic step into a world of competitive physical activity largely considered a masculine world.

Conclusion

The story of the Chinese women athlete is one of continuity as well as of change. Although women's physical difference was acknowledged in sport and women's physical education was focused on the training of healthy mothers so that women would fit smoothly into an integrated family and thus ensure a harmonious society,[106] sportswomen's competitive successes brought a new dimension to femininity, sport and society. Sport could nurture not only a healthy mother but also a strong woman. While sportswomen were expected by many to accommodate themselves to conservative ideas about their physical capabilities, by their actions in competitive sport they effected a change in public opinion about their physical image and the possibilities and meanings associated with it. They used physical activity creatively to promote patriotism in a way which legitimated a freer, more positive physical expression. The biologically determined stereotype of the delicate female was challenged by the more vigorous model of the sporting woman. Eventually, this new image of femininity became predominant. The power of image is essentially ideological – it reflects systems of values and meanings. Sportswomen gave the lie to traditional beliefs about women's physical and psychological abilities. In time their identity became embodied in ideology and action. Their competitive experiences became an authentic reflection of how women could be, and were now in society. They gave a powerful thrust to women's liberation.

A history of women's exercise in China, as elsewhere, is part of the history of women's struggle to control their bodies – and minds – to achieve their freedom. Competitive women athletes in the Nationalist area, as in the Communist area, changed Chinese cultural stereotypes of women for the better. Arguably their success in gaining access to the hitherto masculine domain of competitive sport represented the final act in a long emancipatory drama involving their struggle for physical freedom. However, the final scene of the final act was not to be enacted until after 1949, and its full depiction is the subject for a subsequent study.[107]

Notes

1. See Chapter Two.
2. Turner, B.S., op. cit., p.247.
3. Weber, M., *Economy and Society*. Berkeley and Los Angeles, Vol. 2, 1976, p.1007.
4. Guttmann, A., *From Ritual To Record: The Nature of Modern Sports*, New York: Columbia University Press, 1978, p.34.
5. Ibid.
6. Ibid., p.36.
7. Ibid.
8. See Mangan, J.A. and Park R., op. cit., p.2; Vertinsky, P., *Eternal Wounded Woman*,. op. cit.; Fletcher, S., op. cit.
9. See Hargreaves, Jennifer, *Sporting Females*, London: Routledge, 1994, pp.42–7; Dyhouse, C., 'Social Darwinist Ideas and the Development of Women's Education in England', *History of Education*, Vol. 5, No. 1, 1976, pp.11–27.
10. See Vertinsky, P., 'Body Shapes: the Role of the Medical Establishment in Informing Female Exercise and Physical Education in Nineteenth-century North America'; McCrone K., 'Play up! Play up! And Play the Game! Sport at the late Victorian Girls' Public Schools', in Mangan and Park., op. cit., pp.97–129, 256–81.
11. See Needham, Joseph. *Science and Civilization in China*. op. cit., Vol. 5, pt. V, pp.125, 209; Van Gulik, R.H., op. cit.; Croizier, Ralph C., *Traditional Medicine in Modern China*, Cambridge, MA: Harvard University Press, 1968.

12. The details about McCloy can be found in the Historical Library of the YMCA, New York City. It contains McCloy's letters and personal reports (1915–16).
13. Wu, Chih-kang, op. cit., p.119.
14. Max J. Exner, the first YMCA Physical Director in China, who came to Shanghai in 1908 and returned to the USA in 1911. His major contributions were to establish the pattern for the training of Chinese physical directors in Shanghai in 1909 and the organisation of the First Chinese National Athletic Meeting in Nanjing in 1910. For further details see his 1910 report in the YMCA Historical Library, New York City and his article 'Physical Training in China', *Physical Training*, Vol. VIII, No. 6, April 1911, pp.19–21.
15. A.H. Swan became YMCA Physical Director in Shanghai in 1912. He continued Exner's work and opened one of the first formal vocational physical education training schools in Zhejiang in 1913. He became the Principal of the YMCA School for Physical Education in Shanghai in 1917. For details about his work see A.H. Swan, Annual Report 1913–1915 in the YMCA Historical Library, New York City.
16. See CSHSPE, *Zhongguo jindai tiyu shi* [Modern Chinese Sports History], op. cit., p.179; Shanghai Encyclopedia Press, *Tiyu baike quanshu* [*Sports Encyclopedia*], 1984, p.893; Xiong, Xiaozhen, 'Zai lun zhongguo jindai shi shang de McCloy' [On McCloy's Contribution to Modern Chinese Physical Education], in CSHSPE, *Lunwei ji* [Selected Works], op. cit., Vol. 2, pp.36–7.
17. On 30 Jan. 1952, McCloy wrote to Wu Chih-kang about his journal. He stated: 'In 1923 . . . I was the editor of the *Chinese Journal of Health and Physical Education*. This was published by the Commercial Press in Shanghai for three years until I came home. A good many of the YMCA people contributed things to it and it was a magazine that did a good deal to advance physical education in the YMCA as well as in the schools. So far as I know, it was not published after I left.' Quoted in Wu, Chih-kang, op. cit., pp.165–6. Perhaps McCloy didn't know that the journal was republished by the National Physical Education Promotion Association in Jan. 1935. The editor was Wu Yunrui, who was a student of McCloy in 1918 and obtained his Masters Degree at Columbia University, USA in 1927. The journal continued for three years and stopped in June 1937 as a result of the Japanese invasion.
18. Wu, Chih-kang, ibid.
19. McCloy, H.M., 'The Difference between Men and Women in Physical Education', *Tiyu jikan* [Physical Education Quarterly], Vol. 2, No. 1, Nov. 1923, pp.1–4.
20. This article was called 'Nuzi jinzhen yundong' [On Women's Competitive Sport] and it was published in *Tiyu jikan* [Physical Education Quarterly], Vol. 3, No. 2, Jan. 1924, pp.1–8.
21. Song, Ruhai. 'The Contributions of the YMCA to Modern Chinese Physical Education'. op. cit. and Liang, Xiaochu, *Zhongguo YMCA wu shi nian jianshi* [Fifty Years of the YMCA in China], Shanghai, Shangwu yinshuguan, 1935.
22. Zhu, Shifang, 'Zhongdeng xuexiao nuzi tianjin wenti' [On Girls Athletic Training in Middle Schools], *Qin Fen*, Vol. 1, No. 5, Feb. 1934, pp.37–8.
23. Shun, Shuqiuan, 'Nuzi yundong shi yi zhuyi de shiyiang' [Warning of Women's Physical Exercise], *Qin Fen*, Vol. 4, No. 1, Oct. 1936, pp.59–60.
24. See *Tiyu zhoukan* [Sport Weekly], 4 April 1933.
25. Din, Xueqin, 'Tiyu xunlianshang de liangxin wenti' [The Problem of the Sexes in Physical Exercise], *Tiyu yanjiu yu tongxun* [Sports Research and Information], Vol. 4, Dec. 1936, pp.1–8.
26. See Chapters Six and Seven.

27. The term 'neo-Confucian' refers to the Nationalist attempt infuse the society with Confucianism. However, it was not a naive Confucian revivalism but a sophisticated response to the modern problems of China. See Chapter Seven.
28. Nietzsche, F., *The Gay Science*, New York: Random House, 1974, Section 120.
29. See Prologue and Chapters One and Three.
30. Holis, N.M.W., *The History of Shanghai Rowing Club*, Shanghai, Shangwu yinshuguan, 1938, p.3.
31. One of the earliest references to a basketball game appeared in the Tientsin Bulletin of the municipal YMCA on 11 Jan. 1896: 'A game of basketball will be played this afternoon. All young men interested in athletics are welcome to join the game at 4p.m.' See *Tientsin Bulletin*, Tianjin, 1896, Vol. 3, p.5.
32. Quoted in Wu, Chih-kang, op. cit., p.52.
33. Fan and Wang, *Tiyu shihua* [Sports History], op. cit., pp.185, 211; CSHSPE, *Zhongguo jindai tiyu shi* [Modern Chinese Sports History], op. cit., p.434.
34. The First National Athletic Meeting took place on 18–22 October 1910 in Nanjing. Shanghai YMCA was the organiser. 140 athletes attended the competition. It attracted 40,000 spectators every day. The second meeting took place on 21–22 May 1914 in Beijing. The third took place on 22–24 May 1924 in Wuhan, Hubei province. The organiser was the China National Amateur Athletic Federation. It was the first time that Chinese were referees and staff of the Meeting.
35. The Far Eastern Championship Games were a series of ten international athletic meetings, conducted roughly according to the format of the Olympic Games, in which China, Japan, and the Philippines competed from 1913 to 1934. In the history of Far Eastern sport, these Games stand out as the first international games in which China competed, and, indeed, as the first international team competitions in this part of the world. The activities included track and field, swimming, basketball, volleyball, football, softball and tennis. For details see Ruan, Weicun, *Yuandong yundonghui lishi yu chenji* [The History of the Far Eastern Championship Games], Shanghai, 1935; CSHI, *Zhongguo jindai tiyushi ziliao ji* [Modern Chinese Sports History References], op. cit., pp.531–56; Fan and Wang, *Tiyu shihua* [Sports History], op. cit., pp.189–98.
36. The First Games took place in 1913 in Manila, the Second in 1915 in Shanghai, the Third in 1917 in Tokyo, the Fourth in 1919 in Manila, the Fifth in 1921 in Shanghai, the Sixth in 1923 in Japan, the Seventh in 1925 in Manila, the Eighth in 1927 in Shanghai, the Ninth in 1931 in Tokyo, the Tenth in 1934 in Manila.
37. Brownell, Susan Elaine. 'The Olympic Movement on Its Way into Chinese Culture', Unpublished Ph.D Dissertation, University of California, Santa Barbara, 1990, p.19.
38. The first YMCA group were in Shanghai and Hangzhou in 1885. There were 27 YMCA groups in China by 1896. In December 1896 the 27 groups had a meeting in Shanghai and merged to become a national YMCA called the Student YMCA. In 1902 the name was changed to the YMCA of China. The first YMCA Physical Education Department was set up in Tianjin in 1908 and the first YMCA Physical Education Institute was founded in Shanghai in 1915. In the same year the YWCA of China founded the Women's Physical Education Institute in Shanghai.
39. Including Zhang Huilan, a graduate of 1919, who became successively a member of the National Physical Education Committee and Dean of Physical Education Department of Ginlin Women's University (see Zhang Huilan, 'Wo he Jin nuda tiyuxi' [The Department of Physical Education of Ginlin Women's

University and I], *TWS*, No. 1, 1983, p.36); Gao Zi, a graduate of 1919, was a member of the National Physical Education Committee, the Director of the Department of Physical Education at the Women's Normal University, the Director of Beijing Women's Physical Education Institute. She and her husband, Hao Gensheng, the Director of Physical Education in the Education Ministry, were famous physical educationists in modern China (for details see *Qin Fen*, April 1935, p.84); and Chen Yongshen, a graduate of 1920, who became the Physical Director of a school for girls in Shanghai, the General-Secretary of the YWCA in Hangzhou and a member of the Organising Committee of the Sixth National Athletic Meeting in 1935 (for details see *Qin Fen*, Jan. 1936, p.65).

40. Hong Kong YWCA had a gymnastics class; Hangzhou YWCA opened a tennis class; Shanghai YMCA held women's tennis competitions; Nanjing YWCA organised a women's tennis association; Yantai YWCA offered a swimming class, Guangdong (Canton) YWCA held a women's basketball competition. See *Nu Qinnian* [The Journal of Women], No. 14, 16, 1923; *Qinnian Jinbu* [Progress of Youth], No. 42, 1934; Liang, Tian and Xiang, Qin, 'Guangdong YMCA dui guangdong jindai tiyu fazan de yingxiang' [Guangdong YMCA and Guangdong's Sport Development], in CSHSPE, *Lunwei ji* [Selected Works], op. cit., Vol. 2, p.88.

41. Vera Barger is briefly mentioned in Wu Chih-kang's Ph.D. dissertation 'The Influence of the YMCA', op. cit.; and Hao, Gensheng, *Physical Education in China*, Shanghai: Shangwu yinshuguan, 1926, p. 94. Unfortunately there seems to be no extant record of her contribution to the Chinese YWCA.

42. *North China Herald*, 16 May 1914 and 23 May 1914; Hao, Gensheng, ibid.

43. See Tong, Yilai, 'Man hua zhong ri funu tiyu de fazhan' [On the Development of Chinese Women's and Japanese Women's Physical Activities], *TWS*, No. 2, 1991, p.35.

44. Barol, L. Christensen, 'Basic Exercise Physiology: Myths and Realities', in Cohen, Greatal (ed.), *Women in Sport*, Newbury Park: Sage Publications, 1993, p.123.

45. Donna, A. Lopiano, 'Political Analysis: Gender Equality Strategies for the Future', in Cohen, Greta, op. cit., p.100.

46. See notes 35 and 36 above.

47. See Ruan, Weicun, op. cit., p.81; Wu, Chih-kang, op. cit., pp.163–4; CSHI, *Jindai Zhongguo tiyushi ziliao ji* [Modern Chinese Sports History References], op. cit. pp.538–41.

48. Ibid.

49. Ibid.

50. Zhou, Jiaqi. 'Wu guo chuxi yuandong yundonghui de jinguo' [The Records of China's Participation in the Far Eastern Championship Games], *Tiyu jikan* [Physical Education Quarterly], Vol. 1, No. 1, Jan. 1935, pp.115–21.

51. There were five sectional athletic associations in China at that time. These were North China, South China, East China, West China and Central China. Each section included several provinces. The Central section included Jiangxi, Anhui, Hunan and Hubei provinces. Each section was responsible for organising its athletic competition. For example, the North China Sectional Association held ten sports meetings from 1913 to 1934. The Central section had six sports meetings from 1923 to 1936. For more details, see Dong, Shouyi, 'Huabei tiyu lianhehui de yange' [The History of the North China Sectional Athletic Association], in Tang, Hao, op. cit., Vol. 4, 1958, pp.72–3; Din, Feijie, and Peng, Zhenpu, 'Lijie huazhong yundonghui gaikuang' [The

Outline of the Central China Athletic Competitions], CSHI, *Zhongguo jindai tiyushi ziliao ji* [Modern Chinese Sports History References], op. cit., pp.454–67.

52. Dong, Shouyi, op. cit.
53. CSHI, *Zhongguo jindai tiyushi ziliao ji* [*Modern Chinese Sports History Reference*], op. cit., pp.482, 488.
54. Wu, Chihkang, op. cit., p.183.
55. Ibid., pp.465, 502, 506.
56. For example, the Guangdong provincial sports meetings in 1933 (see Saichang huaxu [The Report of the Sports field], *Tiyu zhoubao* [Sport Weekly], Vol. 2, No. 18, 10 June 1933, p.26); the Zhejiang provincial sports meetings in 1933 and 1937 (see *Tiyu zhoubao*, Vol. 2, No. 18, 10 June 1933, p.26); the Sichuan provincial Games in 1936, (see *Qin Fen*, Vol. 3, No. 10, July 1936, p.1); the Shanghai International Competitions in 1933 and 1935 (see *Tiyu jikan* [Physical Education Quarterly], Vol. 1, No. 3, July 1935, pp.450–51); the Tianjin International Tennis Competition in 1933 (see *Tiyu jikan*, No. 4, Sept. 1933, pp.23–5); and city sports meetings in Zhenjiang (1933) and Jiadin (1933) (see *Tiyu zhoubao*, Vol. 2, No. 2, 10 June 1933, p.26); Jinan (1934), Beijing (1934) (see *Qin Fen*, Vol. 1, No. 5, Feb. 1934, pp.62–4), Wanxian (1934) (see *Qin Fen*, Vol. 2, No. 1, Oct. 1934, pp.52–3); Qindao (1934) (see *Qin Fen*, Vol. 1, No. 10, July 1934, p.67); the Beijing Inter-Universities Games (1936), the Shanghai Inter-College Athletic Championship (1936), and the Shanghai Inter-Schools Competition (1936) (see *Qin Fen*, Vol. 3, No. 9, June 1936, p.50.
57. China was recognised as a member of the IOC in 1922. Song Ruhai, the Secretary of Wuchang YMCA and Honorary Secretary of the China National Amateur Athletic Federation, was present at the Sixth Olympic Games at Amsterdam, Holland in 1928. When he returned to China he wrote a book about the Olympics. However, for the time being there was no intention to send Chinese athletes to the Games since athletic standards were below those of international athletic contestants. When Japanese troops moved into Manchuria and set up the puppet state of Manchuguo in 1932, they tried to bring Manchuguo into all international matters. The first step occurred when the Japanese Athletic Federation tried to include Manchuguo as a regular member of the Tenth Olympic Games at Los Angeles in 1932. This angered the Chinese and the China Athletic Association decided to take part. Liu Changchun, a national athletic champion, was sent as the first Chinese athlete to the Olympics in 1932. China then sent delegations to the 1936 and the 1948 Olympic Games during the Nationalist period.
58. There is some misunderstanding and confusion about the formation of Chinese national athletic associations in Jonathan Kolatch's book *Sports Politics and Ideology in China* (see pp.18–19). It is necessary to explain briefly the process of the formation of the national athletic associations here. In 1915 there were five regional sports associations (The North, South, East, West and Central) founded in China (see note 51 of this chapter). In the spring of 1919 the representatives of North, South and East China appointed a committee to draft a provisional consititution for a national athletic organisation. The fruit of this was the formation of 'Zhonghua yieyu yundong lianhehui' [the China Amateur Athletic Union] which was formally founded on 3 April 1922 in Beijing (the first preparatory meeting was on 4 June 1921 in Shanghai). There were nine members on the Executive Committee, and three of them were foreigners (YMCA physical directors). In 1924, influenced by the May Fourth Movement, in an anti-imperalist atmosphere, the China Amateur Athletic Union was

abolished. The Chinese founded their own national athletic association called 'Zhonghua quanguo tiyu xiejinhui' [China National Amateur Athletic Federation] on 5 July 1924 in Nanjing. There were nine members on the executive committee, all Chinese. This Association and the Physical Education Committee of the Ministry of Education (see Chapter Seven, note 37) were the two major national bodies in charge of development of physical education and sport in the Nationalist area. For details see Shen, Shiliang, 'Zhonghua quanguo tiyu xiejinhui lue shi' [History of the China National Amateur Athletic Federation], *Tiyu jikan* [Physical Education Quarterly], Jan. 1935, pp.10–13. The author was a director and executive member of the Federation from 1924 to 1935. See also CSHSPE, *Zhonguo jindai tiyu shi* [Modern Chinese Sports History], op. cit., pp.161–3; Zhang, Gong, 'Zhonghua yieyu yundong lianhehui jieti yu heshi?' [When did the China Amateur Athletic Union Disappear?], *TWS*, No. 4, 1991, pp.48–9; Zhang, Tianbai, 'Zhonghua quanguo tiyu xiejinhui choubei chenli shi mo' [The History of the Founding of the China National Amateur Athletic Federation], *TWS*, No. 6, 1990, pp.30–3.

59. See *Di sijie quanguo yundonghui zhongbaogao* [The Report of the Fourth National Athletic Meeting], April 1930 (pamphlet).
60. Tang, Hao, op. cit., Vol. 4, 1958, pp.61–8.
61. Kong Xiangxi (1880–1967), a financer/industrialist, obtained a masters degree from Yale in 1907 and became Minister of Finance of the Nationalist government in 1940s.
62. The speech was published in *Qin Fen*, Vol. 3, No. 2 , Nov. 1935, p.135.
63. Wang Jingwei (1883–1947) studied in Japan in 1905 and was a follower of Sun Yat-sen. He later held several top positions in the Nationalist government. In 1940 Wang agreed to be titular head of a collaborationist regime in Nanjing that co-operated with invading Japanese forces.
64. Cited in Kolatch, Jonathan, op. cit., p.43.
65. See *Qin Fen*, the Special Issue of the Sixth National Athletic Meeting, Vol. 3, No. 2, Nov. 1935, p.134.
66. Shao, Rugan, 'Diliujie quanguo yundong dahui de zanwang' [On the Sixth National Athletic Meeting], *Qin Fen*, Vol. 3, No. 2, Nov. 1935, p.1.
67. Xiao, Zhongguo, 'Tichang nuzi tiyu yu zhonghua minzu zhi fuxin' [On the Relationship between the Promotion of Women's Sport and China's Future], *Tiyu jikan* [Physical Education Quarterly], Vol. 3, No. 2, June 1932, pp.145–6.
68. Wang, Jianwu, 'Woguo yi ruhe juxin yundonghui' [How to Hold Athletic Meetings in China], *Qin Fen*, Vol. 3, No. 3, Dec. 1935, pp.241–4.
69. See *Qin Fen*, Vol. 3, No. 2, Nov. 1935, p.6.
70. Cheng Dengke (born in 1902) graduated from the Physical Education Department of Nanjing Dongnan University in 1905 and went to Berlin, Germany to study between 1923–33. He was a professor at Nanjing Central University and the Director of Physical Education Committee of the Youth League of the Nationalist government.
71. Cheng, Dengke. 'Xiegei xinbiyie de tiyu tongxue' [For the New Graduates of the Sport Institute], in *Qin Fen*, July 1935, Vol. 2, No. 10, pp.666–7.
72. Wang, La, 'Jinhou woguo funu tiyu zhi fangxiang' [The Direction of Chinese Women's Sport], *Tianjin tiyu zhoukan* [Tianjin Sport Weekly], No. 1, Dec. 1932, pp.6–9. The author was a female physical educationist and taught gymnastics in several girls' schools in Tianjin.
73. For example, at the Physical Education Department of Ginling Women's University (founded in 1925), Dongya [East Asia] Physical Education Institute (founded in 1918 but extended in 1928), Liangjiang Women's Physical

Education Institute (founded in 1922 and also extended in 1928), Sichuan Women's Physical Education Institute (founded in 1931), the Department of Physical Education, Beijing (Beipin) Women's University (founded in 1931), the Physical Education Division of Beijing Women's Normal College (founded in 1931), the Department of Chongqing Women's Physical Education Institute (founded in 1940), the Baisha Women's Sport College (founded in 1940) and the Women's Physical Education Department of Hebei Normal University (founded in 1946). The source is from CSHSPE, *Zhongguo jindai tiyu shi* [Modern Chinese Sports History], op. cit., p.236–8; Dai, Shizheng, 'Beipin daxue nuzi wenli xueyuan tiyu zhuxiuke gaikuang' [History of the Department of Physical Education, Beipin Women's University], *Beijing tiyu wenshi* [Beijing Sports History Material], No. 1, 1987, pp.49–53; Bai, Shaojie, 'Ji Beijing nuzi shifan xueyuan tiyu zhuaxiuke' [The History of the Physical Education Division of Beijing Women's Normal College], in *Beijing tiyu wenshi* [Beijing Sports History Material], No. 1, 1987, pp.38–44.

74. In March 1934, the Nationalist government issued 'Shifan xuexiao tiyu ke jiaoxue kemu ji ge xueqi meizhou jiaoxue shike biao' [The Curriculum of Physical Education Departments and Institutes]. See CSHSPE, *Zhongguo jindai tiyu shi* [Modern Chinese Sports History], op. cit., pp.212–13.

75. In 1942 the Nationalist government revised the curriculum but the majority of it remained unchanged. The curriculum was published in *Qin Fen*, Vol. 2, No. 1, Oct. 1944, p.93.

76. Lu, Lihua, 'Zhongguo nulanqiu zai quanyunhui geiyu women de yinxiang' [Women's Basketball Competitions at the Fifth National Athletic Meeting], *Qin Fen*, Vol. 1, No. 1, Nov. 1933, pp.7–8.

77. For example, the women's high jump champion, Zhou Shande became the Director of Women's Sport at Shanghai Daxia University, while the discus champion, Ma Yi, became a Director of Physical Education in a middle school.

78. The Department of Physical Education at Ginling Women's University was founded in August 1925. The former YWCA Physical Education Institute merged with it. For details see Zhang Huilan, the Director of the Department, 'Ginling University and I', *TWS*, No. 1, 1983, pp.36–7.

79. For details see Li Jiuan, the Director of the Division, 'Fuxinzhong zi aiguo nuxue tiyuke' [The Development of the Physical Education Division of Shanghai Patrotic Women's School], *Qin Fen*, Vol. 1, No. 1, Oct. 1933, pp.76–9.

80. Dongya Physical Education Institute was founded in August 1918 by Fu Liangzai and Pang Xinyao who studied physical education in Japan and the USA. For details see CSHSPE, *Zhongguo jindai tiyu shi* [Modern Chinese Sports History], op. cit., pp.226–7.

81. Liangjiang Women's Physical Education Institute was founded in 1922 in Shanghai. Lu Lihua, a graduate of the Chinese Women's Physical Education Institute founded in 1912, was the Principal. For details see Lu, Lihua, 'Fuxinqian de Liangjiang nuzi shifang xuexiao shinian de huishu' [The History of Liangjiang Women's Physical Education Institute], *Qin Fen*, Vol., 1, No. 10, July 1934, pp.31–2; Wu, Zhimin, 'Liangjiang nuzi tiyu zhuke xuexiao xiaoshi' [The History of Liangjiang Women's Physical Education Institute], in Tang, Hao, op. cit., pp.7–8.

82. In 1924 Lu Lihua, the Principal of Liangjiang Institute, discovered from a book that British women played football. She believed that if Western women could do it, then so could Chinese women. So she founded a football team in her Institute. For details see Wu, Zimin, 'Woguo diyizi nuzi zhuqiudui' [The First Chinese Women's Football Team], *TWS*, No. 3, 1985, p.30.

83. For example, Qian Xinshu, Chen Yongtang, Chen Jian, Pan Yinchu and Zhen Yijiao, were students of Dongya Physical Education Institute. Qian Xinshu (born in 1913) was a champion at the Fifth and Sixth National Athletic Meeting in 1933 and 1935. She was the member of Chinese team at the Far East Championship Games in 1933. For details see Yue, 'Yundong Nujie' [Athletic Heroine], op. cit.; Chen, Yongtang (born in 1914) was a champion at the Sixth National Athletic Meeting in 1935. For details see *Qin Fen – special issue for the Six National Athletic Meeting*, Vol. 3, No. 3, Dec. 1935; Chen Jian was the only one who attended the Fourth to the Sixth National Athletic meetings. For details see *Qin Fen*, Vol, 3, No. 7, April 1936, p.77; Pan Yinchu (born in 1917) was a champion of the Sixth National Athletic Meeting in 1935. For details see *Qin Fen* Vol. 3, No. 3, Feb. 1936, p.47; Zhen Yijiao (born in 1917) was a champion of the Sixth National Athletic Meeting in 1935. For details see *Qin Fen*, Vol. 3, No. 5, May 1936, p.42.

84. Lu, Lihua, 'Zhongguo nulan zhai quanyunhui geiyi women de yinxiang' [The Women's Basketball Competitions at the Fifth National Athletic Meeting], op. cit.

85. Yang Ren, one of the members of the team, wrote an article entitled 'Dongzhen huiyi pianduan' [My Memory of the Visit to East Asia], *TWS*, No. 3, 1983, pp.39–40.

86. On 18 September 1931 the Japanese troops invaded Manchuria. The puppet regime called Manchuguo was established in 1932. The Japanese made the deposed Qing emperor Puyi 'chief executive' of the government and retained control of the area until the end of the Second World War. On 7 July 1937 the Japanese took control of the Marco Polo bridge near Beijing. The fighting that followed this manoeuvre marked the beginning of open hostilities between China and Japan and can be seen as the first battle of the Second World War.

87. Xu, Fulin, 'Liangjiang nulan zhai Riben' [Recollections of Liangjiang Women's Basketball in Japan], *TWS*, No. 6, 1988, pp.17–18.

88. See the report, 'Liangjiang nulan lanqiudui yuanzheng nanyang ji' [Liangjiang Women's Basketball Team Visiting South Asia], *Qin Fen*, Vol. 2, No. 10, July 1935, pp.77–8.

89. See the report, 'Dongya tizuan nuzibu yuanzheng nanyang ji' [Women's Teams of Dongya Physical Education Institute Visiting South Asia], *Qin Fen*, Vol. 2, No. 8, April 1935, p.45.

90. Chen, Yimin, 'Wo de yundong shenhuo' [My Athletic Life], *Qin Fen*, Vol. 2, No. 2, Nov. 1934, pp.175–6.

91. See Wu Tang's articles 'Huanxiang de pomie' [My Dream] and 'Yuanwei tiyu shiyie xian zhongshen' [My ambition was to devote my life to sport], in *Beijing tiyu wenshi* [Beijing Sports History Material], Vol. 1, 1987, pp.254–6, Vol. 4, 1990, pp.326–35.

92. Shang, Quan, 'Yi nuzi duanpao jianjiang Li Sen' [Recollections of Li Sen], *TWS*, No. 1, 1984, p.13.

93. Some of the better known included Shun Shuquan, Ha Qinchi, Chen Yunlan, Du Yifei, Wang Jinhua and Huang Limin.
    Shun Shuqiuan (born in 1912) graduated from Ginlin Women's University and became a physical educator in a girls' school in Suzhou, Zhejiang province. She was a basketball and tennis player and attended the 1930 National Athletic Meeting. For more details see *Qin Fen*, Dec. 1936, Vol. 4, No. 3, p.257.
    Ha Qinchi (1915–66) came from a wealthy family. Her father was a general in the Nationalist army. She graduated from Ginling Women's University in 1936 and worked in several girls' schools in Beijing. For further details see

Zhan, Meidi, 'Yi haoyou Ha Qinchi' [My Good Friend Ha Qinchi]; Cheng, Yulan, 'Yi wode lianshi Ha Qinchi' [My Good Teacher Ha Qinchi], in *Beijing tiyu wenshi* [Beijing Sports History Material], No. 2, 1988, pp.264–7.

Chen Yunlan, a graduate of Ginling Women's University in 1930, was a member of the Nanjing team and attended the Fourth National Athletic Meeting in 1930. For more details see *Qin Fen*, Vol. 3, No. 10, July 1936, p.43.

Du Yufei (born in 1905) graduated from Ginling Women's University and worked as a physical educator in various schools and colleges. In 1937 she became the Principal of Shanghai Women's Physical Education Institute. She was a member of Chinese delegation to the 1936 Berlin Olympic Games. For more details see *Qin Fen*, Vol. 4, No. 5, Feb. 1937, p.91.

Wang Jinhua (born in 1905) graduated fron Ginling Women's University. She worked in various schools and universities. She became a professor at Beijing Normal University in 1938. For details see Xiao Xinhua's article, 'Ji tiyu jiaoyujia Wang Jinhua' [Physical Educationist Wang Jinhua], *Beijing tiyu wenshi*, No. 4, p.291.

Huan Limin graduated from Ginling Women's University. After obtaining a masters degree in the USA, she worked in the Physical Education Department of Ginlin Women's University and eventually became the Head of the Department. She was a member of Physical Education Committee of the Ministry of Education. For further details see *Qin Fen*, Vol. 3, No. 4, Jan. 1936, p.68.

94. Lu, Lihua, 'Jiqie xujiao zi Zhongguo nuzi tiyu' [Development of Women's Sport was the Top Priority], *Tiyu zhoubao* [Sports Weekly], Vol. 2, No. 20, June 1933, p.1.

95. Sheng, Chijiu, 'Kangzhan si nisn lai de funu yundong' [The Women's Movement in China 1937–1941], in CWF, op. cit., Vol. 3, p.579.

96. Fan and Wang, *Tiyu shihua* [Sports History], op. cit., p.208.

97. See *Qin Fen*, Vol. 1, No. 2, Oct. 1933, p.32–3.

98. See *Qin Fen*, Vol. 3, No. 2, Nov. 1935, pp.157–8.

99. See report in *Qin Fen*, Vol. 1, No. 4, Aug. 1934, p.32.

100. See *Qin Fen*, Vol. 1, No. 2, Nov. 1935, p.2.

101. For examples see *Qin Fen*, Vol. 1, No. 1, Oct. 1933. and *Qin Fen Tiyu huabao* [Qin Fen Sport Pictures], Vol. 1, No. 11, 1934; *Tiyu zhoubao* [Sports Weekly], Vol. 2, No. 9, April 1933.

102. See *Qin Fen*, Vol. 1, No. 2, Nov. 1933, p.5.

103. See *Tiyu zhoubao* [Sports Weekly], Vol. 2, No. 1, Jan. 1933, pp.7–9.

104. In fact, the rumour was inaccurate. Wang Yuan and the Ambassador were only friends. For discussion of the 'marriage', see Zhong Qi, 'Wang Yuan nushi de zou yitaitai wenti' [On Wang Yang's Marriage], in *Tiyu zhoubao*, Vol. 2, No. 5, Feb. 1933, pp.2–3.

105. See Chapters Five and Six.

106. For example, in 1947, two years before the Nationalist era ended in Mainland China, Yao Jiechang, a physical educationist, submitted a proposal to the Ministry of Education entitled 'Shisi woguo nuzi tiyu zhi juti fangan' [A Proposal for the Implementation of Chinese Women's Physical Exercise]. He repeated all the well-rehearsed arguments (from both the West and the East) about women's biological difference. He suggested women's sport should nurture a woman's fit body, hygienic habits and personal characteristics. His proposal was published in *Tiyu* [Physical Education], No. 5, May 1947, pp.241–6.

107. See the Epilogue.

From Cripples to Champions[1]

IN CHINESE HISTORY until the recent past women's bodies have been the focus of their humiliation, exploitation and oppression. This is irrefutable. It is through their bodies that they have been subjugated both physically and psychologically; first and foremost, through the institution of footbinding – a brilliant and brutal instrument of control. Women unable to walk adequately were easy to restrain. Furthermore, the intense physical sufferings brought about by the process of breaking and binding the feet in early childhood produced a passivity, stoicism and fatalism that effectively 'bound' not only the feet but also the mind and the emotions.

In conjunction with this physical restriction was the cultural conditioning brought about by the principles and practices of Confucianism. For centuries Chinese women, in consequence, were constrained by physical restrictions, by ethical precepts, by social custom and by legal sanctions. Therefore, their release from tradition, their freedom from tyranny, but above all the liberation of their bodies were essential requirements for their wider physical, cultural and political freedom.

The central argument of this book has been that physical normality was the prerequisite of political, cultural and physical assertion. The contention is that prior to 1840 the life of virtually every Chinese woman from every class was a life of dependence systematised and sanctioned by society, and that post-1840 this dependence gradually if spasmodically, was inexorably reduced by the influence of various movements.

The first moments of modern self-assertion occurred in the Taiping Rebellion of 1850. Women of the rebellion were accorded equality. These peasant women with unbound feet, robust physiques, militant attitudes and proven courage were committed revolutionaries and successful soldiers. They won respect and admiration from the men of the Revolution. They set a precedent; they represented a new femininity; they offered a new image of women to society.

Unlike the urban origins of the emancipation of women in Europe, the emancipation of Chinese women arose out of a rural revolution. Women warriors of the Taiping Rebellion challenged orthodox ideas of femininity. The Taiping Rebellion was defeated in 1864. Following this defeat, it was the Christian missionaries who then effectively challenged traditional Chinese culture and created the early opportunity for women to free themselves physically and mentally.

Western powers invaded China in the mid-nineteenth century, not only with military forces but also with strong ideological forces in the form of religious dogma. The primary purpose of the Christian missionaries was to convert the Chinese to a superior *weltanschauung*. However, the missionaries' historical function, as it turned out, was to help transmit new ideas and images to Chinese women and to free women from feudal bondage. They saw education as the key by which the door to the social transformation of Chinese society could be opened. Through the practice and promotion of Western education, the missionaries attempted to abolish footbinding and to change cultural attitudes towards Chinese women's bodies, health, education and status. Above all, by caring for bodies (especially tortured feet) and by alleviating physical suffering, they hoped to win souls and to liberate Chinese women from heathen culture. In these ambitions they were not without some success. They initiated the anti-footbinding movement and used the consequent physical freedom, mobility and exercise as major instruments in the erosion of female inequality.

The further significance of the missionaries for Chinese women's physical emancipation was that they brought women's physical emancipatory ideas from the West and drew *Chinese* attention to the harsh traditional ways in which inequality was perpetuated. Their ideas and actions stimulated concern among Chinese reformers about women's issues in China. This eventually produced social change.

Under political pressure from, and military humiliation by, the European powers, the reformers approached the 'women's issue' from a broader patriarchal perspective. Women's traditional bodies became political anomalies. China needed healthy mothers to bear healthy sons in turn to preserve and promote the state. Women's health, therefore, became a form of insurance to guard against the further decline of China. Footbinding was regarded as a major factor in weakening women's health and it had to be abolished. Women's bodies required reconstruction. The anti-footbinding movement, therefore, was widely supported, and spread throughout the country.

It challenged Confucian ideas about, and attitudes towards, women and changed to an extent women's social image in society. This paved the way for their further but still partial physical, economic, cultural and political liberation.

In 1902 the custom of footbinding was officially banned. The general abolition of footbinding was a necessary foundation for women's general participation in physical exercise. In turn, this participation was the prerequisite of sound health, personal vigour and physical fitness. It was the beginning of a long road to the freedom to take part in, to enjoy and to compete in the life-enriching physical, political and economic activities of the modern world. By the end of the nineteenth century missionary and reformer had jointly brought about a reconceptualisation of femininity and a redefinition and reshaping of the female body in accordance with Western perceptions of female normality, desirability, propriety and possibilities. Although initially it mostly touched the lives of only the privileged, it had a profound significance for the relationship between the sexes, the cultural roles of men and women, and the arrangements of social power. The physical emancipation of women, arguably to an extent demonstrated nowhere else in the world given the extraordinary phenomenon of footbinding, has been the prerequisite of all subsequent emancipation in China.

The role of Chinese men in these changes was crucial. In China, the leading early believers in feminism and those first influenced by Western ideas of feminism were men. This role of men as the initiators of the Chinese Women's Movement is indicative of the extreme dependence and powerlessness of Chinese women in traditional society in the nineteenth century, a state of affairs which made it virtually impossible for them to act as innovators.

Women's modern education, first introduced by the missionary, expanded in the first two decades of the twentieth century. Since those most disadvantaged or oppressed in the old society were the ones who most readily felt frustration and bitterness at their position, women, especially educated middle-class women, in the first phase of social revolution (1900–11) were potentially a good source of recruits to the struggle for educational expansion. They were not satisfied with the reformer's narrow perception of their gender role. They attempted, with sympathetic male supporters, to play a crucial part in determining their country's future. They sought modern education abroad and most of them went to Japan. It was in Japan that female, as well as male radicals took their first steps in mastering, among other things, the modern philosophy and practice of physical education – for patriotic purposes. They saw physical exercise as a significant means of developing a national spirit of muscular unity which would enable China to emerge as a modern state capable of defending itself. Physical education was regarded as a nationalistic instrument. Women's physical emancipation, therefore, was closely connected with patriotism and nationalism. With men, these women initiated a campaign: 'Saving China with Exercise'.

The Japanese-educated students set up, or taught in, schools with clear and declared aims: the advancement of women's knowledge and the universalisation of women's education, mental and physical. They created an educational infrastructure to promote these aims. Interestingly, for the first time in Chinese history Chinese women now believed in significant numbers that emancipation would come in large measure through exercise. A new image of radical women steadily emerged: strong in mind and body. These women were confirmed nationalists and feminists, and played an active role in both the national salvation movement and the Women's Movement. They believed that in the long run sexual restrictions would be swept away along with other old evils, and that in a new China driven by liberal values men and women would strive harmoniously together to reach shared goals to the benefit of all. In the short run, the revolutionary movement offered women the opportunity to join in the great work of saving the nation, to prove themselves through heroic action and thus earn the right to full equality. Chinese indigenous female emancipation in the hands of women, from its birth combined feminism, radicalism and nationalism – and optimism. Chinese women now strove to find their own way without paternal 'guidance'. They were determined to think *and* act for themselves. They embodied a *gender* declaration of freedom – in the spirit of the European Enlightenment in China. The first years of the twentieth century were those of Chinese Female Enlightenment.

The 1911 Revolution ended the Chinese feudal social system but did not end the feudal culture. The Women's Movement was halted in its tracks by the conservative rule of Yuan Shikai. Women did not achieve what they had fought for. It proved to be an error of judgement for the Chinese Women's Movement to have subordinated itself to the nationalist movement. When the Republicans came to power women's demands for full equality were rejected. Chinese society needed order and it decided on traditional order. Therefore, traditional female physical images, concepts of femininity and sexual roles were reasserted. Even radical male sympathisers proved unable to resist the cultural influences which were deeply rooted in every psyche and, in the event, they were not prepared to work to change gender rights and roles. Women radicals, for their part, were not strong enough to fight against the male-dominated culture.

Atavistic attitudes fortunately did not last long. The New Culture and the May Fourth Movements again brought fundamental reflection. Broad criticism of Confucianism and advocacy of the Western ideas of democracy, equality and freedom brought reorientations in consciousness that in turn opened up new possibilities for Chinese women. By 1921 modern education was again available in public and private schools; the idea of women's education needed no further justification. The physical ideal in the middle classes had become the natural footed and vigorously healthy woman. Her body became an icon of modernity, reconstruction and rehabilitation in the progressive May Fourth Era. More importantly, the establishment of the Chinese Communist Party in 1921 was a watershed in modern Chinese history. After this date women's physical emancipation divided into two parts. It reflected two ideologies and two practices: Communist and Nationalist.

From the beginning, the Communists, as good Marxists, believed that in merit women were half the Chinese population. They were also brutalised and they were, therefore, ideal recruits to the Communist revolution. The Women's Department was created in 1922. Equality between the sexes was declared in same year. However, although the Communist Party emphasised the importance of women's emancipation it never made this emancipation a top priority. In fact, the Chinese Communists distanced themselves from the feminist movement. They concentrated on traditional Marxist theories of the economic foundations of the oppression and exploitation of women and linked the women's struggle to the wider issue of the proletariat struggle against the forces of capitalism. They asserted that women could not hope to be effectively liberated until the whole evil historical social system was overthrown and *all* the oppressed were liberated. This policy of the Communist Party towards the Women's Movement never changed. The Communist Women's Movement in China was never to be an independent manifestation but part and parcel of the peasant and worker revolutionary liberation movement.

Between 1929 and 1934 the Chinese Communist Party and its Red Army, in retreat from cities held by the Nationalist Army, established the Chinese Soviet Republic in the mountainous area of Jiangxi. Arguably, the Jiangxi period initiated some of the most radical social changes in modern Chinese history. Land was redistributed, new laws were implemented and society was reorganised. Radicalism also involved attempts fundamentally to transform women's legal and social status. At the same time, the harsh physical environment and the constant attacks from the Nationalists and from warlords meant that women had to take strenuous physical exercise and undergo intensive military training in order to fight with the Red Armies. The Communists revived the Taiping Rebellion's concept of liberated women warriors and structured the community around the idea of 'Darwinian' survival through war. They created a formal system of physical exercise for women which for the first time reached worker and peasant women. This system was the Red Sports Movement. The Communist Party promoted the Red Sports Movement in the Soviet area from 1927–34. It was a mass movement in which exercise was viewed as the basis of physical, cultural and military training of people in Soviet areas. Women of every social background were made to exercise with a single purpose – military survival. Access to exercise, available only to the privileged urban few of earlier years, now became available to the poverty-stricken rural many. Female exercise was transformed from a prerogative of the privileged into a pragmatic tool of the proletariat. As a byproduct, it challenged patriarchal tradition. It created opportunities for women's development – mentally and physically. It contributed to the on-going redefinition of the female image and it produced a radical female role-model: the 'iron woman'. Depictions of 'iron' Jiangxi women who fought with the Communist soviet armies are still used today to underline the duties, responsibilities and possibilities of contemporary Chinese women under Communism.

The Jiangxi era ended in October 1934 when the Nationalists occupied the Red area. The Communists lost virtually everything and had to leave the rural soviets. They began the Long March which took them to Shanxi in late 1935. There, the Communists established their new base in Yan'an. The Japanese invasion in 1937 transformed the civil war into a National War and the Communists and the Nationalists formed a United Front. This Front brought to the new Communist area a time of relative tranquillity.

The Communists, therefore, had an opportunity to institutionalise their policy towards the Women's Movement. The principle of the Communist Women's Movement was emancipation without feminism. Yan'an served in a sense as a laboratory for social change, and experiments there were later to determine the course of the Chinese Women's Movement after 1949. Politically, women had equal rights to men. Economically, women were mobilised to participate in productive work. Culturally, women were encouraged to remain true to their traditional duties – that of wife and mother. But now they needed to be strong and healthy. Physical education was systematically promoted in armies, schools, counties and villages. A Physical Education and Sports Committee was established under the leadership of the Communist Party. The Committee supervised clubs and groups, ratified the regulations for games and organised sports events. The Committee promoted a New Sports Movement. Its slogan was 'everybody is to do exercise'. The structure and principles of post-1949 physical exercise were pioneered in Yan'an. Women from all classes were encouraged to participate in exercise. For the first time, in the Communist area, female athletes competed at sports meetings. Consequently, an image of 'Yan'an woman' was successfully created: freed from physical restriction, able to exercise, trained for careers and encouraged to be 'modern wife, mother and daughter-in-law'. This image met the needs of the new Marxist society. It became the model for the updated Communist woman – less militaristic and more domestic than the Jiangxi 'iron woman'.

Although the image changed from the hard Jiangxi women to the softer 'Yan'an woman', women's physical freedom was the key to their participation in revolution in both periods. In the interest of the Party, women were mobilised and women's bodies were exercised. This mobilisation and exercise both necessitated and gave rise to rapid social change and established a new femininity in the Communist area.

Women's physical emancipation in the Nationalist area was another story. The National Party controlled two thirds of China by 1936 (before the Japanese invasion). Its ambitions were to maintain general social order and stability and to unify the country under one-party rule. To achieve these goals the Party, on the one hand, employed traditional morality in order to resist the corrosive influence of Communist and Western ideologies on women; on the other hand, it promoted modern exercise to ensure the production of healthy mothers for the nation. From 1928 to 1949, the Nationalist government developed a national physical-training system for both men *and* women. The government was committed to the long-standing view that the only way to restore the nation's morale was through the promotion of the spirit of nationalism and the creation of strong bodies. The Nationalist Party, therefore, made special efforts to encourage women's participation in exercise. It believed that only through adequate exercise could women efficiently fulfil their duties in the domestic and in the public domain. There was a distinctive Nationalist interpretation of equality: women could serve the country in their special biological way – as strong mothers for the production of strong soldiers. Paradoxically, women's exercise, partially denied women's traditional image and partially confirmed their traditional responsibilities.

Through exercise, however, an important transition occurred. A fit female body assumed a new cultural, social and individual significance. A healthy body became a vehicle of self-promotion. It broke into a world of new roles, new images and new possibilities. In the Nationalist area in the 1930s exercise ensured a new female personality type which sociologists have referred to as 'the performing self'. This new personality required validation from audiences through successful projections of the self. The new self was a visible self and the body, suitably presented, came to symbolise overtly the status of the self. The new self was epitomised *par excellence* by successful sportswomen. They were educated, healthy, independent in mind and in pocket and prepared confidently to share responsibility with men in society. They wanted full access to the man-oriented domain, in particular to competitive sport. This they now attempted and here the ultimate emancipatory dramas associated with exercise were enacted.

Excellence at competitive sport was the ultimate celebration of their bodies' freedom, strength and competence. It was a source of self-esteem, personal autonomy and social success. It symbolised a new femininity. Competitive action and achievements on the sports field denied historic gender shibboleths and ensured a modern sexual identity irrespective of the 'neo-Confucian' cultural atmosphere. While women in general went backwards, pulled firmly by reactionary traditional ideology, sportswomen went forwards sustained by society's pride in their success. They became emancipationist icons. They kept the flag of feminism flying in the face of reactionary social pressure.

What all this amounts to is that the Women's Movement in China, in general, was not an independent movement. It was either dependent on Nationalists or Communists. Under the Nationalists, the Women's Movement comprised an élite, a small but significant sector of the middle class. It shared the élitist concerns of its class, including a belief in the traditional economic order and in the efficiency of education as a cure for many problems. The feminists demanded their rights, for they were denied on the grounds of their sex what middle-class men possessed, access to comprehensive education and the full of rights of citizenship. They appeared little concerned with the rights of women peasants and workers. When they spoke of 'women', they actually meant educated women. Urban and rural working-class women were still greatly exploited and oppressed by imperialism, capitalism and feudalism. Their concerns, therefore, were basic: food, clothing and shelter. The question of how to achieve emancipation was academic: survival was the top priority. Although some middle-class feminists recognised the importance of educating and mobilising these women, they had difficulty communicating with and cultivating their underprivileged counterparts. In this lack of contact with the masses, the Women's Movement produced an isolated and inward-looking middle-class women's movement. Feminism was a luxury only the well-to-do had the opportunity to cultivate.

However, patriotism eventually rescued it from this narrow élitism and provided the impetus for its democratisation. The feminists came to play an integral but subordinate role in the nationalist movement in its various phases. In the Nationalist area, while the Party proscribed the active promotion of the Women's Movement itself and emphasised the traditional domestic responsibilities of women, physical fitness remained an important part of both the Nationalist movement and the feminist movement. This was necessitated by the powerful and practical requirements of Nationalist survival in the face of considerable internal and external threats. Women's exercise, therefore, remained closely associated with the Nationalist movement, and was supported not only by the feminists but also by the government and the masses. Thus, rebuttal of the feminist movement did not mean the end of the process of women's physical liberation. Women's physical liberation served Nationalist Party purposes. It was a means of ensuring political survival.

In contrast to the Nationalists, the Communists concentrated on peasant and working women. Women's liberation was intimately connected with the life and death of the revolutionary cause. At the same time, to win its struggle the Party had to win support from both sexes. The Party, on the one hand, had to avoid the male peasantry's resentment evoked by reform of traditional sexual roles and family institutions, and on the other hand, had to avoid the danger that women would grow strong enough to split from the revolutionary ranks. The Party, therefore, advocated women's freedom but limited its extent. It never shifted from the view that no meaningful change for women could be achieved until the victory of the class struggle. Nevertheless, the revolution needed strong women. For this reason, women's physical emancipation was promoted by the Communists. Traditional femininity was challenged and the new femininity based on a heroic image was eventually established.

In essence, in the first half of the twentieth century Chinese exercise was an instrument of political purpose; it served both Nationalist and Communist. Nationalists and Communists had different ideologies but shared the same desperation and hope. The desperation was over China's fragmented state, compounded by feuding militarist regimes and foreigners' special privileges. The hope lay in drawing on the spiritual, intellectual and physical powers of the Chinese people to create the strength necessary for lasting reunification. Despite competing long-range goals and clashing personalities, Communists and Nationalists at least had one thing in common: a realisation of the need to attempt reunification of the country through a mixture of military force and social reform. Among other things, they used physical exercise as a tool to this end. Thus the physical emancipatory process was inexorable and, to a substantial degree, beyond the control of divergent political ideological principles. The process was driven by the powerful requirements of national survival and national reunification in the face of major internal and external threats to political, and indeed, physical existence. Women's participation in exercise was therefore supported energetically by both Parties. Consequently, women, in both Nationalist and Communist territories, while largely unaware of each other, gradually formed a collective and resistant barrier to past peasant prejudices against women and past bourgeois demands upon women.

In the final analysis, Chinese women's physical emancipation was the result of an Eastern plant grafted onto a Western root and grown to slow maturity in the hothouse atmosphere of Chinese Nationalism and Communism. However, the greatest growth occurred only after

1949 when the People's Republic of China attempted to implement its promise of full equality of the sexes. Then Chinese women athletes for the first time became sports superstars: symbols of full physical liberation. The period after 1949 reveals their triumph over historic adversities but it also reveals a need to triumph over continuing adversities. History is a process of change and continuity and the narrative of the relationship between women's emancipation and exercise in China demonstrates this profoundly. For both these reasons the era of Communist control will now receive brief consideration.

Coda: Continuing Struggle

In 1949 the Communists won the civil war (1945–49). Chiang Kai-shek and his government fled to Taiwan and the Communists took over mainland China. The People's Republic of China was formally established in Beijing on 1 October 1949. In Mao Zedong's words, socialist China was the culmination of the revolution that began with the May Fourth Movement, and continued with the Long March and the Jiangxi and Yan'an eras.[2] What has been the relationship between exercise and emancipation under Communism?[3] Have women received full equality as the Party promised as long ago as 1922 in the second year of its existence? What sort of change has the Communist Party brought to Chinese women's social position?

Women's Emancipation under Communism

In 1949 China's Communist leaders were masters of their own house built on the foundations of a Marxist ideology. Communism promised to give women equal rights in the new society. On 24 March 1949, shortly after Beijing came under Communist control, the First National Women's Congress convened, and the formation of the All-China Federation of Democratic Women was announced.[4] Women revolutionaries of the May Fourth Movement and the Jiangxi and Yan'an eras (such as Cai Chang, Deng Yingchao, Kang Keqing and Ding Ling) became its leaders.[5] In September the Chinese People's Political Consultative Conference met, and its Common Programme contained the following statement: 'The People's Republic of China shall abolish the feudal system that holds women in bondage. Women shall enjoy equal rights with men in political, economic, cultural, educational and social life.'[6]

This ideal of equality described by the Common Programme, was to be attempted in four stages following the establishment of the New China: the enactment and promulgation of the 1950 'Marriage Law', the Great Leap Forward and People's Communes in 1957–59, the Cultural Revolution from 1966 to 1976 and the Economic Reform from 1979 to the present.

The 'Marriage Law of the People's Republic of China' was issued on 1 May 1950. It was the direct descendent of the Jiangxi Marriage Laws of 1933.[7] Women could choose and divorce their husbands. They were no longer family slaves, machines for the production of sons and powerless possessions. For the first time they thus obtained a measure of freedom to live as self-asserting individuals. In short, the Marriage Law finally buried the feudal family system.[8]

However, it would be naive to believe that equality in the context of twentieth century Chinese history would come automatically as a result of the passing of laws. As late as 1980 the Marriage Law was revised and strengthened with freedom of marriage guaranteed and the buying, selling or arranging of marriages forbidden. In fact, six years later, all was still far from well. 'The supportive words about marriage rights for women in the Code of Civil Procedure were echoes of those used in the Marriage Law of 1980, but in fact they were frequently violated. Sale of women and girls into marriage, forcible marriage of widows, purchase of brides, or parental negotiation of children's marriages in exchange for various forms of 'bride price' remained common in China'.[9] In 1994 the Party announced that 'At present, China is still at the primary stage of socialism and remains comparatively underdeveloped in economic and cultural development. Therefore, certain provisions on the legal rights of women and guarantee mechanisms need to be further improved.'[10]

Realistically, the First All-China Women's Congress in April, 1949 recognised that 'only through active participation in production can women raise and consolidate their position, improve . . . their own living standards . . . and free themselves from the feudal yoke'.[11] However, as long as women were restricted to 'domestic labour', they were not engaged in 'socially productive labour'.[12] When the Great Leap Forward and People's Communes were launched in 1957[13], it was the task of the Women's Movement to mobilise all women to take part in 'social labour' and steadily to promote their role in agricultural and industrial production and construction.[14] To achieve this, the government established community agencies such as nurseries and kindergartens, public dining-rooms, and sewing centres to free women from domestic chores. By 1959, in the rural areas there were 4,980,000 nurseries and kindergartens, more than 3,600,000 public dining-rooms and numerous sewing centres.[15] In the large and medium-sized cities some 50,000 community dining-rooms had been established, and some 42,000 kindergartens with more than 1.2 million children in their charge had been set up.[16] Millions of women were able to 'step out of their homes' and to take part in 'social production'. In 1958, 90 per cent of rural women were participating in production and in 26 cities, including Beijing, Guangzhou, Harbin and Taiyuan, 80 per cent of the female population was involved.[17]

The results of the Great Leap Forward were politically intolerable and economically disastrous.[18] However, the policy of mobilising women into production gave women an opportunity to obtain a measure of economic independence. The nationwide upsurge of women leaving their homes to take part in economic production illustrated Chinese women's potential economic power. Once given adequate circumstances, they could exert a striking influence. The failure of the Great Leap Forward put a temporary end to this influence. Of course, women still remained in productive roles outside the home but not as a matter of political priority and not in the numbers seen during the Great Leap Forward. The morale of the Women's Movement sank to a low ebb once again. Since it had submitted itself to the CCP, it had no other choice but to comply with Party directives – to return to the home. Women's vociferous voices were not to be heard again until the Cultural Revolution of 1966.

The Cultural Revolution was launched by Mao Zedong. It became a mass political and social movement throughout the whole of China. During the ten years of the movement, a broad attack on all forms of inequality yet again challenged the conservative view of women. To ensure women's participation in the Revolution their role in Communist China was re-examined. Eight years into the Revolution, in 1973, encouraged and supported by Mao and his wife Jiang Qing, the Anti-Lin Biao and Confucian Campaign was launched. One of the aims of the Campaign was to reconstruct sexual roles in the public and domestic spheres and redefine femininity. The lesson that the Women's Movement had learned from the Great Leap Forward was that 'only by enabling women to obtain their ideological emancipation will it be possible for them to develop their infinite source of power'.[19] The Campaign, Croll has noted, represented a new aggressive stage in the attempted ideological evolution of women.[20] Supporters of the Campaign claimed: 'China was under feudal rule for 2,000 years and the exploiting classes left behind deep-rooted Confucian ideas discriminating against women . . . .Today, classes, and the class struggle, still exist. It has been impossible to eliminate completely the remnants of the old ways of looking down upon women. It is necessary to wage a protracted struggle against them.'[21]

The Campaign sparked off a desire among women to study the origins and development of Confucian ideology and to rediscover their own history. Lin Biao,[22] the Vice-Chairman of the CCP and the leader of the Army, was identified as the living spokesman and representative of the despised Confucius in contemporary China. He was a scapegoat. He symbolised those in power who advocated the idea of male supremacy. Of course, the Party – in its own interest – kept up an old refrain. Women were reminded that the lesson to be drawn from their own history was that women's emancipation was impossible without the victory of the proletarian revolution. They were made to understand that the CCP had always supported the Women's Movement and women's equality. It was diehard Confucianism which denied women. In attacking the idea of male supremacy the women were to draw confidence and support from the fact that they were part of a long 'proletarian' tradition of resistance to Confucian ideology. Throughout the period of the Cultural Revolution, women were encouraged to take part in all kinds of political and cultural actions. They were intended to constitute a great revolutionary force. The Cultural Revolution failed to accomplish what Mao intended – the permanent radicalisation of the nation. It was a national disaster psychologically, culturally, economically and politically. However, from a feminist point of view, the significance of the Revolution lay in the fact that there was an intensive, nationwide attempt to redefine the female role, to change the self-image and expectations of women, to further their emancipation.[23] To an extent these continuing aspirations of the Revolution revealed the relative impotence of laws in the face of tradition.

Mao Zedong died in September 1976 and shortly afterwards the Gang of Four[24] was arrested by his successor, Hua Guofeng. Deng Xiaoping's hour came two years later, at the Third Congress of the

Party's Eleventh Central Committee in December 1978. The Congress claimed that the Cultural Revolution was over. Furthermore, the Congress marked the beginning of modern economic reform. The policy of 'reforming and opening up' to outsiders in order to modernise China set China on a new course. It was, as Deng Xiaoping claimed, 'a second Long March (after 1935) and a second Revolution (after 1949)'.[25] Women as a potential economic force gradually came to the fore once again. In 1992, women in employment made up 72.23 per cent of all females over 15, and in the countryside half the rural labour force consisted of women labourers. The number of urban working women increased from 600,000 in 1949 to 56 million in 1992, while their share of the country's total working population went up from 7.5 per cent to 38 percent.[26] As they are more and more involved in the economy, women's position in society is improving and their future seems reasonably promising.

Nevertheless, as Margery Wolf demonstrates in her book *Revolution Postponed* published in 1987, Chinese women are far from achieving socioeconomic equality with the men. From her interviews with over 300 women she reveals that nothing approximating equality has been achieved in working conditions, pay or educational opportunity.[27] In the 1990s inequality between men and women is actually increasing. Modernisation has brought technological reform and freedom from labour-intensive work. Consequently, female unemployment is rising. In cities female workers are sent home to await work while male workers retain their jobs. In rural areas, since men with machines can do the field-work by themselves, women are instructed to return to their homes to concentrate on household work. And women do not receive equal pay for equal work. In urban areas they receive only 77.4 per cent of the pay given to men; in rural areas the figure is 81.4 per cent. In 1990, female graduates from college found it more difficult to obtain a suitable job than men. About 8 per cent of children, who dropped out of school in rural areas, were girls.[28] Concubinage and prostitution, which the CCP fought hard to eliminate in the revolutionary years and which largely vanished after 1949, have reappeared. The belief that women 'can hold up half the sky' is questioned by women themselves and by society. A survey in 1991 showed that more than half of the respondents (both men and women) believed that men were superior to women.[29]

Why have Chinese women failed to achieve equality under Communism? The common answer is because of the continuing

303

influence of Confucianism.[30] However, arguably, it is the ideology of Marxism as much as Confucianism which has protected male supremacy from fully successful challenge in modern China. Marxist writing, with few exceptions, has tended to be mostly silent on the question of gender relations.[31] In Marxist theory the causality of the economic context takes primacy, leaving the concept of gender to be treated as a byproduct of changing economic structures. It difficult to see historically how economic systems exclusively determine gender relationships. Marxists believed that once the oppressing class was destroyed, private ownership and profit abolished, and the means of economic production redistributed to the society as a whole, the oppression of women would disappear.[32] Gender, therefore, tends to lack an independent analytical status of its own and Marxist analysis seems unable to accommodate the complexities of the interaction between patriarchal society, women and emancipation.[33] Under the dominance of Marxist theories, Chinese women's analytical self-consciousness has never fully awakened. Although they have challenged feudal concepts of women continuously this century, their emancipation movements have been linked to, and submissive to, political revolution and patriotic war before 1949, and to class struggle afterwards. An independent character to the women's movement has never been allowed. Consequently, once immediate revolutionary aims were fulfilled women would be sent home to maintain society in traditional style, and the problem of the causes of their lack of full emancipation would remain unsolved.[34] The situation of women in China has proved that socialist revolution cannot automatically result in an equal relationship between sexes. Chinese women will never achieve full equality without challenging the simplistic reductionism of Marxism itself.

Women's Physical Emancipation under Communism

However, there seems to be one exception: women in sport. The Communists believed, from their early experience, that exercise would produce a strong and healthy female labour force for the construction of the new China. They also learned that sports success would transform the worldwide image of the nation. Women enjoyed equal rights in physical education and sport. They were advocated in the Communist Common Programme.[35] Chinese women and men have

304

had equal opportunities in élite sports since the establishment of sports schools in 1955. Susan Brownell has written, 'If one takes the establishment of college athletic scholarships as the point when American sportswomen began to achieve the semblance of parity with men, then 1977 was the year when the American situation approached the Chinese. American women lagged 22 years behind the Chinese.'[36] It is not just élite athletes who have benefited from Party policy. When the Chinese government withdrew from eight international sport federations and the Olympic Games between 1956 and 1979, over the 'two Chinas' question, the mass sports movement, the legacy of Jiangxi and Yan'an, developed rapidly. 'To develop sport and build and defend the motherland' was its slogan.[37] All women were encouraged to participate in exercises. A ten-year plan for exercise was formulated in 1958, in which two hundred million men and women were expected to pass the fitness grade 'People's Labour and Defence Standard System'.[38]

While the Cultural Revolution (1966–76) had an adverse effect on some aspects of sport, especially major competitive games, activities and events[39] – because they smacked of élitism – the Revolution brought the mass sports movement to its zenith. Most of villages, cities and factories had their sports activities. Sport events took place frequently in every city and some factories and villages.[40] They were a major pastime for most of the Chinese people. Throughout the whole country, exercise to radio music was practised every morning and mass cross-river swimming took place once every year. Many parents encouraged their children to engage in sport in order to stay in the city and find jobs since many factories needed players. Sport was regarded generally as a means of achieving security *and* social mobility. The First National Students Sports Meeting was held in 1973. The Third Army's Sports Meeting and the Third National Games took place in 1975. In the same year the Women's Table-Tennis Team became world champions and the Women's Volleyball Team took the fourth place in the world championships.[41] 'Sport crazy' became one of the distinguishing characteristics of the Cultural Revolution.[42] Furthermore, when China eventually wanted to escape its long isolation from the international community, sport served as a means of diplomatic communication in 1972. 'Ping-pong diplomacy' was the strategy used to re-establish diplomatic contacts.[43]

When China rejoined the international athletic community after 1979 sport was an effective way of publicising the nation to the world. In this regard women athletes brilliantly made their mark. In 1987 China won 70 world titles and broke 23 world records 44 times. Of these, 61 per cent of the world titles were won by women and approximately 50 per cent of the world records were broken by them.[44] Their success in Olympic events was even more marked: in track and field, seven of the eight athletes ranked in the world's top ten were women. In swimming, while only one Chinese was ranked in the top ten, it was a woman. In winter sports, a Chinese woman won China's first Olympic gold medal in short-track speed skating, an exhibition event. In the First Women's Weightlifting Championships, China claimed 22 of 27 gold medals. In fact, in almost every sport women have done better in international competitions than men. From 1985 to 1993 China had 404 top sportswomen at international level, accounting for 51 per cent of all Chinese athletes at that rank. Between 1949 and 1993 Chinese athletes won 775 world championships, of which 460 or 59 per cent, were won by women. Chinese athletes broke world records 725 times, with women accounting for 458 of these, or about 63 per cent of the total.[45] At the 25th Olympic Games held in 1992, Chinese women athletes 'scooped' 12 gold medals, three-quarters of China's gold medals. Hu Yiaobang, the General-Secretary of the Party pointed out that the indomitable and tenacious character displayed by Chinese women athletes embodied the new Chinese nation and brought it to the notice of the whole world.[46] In 1981 the State Council announced that the whole nation should learn from women athletes and use their spirit in sport to create the new face of socialist modernisation and reconstruction.[47] Women athletes are not only models for new Chinese women but for new Chinese men! In 1983 the National Women's Congress used women athletes as an illustration of women's superiority over men.[48] The Sports Ministry announced proudly in 1990 that women athletes had established a new inspirational femininity.[49]

New Femininity

Women have certainly done themselves and the nation proud in international sports areas. A frequent topic for discussion in the 1990s has been why 'the Phoenix (the symbol for women) can fly higher than the dragon (the symbol for men)'. One analyst offers three reasons: the socialist ideology of equality in sport training, funding and facilities, women's easy access to sport, the consequence of its low traditional status in society if not in Communist ideology; and Chinese women's ability 'to eat more bitterness' and endure more hard labour than men.[50] However, this view lacks an adequate historical perspective. To find the truth we must go back to the past and we must look at the long efforts of Chinese women and their sympathisers and supporters to achieve physical freedom. Here is the foundation of their present success. The glory of the modern victories of Chinese women athletes is the consequence of generation after generation of Chinese women who fought for the emancipation of their bodies for over a century.

Central to the history of Chinese women's emancipation, has been the long-standing hegemonic control that men have claimed over women's bodies. For centuries a woman's body was a site of oppression, exploitation and control. The nineteenth century struggle for women to take conscious control of their own bodies was one of confrontation, transformation and liberation. The Taiping women set a heroic if tragic precedent. They did not bind their feet and fought for equality. The Christian missionaries and Chinese reformers released many women from the physically, psychologically and symbolically repressive practice of footbinding. The female emancipationists in the first decades of the twentieth century used physical activity to establish physiological and psychological confidence and competence. The women of the May Fourth Era, after the set-back of 'neo-Confucianism', claimed women's right to exercise, to repossess themselves and to intervene on their own behalf to counter re-established, restrictive 'patriarchal' practices. Throughout the twentieth century, physical empowerment through exercise served as a metaphor for cultural empowerment. Then from 1920 to 1940, Nationalist and Communist political involvement in, and concern for women's physical freedom in the interest of party and national salvation, was a springboard for the transformation of gender relations by gradually, if not completely, dislodging the gender hierarchy and dismantling gender stereotypes.

Conclusion

Women athletes' considerable success in Communist China and, less completely, their social emancipation, has been in a real sense the consequence of the liberation of women's bodies, the reconstruction of the female physique, and the redefinition of femininity which started over a century ago and still continues. This revolution has been a significant and successful Chinese *cultural revolution*; one that has not yet run its course.

Notes

1. I am grateful to J.A. Mangan for letting me use this title.
2. Mao, Zedong, 'Xin minzhu zhuyi lun' [On the New Democracy], in *Mao Zedong xuanji* [Selected Works of Mao Zedong], op. cit., Vol. 4, p. 35.
3. Vertinsky, P., 'The Social Construction of the Gendered Body: Exercise and the Exercise of Power', *The International Journal of the History of Sport*, Vol. 11, No. 2, Aug. 1994, p.147.
4. The documents of the First All-China Congress of Women have been collected in *Zhongguo funu diyici quanguo daibiao dahui* [The First All-China Congress of Women], Hong Kong: Xin minzhu chubanshe, 1949.
5. Ibid.
6. The English translation is in Blaustein, Albert P. (ed.), *Fundamental Legal Documents of Communist China*, South Hackebsack: N.J. Rothman, 1962, pp.36–7.
7. See Chapter Five.
8. For more details about the relationship between the Marriage Law and women's emancipation see Ono Kazuko, op, cit., pp.177–86; see also Davin, Delia, *Women-Work*, op. cit., pp.87–114.
9. Spence, Jonathan D., *The Search for Modern China*, op. cit., pp.707–708.
10. Information Office of the State Council of the People's Republic of China, [hereafter IOSCPRC], 'The Situation of Chinese Women', *Beijing Review*, June 1994, p.13.
11. Zhonghua quanguo minzhu funu lianhehui [All-China Democratic Women's Federation], (ed.), *Zhongguo funu yundong ziliaoji* [Documents of the Women's Movement of China], Beijing (n.p.), 1952, pp.41–2.
12. Davin, Delia, 'Women in the Countryside of China', in Wolf and Witke (eds), *Women in Chinese Society*, op. cit., p.244.
13. In 1957 Mao proclaimed that China needed continuing revolution: 'Now we must start a technological revolution so that we may overtake Britain in fifteen years . . . .After fifteen years, when our foodstuffs and iron and steel became plentiful, we shall take a much greater initiative. Our revolutions are like battles. After a victory, we must at once put forward a new task.' Therefore, attempts were launched by Mao Zedong to heighten economic productivity dramatically in China through mass organisation and the inspiration of revolutionary fever among the people. It was known as the Great Leap Forward and the People's Commune. As a result of a lack of effective central planning, combined with a three-year drought and the withdrawal of Soviet aid and technical expertise, the Great Leap Forward turned into an economic disaster.
14. See 'Funu liaohehui gongzuo baogao' [Report Secretariat of the Women], *Renmin ribao* [People's Daily], 2 June 1958; 'Zhi quanguo funu de gongkaixin' [Open Letter to All Women], *Xinhua she* [New China News Agency], 16 Dec. 1958, 'Funu dahui gongzuo baogao' [Report on National Conference on Women

Work], *Xinhua she*, 31 July 1958.

15. *Renmin ribao* [People's Daily], 8 March 1958.
16. Li, Chiepo, 'Urban People's Communes', *Peking Review*, April 1960, p.19.
17. *Xinhua she* [New China News Agency], 31 July 1958.
18. Andors, Phylis, 'Politics of Chinese Development: The Case of Women, 1960–1966', Signs, Vol. 2, No. 1, 1976, pp.89–119; Spence, Jonathan D., The Search for Modern China, op. cit., pp.574–83.
19. *Renmin ribao* [People's Daily], 2 Jan. 1958.
20. Croll, E., 'The Anti-Lin Biao and Confucius: a New Stage in the Ideological Evolution of Women', *Australia and New Zealand Journal of Sociology*, Vol. 2, No. 1, 1976, pp.35–41.
21. *Renmin ribao* [People's Daily], 8 March 1973.
22. Lin Biao (1908–71) was the military leader who helped to transform the People's Liberation Army into a conventional modern army. He became Minister of Defence in 1958. As ardent supporter of Mao Zedong, Lin compiled the influential little red book *Mao zhuxi yulu* [Quotations from Chairman Mao] and was named as Mao's successor in 1969. Supposedly, he died two years later in an aeroplane crash after having escaped a failed coup against Mao.
23. Croll, E., 'The Anti-Lin Biao and Confucius . . .', op. cit., p.41.
24. See Wolf, Margery, *Revolution Postponed: Women in Contemporary China*, London: Methuen, 1987, *passim*.
25. See Pan, Lynn, *New Chinese Revolution*, Sphere Books Limited, 1988, p.1.
26. IOSCPRC, op. cit., p.13.
27. Wolf, Margery, *Revolution Postponed: Women in Contemporary China*, op. cit.
28. Ibid.
29. Wang, Jia, '40,000 diaocabiao xiansi zhongguo funu de shehui diwei' [Data Illustration of the Social Status of Chinese Women: the Investigation of 40,000 Questionnaires], *Zhongguo funu* [Chinese Women]; no. 1, 1992, pp.24–5.
30. IOSCPRC, op. cit., p.13.
31. Vertinsky, P., 'Gender Relations, Women's History and Sport History: A Decade of Changing Enquiry 1983–1993', *Journal of Sport History*, Vol. 21, No. 1, spring 1994, p.321.
32. Boutilier, Mary A and SanGiovanni, Lucinda F., 'Politics, Public Policy and Title IX: Some Limitation of Liberal Feminism', in Birrell, Susan and Cole, Cheryl L. (eds), *Women, Sport and Culture*, Human Kinetics, 1994, p.98.
33. Scott, Joan Wallach, *Gender and the Politics of History*, op. cit., p.37.
34. The mouthpiece of the CCP, *Hongqi* [Red Flag], acknowledged that many associations and enterprises were said to believe that so long as overall revolutionary aims were fulfilled, there was no need to pay particular attention to the position of women. See *Hongqi*, 1 Feb. 1971. Also see Chow, Rey, 'Violence in the Other Country: China, as Crisis Spectacle, and Women', in Mahanty, Chandra Talpade (ed.), *Third World Women and the Politics of Feminism*, Indiana University Press, 1991, p.35.
35. The Common Programme for China was announced by a group of delegates convened in September 1949 by Mao Zedong as the People's Political Consultative Conference. It promised equal rights to women and the end of their lives of 'bondage'. It also promoted physical education and sport to all men and women. See Spence, *The Search for Modern China*, p.515; Yong, Gaotang *et al.*, (eds), *Dangdai zhongguo tiyu* [Contemporary Chinese Sport], Beijing: Zhongguo shehui kexue chubanshe, 1987, pp.48–69.
36. Brownell, Susan, op. cit., p.227.
37. Su, Jingchun, 'Xuexiao tiyu sishi nian' [The Development of Physical Education

in Chinese Schools in the Past Forty Years], *TWS*, No. 4, 1989, p.2.

38. Yong, Gaotang, pp.16–18, 589.

39. During the Cultural Revolution, the Party's attitude towards competitive sport was negative. Competitive sport was regarded as the élite sport. The spirit of competitive sport was replaced by the slogan 'friendship first, competition second'. For further details see Rong Gaotang, op. cit., pp.78–82.

40. Ibid., p.73.

41. Some Chinese teams and individuals still participated in international competitions with the agreement of the Party. Ibid., pp.575–81.

42. Susan Brownell misunderstood the situation in the Cultural Revolution. She claimed that 'at the height of the Cultural Revolution, sport and games were attacked'. (See her dissertation, 'The Olympic Movement on its Way into Chinese Culture', op. cit., p. 358.) The truth is that competitive sport on the international level was attacked and revisionist. However, the development of mass sport and exercise remained unattacked. Sport in the Cultural Revolution is still a research area which needs to be explored. See Editor's article, 'Jiji you buchou de kaizhan longchun tiyu huodong' [On the Development of Sports Activities in the Countryside], *Xin tiyu* [New Sports], No. 1, 1973, pp.1–2; Reporter's article, 'Jianchi duanlian, yifeng yisu' [Doing Exercise and Changing Old Custom], *Xin tiyu*, No. 9, 1973, pp.11–12; Fu, Lianlong, 'Wenge zhong longchun tiyu xinshen xianxiang de shikao' [On the Development of the Mass Sports Movement in the Countryside in the Cultural Revolution], *TWS*, No. 4, 1991, pp.40–42; Rong, Gaotang, op. cit., p.73.

43. Rong, Gaotang, op. cit., p.394.

44. See the report, 'China's winning year', *China Daily*, 28 Dec. 1987.

45. IOSCPRC, op. cit., p.17.

46. Hu, Yiaobang, 'Dui tiyu zhanxian de tongzimen de jianhua' ['The Speech to Sports Ministry], The document can be seen in Zhongguo tiyu bowuguan [Chinese Sports Museum], Beijing, China.

47. Quoted in Yong, Gaotang, op. cit., p.199.

48. Wolf, Margery, *Revolution Postponed*, op. cit., p.262.

49. Zhang, Caizheng, 'Ya yunhui dailaide wuda bianhua' [On the Beijing Asian Games], in *90 Yayunhui* [The Asian Games in 1990], Wuhan: Wuhan chubanshe, 1990, p.8.

50. Brownell, Susan, op. cit., pp.229–35.

On Women's Participation in Physical Education and Exercise
[Lun nuzi yijiang tiyu]
April 1903
Chen Jiefen

≭ℒ⊛ℒ≭

MEN AND WOMEN both need physical education and exercise. They are as important as moral and intellectual education. However, Chinese women are not only excluded from physical development but also suffer physical torture. They have to pierce their ears, bind their waists and their feet and put on make-up. In the past they had no tradition of exercise so they did violence to their bodies through footbinding, inactivity and ignorance. Our women accept too readily the male ideal of feminine beauty as physical fragility because in their hearts they wish to please men.

I want our women to understand what beauty is. A beautiful woman should have a healthy body. A pale skin with a lot of make-up and a fragile body with bound feet are not beautiful. Real beauty depends on good health. The popular image of beauty is simply that favoured by dead-hearted, foolish males to make it easy to treat women without respect and to oppress them. If these men who created this ideal really consider it desirable, why don't they apply it to themselves instead of making only women follow it?

A long time ago our ancestors told us that a healthy body was beautiful. Why did we forget their words and follow men's ideal of feminine beauty? Why do we always torture our bodies to please men? Physical education is as important as moral and intellectual education. We should adopt it so that we will not mistreat our bodies.

Chen Jiefen was a journalist, feminist and revolutionary of the early twentieth century. This article was published in *Nuxue bao* [Journal of Women's Education], No. 2, April 1903. It was the first women's article which directly advocated women's participation in physical education and exercise. For more details about the author see note 96, Chapter 3 of this book.

Physical education is not simply as important as moral and intellectual education, it forms their very basis. For women in a physically weak condition can do nothing, not even perform their traditional duties of companion and mother. A woman with bound feet and fragile body is like a woman in a picture who can do nothing. I don't understand why men like women to be useless pictures. And I don't know why women permit themselves to be the pictures.

A physically mutilated woman is not a beauty. Men forced women to accept their ideal of feminine beauty because they wanted to destroy women's physical health, and subsequently women's intellectual development and moral growth. These men were not unaware that this would be the case. They knew it would be easier to oppress women if it were this way. They could not treat women so if they had not destroyed their bodies. I hope that my two million women comrades – poor worms – will realise henceforth their predicament and turn, and encourage each other to turn. For several thousand years we have been sunk in a dark hell. Only since the importation of women's rights has there been a ray of light. But if we wish to escape the status of slaves and dogs and horses, we must reform ourselves, and the way forward lies with physical education and exercise. Women's emancipation should start from physical release through physical education. Let Chinese women have healthy bodies to shoulder the responsibilities of society and themselves.

APPENDIX 2

On Physical Education and Exercise
1 April 1917
Mao Zedong

✕✦✕

THE COUNTRY IS in crisis. The military is weak. People's bodies are degenerating. Certain reformers wished to solve these problems by learning to use Western technology. They do not understand that what is fundamental is to promote physical exercise. Only when their bodies are strong can people defend their country. Some reformers have promoted physical education. They have failed too. For they have omitted to explain the value of physical exercise. Only when people know the importance of exercise can they participate in it actively and effectively. A new system of physical education and a new recognition of the need for exercise are urgently required. I would like to offer my opinions on both these matters and discuss them with my colleagues.

1. What is Physical Education?

When humans became human, some were clever and some stupid, but they all knew how to exercise and defend themselves. . . . Physically, the bodies of animals and human beings are similar. However, humans can live longer than animals because they know how to exercise and control their bodies consciously. The method of

---

This is an extract from an article published in *Xin qingnian* [New Youth], Vol. 3, No. 2, 1 April 1917. It is not included in Mao's collected works or selected works. Perhaps Mao was not a Marxist at that time. Although the specific theme of the article has not been repeated in any of Mao's subsequent writings, the connection between China's ability to defend her borders and a physically fit nation continued to be made by him in practice. Mao's article foreshadows the general consistency of thought of Chinese Communist leaders down the years with respect to physical exercise. It is not a coincidence that physical exercise played an important part in the Communist areas before 1949, and played the same role in Communist China after 1949. The principles were laid down by Mao in 1917.

exercising and controlling the body is physical education. . . . In short, physical education is the method employed by human beings to develop their bodies in a systematic manner and prolong their life.

2. The Position of Physical Education and Exercise

It is the body which is the source of morality and knowledge. If there is no body there is no moral and intellectual development. Not many people appreciate this simple truth. People always focus on the development of the moral or intellectual. Intellectual development is important. It distinguishes humans from animals. But where do human beings store knowledge? Moral development is important. It improves the quality of men and women. But where do they store morality? The body contains both. It is a carriage for knowledge; it is a warehouse for morality. Therefore, pupils in school should concentrate on the development of their bodies. Physical education should have priority in their education, and moral and intellectual education should be given lower consideration. Few educationists appreciate this. And so in primary schools, children know how to read but not how to exercise. They are unhealthy and die early. In the middle school, education should be physical, moral and intellectual. However, schools always emphasise the intellectual. Pupils' physical education is neglected. In school, every hour is occupied by academic subjects. An adult couldn't cope with this, let alone children. Educationists plan the curriculum to torture pupils. If pupils do not complete their courses they are punished. If they do finish them, they are asked to read yet more books. To be a pupil means to be in (academic) prison with no chance of being released. What a nightmare! If one finds methods to improve the body, mind and morality will improve automatically. To get the body into condition, there is nothing better than exercise. Physical education should occupy the first place in one's life. When the body is strong one can advance rapidly in studies and in virtue and attain one's full potential. In my study this is an important point. . . .

3. The Shortcomings of the Present Physical Education System

Physical, moral and intellectual education are all important, but the old scholars neglected physical education. . . .

However, the situation changed for the better when the modern schools modelled themselves on foreign countries. But the old culture dies hard. Physical education became a course but not a properly implemented one. We now have gymnastic courses and teachers in schools but our pupils' bodies haven't developed healthily. In class the teacher gives his order and the pupils obey. They suffer both physically and mentally. At the end of the class the pupils are exhausted. In addition, their food is poor, their classrooms are dark, their facilities are inadequate. Consequently the physical condition of pupils is very unsatisfactory.

How can we change the situation? . . . It is not easy to promote the value of physical education. However, only when our educationists fully appreciate the importance of exercise can educational shortcomings be overcome and the situation improved. . . .

4. The Effect of Physical Education

A man is a physical creature. He needs to participate in activities involving motion. As a being of reason, his movement should be systematic. It is through systematic movement – a part of physical education – that the body is built up. . . . Systematic movement is the role of man and universe.

Systematic movement for a man is physical education. As mentioned above, the aim of physical education is to strengthen the body. The old belief which holds that after the age of 25 man's body is unchangeable is incorrect. The body never loses its capacity. It changes every day. It undergoes a process of metabolism. A weak body can become a healthy one and vice versa. The key is exercise. . . . Someone born weak can become strong through activity, and someone born strong can become weak through inactivity. Further, there is no truth to the view that a superior physical condition adversely affects one's mental condition. . . . History, both modern and ancient, is replete with people who advocated physical exercise without detriment to their intellect. . . . In short, participation in exercise can improve a man's physique. Physique depends on man's effort not God's will.

Participation in exercise serves not only to strengthen the body, but indirectly improves intellectual development. . . . A strong body can contain modern knowledge effectively by rendering healthy those organs of the body which are responsible for the absorption of this knowledge.

Perhaps the greatest value in exercise lies in strengthening the will. The main practical purpose of exercise is military heroism. Fearlessness, daring, tenaciousness and courage cannot be achieved without control over the will developed through exercise. . . .

In short, participation in exercise can strengthen the body, stimulate the learning of knowledge, conquer uncertainty and train determination. . . .

5. The Reasons for the Lack of Exercise

Physical exercise is most important but most scholars still show little or no interest in it. There are four reasons: firstly, they have not recognised the value of exercise for others or for themselves. They do not feel the need for physical fitness. Secondly, cultural attitudes passed down through the ages have favoured 'civil' careers, and approved of slow-flowing movement rather than the rapid motion inherent in exercise. Such aphorisms as 'a good man doesn't undertake the occupation of a soldier' have lodged themselves in the subconscious. Thirdly, educationists have failed to delve into the subject of exercise in sufficient depth. Instructors lack knowledge about exercise. Their teaching is boring. Fourthly, old cultural habits are very hard to break. Many people are ashamed to be seen exercising. . . . These are the four reasons. The first and the fourth are subjective and can be changed by people themselves. The second and the third are objective and depend on others' change of attitude. People should change themselves not depend on others.

6. The Method of Exercise – Simplicity

I was an unhealthy boy. So I was very interested in fitness. I read ancient books at home and modern books at school about physical exercise methods. However, I made little progress. For exercise is not only preaching but practise. . . . There are hundreds of methods of exercise. One only needs to stick to one method and practise it. The importance of exercise is to let the blood flow which can drive away disease. To achieve this one method can do. The point is to exercise assiduously and perseveringly. . . .

7. The Instruction of Exercise

Participation in frequent exercise is very important. Regularity is the essence. . . . First, regularity produces interest . . . One should exercise twice a day: after rising in the morning and before going to bed in the evening. . . . A regular programme of thirty minutes per day is necessary. Second, regularity produces pleasure. The person who exercises regularly will begin to get pleasure from his performance, experience improvement and feel an inner urge to maintain the regime. In short, interest motivates people. It is the beginning of exercise. Pleasure pleases people. It is the result of exercise. . . .

In conclusion, there are three rules of exercise: the first is consistency, the second is concentration and the third is severity of the programme if a powerful physique is to be developed. . . .

Open Telegram to the Nation: Promotion of Sport and Exercise
[Tichang tiyu tongdian]
2 March 1935
Chiang Kai-shek

To Director of every region,
Commander of every Army Regiment,
Party committee, government and education council of every province:

To strengthen people's bodies we should promote and develop physical exercise and sport so as to improve our race and save our country. In ancient China, hunting and archery were compulsory in schools. In modern times, exercise and sport are practised in powerful Western countries. Their people, men and women, the old and the young, all participate in exercise. In our country, although there is some progress in schools in recent years the situation is far from satisfactory. Some schools have concentrated on training top athletes and have ignored the majority's physical education. The staff of Party offices, the social services and the army is too lazy to engage in any physical activity. They don't show any interest in exercise. If this situation continues, it will destroy our nation.

We must have a mass physical exercise campaign. From now on all the students and teachers of primary and middle schools, all staff of Party offices, the social services and the army must participate in physical exercise. Without delay they must choose one event as their regular exercise and have their daily exercise time fixed between five to six o'clock every day. They are to be encouraged to take up outdoor activities but they can take indoor exercise if the weather is not good.

This speech was published in *Qin Fen Sport Monthly*, Vol. 2, No. 7, April 1935.

Physical training must be constant. The principals of schools, the heads of government office and army officers must supervise and discipline their pupils and staff and report to their superior. Their reports will be on record and monitored.

The Law of Sport for Citizens
[Guomin tiyu fa]
Issued by the Nationalist Government
on 16 April 1929

❧❧◆❧❧

1. Boys and girls must take part in physical education and sport. Their parents and guardians are responsible for their supervision.
2. The aim of physical education and sport is to develop the bodies of men and women for the good of the country.
3. Every male and female should participate in physical activity in which scientific sports methods are applied.
4. Old customs which present an obstacle to the physical fitness of men and women must be banned by the local authority.
5. Every town, city and region must have public sports stadiums.
6. Physical education should be an obligatory course in middle schools and colleges. Students will not be allowed to graduate unless they pass their physical education test.
7. All sports committees must be registered with and under the supervision of the local authority, and apply to the Ministry of the Interior, and consult with the Training Commissioner's Department. However, those who are serving the people's physical education in scientific research and in the monitoring of teaching materials are not bound by this limitation. In the matter of budgets, efficient unofficial sports organisations would benefit from financial incentives from the government.
8. Sports societies organised in each county, municipality, village, town and hamlet must accept the control of the local government and be under that organisation.
9. Physical education teachers and instructors should be qualified. The regulations regarding the nature of the credentials should be drawn up by the Training Commissioner's office.
10. All physical education personnel who have served for three years

or more in good standing should be given suitable incentives by the Training Commissioner's Department, with the Department to work out details.

11. The Training Commissioner's Department should set up a special high-level physical education committee to deal with the research findings of specialist organisations and to examine foreign practices so as to serve the objective of promoting the people's sport and physical education.
12. All sports groups must comply with directives in the government programme.
13. This law takes effect from the day on which it is issued.

The Revised Law of Sport for Citizens
[Xiuzheng guomin tiyu fa]
Issued by the Nationalist Government
on 9 September 1941

⋇⁓⊙⁓⋇

1. The aim of physical education and sport is to develop the bodies of men and women and build national character so as to save the country.
2. Every citizen of the Republic of China regardless of age, sex and race must take part in physical education and sport. Their parents. teachers and authorities are responsible for their supervision to ensure that national physical education and sport can develop quickly and widely.
3. The Ministry of Education is in charge of administration matters. The planning, supervision and monitoring of the development of physical education and sports are to be the responsibility of the Ministry of Education and the department concerned.
4. The central and local educational councils should have physical education personnel who are responsible for the development of physical education and sport.
5. The regulations associated with the implementation of the Law of Sport for Citizens should be drafted by the Ministry of Education and the department concerned and issued by the State Council.
6. The Ministry of Education and local education councils should also formulate the regulations concerning the training of physical education personnel, teachers and instructors. Teacher training colleges, physical education institutions and physical education department of universities at all levels should be responsible for training physical education personnel, teachers and instructors. The Ministry of Education will be responsible for the curricula.
7. The syllabus for physical education teachers' and instructors'

vocational studies should be drafted by the Ministry of Education and issued by the State Council.

8. All spending on physical education and sport authorities will be under the budgetary control of local governments.

9. Unofficial sports organisations and societies should be supervised and monitored by the local education council. Those in good standing should be given suitable incentives and financial support from the government.

10. The Ministry should enact a decree to ensure the monitoring of the people's physical condition so as to improve people's health.

11 This law should take effect from the day on which it is issued.

Selected Bibliography

჻

This selected bibliography represents merely a fraction of the English sources considered. The complete bibliography which includes primary and secondary sources in *both* Chinese and English can be found in my doctoral thesis: 'The Physical Reconstruction of the Female Body and the Reconceptualisation of Femininity in Modern China: 1840–1949' at the International Research Centre for Socialisation, Sport and Society, Faculty of Education, University of Strathclyde, Glasgow, UK.

Ayscough, Florence, *Chinese Women's Yesterday and Today*, London: Jonathan Cape, 1938.

Band, Clare and William, *Two Years with the Chinese Communists*, New Haven: Yale University Press, 1948.

Beldon, Jack, *China Shakes the World*, New York: Harper & Bros., 1949.

Bird, Isabella, *The Yangtze Valley and Beyond*, first published in 1899 by John Murray and reprinted by Virago (London) in 1985.

Boardman, Eugene Powers, *Christian Influence Upon the Ideology of the Taiping Rebellion*, Wisconsin: University of Wisconsin Press, 1952.

Brabdt, Conrad, Schwartz, Benjamin and Fairbank, John K., *A Documentary History of Chinese Communism*, London: George Allen & Unwin, 1952.

Burton, Margaret E., *The Education of Women in China*, New York: F. H. Revell, 1911.

Ch'ien, Tuan-sheng, *The Government and Politics of China, 1912–1949*, Stanford: Stanford University Press, 1950.

Chalmers Johnson, *Peasant Nationalism and Communist Power*, Stanford: Stanford University press, 1962.

Chan, F. Gilbert and Etzold, Thomas H. (eds.), *China in the 1920s*, New York: New Viewpoints, 1976.

Chao Buwei, *Autobiography of a Chinese Woman* (trans. by her husband

(Chao Yuanren), New York: John Day, 1947.

Chen, Jerome, *China and the West: Society and Culture 1815–1937*, London: Hutchinson, 1979.

Chen, Sophia H. (ed.), *Symposium on Chinese Culture*, Shanghai: China Institute of Pacific Relations, 1931.

Ching, Jujia, *Confucianism and Christianity*, Tokyo: Kodansha, 1977.

Chow, Tse-tung, *The May Fourth Movement: Intellectual Revolution in Modern China*, Cambridge, MA: Harvard University Press, 1960.

Christian Education in China: A Study, edited by an Educational Commission representing the Mission Board and Societies conducting work in China, New York: Committee of Reference and Council of the Foreign Missions Conference of North America, 1922.

Cohen, Paul A., *China and Christianity: the Missionary Movement and the Growth of Chinese Anti-Foreignism 1860–1870*, Cambridge, MA: Harvard University Press, 1963.

Compton, Boyd, *Mao's China: Party Reform Documents 1942–1944*, Seattle and London: University of Washington Press, 1966.

Croll, E., *Feminism and Socialism in China*, London: Routledge & Kegan Paul, 1978.

Curtin, K., *Women in China*, New York: Pathfinder Press, 1979.

Cusack, Dymphna, *Chinese Women Speak*, Sydney: Angus and Robertson, 1958.

Davin, Delia, *Women-Work: Women and the Party in Revolutionary China*, Oxford: The Clarendon Press, 1976.

Dean, William, *The China Mission: Embracing a History of the Various Missions of All Denominations among the Chinese*, New York: Sheldon, 1859.

Dennis, James S., *Christian Missions and Social Progress*, Edinburgh: Anderson & Ferrier, 1906.

Dorries, Carl E., 'Peasant Mobilisation in North China and the Origins of Yan'an Communism', *China Quarterly*, Vol. 68, Dec. 1976, pp.696–721.

Eide, Elisabeth, 'Ibsen's Nora and Chinese Interpretations of Female Emancipation', in Malmgvist, Goran (ed.), *Literature and Its Social Context*, New York: Nobel Foundation and Plenum Press, 1978, pp.140–61.

Fairbank, John K., *The Cambridge History of China: Late Ching, 1800–1911*, Cambridge: Cambridge University Press, 1978.

Five Years of Progress, edited and published by the National Committee of the YMCA of China, Shanghai, 1912.

Forman, Harrison, *Report from Red China*, New York: H. Holt, 1945.

Freedman, Maurice, (ed.), *Family and Kinship in Chinese Society*, Stanford: Stanford University Press, 1970.

Gilmartin, Christina K. *et al.* (eds), *Engendering China*, Cambridge, MA: Harvard University Press, 1994.

Grieder, Jerome, *Hu Shih and the Chinese Renaissance: Liberalism and the Chinese Revolution, 1917–1937*, Cambridge, MA: Harvard University Press, 1970.

Hao, Gensen, *Physical Education in China*, Shanghai: Commercial Press, 1926.

Harrison, E. Salisbury, *The Long March*, London: Macmillan, 1985.

Headland, Isaac Taylor, *Court Life in China*, New York: Fleming H. Revell, 1909.

Honig, Emily, *Sisters and Strangers – Women in the Shanghai Cotton Mills, 1919–1949*, Stanford: Stanford University Press, 1986.

Hsu, Francis L.K., *Under the Ancestor's Shadow: Chinese Culture and Personality*, London: Routledge, 1949.

Hu, Chi-hsi, 'The Sexual Revolution in the Kiangsi Soviet', *China Quarterly*, Vol. 59, July 1974, pp.477–490.

Hunter, Jane, *The Gospel of Gentility, American Women Missionaries in Turn-of-the-Century China*, London: Yale University Press, 1986.

Israel, John, *Student Nationalism in China, 1927–1937*, Stanford: Stanford University Press, 1966.

Jen, Yuwen, *The Taiping Revolutionary Movement*, New Haven: Yale University Press, 1973.

Johnson, Ann, *Women, the Family and the Peasant Revolution in China*, Chicago: University of Chicago Press, 1983.

Kim, Ilpyong J., *The Politics of Chinese Communism: Kiangsi under the Soviets*, Berkeley: University of California, 1973.

Kristeva, J., *About Chinese Women*, London: Marion Boyars, 1977.

Levy, Marion, *The Family Revolution in Modern China*, New York: Octagon Books 1963 (first published in 1949).

Levy, H.S., *Chinese Footbinding: The History of a Chinese Erotic Custom*, London: Neville Spearman, 1966.

Lewis, Charlton M., *Prologue to the Chinese Revolution: The Transformation of Ideas and Institutions in Hunan Province, 1891–1907*, Cambridge, MA: Harvard University Press, 1976.

Lin, Meihua, 'Activities of Women Revolutionaries in the Tongmenghui Period', *China Forum*, Vol. 2, July, 1975, pp.245–99.

Lin, Yu-sheng, *The Crisis of Chinese Consciousness: Radical Anti-*

traditionalism in the May Fourth Era, Madison: University of Wisconsin Press, 1979.

Lin, Yutang, *My Country and My People*, London: Williams, 1936.

Lindsay, Michael, *Notes on Educational Problems in Communist China, 1941–1947*, New York: Greenwood Press, 1978.

Little, Archibald, *In the Land of the Blue Gown*, New York: D. Appleson, 1909.

Little, Archibald, *Intimate China: The Chinese As I Have Seen Them*, London (n.d.).

Lo, R.Y., *China's Revolution from the Inside*, New York: The Abingolon, 1930.

Lutz, Jessie G. (ed.), *Christian Missions in China, Evangelists of What?*, Boston: D.C. Heath, 1965.

Lyon, D.W., *The First Quarter Century of the YMCA in China, 1895–1920*, Shanghai: The Association Press, 1920.

Mangan, J.A. and Park, R. (eds), *From 'Fair Sex' to Feminism*, London: Frank Cass, 1987.

McDougall, Bonnie, *Mao Zedong's 'Talk at the Yenan Conference on Literature and Art': A Translation of the 1943 Speech with Commentary*, Ann Arbor: University of Michigan Press, 1980.

Michael, Franz and Chang, Chung-li, *The Taiping Rebellion: History and Documents*, Seattle: University of Washington Press, 1966 (3 vols.).

Needham, J., *Within the Four Seas*, London: Allen & Unwin, 1969.

New Women in New China, edited and published by Beijing Foreign Language Press, 1972.

North, Robert C., *Chinese Communism*, London: World University Library, 1966.

O'Hara, Albert, S.J., *The Position of Women in Early China*, Washington: (n.p.), 1946.

Ono Kasuko, *Chinese Women in a Century of Revolution*, Stanford: Stanford University Press, 1989.

Payne, Robert, *China Awake*, New York: Dodd Mead, 1947.

Peake, Cyrus H., *Nationalism and Education in Modern China*, New York: Columbia University Press, 1932.

Pong, David and Fung, Edmond S.K. (eds), *Ideal and Reality: Social and Political Change in Modern China 1860–1949*, Lanham: University Press of America, 1985.

Pruitt, I., *A Daughter of Han: An Autobiography of a Working Woman*, Stanford: Stanford University Press, 1967.

Purcell, Victor, *The Boxer Uprising, A Background Study*, Cambridge:

Cambridge University Press, 1963.

Rankin, Mary B., *Early Chinese Revolutionaries: Radical Intellectuals in Shanghai and Chekiang, 1902–1911*, Cambridge, MA: Harvard University Press, 1972.

Reason, Joyce, *Chiang Kai-shek and the Unity of China*, Edinburgh: Edinburgh House Press, 1943.

Rong, Tiesheng, 'The Women's Movement in China before and after the 1911 Revolution', *Chinese Studies in History*, Nos. 3–4, 1983, pp.159–200.

Ropp, Paul S., 'The Seeds of Change: Reflections on the Condition of Women in the Early and Mid Ch'ing', *Signs: Journal of Women in Culture and Society*, Vol. 2, No. 1, 1976, pp.5–26.

Salatt, Janet Weitzner and Merkle, Judith, 'Women in Revolution: the Lessons of the Soviet Union and China', *Socialist Revolution*, Vol. 1, No. 6, pp.37–62.

Schwarcz, Vera, *The Chinese Enlightenment: Intellectuals and the Legacy of the May Fourth Movement of 1919*, Berkeley: University of California Press, 1986.

Selden, Mark, *The Yenan Way in Revolutionary China*, Cambridge, MA: Harvard University Press, 1971.

Shieh, Milton J.T., *The Kuomintang: Selected Historical Documents 1894–1969*, New York: St. John's University Press, 1970.

Siu, Bobby, *Women of China, Imperialism and Women's Resistance 1900–1949*, London: Zed, 1981.

Smedley, Agnes, *China's Red Army Marches*, London: Lawrence and Wishart,1934.

Smith, D.H., *Confucians*, London: Temple Smith, 1973.

Snow, Edgar, *Red Star Over China*, New York: Grove Press, 1938.

Snow, Foster Helen (pseud. Nym Wales), *Inside Red China*, New York: Double Day, 1939.

Snow, Foster Helen, *Women in Modern China*, The Netherlands: Monton, 1967.

Soong, Ching-ling, *The Struggle for New China*, Beijing: Foreign Language Press, 1952.

Spence, Jonathan D., *The Gate of Heavenly Peace: the Chinese and their Revolution*, New York: the Viking Press, 1987.

Spence, Jonathan D., *The Search for Modern China*, London: Hutchinson, 1990.

Stacey, Judith, 'When Patriarchy Kow-tows: the Significance of the Chinese Family Revolution for Feminist Theory', *Feminist Studies*,

Vol. 2, 1975, pp.65–77.

Stein, Guenther, *The Challenge of Red China*, London: Pilot Press, 1945.

Teng, Ssu-yu and Fairbank, John K., *China's Response to the West: A Documentary Survey, 1839–1923*, New York: the Viking Press, 1967.

Van Gulik, R.H., *Sexual Life in Ancient China: A Preliminary Survey of Chinese Sex and Society from ca. 1200 BC. till 1644 AD*, Leiden: E.J. Brill, 1961.

Wang, Suling and Cressey, Earl, *Daughter of Confucians : A Personal History*, New York: Farrar, Strauss & Young, 1952.

Wang, Y.C., *Chinese Intellectuals and the West 1872–1949*, Chapel Hill: University of North Carolina Press, 1966.

Wang, T.C., *The Youth Movement in China*, New York: New Public Inc., 1927.

Wei, Cheng yu-hsiu (Mme Wei Tao-ming), *My Revolutionary Years*, New York: Charles Scribner, 1943.

Wolf, M, *Revolution Postponed: Women in Contemporary China*, London: Methuen, 1987.

Wolf, M. and Witke, R., (eds), *Women in Chinese Society*, Stanford: Stanford University Press, 1975.

Wright, Mary C., (ed.), *China in Revolution: The First Phase, 1900–1913*, New Haven: Yale University Press, 1968.

Yakhontoff, Victor A., *The Chinese Soviets*, New York: Coward-McCann, 1934.

Yang, C.K., *The Chinese Family in the Communist Revolution*, Cambridge, MA: MIT Press, 1959.

Young, Marilyn B., (ed.) *Women in China: Studies in Social Change and Feminism*, Ann Arbor: Centre for Chinese Studies, the University of Michigan, 1973.

Index

❧❧❧

Note: Bold figures indicate an illustration on the page.

changed outlook for women 53–4;
Chinese women's education and 43,
62–3, 86, 290–1; communists followed
path of 198; girls' schools 54, 58, 264,
291; permission to live in China 50–1;
reaction to self-assertion of Chinese girls
60–1; stimulated Chinese reformers 61–2
Mitchell, Juliet 196
Model District Sports Movement (1932)
233–4
'Model of Soviet Work in Changgang Village,
The' 165
'My Athletic Life' 272

Nanjing Normal University, women and
133, 257
Nanjing Provisional Government (1911) 98
National Amateur Sports Association 257,
267
National American Athletic Federation (USA)
256
National Education Conference (1928,
Nanjing) 230
National Educational Council orders 243
National New Life Movement Promotion
Committee 237–8
National Physical Education Committee 232,
249
National Physical Education and Sports
Committee (1927) 230
National Provisional Parliament 99–100,
116
National Research Society of Physical
Education 257
National Revolutionary Army 226
National Women's Congress (1949) 299
nationalism: exercise and 242–6; feminism
and 88, 104
Nationalism and Modern Education in China
231
Nationalist Area (1928–49): education in
270–1, 284–5; emancipation and exercise
225–9, 295; National Games (1910–19)
102, 118; (1924, Wuchang) and women
athletes 136; (1930) 267–8; (1933)
267, 271–2, 275; (1935) 268–9, 274;
peasant women 239–40; schools for
middle-class girls 230; sports meetings
233; sportswomen and women's
emancipation 278; Women's Movement,
middle class 240
Nationalist Chinese schools, McCloy and
physical education 256–65
Nationalist government in Nanjing 226,
247; physical training system 234;
women and 227, 307
nationalist movement, schools and 88, 103

Nationalist Party 149; attitude to women
101, 153; coup (1927) 151, 177;
Women's Movement and feminism
227–8
Nationalist women, definition 234
Nationalists: China and 120, 164;
encirclement of Communists 174;
McCloy's influence on women's exercise
256–65; selective emancipation for
women 246; tradition and 225;
women's exercise and 10, 296
Natural-foot Societies 55–7, 65
'neo-Confucian' ideas 261, 266, 281, 296,
307
New Culture Movement (1915) 119–20,
126, 128, 135, 137, 293
New Curriculum (1923) 134
new femininity 296, 306–7
New Life Movement 235–42, 244, 276
New Life Promotion Committee, Physical
Education and Sports Department (1935)
243–4
New Life Promotional Associations 236
New Mission of Chinese Sports (1934) 244
'New People's Study Society' 126
New Sports Movement 205, 207, 223, 295
New Sports Society (1942) 205
'new women' 242, 276
Nie Rongzhen 158
Ningpo Girls' School (1844) 53
'non-essentials' 79–80
North China Herald 88
North China Sectional Athletic Competition
(eighth, 1929) 266, 282
North China Sport Association 266
North China Union Women's College 59
North Herald, The 36
North Western Navy Academy, physical
education in 31
North–South YMCA, Physical Education
School (1916) 135
Nu bao (Women's Daily) 128
Nu jie zhong (Women's Bell) 128
Nu jie zhong xu (Preface to the Bell of Women,
1903) 98
Nubao (Women's Journal) 89, 111
Nusheng (Women's Voice, 1932) 229, 248

'objectification' of women 3
Occidental ideals, influence on Chinese feudal
philosophy 9, 292
Olympic Games: Chinese sportswomen and
10–11; (1936) 266, **273**–4, 275; (1948)
266; (1992) 306
'On Chastity' 127
'On Physical Education and Exercise' (1917)
313–17